Y0-DYT-700

Gertrude Hoyt Memorial

Mergers and Acquisitions

Mergers and Acquisitions

Current Problems in Perspective

Edited by
Michael Keenan
Lawrence J. White
New York University

LexingtonBooks
D.C. Heath and Company
Lexington, Massachusetts
Toronto

69340

Library of Congress Cataloging in Publication Data
Main entry under title:

Mergers and acquisitions.

1. Consolidation and merger of corporations. I. Keenan, Michael,
1938–   . II. White, Lawrence J.
HD2746.5.M46   338.8'3   81–47691
ISBN 0-669-04719-8   AACR2

Copyright © 1982 by D.C. Heath and Company

Published simultaneously in Canada

Printed in the United States of America

International Standard Book Number: 0-669-04719-8

Library of Congress Catalog Card Number: 81-47691

Contents

v

Preface and Acknowledgments

On January 8–9, 1981, the Salomon Brothers Center for the Study of Financial Institutions, Graduate School of Business, New York University, sponsored a two-day conference entitled "Mergers and Acquisitions: Current Problems in Perspective." The conference participants included academics, practicing professionals in finance, corporate executives, and government regulators. The two editors of this book were the organizers of the conference. The conference sessions provided a forum for an interesting interchange of ideas and viewpoints. This book is the outcome of that conference.

Special thanks are due to a number of people who assisted with the organization and running of the conference. Edward Altman, Ernest Bloch, Eleanor Fox, and George Sorter served as able moderators of the four sessions. Mary Jaffier and Ligija Roze provided their usual superb performance in managing the details of the conference arrangements. Finally, Arnold Sametz, director of the Center, provided constant encouragement and support.

1 Introduction

Michael Keenan and
Lawrence J. White

Mergers and acquisitions continue to be important phenomena in the U.S. economy. They are the subject of continuing concern of business executives who are looking for (or hoping to elude) potential merger partners, by investment bankers who manage the mergers, of lawyers who advise the parties, by government regulators concerned with the operation of securities markets or with fears of growing aggregate corporate concentration in the economy, and by academic researchers who want to understand these phenomena better.

The 1970s were an active era for mergers and acquisitions and for research on them. During this decade, economics-finance researchers made great strides in understanding the operations of capital markets and the ways in which the causes and effects of mergers and acquisitions might be modeled and measured.

In January 1981, the Salomon Brothers Center for the Study of Financial Institutions at New York University's Graduate School of Business Administration held a conference to explore a wide range of issues concerning mergers and acquisitions. The conference brought together academic researchers, lawyers, government regulators, securities-industry participants, and representatives from companies actively involved in the merger process. This book is the product of that conference.

Before summarizing the individual chapters in this book, we believe that it is worthwhile to state a few of the broad themes that emerged from the conference concerning merger rationales, social consequences, and the increasing importance of divestitures.

First, the reasons why mergers take place are of continuing research interest. There are, of course, always idiosyncratic reasons that appear to apply to each individual merger, but researchers usually are searching for a few general principles that could explain the broad patterns of merger activity. Among the explanations offered at various times have been the exploitation of economies of scale, synergy, the acquisition of market power, diversification, the acquisition of undervalued assets, and the "urge to merge" on the part of some business executives. Two additional motives emerge from some of the chapters in this volume: (1) diversification that reduces the likelihood of bankruptcy (and the costs associated with bankruptcy), and (2) achieving a better fit between the talents of corporate

1

managers and the resources at their disposal either by acquisition or divestiture.

Second, concern still exists about the noneconomic consequences of mergers and acquisitions that do take place. Many individuals are not convinced that the economic-efficiency gains from mergers are great; at the same time, they are quite uneasy about the political and social consequences of the greater corporate size that occurs because of mergers. This group stands in sharp contrast with the group that sees substantial efficiency gains from mergers, that sees the operations of the securities markets in arranging and facilitating mergers as just another manifestation of efficient markets at work, and that sees little or no social or political threat. This tension of diverse philosophies has not been resolved by merger or antitrust legislation passed in the 1970s, nor is it likely to be resolved in the near future.

Third, though corporate spin-offs and divestitures have been occurring at (apparently) a substantial pace in the 1970s and 1980s, few data are available to allow us to keep track of this important activity, and no theories have been developed that would yield testable hypotheses concerning spin-offs and divestitures. This area may well be a promising one for research in the 1980s.

We now turn to a summary of the chapters in this book. The conference was organized into four broad sessions. The first session's papers discussed some theoretical questions concerning mergers and acquisitions. The second session raised some legal and social concerns. The third session focused on empirical work that tries to explain the patterns of mergers and acquisitions. The fourth session dealt with mergers in the context of corporate strategic planning.

In the next chapter, Richard C. Stapleton argues that an important motive for mergers must be to increase the debt capacity of the merged firm. He points out that the stock equity of a firm can be considered to be the equivalent of a call option on the cash flow and assets of the firm. When two companies merge, the combined equity is a call option on the portfolio of the combined firm. Since an option on a portfolio is generally worth less than a portfolio of options, ceteris paribus stockholders suffer a loss at the time of a merger and bondholders gain. However, the bondholders' gain yields a greater debt capacity for the firm, which allows greater leverage and ultimately, perhaps, greater gains for stockholders. Michael Keenan discusses some valuation problems in mergers, especially service-sector acquisitions. He argues that acquisitions may involve the capitalization of the value of the specialized labor in service-sector firms. But the capitalization process itself may provide those employees with new information as to their value and worth; and this type of human capital is frequently quite mobile. Hence, the acquiring firm may end up with lower earnings from its purchase than it had expected. This process, Keenan concludes, raises problems for value determination and accounting standards in acquisitions. Joshua Ronen points out that a merger creates the possibility of a loss of financial information concerning the operation of the individual components of the merged firm. Whether the merged firm's management chooses to reveal as much information as was revealed by the individual firms prior to the merger will depend on how the information affects the merged firm's stock prices and hence the welfare of the firm's stockholders. In some cases, as much information may be forthcoming as occurred prior to the merger; in others, however, less information will be yielded, and a social loss may occur.

In chapter 5, John J. Siegfried and Jane Barr Sweeney review the hypotheses that relate the large size of firms (of which mergers and acquisitions are an important cause) to various noneconomic social goals and concerns, and they survey the available empirical evidence on these hypotheses. They make the important distinctions among the effects of pure size, market concentration, and diversification. They also distinguish between the incentives for large firms to try to influence social outcomes and the efficiency with which they can actually mobilize their resources to achieve those outcomes. This distinction in turn allows Siegfried and Sweeney to distinguish between empirical tests of *efforts* (for example, lobbying) to achieve outcomes and of *results* (for example, differential tax rates). Lawrence J. White focuses on the question of aggregate concentration of economic activity in a few large corporations in chapter 6. He points out that many such measurements in the past have examined only the manufacturing sector but that manufacturing is less than a quarter of gross national product (GNP) and its percentage is declining. He argues that aggregate concentration, when measured across the entire private sector, was probably constant or even may have declined in the 1970s. This evidence greatly weakens the arguments of those who oppose large conglomerate mergers on the grounds that the problems of aggregate concentration are getting worse. In chapter 7, W. Scott Cooper, John J. Huber, and Benjamin M. Vandegrift discuss the legal issues surrounding insider information and securities trading, especially in the context of merger announcements. They provide an analysis of a recent Supreme Court decision (in *United States* v. *Chiarella*), which held that existing Securities and Exchange Commission (SEC) regulations (Rule 10b–5) did not apply to transactors who had no fiduciary obligations and who were trading in anonymous markets. They then explain the development and logic of the SEC's new rule 14e–3, which is designed to close this breach. The new rule makes it more difficult for individuals with insider information, regardless of their position, to trade and profit from this information. Dennis C. Mueller reviews in chapter 8 the evidence on the determinants and effects of mergers. He concludes that mergers in general do not bring important efficiency gains. Hence, he is prepared to consider some restrictions on conglomerate merger activity, and he provides a summary of the major possible restrictive policies.

In chapter 9, Ivan E. Brick, Lawrence J. Haber, and Daniel Weaver argue that diversification, especially in the presence of substantial financial leverage, is an important motive for conglomerate mergers. They develop a finance model of diversification benefits and test it on a sample of fifty-seven conglomerate mergers. They find that the interaction between diversification and leverage is an important factor in explaining the increases in stock market value (the merger premium) that occurred as a consequence of the mergers. In chapter 10, Robert S. Harris, John F. Stewart, and Willard T. Carleton focus on the characteristics of the acquired firms in the merger process. Using probit analysis on a sample of acquired and nonacquired firms, they find that small size and low price-earnings ratios are important characteristics of firms that are likely to be acquired. John B. Guerard, Jr., explores the relationship between mergers and the capital expenditures and employment of the merging firms in chapter 11. He finds that a capital-expenditures variable is a significant discriminant between the acquiring and acquired firms, whereas employment is not; apparently merger partners look for a fit in their capital-expenditures characteristics. He also finds that the merged firms appear to economize on capital expenditures after the merger; thus, there may be economies of scale in the use of capital. In chapter 12, Michael Bradley focuses on interfirm cash-tender offers. He argues that the bidding companies are not simply trying to make a capital gain on the shares they buy; in fact, they usually make a capital loss on those shares. Instead, the bidding companies achieve their gains through the successful control of the target companies and the efficiency synergies that follow. His examination of 258 tender offers provides evidence to support these conclusions.

In chapter 13, Kwang S. Chung and J. Fred Weston approach the question of conglomerate mergers from the perspective of corporate strategic planning. They argue that corporate planners are likely to be looking for both financial and managerial synergies and complementarities when seeking merger partners. They argue that the past studies of the determinants of mergers are consistent with this view, and they provide fresh evidence that supports their hypotheses. Finally, in chapter 14, Richard B. Curtiss offers a description of how the mergers and acquisitions program at United Technologies is actually managed. The company has focused on merger partners that were in high-technology areas, that were market leaders, and that had strong management capabilities. The company has in fact had an active program of acquisitions and, where appropriate, divestitures.

The chapters in this book represent a diversity of perspectives, disciplines, approaches, arguments, and conclusions. Many of the chapters are in harmony with each other; some are in sharp disagreement. As editors, we have not tried to use our editorial prerogative to try to shape a completely consistent whole. Rather, we believe that to understand fully the current questions and problems concerning mergers and acquisitions, one must understand these differences.

Part I
Some Issues in Merger Theory

2

Mergers, Debt Capacity, and the Valuation of Corporate Loans

R.C. Stapleton

Perhaps the most significant advance in the theory of finance in recent years has been the development of option-pricing theory. Since most corporate liabilities can be modeled as call options of various types, this theory has many applications in corporate finance. This chapter looks at some applications in option-pricing theory to the analysis of corporate mergers and acquisitions.[1]

Given limited liability, the equity of a firm is a call option on the cash flow and assets of the firm with an exercise price equal to the obligations to the bondholders. When two companies merge, the joint company normally becomes responsible for the combined debts. The equity of the merged firm is therefore a call option on a portfolio of cash flows and assets at an exercise price equal to the sum of the two separate bondholder obligations. It can be shown that an option on a portfolio is worth less than, or (in very special circumstances) the same as, a portfolio of options. Hence, in the case of a pure conglomerate merger in which no change in earnings is expected, the equity of the merged firm is likely to be less than the sum of the individual equity values. The size of this disincentive to merge can be estimated using option-pricing theory.[2]

The effect of mergers on existing debts may be a relatively unimportant effect for two reasons. First, if the merging firms have relatively small debt ratios and correspondingly low probabilities of defaulting, their debts will be selling near default-free yields, and merger will have little effect on debt values. Second, if one or the other of the firms has debt that is selling significantly above the default-free yield level, a determined management could reduce or avoid the disincentive effect by either purchasing the debt in the marketplace or by inserting me-first clauses into the merger agreement, thereby protecting its own stockholders from obligations to the acquiree's bondholders.[3] There is, however, a related merger effect that has perhaps greater practical importance—namely, the effect on debt capacity. Debt

I am grateful to Marti Subrahmanyam for suggesting the idea of simulating the effect of mergers on debt values. It goes without saying that the results derived in this chapter rely heavily on past joint work, especially that in Stapleton and Subrahmanyam (1980).

9

capacity—the amount of debt that a firm can raise at a given rate of inter-est—is important because of the discriminatory tax treatment of debt in-terest payments. Again, debt capacity can be investigated after recognizing explicitly that debt is a form of option contract and that the option, after the merger, is written on a portfolio rather than on separate assets.[4]

In this survey of the impact of merger on debt values and capacity, two important points are emphasized throughout. First is the distinction made previously between the impact of merger on the value of existing debts of the firm and the impact on the capacity to raise future debt. This distinction is often blurred in the literature. However, although closely connected, these are distinct issues, and it is easy to construct examples in which a merger would have no effect on debt capacity while significantly affecting the value of existing debts.

The second point is a methodological one. There is little point in using a sophisticated option-pricing model to demonstrate results that are true even under universal risk neutrality. Hence, the effect of mergers on debt values and capacity is looked at first under the assumption of risk neutrality. In order to capture the effects of risk aversion in the simplest possible way, models assuming quadratic utility are then investigated. In spite of the well-known problems with this assumption, certain issues can be neatly analyzed at this level.[5] At the most sophisticated level, an option-pricing model assuming multivariate normality of the underlying cash flows and constant absolute risk aversion is used to analyze debt capacity.[6]

Portfolios of Options and Options on Portfolios

Throughout this chapter we assume a one-period model.[7] Normally it is suf-ficient also to consider the merger of just two firms with cash flows at the end of the period (including the liquidation value of the assets), denoted by X_1 and X_2. If Y_j is the debt obligation of firms, due at the end of the period, then the return on the equity stock of the firm (given limited liability) is

$$E_j = \max(X_j - Y_j, 0). \qquad (2.1)$$

Correspondingly, the return on the debt securities is

$$Z_j = X_j - E_j = \min(Y_j, X_j). \qquad (2.2)$$

The return on the equity of the firm is the return on a European call option on X_j at an exercise price of Y_j. Correspondingly, the return on the debt securities is the return from writing such a covered call option on X_j at an exercise price of Y_j.

Consider now a pure conglomerate merger of firms 1 and 2 in which (by definition) the cash flow of the merged firm is

$$X = X_1 + X_2. \tag{2.3}$$

The return on the stock of the merged firm, if it has debt obligations Y, is

$$E = \max(X_1 + X_2 - Y, 0), \tag{2.4}$$

and the return on the debt obligation is

$$Z = X - E = \min(Y, X_1 + X_2). \tag{2.5}$$

Clearly, the return on the equity is a call option at exercise price Y on a portfolio of cash flows, and the debt return is the return from writing such an option.

An important case to consider is that in which Y is the sum of the individual firm debt obligations and represents a single obligation. In this case it can easily be shown that

$$E \leq E_1 + E_2 \tag{2.6}$$

since it is a property of the max operator that[8]

$$\max[X_1 + X_2 - (Y_1 + Y_2), 0] \leq \max(X_1 - Y_1, 0)$$
$$+ \max(X_2 - Y_2, 0). \tag{2.7}$$

Inequality 2.7 states that the return from an option on a portfolio is less than or equal to the return from a portfolio of options in which the exercise price of the former option is the sum of the exercise prices on the individual options.

The equity of the merged firm will be worth less than that of the individual firms because the merger effectively reduces the advantages to stockholders of limited liability. The corollary is that the bondholders' joint return is likely to be enhanced. In fact, because the sum of equity and bond returns are constant,

$$Z \geq Z_1 + Z_2, \tag{2.8}$$

which can be seen from

$$\min(Y_1 + Y_2, X_1 + X_2) \geq \min(Y_1, X_1) + \min(Y_2, X_2). \tag{2.9}$$

These conclusions are unaffected by the priority structure of the debt obligations. For example, perhaps the terms of the merger agreement give priority to the debt of, say, firm 2 or that after the merger there are two newly issued debts with differing priority. In this case, the equity of the merged firm has a return

$$E = \max[\max(X_1 + X_2 - Y_1, 0) - Y_2, 0]. \qquad (2.10)$$

However, in the single-period case, a compound option such as equation 2.10 is identical to a simple option at the sum of the two exercise prices. The right-hand side of equation 2.10 is identical to the left-hand side of equation 2.7. Clearly, the order of priorities within the debts of the firm has no influence on equity returns. It follows that the sum of the two debt returns is also the same as the debt return in equation 2.9, while the individual debt returns are quite different.

Valuation of Loans and Debt Capacity: The Case of Risk Neutrality

The essential coinsurance effect of mergers on debt and equity returns is captured by the first-order stochastic-dominance inequalities 2.7 and 2.9. Whatever the valuation model used, simple arbitrage considerations guarantee that the value of given-sized debt obligations must either rise or stay the same when guaranteed against the merged firm's cash flow. Since this is a first-order effect, it can be captured most simply by looking at expected values of the debt or equity returns and the effect on market values in a world of universal risk neutrality. The second-order effects can be analyzed using risk-aversion models after the primary effect has first been examined.[9]

The value, under risk neutrality, of a loan (D) that promises to pay Y_j against a cash flow X_j is (using equation 2.2)

$$D_j = r^{-1}E\,[\min(Y_j, X_j)]$$

$$= r^{-1}\left[\int_{-\infty}^{\infty} \min(Y_j, X_j)f(X_j)dX_j\right]$$

$$= r^{-1}\left[\int_{-\infty}^{Y_j} X_j f(X_j)dX_j + \int_{Y_j}^{\infty} Y_j f(X_j)dX_j\right], \qquad (2.11)$$

where r is a one plus the risk-free rate of interest and $f(X_j)$ is the density function of X_j. Equation 2.11 is tabulated, assuming that X_j is normally distributed, for various values of $f(X_j)$ and Y_j, with $r = 1.1$ in table 2-1.

Table 2-1
Debt Values under Risk Neutrality

Cash Flow	Firm A				Firm B				Firm C				Firm D			
Mean μ	100				100				100				100			
Standard deviation σ	25				30				35				40			
i percent	Y_A	D_A	$\frac{Y_A}{D_A}$	$P(X_A<Y_A)$	Y_B	D_B	$\frac{Y_B}{D_B}$	$P(X_B<Y_B)$	Y_C	D_C	$\frac{Y_C}{D_C}$	$P(X_C<Y_C)$	Y_D	D_D	$\frac{Y_D}{D_D}$	$P(X_D<Y_D)$
Debt level 1 12	68	60.7	1.12	.10	57	50.9	1.12	.08	42	38.4	1.12	.05	23	20.5	1.12	.03
Debt level 2 14	79	69.3	1.14	.20	70	61.4	1.14	.16	59	51.8	1.14	.12	45	39.5	1.14	.08
Debt level 3 16	86	74.1	1.16	.27	78	67.2	1.16	.23	70	60.3	1.16	.20	58	50.0	1.16	.15

Note: $D_j = r^{-1}[\mu_j F^*(Y_j) - \sigma_\pi f^*(Y_j) + Y_j[1 - F^*(Y_j)]]$, and $r = 1.1$.

Debt capacity can now be defined precisely and illustrated with the numerical examples of table 2-1. Debt capacity will be defined as a function

$$D_j^* = D_j^*(i), \qquad (2.12)$$

where

$$i = \frac{Y_j}{D_j}$$

and D_j is given by equation 2.11. The variable i is the nominal (promised) yield on the debt. $D_j^*(i)$ is the maximum debt that can be sold at a given promised yield i.

Debt capacity must be defined as a function since the amount of debt that can be raised is clearly dependent on the rate of interest offered. In practice what matters is the amount that can be raised at reasonable interest rates—that is, within (say) 2-4 percent of the prime (or risk-free) rate. It is just not normal practice to raise debt at very high rates, mainly because of the agency costs associated with a risky debt contract and perhaps because of the doubts that attend the tax deductibility of high interest payments. Hence, the definitions of debt capacity used by Kim (1978) and Turnbull (1979), where the absolute maximum of the function 2.12 is used, seem impractical. Defining debt capacity as the maximum amount of debt that can be raised at any price is just not very interesting.

This approach to debt capacity is closer to that of Lewellen (1971), who also considers debt capacity to be a function. However, his definition did not explicitly look at market values and resulting interest rates. He sees debt capacity as basically a lender's decision. Lenders are then assumed to set limits to debt raising by limiting the probability of default. In Lewellen's model, debt capacity is determined by solving

$$\int_{-\infty}^{Y_j} f(X_j)dX_j \le \alpha, \qquad (2.13)$$

where the left-hand side is the probability of default and α is the prescribed limit.

Lewellen's model actually implies that lenders ignore the returns that accrue to them in the event of a partial default. This would be reasonable as an approximation if bankruptcy costs are so large that lenders are effectively wiped out in the event of a default. Alternatively, if default probabilities are linearly related to expected debt returns, control by default probability might be effectively the same as control by given promised interest-rate yields. However, the following simulations show that this is not the case if cash flows are normally distributed. The Lewellen approach can be thought of as a rather crude version of the market-value–interest-rate approach to debt capacity.

Simulations of Debt Capacity: The Normal Distribution

Note that when X_j is normally distributed, equation 2.11 can be rewritten

$$rD_j = \mu_j F^*(Y_j) - \sigma_j f^*(Y_j) + Y_j[1 - F^*(Y_j)], \qquad (2.14)$$

where $f^*(Y_j)$ and $F^*(Y_j)$ are the standard normal density function and distribution function and μ_j and σ_j are the mean and standard deviation of X_j.[10]

In Table 2–1, D_j values are recorded for four firms with differing risk levels. If firm A, which has a single-period cash flow with mean $100 and standard deviation $25, promises debt obligations of $68, it can sell them for $60.70 if the risk-free interest rate is 10 percent. In fact, the maximum amount of debt that could be raised at a promised coupon yield of 12 percent is $60.70. At this level the ratio of Y_j to D_j is exactly 1.12, whereas at higher debt levels it is higher (for example, if $Y_j = 79$, the ratio is 1.14) and at lower levels it would be lower. The figures for D_j and Y_j in table 2–1 represent solutions to equation 2.14 with the additional constraint that $Y_j/D_j = 1 + i$, where i is fixed at 12 percent, 14 percent, and 16 percent. It can readily be seen that D_j^*, the debt capacity, increases at a diminishing rate as the promised coupon increases. Also, at any given coupon rate the amount of debt obtainable declines at an increasing rate as the risk of the underlying cash flow increases.

Mergers, Debt Capacity, and Loan Values: Risk Neutrality

In the section on options we saw (in equations 2.8 and 2.9) that the return to lenders to a conglomerate was greater than or equal to the sum of the returns to lenders, of the same aggregate amount, to independent firms. It follows that the value of the loans is likely to be greater and the required coupon rate less. Alternatively, the conglomerate can raise more debt at a given coupon rate than its constituent parts could. In this section we look at some simulations of this effect under the assumption of risk neutrality.

From equations 2.8 and 2.9, we know that if a conglomerate promises the same aggregate loan payment $Y = Y_1 + Y_2$ against earnings $X = X_1 + X_2$, then $Z \geq Z_1 + Z_2$. Under risk neutrality,

$$D = r^{-1}E(Z)$$
$$\geq r^{-1}E(Z_1) + r^{-1}E(Z_2)$$
$$= D_1 + D_2. \tag{2.15}$$

It follows that, if Y_1 and Y_2 are at premerger debt-capacity levels such that

$$\frac{Y_1}{D_1} = \frac{Y_2}{D_2} = 1 + i, \tag{2.16}$$

then, if the same total debt obligation is outstanding after merger,

$$\frac{Y_1 + Y_2}{D} \leq 1 + i. \tag{2.17}$$

If 2.17 is a strict inequality, then the amount of debt could be expanded while maintaining the coupon rate i. The following examples show that the effect of merger on debt capacity is dependent on the relative risks of the merging firms as well as the correlation between the firms' earnings.

It is convenient to talk of debt capacity as the amount of debt obligation Y_j that can be supported at a given coupon rate i rather than the amount of debt D_j that can be raised. Since for a given i, D_j is proportional to Y_j, this is an equivalent definition of debt capacity. Table 2–2 shows the debt capacity of firms B and D at three levels of coupon rate i: 12 percent, 14 percent, and 16 percent. The sum of their individual debt capacities is $80 at $i = 12$ percent. It then shows the effect of merging the firms to form firm BD, assuming that the cash flows of the firms are uncorrelated, correlated, and perfectly correlated.

Under Lewellen's (1971) definition of debt capacity, a merger between firms with perfectly correlated cash flows has no effect on debt capacity. If the probability limit is held at $\alpha = .043$, for example, firm B can raise debt with obligation $Y_B = 48.6$. Firm D can raise $Y_D = 31.4$. If the earnings streams of B and D are uncorrelated, BD can raise $Y_{BD} = 114.3$, a considerable increase on the sum of Y_B and Y_D. However, if B's and D's cash flows are positively correlated, the increase is smaller, and in the limit, if $\rho = 1$, the debt capacity is $Y_{BD} = 80$, exactly equal to the sum of the individual debt capacities.

If debt capacity is defined taking into account the payments to bondholders in the event of a default, this result does not hold. Even if the earn-

Table 2-2
Debt Capacity and Merger under Risk Neutrality

| | Firm B | Firm D | | Firm BD | | |
				$\rho = 0$	$\rho = 0.46$	$\rho = 1$
Mean μ	100	100		200	200	200
Standard deviation σ	30	40		50	60	70
i percent	Y_B	Y_D	$Y_B + Y_D$	Y_{BD}	Y_{BD}	Y_{BD}
Debt capacity[a]						
12	57	23	80	136	114	84
14	70	45	115	158	140	118
16	78	58	136	172	156	140
Debt capacity[b] ($\alpha = .043$)	48.6	31.4	80	114.3	97.2	80

[a]Debt capacity is defined as in table 2-1.
[b]Debt capacity defined, as in Lewellen (1971), as the level of promised payments such that $P(X_j < Y_j) \leq \alpha$. Here, α is chosen so that the total debt of firms B and D is the same as that generated by a 12 percent interest-rate limit.

ings are perfectly correlated, there is an increase in debt capacity upon merger. For example, at the 12 percent interest-rate level, B can raise $Y_B = 57$ and D can raise $Y_D = 23$, whereas the merged firm can raise $Y_{BD} = 84$. The phenomenon is explained by the nonlinear effect of risk (as measured by standard deviation) on debt capacity noted earlier in table 2–1.

The other feature of table 2–2 that should be noted is that the size of the debt-capacity effect is far larger than in the Lewellen model. For example, at the 12 percent level with $\rho = 0$, debt capacity rises from a total of $Y_B + Y_D = 80$ to $Y_{BD} = 136$, compared with the Lewellen increase from 80 to 114.3. This is because merger has a fairly radical effect on the size of bondholder returns in the event of a default. Finally, it should be noted that the debt-capacity effect of merger is larger if debt capacity is defined stringently. At the 12 percent interest level, the absolute increase in debt capacity is larger [$Y_{BD} - (Y_B + Y_D) = 56$] than at the more-liberal 14 percent and 16 percent levels.

Mergers and the Value of Existing Debt

The important effect of conglomerate mergers is on the capacity to raise debt since this can constitute a significant motive for merger. Existing debts are of subsidiary importance since they can, of course, normally be paid off before the merger is effected. However, it is often inconvenient to repay such debts, so an analysis of the effect of merger on them is relevant. Also it might be of interest to consider the terms on which a merged firm could raise the same quantity of debt as the independent enterprises. Table 2–3, then, looks at the effect of merger on the value and yields of debt when the total outstanding obligations remain constant after the merger.

In table 2–3, firm B has debt obligations $Y_B = 78$ promising 16 percent, and firm D has obligations of $Y_D = 58$, also promising 16 percent. The value and yield of the obligation $Y_{BD} = 136$ after merger depends on the correlation of the earnings. If $\rho = 0$ the yield drops to 12 percent. If $\rho = 0.46$ the yield drops to 14 percent, and if $\rho = 1$ it stays unchanged at 16 percent. Table 2–3 results are a direct reflection of the analysis of the second section of this chapter. Merger provides protection for debtors, and this is reflected in bond yields.

The effect of merger on bond yields is not simply due to the correlation structure of the earnings. It is clear that even if cash flows are perfectly correlated, then added protection is afforded to debtors if one of the two companies is below its debt capacity at the time of merger. For example, if D has no debt, the obligation of B is increased in value by merger with D even if earnings are perfectly correlated, and the yield is reduced to 12 percent.[11]

Table 2-3
Interest Rates, Debt Values, and Merger under Risk Neutrality

		Firm B	Firm D	Firm B + Firm D	Firm BD $\rho = 0$	Firm BD $\rho = 0.46$	Firm BD $\rho = 1$
Premerger Y_j at same debt capacity (i = 16 percent):	Y_j	78	58	136	136	136	136
Debt values[a]	D_j	67.2	50	117.2	121.4	119.3	117.2
Yield (percentage)	i	16	16	16	12	14	16
Premerger Y_j not at same debt capacity:	Y_j	78	0	78	—	—	78
Debt values[a]	D_j	67.2	0	67.2	—	—	69.6
Yield (percentage)	i	16	—	16	—	—	12

[a]To nearest whole percentage yield.

Mergers and the Value of Debt under Risk Aversion

The analysis of the previous section can be extended to risk aversion by using a contingent-claims-valuation model. Several possibilities exist:

Black and Scholes (1973)	Continuous time model;
Rubinstein (1976)	Lognormal distribution, discrete time model;
Kim (1978)	Normal distribution, quadratic utility model;
Brennan (1979)	Normal distribution, exponential utility model;
Cox, Ross, and Rubinstein (1979)	Binomial distribution model.

The continuous time model was used as background for a rather loose analysis of merger by Galai and Masulis (1976). In actual fact, a rigorous analysis of merger using this model is not possible since the model assumes that the end-period value of the firm is lognormally distributed. Unfortunately, the lognormal distribution is not a member of the stable class of distributions—that is, linear combinations of lognormal random variables are not lognormally distributed (except in the uninteresting special case in which the variables are perfectly correlated). Thus, it is not possible to assume that the merged firm's earnings are lognormally distributed if the merging firm's earnings are so distributed. The same problem exists with the Rubinstein's (1976) lognormal distribution, discrete time model. Essentially, if the model were used to value the individual debts, a different model would be needed to evaluate the merged firm's debt. Unfortunately, the very simple model in Cox, Ross, and Rubinstein (1979) suffers from the same nonstability problem. The choice of model reduces, therefore, to two approaches based on the normal distribution. Of course, the sum of two normally distributed cash flows is normal, and this stability allows us to value the merged company's debt with the same model used for the independent companies.

Kim (1978) uses the mean-variance capital-asset-pricing model (CAMP) to value risky debt. One possibility is simply to extend his model to value the debt of the merged company. However, as will be shown, this model has two disadvantages compared with the exponential utility model of Brennan (1979). First, the quadratic utility function, which is required since debt and equity returns are truncated distributions, has well-known problems associated with it.[12] Second, it turns out that the Brennan (1979) model is simpler, from a computational point of view, than the quadratic utility model.

It follows from state-preference theory that the value of a bond with payoff Z_j, which is a contingent claim on a cash flow X_j (see equation 2.2), has a value[13]

$$D_j = \frac{1}{r} E[Z_j \phi(W)] \qquad (2.18)$$

that, given the definition of covariance, yields

$$D_j = \frac{1}{r} \{ E(Z_j) E(\phi) + \text{cov}[Z_j, \phi(W)] \}. \qquad (2.19)$$

$\phi(W)$ is an aggregate marginal utility of wealth function for end-period wealth W.

In the special case in which utility is quadratic and marginal utility is linear with parameter b, the covariance in equation 2.19 can be written

$$\text{cov}[Z_j, \phi(W)] = b \, \text{cov}(Z_j, W). \qquad (2.20)$$

Furthermore, if X_j and W are joint normal, this term can be further simplified using results for the partial moments of the normal distribution. Since Z_j is a simple function of X_j, we have

$$\text{cov}(Z_j, W) = E\left(\frac{dZ_j}{dX_j}\right) \text{cov}(X_j, W)$$

$$= F(Y_j) \, \text{cov}(X_j, W), \qquad (2.21)$$

where $F(Y_j)$ is the probability of default on the loan.[14]

Substitution of equations 2.21 and 2.20 into equation 2.19 yields an analytic formula for evaluating the value of a bond. This is in fact the basis for the formula used by Kim (1978) to evaluate bond values. Since the effect of conglomerate mergers on $E(Z_j)$ has been analyzed previously, as well as the effect on $F(Y_j)$, and the effect on $\text{cov}(X_j, W)$ is a simple additive one, it would be a straightforward extension of the previous analysis to show the effects of merger on debt capacity and bond values in the quadratic-utility case.

Although the quadratic-utility model is a simple one, Brennan (1979) has shown that if cash flows are normally distributed and utility exponential, an even simpler valuation of contingent claims results. Brennan shows that in this case equation 2.18 can be evaluated by shifting the mean of X_j.

The size of the mean shift is given by the certainty equivalent of X_j in the mean-variance CAPM. Because of its simplicity and its close relationship to the risk-neutrality analysis of the previous section, the normal distribution, exponential utility model is used in the following simulation of debt capacity under risk aversion.

**Mergers and Debt Capacity: Simulations of the
Exponential Utility Model**

In the special case in which the underlying cash flow X_j is normally distributed and utility is exponential, the effect of risk aversion on bond values is entirely captured by its effect on the value of the underlying cash flow. After this effect has been computed, the contingent claim can be valued in relation to this underlying value using the procedure in the section on risk neutrality, as if investors were risk neutral. Brennan (1979) shows that, in the context of a bond,

$$rD_j \quad = \int_{-\infty}^{\infty} \min(Y_j, X_j) \hat{f}(X_j) dX_j, \qquad (2.22)$$

where

$$\hat{f}(X_j) = \frac{1}{\sqrt{2\pi}\,\sigma} \; e^{-(X_j - Vr)}$$

and where V is the value of X_j at $t = 0$ and Vr is the certainty equivalent of X_j. Compared to the risk-neutral case, this certainty equivalent has been substituted for the mean of X_j.

In the numerical simulations in table 2–4, the mean of X_j is 100 for each of the firms B, C, and D. From the CAPM we have the certainty equivalent of X_j:

$$Vr = \mu_j - \lambda(\phi_j \rho_{jM}), \qquad (2.23)$$

where ρ_{jM} is the correlation between X_j and the return on the market portfolio and λ is the market price of risk. In the simulations, ρ_{BM} is at three levels (1, 0.75, and 0) in order to illustrate the effects of covariance on the bond values. Firms C and D have a correlation of 0.75 with the market. The market price of risk parameter is $\lambda = \frac{1}{3}$, and hence for firm C, for example, the certainty equivalent cash flow is

$$Vr = 100 - \frac{1}{3}(35 \times 0.75) = 91.25. \qquad (2.24)$$

Debt Capacity/Corporate Loans 23

Table 2-4
Debt Capacity under Risk Aversion

Cash Flow		Firm B			Firm C	Firm D
Mean μ			100		100	100
Standard deviation σ			30		35	40
Correlation with market ρ_m		1	0.75	0	0.75	0.75
	i percent	Y_B	Y_B	Y_B	Y_C	Y_D
Debt level 1	12	44	47	57	28	0
Debt level 2	14	56	60	70	46	22
Debt level 3	16	63	68	78	56	41

Using these certainty equivalents, debt values were calculated, and the resulting debt capacities at the 12 percent, 14 percent, and 16 percent levels are presented in table 2-4. Note first that debt capacity is a declining function of the correlation between the underlying cash flow and the market. If there is zero correlation, debt capacity and debt values are the same as they were under risk neutrality since, in this case, the underlying cash flow is valued as if investors were risk neutral. The debt capacities for firm B show that the higher the correlation, the lower the debt capacity of the firm at a given interest rate. Compared with the risk-neutral debt capacities of table 2-1, the debt capacities under risk aversion are considerably lower. Thus, firm D, for example, can raise no debt at all at 12 percent, whereas under risk neutrality, it could raise debt with an obligation $Y_D = 23$. As before, debt capacity (given the degree of correlation) falls more than proportionately as ϕ_j increases and rises less than proportionately as the maximum interest rate is increased.

In table 2-5, the effect on debt capacity of merging firms B (with $\rho_{BM} = 0.75$) and D is simulated, first assuming that the correlation between B and D is $\rho = 1$ and second assuming that $\rho = 0.46$. The first assumption implies that the correlation between BD and the market remains at 0.75, and the second implies that it increases to 0.875. Again it is apparent that, even when the earnings are perfectly correlated, merger does affect debt capacity. At the 12 percent level, debt capacity rises from a combined $Y_B + Y_D = 47$ to $Y_{BD} = 56$. As before, this is due to the nonlinear relationship between risk and debt capacity. Lenders will lend more at a given rate of interest to a medium-risk firm than they would to high- and low-risk independent concerns.

Comparison of tables 2-2 and 2-5 shows that under risk aversion the effect of merger on debt capacity is far more significant. In the case in which $\rho_{BD} = 0.46$, the increase in debt capacity is larger in absolute as well as relative terms, even though debt capacities are far smaller. Thus, at the $i = 14$ percent level, debt capacity rises from 82 to 116, whereas under risk neutrality the rise was only from 115 to 140.

Finally, it should be noted that the effect of merger on the ability to raise a given amount of debt is similar to that in the risk-neutral case. A separate table has not been prepared to show this since it is readily apparent from the figures in table 2-5. Note, for example, that B and D could raise a total of 109 at 16 percent, whereas rather more (116) could be raised after merger at 14 percent. The effect of merger on existing debt would be to reduce yields in this case from 16 percent to slightly less than 14 percent.

Conclusions

The use of option-pricing theory in this chapter has shown that an effect of merger on debt capacity may exist even when earnings are perfectly cor-

Table 2-5
Debt Capacity and Merger under Risk Aversion

				Firm BD	
	Firm B		Firm D	$\rho = 0.46$	$\rho = 1$
Mean μ	100		100	200	200
Standard deviation σ	30		40	60	70
Correlation with market ρ_m	0.75		0.75	0.875	0.75
		Y_B	Y_D	$Y_B + Y_D$	
Debt capacity	12	47	0	47	91	56
Debt capacity	14	60	22	82	116	92
Debt capacity	16	68	41	109	133	112

related. Also, the Lewellen definition of debt capacity tends to underestimate the effects of merger. The use of a discrete-time bond-valuation model assuming normally distributed cash flows and exponential utility suggested that the debt-capacity effects of merger can be underestimated using simple risk-neutral models.

Notes

1. Modern option-pricing theory owes much to papers by Black and Scholes (1973) and Merton (1973). Rubinstein (1976) and Brennan (1979) have generalized the continuous-time approach of the early papers to the valuation of options in discrete time. The simplest approach (implied by its title) is that of Cox, Ross, and Rubinstein (1979), who show that, if the underlying asset follows a binomial process, a particularly simple valuation of an option on the asset results from a hedging argument.

2. Merton (1974) used the continuous-time option-pricing model to value single-period debt obligations. Geske (1977; 1979) analyzes compound options to value bonds with coupons. Stapleton and Subrahmanyam (1980) extend Brennan's (1979) discrete-time model to a multiperiod scenario and value bonds and equities assuming that underlying cash flows are normally distributed. Galai and Masulis (1976) were the first to recognize that conglomerate mergers could be analyzed using option-pricing theory. This chapter represents an in-depth extension of their analysis. The coinsurance effect of the corporate merger was recognized and analyzed in a non-options-pricing theory context by Stapleton (1972; 1973), Higgins and Schall (1975), and Kim and McConnell (1977). Essentially, these papers pointed out the effect of mergers on expected equity returns.

3. Alternatively, Kim and McConnell (1977) argue that the merged firm may expand its debt outstanding and negate any wealth transfer to

bondholders. However, this would require issuing new bonds with priority over or equal priority with existing bonds. This may well be prevented by the indenture provisions of the existing bonds.

4. Lewellen (1971) and Stapleton (1973) look at the affect of mergers on debt capacity. Neither of these analyses takes account of the fact that the return on bonds corresponds to that of the writer of a covered call option on the cash flow and assets of the firm. Turnbull (1979) uses the Black and Scholes (1973) framework to look at the debt capacity of a single firm. However, his definition of debt capacity is different from that used in this chapter. Turnbull defines debt capacity to be the level of debt interest payments that maximize the value of the debt. This ignores the fact that the tax deductability of debt interest is, in practice, restricted to reasonable interest-rate levels.

5. The analysis assuming quadratic utility follows that of Kim (1974; 1978) and Chen, Kim, and Kon (1975). Although these papers do not state it explicitly, they assume quadratic utility by using mean-variance models to analyze bonds subject to default risk. The problems associated with this assumption have been pointed out by Gonzalez, Litzenberger, and Rolfo (1977).

6. The continuous-time methodology of Black and Scholes (1973) is not appropriate for the evaluation of conglomerate mergers and is not used here. The fundamental problem is that, in their model, firm value at the end of a finite period is lognormal. However, if two firms with lognormal values (or cash flows) are merged, the combination cannot be lognormal unless the two are perfectly correlated. This problem, which also applies to Rubinstein's (1976) discrete-time, lognormal, option-pricing model, may be of small relevance when valuing options on individual assets is fundamental and when the effect of merger is the issue under consideration.

7. The multiperiod case is a nontrivial extension of the single-period bond-valuation problem. In the multiperiod case, options are invariably written on portfolios of multiperiod cash flows. For an investigation of these issues in a nonmerger context, see Stapleton and Subrahmanyam (1980).

8. See Merton (1973, Theorem 7). The max function is convex, and the inequality is a property of convex functions.

9. This first-order effect is essentially the one that Lewellen (1971), Stapleton (1972), and Higgins and Schall (1975) analyze without resort to option-pricing theory.

10. This follows from Winkler, Roodman, and Britney (1972). The result is used by Kim (1978) and Brennan (1979). The analogue for the case where X_j is lognormal is used to derive the Black and Scholes (1973) formula for the value of a call option.

11. In option-pricing parlance, this is the striking price effect of combining two options.

12. These problems were pointed out in the context of risky debt by Gonzalez, Litzenberger, and Rolfo (1977).

13. See Rubinstein (1976) or Brennan (1979, equation 5).

14. Note that $dZ_j/dX_j = 1$ if $Y_j > X_j$ and that $dZ_j/dX_j = 0$ if $Y_j < X_j$. Hence, equation 2.21 follows from Rubinstein (1976). Alternatively, Kim (1978) proves the same result using properties of lower partial moments of the normal distribution.

References

Black, Fischer, and Scholes, Myron. "The Pricing Options and Corporate Liabilities." *Journal of Political Economy* 81 (May/June 1973): 637–654.

Brennan, Michael J. "The Pricing of Contingent Claims in Discrete Time Models." *Journal of Finance* 34 (March 1979):53–68.

Chen, Andrew H.; Kim, Han E.; and Kon, Stanley. "Cash Demand, Liquidation Costs and Capital Market Equilibrium under Uncertainty." *Journal of Financial Economics* 2 (1975):293–308.

Cox, John C.; Ross, Stephen A.; and Rubinstein, Mark E. "Option Pricing: A Simplified Approach." *Journal of Fiancial Economics* 7 (September 1979):229–263.

Galai, Dan, and Masulis, Ronald W. "The Option Pricing Model and the Risk Factor of Stock." *Journal of Financial Economics* 3 (1976):53–82.

Geske, Robert E. "The Valuation of Corporate Liabilities as Compound Options." *Journal of Financial and Quantitative Analysis* 12 (November 1977):541–552.

———. "The Valuation of Compound Options." *Journal of Financial Economics* 7 (March 1979):63–81.

Gonzalez, Nestor; Litzenberger, Robert; and Rolfo, Jacques. "On Mean Variance Models of Capital Structure and the Absurdity of their Predictions." *Journal of Financial and Quantitative Analysis* 13(June 1977):165–179.

Higgins, Robert C., and Schall, Lawrence D. "Corporate Bankruptcy and Conglomerate Merger." *Journal of Finance* 30 (March 1975):93–113.

Kim, Han E. "A Theory of Optimal Financial Structure in Market Equilibrium: A Critical Examination of the Effects of Bankruptcy and Corporate Income Taxation. Ph. D. dissertation, State University of New York at Buffalo, 1974.

————. "A Mean-Variance Theory of Optimal Capital Structure and Corporate Debt Capacity." *Journal of Finance* 33 (1978):45–63.

Kin, Han E., and McConnell, John J. "Corporate Mergers and the Coinsurance of Corporate Debt." *Journal of Finance* 32 (May 1977): 349–353.

Lewellen, Wilbur G. "A Pure Financial Rationale for the Conglomerate Merger." *Journal of Finance* 26 (May 1971):521–537.

Merton, Robert C. "Theory of Rational Option Pricing." *Bell Journal of Economics and Management Science* 4 (Spring 1973):141–183.

————. "On the Pricing of Corporate Debt: The Risk Structure of Interest Rates." *Journal of Finance* 29 (May 1974):449–484.

Myers, Stewart C. "Determinants of Corporate Borrowing." *Journal of Financial Economics* 5 (1977):147–175.

Rubinstein, Mark E. "The Valuation of Uncertain Income Streams and the Pricing of Options." *Bell Journal of Economics* 7 (Autumn 1976): 407–425.

Stapleton, Richard C., "Conglomerate Mergers and Corporate Debt Capacity." Unpublished manuscript. 1973.

Stapleton, Richard C., and Subrahmanyam, Marti G. "Default Risk, Debt Capacity and the Valuation of Corporate Loans." Manchester Business School, August 1980.

Turnbull, Stuart M. "Debt Capacity." *Journal of Finance* 34 (September 1979):931–940.

Winkler, Robert L.; Roodman, Gary M.; and Britney, Robert R. "The Determination of Partial Moments." *Management Science* 19 (1972): 290–296.

3 Valuation Problems in Service-Sector Mergers

Michael Keenan

Modern analysis of the financial impact of a merger between two firms has focused almost exclusively on the risk-redistribution impact of a conglomerate-type merger, having zero synergistic benefits, in equilibrium capital markets. This chapter examines the other, and we believe more-pervasive, situation in which real economic adjustments evolve from the merger.

Our focus is on the valuation problem associated with real synergistic benefits arising from the acquisition of a service-sector firm. Of particular interest is the value of labor in an acquired firm in which the alternative mechanism for the acquiring firm is entry into the industry by starting a new firm. It would appear, particularly in service-sector acquisitions, that the value of labor is being capitalized. Since the capital markets are not assumed to capitalize the inherent value of the labor force (only its marginal product), this poses a number of questions for the financial manager.

Some might argue that, since mergers are a particularization of the capital-budgeting process, there is really no issue to consider. At least two answers are offered to such assertions. First, capital-budgeting theory has not been very well developed for the typical multiperiod problem where risk levels are shifting and where project-tied financing considerations exist (and these are the typical parameters of a merger decision). Despite its cavalier use in some textbooks and even some professional journals, it is usually recognized that CAPM cannot easily be applied to many capital-budgeting projects without violating critical one-period-horizon, full-equilibrium assumptions. Second, to the extent existing theory is applicable, it remains uncomfortably generalized for application at the firm level—for example, telling a firm its product prices can be best determined by solving the simultaneous system of equations for all demand, supply, and budget constraints in the economy. In the merger area the analogous statement suggests that if the capital markets are strongly efficient and all investors hold their desired (leveraged where necessary) portion of the market portfolio, then the valuation impact of merger and the amount of securities exchanged between firms is a matter of indifference to investors.[1] However, some evidence shows that the real economic markets for labor and capital are not strongly efficient, which complicates matters even if the financial-securities markets should appear to be highly efficient.

In the rest of this chapter, we look first at the drift of current research in the mergers and acquisitions area and why that research has limited applicability to the question at hand. The following section reviews general valuation alternatives and how they relate to synergistic merger opportunities. In the last section we look at some simple examples of the acquisition of a firm in which current wages may understate the value of labor. Throughout, the focus is on the expected value of cash flows and not their distributions. We leave for another book the further complication of what happens if disequilibrium exists in the price of risk in addition to the disequilibrium in the factor prices.

Drift of Research on Mergers and Acquisitions

Most of the research on mergers and acquisitions since the early 1960s has focused on two questions: (1) Are there any real benefits to conglomerate-type mergers, and (2) what are the portfolio implications of a merger between two firms? Even in this latter question the analysis has tended to focus on portfolio implications of a merger between two firms for which no positive or negative economic benefits accrue. For example, Bierman and Hass (1970) argue that merger-created growth in per-share earnings should be a valuation fiction; the value of a merged firm (with zero net benefits) is the sum of the economic values of the two premerged firms so that two firms with different price-earnings ratios merging through share exchange must have an intermediate price-earnings ratio after the merger. Levy and Sarnat (1970) suggest that, under standard Markowitz portfolio theory, there may be no risk-reducing benefits in such mergers, and Myers (1976) and Mossin (1968) suggest that, under standard equilibrium conditions for CAPM, there are no valuation or risk-reducing benefits to mergers. Lewellen (1971) argues that while stockholders cannot gain, creditors may benefit from this type of merger, but Higgins (1971) Stapleton (1975), and Elton, Gruber, and Lightstone (1977), all suggest in different ways that the bankruptcy-creditor risks are not as simple as suggested and come entirely at the expense of stockholder returns.

As to the question of whether there have been any real benefits to con-glomerate mergers, Reid (1968); Steiner (1975); Franks, Broyles, and Hecht (1977); and others argue that statistically there are few apparent valuation benefits to mergers observed and that much merger activity may actually be to the detriment of standard profit-maximizing goals. Mandelker (1974) and Dodd and Ruback (1977) reinforce this conclusion with short-run efficient market tests of abnormal stock returns associated with mergers; while the stockholders of acquired firms appear to reap some benefits (and hence violate equilibrium-CAPM assumptions used to make the tests), the shareholders of acquiring firms basically do not.

One can easily get the impression from this research that a merger or acquisition decision makes little difference, except perhaps to the employment of antitrust lawyers. From a valuation viewpoint, or a cost-of-capital evaluation, or a financial-structure consideration, merger appears to be a mere detail of currently received theory. Unfortunately, as Myers (1976) and other researchers have indicated, existing theory can explain very few of the facts of real merger activity: for example, why there have been great merger waves in the United States rather than continuous random activity; why some merger financial strategies are preferred to others and how these are related to business-cycle conditions; and most important, when there are real economic increments (positive or negative) associated with consolidation, what the relevant financial theory and industrial organization implications are. Part of this last issue is what concerns us in this chapter.

Unfortunately, as table 3-1 indicates, there is not even a clear picture of overall merger activity in the United States. The most widely quoted series is one released by the Federal Trade Commission (FTC), but this series focuses primarily on the mining and manufacturing firms over which the FTC has jurisdiction. Most finance-sector industries—banking, securities firms, and some insurance—most regulated industries, and many small service-sector firms, are apparently omitted. While many of these acquisitions are small in dollar value, they may portend trends in an increasingly service-sector-oriented economy.

Some Merger-Valuation Possibilities

Before looking at a simple example of what might happen in a merger in which the cost of the labor factor is not in equilibrium, it may be useful to consider some of the possible valuation outcomes in the merger process. In this way the reader may get some feel for the scope of the whole process and for what a very small piece of it we are actually addressing here (and what a small piece most research in the 1960s and 1970s has addressed). To keep the situation as simple as possible, we will assume firm A acquires firm B for a payment vector that might include cash, securities, or future considerations of some sort. Each firm generates cash flows that are the basis of valuation.[2] The *expected value* of a firm is assumed to be a properly discounted sum of the cash flows being distributed directly or indirectly to the various suppliers of capital. The discount rates applied to the streams of each firm are a function of risk-free-interest-rate term structures and risk premiums applied for things like capital structure, market covariance, inflation, extreme value potential, and so forth.

The *market value* of either firm may be higher, lower, or equal to the rational-expectations-equilibrium value described as the expected value in the previous paragraph. Existing studies suggest that premiums of more

Table 3-1
Overall Merger Activity in the United States

Year	Total Transactions[a]	Total Transactions[b]
1965	1893	2125
1966	1746	2377
1967	2384	2975
1968	3932	4462
1969	4542	6107
1970	3089	5152
1971	2633	4608
1972	2839	4801
1973	2359	4040
1974	1474	2861
1975	1047	2297
1976	1171	2276
1977	1183	2244
1978	1245	2106

[a]Series of completed mergers and acquisitions from the Bureau of Economics, Federal Trade Commission, 1980.
[b]Series of total publicly announced transactions, including the acquisitions of divisions of other firms with a value of more than one-half million dollars as reported by W.T. Grimm & Company (data from Joseph M. Sheer, "Divestitures and Spin-Offs," MBA thesis, New York University, 1978).

than 30 percent may be commonly paid to acquire another firm. Since related studies suggest that for conglomerate mergers there may be few real economic benefits, the implication is that short-run market-value disequilibrium exists either before the merger (if the market value of B is less than the expected value) or after the merger (if A paid too much for B) for at least some types of mergers. One of the assumptions of this chapter is that short-run demand, supply conditions, or noneconomic psychological pressures may cause the market value of individual firms (or even the market as a whole) to deviate from the full-horizon expected values. That is, the market provides real merger opportunities from time to time in addition to the real opportunities always present if there are positive synergistic benefits.

After the merger, the new firm C has a cash-flow vector that has its own risk characteristics. There is an expected value for this stream and a market value for firm C that at any point in time may again be higher or lower than the expected value determined from marketwide parameters (the expected value calculated from the discounting of the cash flows at rates set by the prices of the various risk premiums). Since the cash-flow vector of firm C may be (less than, equal to, greater than) the sum of the premerger vectors, and the same is true for the market value of C relative to the premerger values of A and B, there are already nine possible states to analyze. A summary of the stages of this decision process is described in figure 3-1.

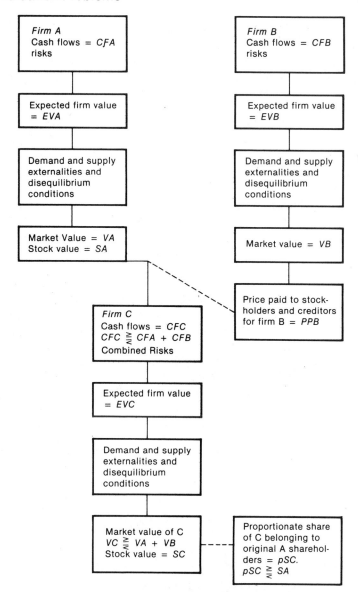

Figure 3-1. Valuation Factors in Mergers

Mergers and acquisitions research has customarily stated null hypotheses in terms of premerger and postmerger cash flows ($CFC = CFA + CFB$—that is, there are no real economic benefits), or in terms of similar market-value conditions ($VC = VA + VB$—that is, there are no financial markets benefits). Research findings seem to support the cash-flow null hypotheses for pure conglomerate mergers between firms already having adequate access to the capital markets. The hypothesis has never been adequately tested for other types of acquisitions and, as we shall argue later, probably not even for conglomerates since the process of merging two disparate flows is more complex than the simple valuation models have made it out to be. For the market-value hypothesis, the evidence is mixed. On the one hand, the acquiring firms seem to be paying significant premiums for the firms acquired. On the other hand, there seem to be no significant negative returns for the firm As or firm Cs around the merger date, even for pure conglomerate mergers. Yet the consensus seems to be that the null valuation hypothesis cannot be rejected.

Actually, if the goal of maximizing shareholder wealth is taken as the prime objective [and Reid (1968) and other provide ample evidence that this is not the case in many mergers], the situation becomes even more complex, for the null hypothesis becomes: "The proportionate share of firm A's stockholders' market value in firm C is equal to their premerger value in firm A." It is entirely possible that the stockholders of firm A would be better off after a merger with firm B even though the cash flows of firm C are less than $CFA + CFB$ and the market value of firm C is less than $VA + VB$. Somebody will be a loser—the stockholders of B or the creditors— but exactly who depends on the terms offered or securities used in the acquisition.[3]

Even the simplest cases have complications. Suppose firms A and B are simple Gordon-model firms—that is, all equity firms whose cash flows are growing at different constant rates, where each has an established dividend policy and a constant marginal rate of return on its investment opportunities (see Gordon 1962). Thus we might have for the expected prices of these firms:

$$E(P_A) = \frac{dv_A}{k_A - g_A} \qquad E(P_B) = \frac{dv_B}{k_B - g_B} \, ,$$

where $E(P)$ = expected stock price,

$\quad dv$ = expected per-share dividends,

$\quad k$ = return required by stockholders,

$\quad g$ = long-run growth rate in dividends.

If these two firms are merged, one does not get a simple Gordon-model firm. The merger of two firms with different constant growth rates yields a firm that *does not* have a constant growth rate. Thus,

$$E(P_C) = f(dv_C, k_C),$$

where dV_C = full vector of specified dividends,

$k_C = f(i^*, \beta_A, \beta_B,$ capital structure, and so on).

Since these complications seem to have been ignored in empirical studies to date, it is not surprising that we have trouble discerning whether or not real economic benefits accrue in mergers, let alone market-value benefits.

Acquisition of Labor-Intensive Firms

The objective of the previous section was to suggest how difficult it is to trace through a reasonable number of states in the merger decision process. However, such a trace is necessary if macro market inferences are to be drawn. In this section we do not attempt such a complete trace, but we use some simple examples to illustrate what may be an increasingly serious problem in the merger and acquisition of service-sector firms. Without the full trace, we cannot make inferences about market-equilibrium states, but we may be able to draw inferences about individual firms.

The problem that must be faced in acquiring a labor-intensive firm can be described by a simple scenario: Firm A has decided to acquire firm B, which happens to be a baseball team. Firm B could just as easily be a brokerage firm, an advertising agency, a law firm, a hospital-management company, a computer-software firm, a bank, or any of a host of other service-sector firms in which management or key labor is the critical input factor. Firm A has excess cash at the moment and has decided to make the acquisition for cash. Thus it will go through as a purchase type of merger accounting treatment. If the acquisition had been a simple exchange of stock, and if other conditions were met, it would be possible for the acquisition to be treated as a pooling-of-interest type of accounting treatment. The problems described later would still exist under a pooling treatment, though they would appear on the surface to be slightly less dramatic. In order to make the point more sharply, and because there is some probability that pooling accounting will be completely banished within the next five years, we restrict the example to the purchase accounting treatment.

Summary balance-sheet data and income-statement data for firm B are indicated in table 3-2. Although B has only a book-value net worth of $100,000, it is currently generating $500,000 in net income. The public market for the firm's stock is limited, and the current market value of that stock is about $3 million. Thus, the total value of firm B at the moment is slightly under $4 million.[4]

Table 3–2
Financial Statements for a Service-Sector, Labor-Intensive Firm B
(thousands of dollars)

Income Statement		Scenario 1[a]	Scenario 2[b]	Scenario 3[c]
Total revenues		2,000	2,000	1,500
Labor costs		600	1,200	600
Depreciation		50	50	50
Interest		50	50	50
Other costs		300	300	300
Operating income		1,000	400	500
Taxes		500	200	250
Preliminary net income		500	200	250
Goodwill expense		150	150	150
Reported net income		350	50	100
Cash flow		550	250	300
Expected market value		5,500	2,500	3,000

Balance Sheet			
Current assets	800	Current Liabilities	600
Net fixed income	200	Long-term debt	300
		Net worth	100
Total	1,000		1,000

[a]Firm B as it exists at the time of its acquisition.
[b]Firm B if labor captures all of its real value.
[c]Firm B if existing employees are replaced by other labor.

Firm A believes that, with some help in the public relations department and with computerized scouting reports that A can help B generate, firm B could be made even more profitable. As it stands, B is not perceived by A to be a high-risk investment so A is willing to capitalize cash flows at 10 percent. We also assume that in the long run this in fact might be a reasonable rate at which to capitalize flows for this baseball team. Thus the current expected value of this team is about $5.5 million and, with positive synergy, firm A believes an expected value of $7 million is reasonable (given the expanded cash flows).[5]

Though firm B seems to be currently undervalued by the market, the owners drive a hard bargain and receive an offer of $6 million cash for their firm—which works out to be twelve times the current reported net income of $500,000. At this point our scenario branches into three possible directions. In the best of all worlds (scenario 1), we assume that no positive synergy develops but that firm B continues operating as a division as it has in the past as a firm; thus cash flows remain the same. Since it is not usually possible to capitalize the true value of labor, firm A must write off almost the whole $6 million as a goodwill expense so reported earnings from division B (or firm A as a whole) would decline by about $150,000 to $350,000 even though actual earnings are the same. (In the real world it turns out to be possible to capitalize part of the value of players' current contracts for professional sport teams; in general, even this is not possible for management or key employees of most firms acquired).

It is entirely possible the world will not turn out to be so nice. In our second scenario (2), key players and managers decide that the sale of the team is a good time to renegotiate their contracts. The price paid for the firm acts as a trigger—if the firm is really worth that much to stockholders, why should they not get salaries that more closely reflect the value of their contribution? Because firm A believes these key managers and players are critical to the success of the team, labor contracts are altered so that the current wage bill doubles. The results are summarized in scenario 2 of table 3-2. Real cash flows drop substantially; reported earnings are now, in effect, reflecting the fact that the firm is paying twice for the value of the labor in firm B—once as part of the capitalized value of the goodwill deduction and again in the increased labor expenses. In addition, the tax status of the two deductions is not even the same. Any new firm that came along and offered to purchase division B would now see a division with expected cash flows of $250,000 and hence an expected stock value of about $2 million. At this point, firm A may in fact have a positive incentive to sell division B, take the real capital loss, and reinvest the remaining funds elsewhere.

Of course firm A might refuse to negotiate salaries, saying the players are already well paid and that other players can be found for similar wages. The key managers and players quit, and firm A does hire new employees at comparable wages, but things are not the same. The combination of new players does not work as well for the existing team so that revenues drop substantially; see scenario 3 of table 3-2. Firm A is again faced with a lower cash-flow and reported-earnings situation and now must deduct the capitalized value of an incremental labor product that it no longer owns and for which it received no payment when the labor departed. Further, under current accounting standards, it is not permitted to write off all the goodwill created by the purchase of this departed labor capital immediately against the firm's capital account.

The scenarios described in this section suggest to us that there may be serious problems in the expected-value determination, negotiated-price determination, and accounting standards applied to the acquisition of a service-sector firm where the value of the labor product is greater than the wage rate paid. We believe this type of market disequilibrium may be fairly pervasive among key personnel of service-sector firms. There are suggestive data in the brokerage industry, for example, to indicate that the pattern described in scenarios 2 or 3 is happening in some of the acquisitions being made. Key partner salaries and bonuses are altered, and the best salesmen renegotiate their cuts or are bid away by other firms. For the reasons outlined in the merger-valuation section, it will not be easy to develop empirical tests to validate this trend or its impact, but it may be possible to do something with a firm-by-firm analysis.

Conclusion

It is not obvious how to resolve these problems. The goodwill accounting requirements seem to be even more misleading here than in the typical acquisition, so some new accounting procedure should be designed that reflects the noncapitalization of labor product and the mobility of labor despite firm contractual agreements. The valuation problems are more difficult. Some researchers might argue that the original $3 million market value for firm B was a more correct value since it reflected the anticipated wage increase or labor transfer that happened in scenarios 2 and 3. A firm selling at six times earnings in the long run, however, will always turn out to be an attractive takeover target. Some might argue that some intermediate value that reflected the probabilities of key labor shifts might be appropriate (ending up with an expected value of, say, $4.5 million). Something is disturbing in a macro sense in this resolution, for it would seem to imply that, while on average all firms were correctly valued, in fact every individual firm would be incorrectly valued depending on whether the labor product was captured by the stockholders or the workers. Finally, some might argue that, as part of the acquisition process and final price, negotiations should go on simultaneously with the executives of firm B as representatives of the stockholders and with the executives and other key personnel as representatives of the wage bill. This of course would create a whole new vector of possibilities in the valuation framework described in that section when we are not yet able to handle fully even that limited framework.

Notes

1. It is interesting to note that some have argued that the principal reason for increased merger activity in recent years is that many firms are undervalued—that is, the capital markets are not efficient in pricing real resources controlled by corporate securities. For comments by selected professionals, see Boucher (1980).

2. Even this assertion is debatable. While received-capital-budgeting theory focuses on the valuation of a cash-flow vector (excluding financing costs), much of the professional approach in equity valuation is focused on the valuation of a net-income stream.

3. An increasing part of mergers and acquisitions business involves reversing the process—divestitures, spin-offs, leveraged buy-outs, and similar activities. Analogous valuation procedures (in a reverse order) to table 3-1 can be developed for such activities. Very little research has been devoted to this side of the merger process.

4. Our numbers in the illustration are obviously somewhat exaggerated for effect, but they are really combinations from two types of firms that exist: (1) a highly leveraged (and profitable) brokerage firm, and (2) a very profitable advertising agency.

5. To keep the illustration simple, we refer to these valuations as the value of the equity for firm B. Thus, the 10 percent capitalization rate should not be considered the cost of capital for A but a kind of modified equity-capitalization parameter appropriate for the cash flows as defined in the example.

References

Bierman, H., and J. Hass. "The Use and Misuse of the P/E Ratio in Acquisition and Merger Decisions." *Financial Executive* (October 1970):62–68.

Boucher, Wayne I. *The Process of Conglomerate Merger.* Prepared for Federal Trade Commission, Bureau of Competition, Washington, D.C. June 1980.

Dodd, Peter, and Richard Ruback. "Tender Offers and Stockholder Returns." *Journal of Financial Economics,* December 1977, pp. 351–374.

Elton, E.; M. Gruber; and J. Lightstone. "The Impact of Bankruptcy on the Firm's Capital Structure, the Reasonableness of Mergers, and the Risk Independence of Projects." New York University Graduate School of Business Working Paper 134, December 1977.

Federal Trade Commission. *Statistical Report on Mergers and Acquisitions.* Washington, D.C.: Bureau of Economics, August 1980.

Financial Accounting Standards Board. *Financial Accounting Standards.* rev. (July 1978) Stamford, Conn.

Franks, J.R.; J.E. Broyles; and M.J. Hecht. "An Industry Study of the Profitability of Mergers in the United Kingdom." *Journal of Finance,* December 1977, pp. 1513–1525.

Gordon, Myron J. *The Investment, Financing, and Valuation of the Corporation.* Homewood, Ill.: Richard O. Irwin, 1962.

Halpern, P.J. "Empirical Estimates of the Amount and Distribution of Gains to Companies in Mergers." *Journal of Business,* October 1973, pp. 554–575.

Higgins, R. "Reply to Lewellen." *Journal of Finance* (May 1971):543–545.

Kummer, D., and J. Haffmeister. "Valuation Consequences of Cash Tender Offers." *Journal of Finance,* May 1978, pp. 505–516.

Levy, H., and M. Sarnat. "Diversification, Portfolio Analysis, and the Uneasy Case of Conglomerate Mergers." *Journal of Finance,* September 1970, pp. 795–802.

Lewellen, W.G., "A Pure Financial Rationale for the Conglomerate Merger." *Journal of Finance,* May 1971, pp. 521–537.

Mandelker, G. "Risk and Return: the Case of Merging Firms." *Journal of Financial Economics* (December 1974):303–335.

Mossin, J. "Merger Agreements: Some Game Theoretic Considerations." *Journal of Business,* October 1968, pp. 460–477.

Myers, S. "Introduction to Mergers. In *Modern Developments in Financial Management,* ed. S. Myers, pp. 633–645. New York: Praeger Publishers, 1976.

———. "Procedures for Capital Budgeting under Certainty." *Industrial Management Review,* Spring 1968, pp. 1–20.

Rappaport, A. "Financial Analysis for Mergers and Acquisitions."*Mergers and Acquisitions Journal* (Winter, 1976):18–36.

Reid, S.R. *Mergers, Managers, and the Economy.* New York: McGraw-Hill, 1968.

Stapleton, R. "The Acquisition Decision as a Capital Budgeting Problem." *Journal of Business, Finance, and Accounting* (Summer 1975): 187–199.

Steiner, Peter O. *Mergers: Motives, Effects, Policies.* Ann Arbor: University of Michigan Press, 1975.

4

Effects of Mergers on Information Production and Dissemination

Joshua Ronen

The motivation for mergers and their impact on market valuations of the merging companies have received considerable attention in the literature (Boyle 1970; Conn 1976; Ellert 1976; Fox and Fox 1976; Gort 1966; Halpern 1973; Higgins and Schall 1975; Langetieg 1978; Levy and Sarnat 1970; Lewellen 1971; Lintner 1971; Mandelker 1974; Manne 1965; Mueller 1969; Sinrich 1970; Steiner 1975; Stevens 1973). Rationales for mergers discussed in the literature include such diverse explanations as market power (Steiner 1975), gains from operating scale economies (Jacoby 1969), diversification (Gort 1966), tax reduction (Sinrich 1970), growth maximization (Mueller 1969), and bankruptcy avoidance (Higgins and Schall 1975; Lewellen 1971; and Lintner 1971).

Empirical studies of the effects of mergers on the stock prices of the merged firms mostly found that the public announcement of a merger had a positive effect on abnormal returns earned by stockholders of the acquired firm. Mandelker (1974), Ellert (1976), and Langetieg (1978) all selected, for the purpose of observing abnormal price relatives, the effective date of the merger as the announcement date. Dodd (1980) used the earlier date of the public announcement of negotiations or proposed terms as the announcement date for the purpose of observing market reaction; he found that stockholders of target (acquired) firms earned a large, positive abnormal return upon the announcement of merger proposals irrespective of the proposal outcome. Stockholders of the bidding firms, however, do not earn abnormal returns. But while stockholders of target firms lose all of this abnormal return when the negotiations are terminated by the bidding firm's management, some of the abnormal return is retained when cancellation of the proposal is brought about by the incumbent management.

To date, no study has assessed directly the impact of mergers on the production of information about the firm's operating and financing activities and the dissemination of such information to capital-market participants. This chapter offers an analysis of the impact of the merger on the production of information about the two merging segments (the acquired

---

This chapter contains an example and empirical results that are also reported in Ronen and Livnat (in press).

41

and the acquiring firms). The discussion contends that, on balance, mergers result in loss of information in that data pertaining to the individual segments that were previously revealed because the segments were separate legal entities would be provided only in the aggregate as they relate to the conglomerate entity after the merger. Premerger information sets will not be lost in all cases, however. In some cases, managers of the conglomerate entities would continue to provide information on the merged segments; their decision to disclose such information voluntarily would be induced by the expected impact of the disclosure on the wealth of the conglomerate-entity stockholders and, thus, indirectly on the welfare of managers.[1]

In their efforts to reduce the cost of agencies, stockholders often choose to induce managers to act so as to maximize the value of the firm (and thus the stockholders' wealth) by compensation schemes that relate a manager's remuneration to the firm's value (such as stock options and other schemes). In this way managers will choose to produce and disseminate information about the firm that is most consistent with maximization of the firm's value; for a publicly treated firm, this implies that information-production and -dissemination decisions would be guided by the anticipated effects of those decisions on the price of the stock. For a conglomerate such as a firm created as a result of a merger, the disclosure of segment information (separate information on the merged entities) may or may not have favorable effects on stock prices (in the sense of causing upward movement), depending on how the disclosure of the segment information affects market transactors' expectations regarding the future earnings of the separate entities and thus the future earnings of the conglomerate and how these expectations in turn act to change stock prices through investors' trading activities. In other words, the disclosure of segment information will usually induce a different revision of investors' expectations regarding future earnings than would the disclosure of only conglomerate information, and this revision-of-expectations effect can be either favorable or nonfavorable (from the standpoint of the induced changes in the stock prices). The anticipated effect of the disclosure on stock prices will determine partially (managers must also consider the cost of the information) whether the manager will decide to disclose or suppress segment information. The sign (whether causing upward or downward movement in stock prices) and the magnitude of the revision-of-expectations effect depend on the structure of the segments' information—that is, the variance-covariance matrix of the segments' reported numbers with reported numbers by other firms in the market and the values of those firms. While not addressed specifically in this chapter, it is intuitively plausible to expect the revision-of-expectations effect to be the more pronounced (whether positive or negative) the less positively intercorrelated the segments' reported-earnings streams.

However, suppression of segment information is most likely to cause a decrement in social welfare—that is, it would cause Pareto-inferior alloca-

tions. Thus, segment information, the disclosure of which is *socially* beneficial, could be suppressed by the firm's management because it is *privately*
beneficial to do that. This possibility is apparently what triggered the mandatory-disclosure requirements imposed by the SEC and the Financial
Accounting Standards Board (FASB).[2]

Statement no. 14 (1976), issued by the FASB, requires the disclosure of
segment information. The statement requires that all enterprises operating
in different segments of business and in foreign countries and that engage in
exports disclose information about their segments of business, exports, and
major customers. The FASB's efforts followed an extensive activity by
various individuals and institutions that centered around the provision of
segment data by companies. Professional organizations issued pronounce-
ments that essentially support segment reporting. For example, the
Accounting Principles Board urged companies to report segment information voluntarily in its Statement no. 2 (1967); support for segment reporting
has also been expressed by the Financial Accounting Policy Committee of
the Financial Analysts Federation, the Financial Executives Institute, the
Committee on Management Accounting Practices of the National Association of Accountants, and the Accountants International Study Group (see
FASB 1976).

In 1969 the SEC issued requirements for reporting line-of-business
information in registration statements. These requirements were extended
in 1970 to annual reports filed with the SEC on form 10-K, and in October
1974 they were further extended to the annual reports to security-holders of
companies filing with the SEC. The New York Stock Exchange issued a
white paper in 1973 urging line-of-business information, at least as extensive as that required in the 10-K, to be included in annual reports to stockholders. In 1974, the Federal Trade Commission (FTC) initiated an annual
line-of-business reporting program to enable it to obtain disaggregated data
on U.S. corporations. Under this program, large manufacturing companies
are required to report detailed financial information for each line of
business as defined by the commission. These efforts, combined with the
FASB's statement no. 14, indicate a widespread belief that segment information is beneficial.

Indeed, several research studies support the contention that segment
information could be socially useful. Studies that elicited opinions of investors in general and financial analysts in particular on the usefulness of segment information showed that the majority of respondents asked for and
supported the provision of information on segments (Mautz 1968; Backer
and McFarland 1968; Financial Analysts Federation 1972; and Bradish
1965). A field experiment by Stallman (1969) demonstrated that analysts
with segment-based data tended to approximate the stock value much better
than those furnished with only consolidated-based data.

The relative ability to predict consolidated earnings by using segment data as compared with only consolidated data was tested by Kinney (1971) and Collins (1976). Both researchers conclude that segment data improve the predictive ability but that disclosure of segment *earnings* does not improve prediction significantly beyond segment-*revenue* data. Kochanek (1974) infers greater relative predictive ability of segment information from lagged association tests between market price changes and earning changes. Tests of effects of segment information on stock price changes were made by Collins (1975) and Horwitz and Kolodny (1977). Collins shows that inside information on segment earnings can result in superior portfolio returns to those obtained by constructing portfolios on the basis of consolidated earnings only. However, portfolios that were constructed using differences between segment-earnings-based consolidated-income prediction and consolidated-earnings-based prediction failed to yield abnormal returns with respect to companies that had previously been disclosing segment-revenue data. Consistent with Collins's findings, Horwitz and Kolodny report that data on segments' earnings have no incremental effect when assessed with respect to price movements of companies that have already disclosed segment-revenue data.

What emerges from this discussion is that some socially valuable segment information was suppressed as the result of mergers and acquisitions prior to the mandatory requirements to disclose such information. Even after such mandatory requirements, some information would be lost since the requirements are not comprehensive and do not cause the reproduction of all the premerger information; furthermore, it is not clear that mandatory requirements do not cause more social costs (for example, cost of regulation) than the benefits produced by the forced disclosure of partial segment information. More important, the gain in private value from suppression of segment information could well have been another contributing factor (along with others mentioned previously) to the decision by firms to merge.

The next section is devoted to the analysis of incentives for voluntary disclosure of information on individual firms (segments) that had merged into a conglomerate. The third section models the impact on stock prices of disclosure of segment information. The fourth section provides results of an empirical test that adopts a simplified version of the model. Discussion and conclusions follow in the fifth and last section.

Analysis of the Information Loss Following Merger

The prices of capital-market assets are determined by market participants' initial endowments, utility functions, the vector of pertinent states of the world they perceive, and the probabilities attached to these. Merger of two component entities (an acquiring firm and an acquired firm) restrict the information previously disseminated with respect to individual entities into a coarser partition pertaining to the conglomerate entity only. This will in turn decrease the number of financial instruments in the marketplace, thus possibly causing inferior reallocation of resources. Whether this happens in fact depends on whether the management of the conglomerate entity voluntarily chooses to continue producing and disseminating information on the individual segments that previously had been autonomous entities and with respect to which separate and distinct sets of information were provided.

Assume that two firms (A and B) merge into firm C. To understand how the information suppression occurs, A and B should be viewed as segments of the conglomerate entity C. The impact of information suppression can best be understood by considering the private (to the entity) benefits and costs of partitioning the information regarding the conglomerate entity C into separate subsets, one concerning segment A and the other concerning segment B. Such information partitioning could serve two roles:

1. Informing stockholders about the outcomes of states of the world that are suppressed in conglomerate-based information;
2. Inducing market participants to revise their assessments of probabilities attached to the pertinent states of the world. This revision is termed positive (negative) if it has a favorable (unfavorable) effect on the expected utility of stockholders.

The observation that the revision of probability assessments depends on whether segment information or conglomerate information only is provided is devoid of implications for trading in capital markets unless potential transactors are led to expect that segment information *will* be provided. If investors do not expect such information, no contracts on contingent claims can be executed since the states of the world giving rise to the segments' separate income streams would then not be identifiable. In this case, potential purchasers of the claims would not be assured of the existence of means to monitor and to enforce the terms of the contracts. Thus, compression of the information on two separate merging firms into a set that pertains only to the conglomerate decreases the number of trades in contingent claims. This is akin to nonsynergistic corporate mergers that preserve strong endowment neutrality as defined by Hakansson (1979)—that is, it constitutes a market-structure change in the sense that the set of instruments available for investment is decreased.[3] In particular, it is decreased by integrating existing financial-market instruments into a coarser and thus a smaller set of linearly independent securities while preserving the initial endowments. Hakansson (1979) has shown that, other things equal, this kind of structural change cannot be Pareto superior (and may be Pareto inferior) provided that the initial endowments in the first market (premerger market) constitute an equilibrium in that market.

When the information on segments (individual merged entities) is provided by management of the conglomerate, the information *content* is used to assess, and hence price, the contracts. The implication of the information for the pricing of financial instruments is what determines whether the management of the conglomerate will continue to provide information on the individual managed entities and thus whether or not an information loss will ensue.

Let us provide an example. The scenario starts at the beginning of period 0 when individuals trade to reach equilibrium. At the beginning of period 1, a report is issued, signaling information about the prevailing states. The signals are used to revise probability beliefs, which in turn induce new prices and trading decisions. Once a new equilibrium is reached, no trading occurs until the issuance of the next report at the beginning of period 2. Then the process starts all over again.

The periods are viewed not as interim periods but as single and independent. More than one period is needed to illustrate the effects of different realizations of segment information.

In this stylized economy, two individuals have claims on two firms and one bond. Table 4-1 provides the contingent cash outcomes for the merged entities (A and B) and the conglomerate (C) that results from the nonsynergistic merger of A and B, the initial claims (endowment) each individual holds in the firms, and the initial probability assessments (different for each of the individuals).

Each firm produces a report that shows net income of -2, -1, 0, 1, or 2. The individuals observe only the signal, not the cash outcome, and assess the probabilities of signals conditional on the state of the world and the accounting method used (table 4-2).

Two cases are discussed. Conditional assessments are (1) homogeneous and (2) heterogeneous. The two individuals are understood to operate with the same information structure except that, in the heterogeneous case, they differ in their probability assessments regarding the use of accounting method X and Y as a basis for preparation of the report. The probability revision is illustrated in appendix 4A. Each individual is endowed with a logarithmic utility function and maximizes expected utility of terminal wealth at each period.

The new equilibrium prices, holdings, wealth, and expected utilities at each trading point are shown for the heterogeneous case (tables 4-3 and 4-4) and for the homogeneous case (table 4-5) under different accounting reports at each period. The period-0 column in table 4-3 demonstrates the superiority of the market with a larger set of financial instruments since at

Table 4-1

Cash Outcomes per Claim and Initial Endowments

		States			Initial Endowments	
Cash Outcomes	Firm	1	2	3	Individual 1	Individual 2
Segments	A	1	2	4	20	0
	B	2	0	1	20	0
	Bond	1	1	1	0	10
Conglomerate	C	3	2	5	20	0
	Bond	1	1	1	0	10
Initial probability	Individual 1	.4	.3	.3		
assessments	Individual 2	.2	.35	.45		

Table 4-2

Conditional Probability Matrix

		Accounting Method X			Accounting Method Y		
	Signal	State 1	State 2	State 3	State 1	State 2	State 3
Firm A	-2	.01	.01	.10	.05	.01	.10
	-1	.10	.05	.01	.20	.12	.02
	0	.2	.10	.05	.25	.22	.25
	1	.4	.24	.34	.25	.25	.33
	2	.29	.60	.50	.25	.40	.30
Firm B	-2	.01	.10	.10	.10	.20	.05
	-1	.10	.20	.20	.20	.30	.30
	0	.20	.40	.20	.20	.30	.30
	1	.30	.20	.20	.20	.10	.30
	2	.39	.10	.30	.30	.10	.05

Note: The probability of using accounting method X is

$$\text{Prob}(X) = .4 \text{ for individual 1;}$$

$$\text{Prob}(X) = \begin{cases} .4 \text{ for individual 2 in the Homogeneous case;} \\ .7 \text{ for individual 2 in the Heterogeneous case.} \end{cases}$$

(The heterogeneous case could be complicated even further if we assume different conditional probability matrixes as well.)

this time the traders know only that segment information will be forthcoming but not its content. Still, this effect is positive and is equal to .0038.

An examination of the remainder of table 4-3 shows how the disclosure of the segment information can cause a revision of expectations that results either in an increase or decrease in the value of the firm. These value changes

Table 4-3
Optimal Holdings and Prices under Heterogeneous Revision of Expectations

				Trading Period and Signal			
		0	*1*	*2*	*3*	*4*
			(0,1,1)	(−1, −1, −2)	(−1, 0, −1)	(1, 2, 3)
			Optimal Holdings—Individual 1			
Segment information	A	13.87	16.32	15.99	16.72	15.09
	B	18.32	19.47	19.39	19.87	18.26
	Bond	14.07	7.78	8.37	6.75	11.47
	Beliefs	(.4,.3,.3)	(.51,.15,.34)	(.73,.20,.07)	(.79,.20,.01)	(.94,.05,.01)
Conglomerate information	C	16.36	16.80	16.55	16.45	16.29
	Bond	10.83	9.53	10.24	10.51	10.97
	Beliefs	(.4,.3,.3)	(.38,.31,.31)	(.38,.37,.25)	(.34,.42,.24)	(.44,.30,.26)
			Optimal Holdings—Individual 2			
Segment information	A	6.13	3.68	4.01	3.28	4.91
	B	1.68	.53	.61	.13	1.74
	Bond	−4.07	2.22	1.63	3.25	−1.47
	Beliefs	(.2,.35,.45)	(.36,.23,.41)	(.56,.33,.11)	(.63,.36,.01)	(.89,.09,.02)
Conglomerate information	C	3.64	3.20	3.45	3.55	3.71
	Bond	−.83	.47	−.24	−.51	−.97
	Beliefs	(.2,.35,.45)	(.19,.38,.43)	(.17,.44,.39)	(.4,.47,.39)	(.19,.37,.44)
			Prices			
	A	2.03777	1.96219	1.42952	1.30071	1.09253
	B	.94155	1.28125	1.38718	1.43404	1.83722
	C	2.97552	2.96232	2.81409	2.75305	2.92545
	A + B − C	.00380	.28112	.00261	−.01830	.00430

Note: Prices are relative to the price of bond, which is arbitrarily set to 1.

Table 4–4
Wealth and Expected Utility under Heterogeneous Revision of Expectations

	Individual	Trading Period				
		0	1	2	3	4
		Wealth				
Segment information	1	59.59	64.76	58.13	56.98	61.51
	2	10.00	10.11	8.20	7.72	7.09
	1 + 2	69.59	74.87	66.33	64.70	68.60
Conglomerate information	1	59.51	59.29	56.80	55.79	58.63
	2	10.00	9.95	9.48	9.27	9.88
	1 + 2	69.51	69.24	66.28	65.06	68.51
		Expected Utility				
Segment information	1	4.13	4.21	4.09	4.06	4.13
	2	2.47	2.39	2.15	2.06	1.96
Conglomerate information	1	4.13	4.13	4.08	4.06	4.11
	2	2.40	2.37	2.34	2.32	2.39

Note: In period 3, aggregate wealth under consolidation is higher than under segment-based reporting.

are manifestations of the joint effect of the increase in the number of financial instruments made possible upon segment-information disclosure and the revision of expectations based on the content of the information disclosed. Since the first effect is always nonnegative, the revision-of-expectation effect could have been either positive or negative in period 1, 2, and 4 but was clearly negative in period 3.

Table 4–4 shows these effects on wealth and the expected utility of the two individuals. Consistent with the effect on prices, stockholders' wealth in the aggregate is higher in periods 0, 1, 2, and 4 and lower in period 3 when segment information is provided, but in some cases one individual is better off and the other is worse off. Thus, providing postmerger segment information may or may not induce greater *total* wealth, and in either case, the wealth of each owner may or may not increase.

A similar (although not identical) pattern prevails in the case of expected utility. Only in periods 0 and 1 can the provision of postmerger segment information be said to be Pareto optimal, in that each individual's expected utility is enhanced. Table 4–5 reveals a similar pattern in the sense of indeterminancy of the results under homogeneous information structure.

Table 4-5
Equilibrium Beliefs, Prices, Wealth, and Expected Utility under Homogeneous Revision of Expectations

		Period and Signal				
		$t = 0$	$t = 1$ (0, 1, 1)	$t = 2$ (−1, −1, −2)	$t = 3$ (−1, 0, −1)	$t = 4$ (1, 2, 3)
				Individual 1		
Segment information	Beliefs	(.4,.3,.3)	(.51,.15,.34)	(.73,.20,.06)	(.79,.20,.01)	(.94,.05,.01)
	Wealth	59.59	65.25	59.47	58.49	62.86
	Expected utility	4.13	4.21	4.11	4.09	4.15
Conglomerate information	Beliefs	(.4,.3,.3)	(.37,.32,.25)	(.38,.37,.25)	(.34,.42,.24)	(.44,.30,.26)
	Wealth	59.51	59.42	56.83	55.77	58.69
	Expected utility	4.13	4.13	4.08	4.07	4.11
				Individual 2		
Segment information	Beliefs	(.2,.35,.45)	(.27,.18,.55)	(.51,.32,.17)	(.62,.36,.02)	(.87,.11,.02)
	Wealth	10	10.34	7.07	6.31	5.72
	Expected utility	2.47	2.54	2.05	1.88	1.76
Conglomerate information	Beliefs	(.2,.35,.45)	(.18,.36,.46)	(.19,.44,.37)	(.17,.48,.35)	(.23,.37,.40)
	Wealth	10	9.98	9.41	9.20	9.76
	Expected utility	2.40	2.40	2.32	2.29	2.36
				Price		
Firm A		2.038	2.000	1.436	1.299	1.095
Firm B		.942	1.279	1.391	1.441	1.834
Firm C		2.976	2.970	2.812	2.748	2.922
				Aggregated Wealth		
Segment		69.59	75.58	66.54	64.80	68.58
Consolidated		69.51	69.40	66.24	64.97	68.45

Note: Holdings will not be revised in the homogeneous case (see appendix 4A).

Analysis of the Conglomerate Manager's Disclosure Choice

Assume that the prevailing rules require conglomerate reports only and that the manager's decision problem is whether to provide segment information as well, either for the current period only or for past periods retroactively in addition. Further, the decision is assumed to be reached prior to the knowledge of signal realization. (Otherwise, a negative signal would be transmitted if realization is followed by nondisclosure.)

The revision of state probabilities conditional on signals, the resulting trading activity, and the subsequent induced changes in wealth and expected utility is illustrated schematically in figure 4-1.

The expectation over all signals of the pairs of expected utilities (individuals one and two) would now become the basis for the manager's decision of the reporting mode. In the case of dominance—that is, when one pair dominates the other—the reporting mode (segment versus conglomerate only) would be the one associated with the higher expected utilities. When there is no clear dominance—that is, one individual's expected utility is higher but the other's is lower for a given mode—the decision will depend on the feasibility and costs of contracting to effect wealth transfers.

At each point of time, the manager can decide to disclose segment information as of the start of the next period for that period and prospectively, or also retroactively to disclose segment information for past periods. It is assumed, however, that once a decision to report segment information is reached, it cannot be reversed at a subsequent date.

The equilibrium results differ when retroactive information as well is provided because probabilities are then revised to the same level that would have been reached had segment information been provided all along. In the current information case, the prior probabilities are the updated conglomerate-only probabilities, which will be revised by the newly supplied segment information. Clearly, this distinction does not hold in the first period.

Tables 4–6 and 4–7 summarize the information the manager needs for making his disclosure decisions at the four periods for the heterogeneous and homogeneous cases respectively. The manager will be induced to disclose segment information at the beginning of the first period. His decision is supported by the clear dominance in both expected wealth and expected utility for both the homogeneous and heterogeneous cases. At the beginning of period 2, he supplies retroactive segment information as this would produce higher expected wealth and utility. This will not be the case for periods 3 and 4, in which a strong dominance for disclosing only current information exists. An identical pattern is described in table 4–7 for the homogeneous case. In all periods, the provision of segment information, either prospectively or retroactively, dominates the conglomerate-only alternative.

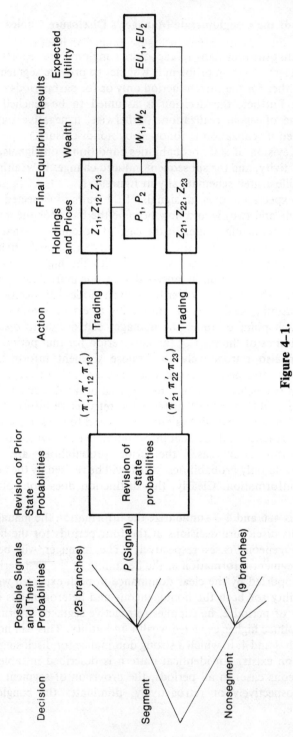

Figure 4–1.

Table 4-6
Wealth and Utility Expectations in the Beginning of the Period under Heterogeneous Revisions of Probabilities

			Period		
	Individual	1	2	3	4
			Wealth		
Conglomerate information only	1	59.53	59.32	56.83	55.83
	2	10.04	9.98	9.51	9.31
Segment information, current	1	59.93	59.73	57.23	56.24
	2	10.14	10.06	9.58	9.39
Segment information, retroactive	1	59.93	64.27	56.99	55.62
	2	10.14	10.93	9.48	9.17
			Expected Utility		
Conglomerate information only	1	4.13	4.13	4.08	4.06
	2	2.40	2.38	2.34	2.32
Segment information, current	1	4.13	4.13	4.08	4.07
	2	2.47	2.43	2.42	2.40
Segment information, retroactive	1	4.13	4.20	4.07	4.04
	2	2.47	2.47	2.29	2.23

Table 4-7
Wealth and Utility Expectations in the Beginning of the Period under Homogeneous Revisions of Probabilities

			Period		
	Individual	1	2	3	4
			Wealth		
Conglomerate information only	1	59.55	59.47	56.88	55.83
	2	10	9.99	9.41	9.20
Segment information, current	1	59.98	59.92	57.29	56.24
	2	10.12	10.11	9.49	9.28
Segment information, retroactive	1	59.98	64.75	57.23	55.71
	2	10.12	11.25	9.43	9.11
			Expected Utility		
Conglomerate information only	1	4.13	4.13	4.08	4.07
	2	2.40	2.40	2.32	2.30
Segment information, current	1	4.13	4.13	4.08	4.07
	2	2.46	2.46	2.38	2.35
Segment information, retroactive	1	4.13	4.20	4.07	4.04
	2	2.46	2.60	2.33	2.23

Some Empirical Evidence

Ronen and Livnat (1981) empirically tested the hypothesis that voluntary disclosure of segment information is predicated on the anticipated effects on stock prices. The previous discussion has shown the incentives to disclose segment information to be derived from the expected effect of disclosure on expected utility and wealth. However, since expected utility and wealth are unobservable, expected price changes can be used as surrogate predictors of voluntary disclosures. The model Ronen and Livnat used for the purposes of testing is described in appendix 4B.

In order to identify a sample of voluntary disclosures and nonvoluntary disclosures, the lists prepared by the *Accounting Trends and Techniques* for 1968-1970 were used by Ronen and Livnat (1981). Three subsamples were obtained according to whether the segment earnings were voluntarily disclosed during all three years (1968-1970), during the last two years, or during 1970 only. Each firm included in the sample had to satisfy certain data-availability criteria. A fourth random subsample was selected from among firms that had not previously disclosed segment earnings. For each firm in any of the subsamples, segment earnings and security price changes (including divided distributions) in the years 1967-1977 were obtained. For each firm, ten observations of earning changes were available. The first three observations (1968-1970) made up the prediction period, and the last seven (1971-1977) composed the estimation period.

For each of the three years in the prediction period, the predicted price changes under segment reporting were compared with the predictions under conglomerate-only earnings. If the predicted price change under segment reporting was algebraically larger (smaller) than the change predicted under a conglomerate-only reporting, a favorable (unfavorable) effect is indicated.

The results were consistent with the hypothesis that firms provided segment information when they expected a favorable price change to be induced by the information.

Conclusions

In general, a positive incentive for segment reporting, when based on the criterion of expected wealth or utility, implies that *ex ante* the anticipated positive effects outweigh the anticipated negative effects over the planning horizon. Symmetrically, a negative expected effect of segment reporting implies that the anticipated negative effect outweighs the expected positive effect over the horizon and would induce the decision not to disclose segment data. The empirical evidence cited produced results consistent with this analysis.

Mergers suppress information on the merging segments unless the conglomerate manager has incentives to provide the information. As we have seen, only some conglomerate managers will find it in their self-interest to do so in the absence of a mandatory requirement to disclose segment information. Even under the mandatory requirements, however, only some of the segment information would be provided since the requirements are not comprehensive and do not cause reproduction of all the premerger information set. Moreover, conglomerates formed by mergers would not disclose segment information whenever the suppression of the information was a contributing factor to the merger decision in the first place. But even when segment information is disclosed, it is not clear that contingency claims would be traded, even though it is theoretically possible to do so, because of the transaction and monitoring costs involved. This requires further explanation.

Theoretically it is possible to trade in contingency claims when segment information is disclosed because, even though contingencies associated with segments of a conglomerate are not traded separately, linear combinations of securities could possibly be found (if the spanning property holds) to replicate the initial holdings (in the premerged entities) once the information on the segments is provided. This trading is possible only if it is known in advance that the realizations (of the segment's earnings) would be eventually observed so that the separate segments can be appropriately priced and the expected return can be realized. If no separate information on the segments is provided, the segments will not be properly priced and trading would be restricted. But even if information continues to be provided, mergers can cause a diminution in trading because (a) linear combinations constituting perfect substitutes do not exist and (b) even if such combinations do exist, additional transaction costs are incurred when they are incorporated into portfolios, causing diminution in the volume of trading. Thus, the mandatory disclosure of segment information imposed by the FASB and the SEC mitigates, but does not eliminate, the information loss brought about by nonsynergistic mergers.

Another problem caused by the mandatory-disclosure requirement, which inevitably must involve arbitrary allocations of costs by management of the conglomerate to the segments, is the introduction of moral hazard coincidently with such cost allocations: Among the set of possible arbitrary-allocation mechanisms, managements of firms that did not choose voluntarily to provide segment information will tend to select the mechanism that is likely to produce the most favorable effect on stock prices. For a merged conglomerate that, in the absence of mandatory disclosure chooses to suppress segment information, the allocation mechanism selected would result in restricting the information field—that is, the partition of the events disclosed would be coarser. Since no built-in market penalty exists for the potential incentive of management to mislead investors (moral hazard) embedded in the discretion management has over allocation mechanisms, a diminution in the volume of potential trading might ensure. This expected diminution is an example of the consequence of adverse selection (Akerlof 1970; Ronen 1979). Additionally, the mandatory disclosure and its regulation involves nontrivial social costs. Whatever the motivation for the two firms to merge could be, the act of nonsynergistic merger diminishes the set of potentially tradable contingent claims, thus producing external diseconomies coincident with information loss.

The analysis and the results presented in this chapter suggest the following potentially testable implications:

1. To the extent that the expected private value from suppressing segment information constitutes a contributing factor to the decision to merge, one would expect the equilibrium number of mergers and acquisitions to decrease as a result of the mandatory requirement to disclose segment information. Empirical models constructed to explain mergers can now be enriched by introducing the segment-information-disclosure requirements as a possible explanatory factor that depresses the number of mergers in the post-requirement imposition period.

2. If the private value of segment-information suppression is unbiasedly expected by market transactors, one would expect the mandatory requirement of segment-information disclosure to have a negative effect on the stock prices of conglomerates that did not previously disclose segment information voluntarily and, more significantly, of conglomerates that were recently formed as a result of merger and that did not voluntarily disclose segment information immediately after the merger.

3. Conglomerates that were formed by mergers tend to suppress segment information relatively more than conglomerates that were not formed as a result of merger—that is, the pre-mandatory-disclosure-requirement incidence of voluntary segment-information disclosure is expected to have been higher in nonmerged conglomerates than in merged conglomerates.

4. The incidence of mergers would be expected to be higher among companies that stand to benefit privately from the suppression of information on their separate activities than among companies for which such suppression produces either a decrement in value or a zero increment in value. To test this implication, the model presented in this paper could be used to divide companies into two groups: one which the segment-information disclosure is expected to be beneficial and a second group for which the segment-information disclosure is expected to be harmful. The test could then be applied either *ex post,* by comparing a sample of merged companies with a control group of nonmerged companies (matched with respect to pertinent parameters such as risk, industry, size, and so forth) with respect to the model-predicted effect of disclosure on the stock price, or *ex ante,* by examining the incidence of mergers among a group for which the model pre-

dicts beneficial effects and another for which the model predicts harmful effects. The groups to which the model is to be applied would be randomly selected pairings of companies.

Notes

1. In fact, it is interesting to note that voluntary disclosure of segment revenues was common prior to the imposition of the disclosure requirement by the SEC in 1969. Hobgood (1971) reports that in the years 1967–1969, about one-half of a sample of 614 companies out of a population of 1,500 companies whose annual reports are received by the Financial Executives Institute Library disclosed segment revenues voluntarily (only 15 percent of the sample also disclosed segment-earnings information).

2. The issue of the desirability of mandatory segment-disclosure requirements is not addressed in this chapter but is dealt with at some length in Ronen and Livnat (1981).

3. Strong endowment neutrality requires that each consumer-investor's initial claims to current compensation remain unchanged between the two markets (premerger and postmerger markets) and also that initial claims to end-of-period wealth *in each state* be the same in these two markets (see Hakansson 1979, p. 13).

References

Accounting Principles Board. *Statement No. 2.* Stamford, Conn., 1967.

Akerlof, George A. "The Market for Internal 'Lemons': Qualitative Uncertainty in the Market Mechanism." *Quarterly Journal of Economics,* 84 (August 1970):488–500.

Backer, Morton, and McFarland, Walter B. *External Reporting for Segments of a Business.* New York: NAA, 1968.

Boyle, S.E. "Premerger Growth and Profit Characteristics of Large Conglomerate Mergers in the United States: 1948–1969." *St. John's Law Review* 44 (special ed.) (Spring 1970):152–170.

Bradish, Richard D. "Corporate Reporting and the Financial Analyst." *The Accounting Review* 40 (October 1965):757–766.

Collins, Daniel W. "SEC Product Line Reporting and Market Efficency." *Journal of Financial Economics* 2 (June 1975):125–164.

———. "Predicting Earnings with Sub-Entity Data: Some Further Evidence." *Journal of Accounting Research* 14 (Spring 1976):163–177.

Conn, R.L. "The Failing Firm/Industry Doctrine in Conglomerate Mergers." *Journal of Industrial Economics* 24 (March 1976):181–187.

Dodd, P. "Merger Proposals, Management Discretion and Stockholder Wealth." *Journal of Financial Economics* 8 (June 1980):105–138.

Ellert, J.C. "Mergers, Anti-trust Law Enforcement and Stockholder Returns." *Journal of Finance,* 31 (May 1976):715–732.

Financial Accounting Standards Board *Statement no. 14* Stamford, Conn., December 1976.

Financial Analysts Federation, *Evaluation of Corporate Financial Reporting in Selected Industries for the Year 1971.* New York: FAF, 15 November 1972.

Fox, B.E., and E.D. Fox. *Corporate Acquisitions and Mergers.* New York: Matthew Bender, 1976.

Gort, M. "Diversification, Mergers, and Profits." In *The Corporate Merger,* edited by W. Alberts and J. Segal pp. 31–44. Chicago: University of Chicago Press, 1966.

Hakansson, Nils H. "Welfare Comparisons and Financial Markets and the Basic Theorems of Value Conservation." Working Paper No. 91. Institute of Business of the Economic Research, University of California, Berkeley, June 1979.

Halpern, B. "Empirical Estimates of the Amount and Distribution of Gains to Companies in Mergers." *Journal of Business* 46 (1973):554–575.

Higgins, R.C., and L.D. Schall. "Corporate Bankruptcy and Conglomerate Mergers." *Journal of Finance* (March 1975):93–114.

Hobgood, George. "Segmented Disclosure in 1970 Annual Reports." *Financial Executive* 31 (August 1971):18–22.

Horwitz, Bertrand, and Richard Kolodny. "Line of Business Reporting and Security Prices: An Analysis of an SEC Disclosure Rule." *Bell Journal of Economics* 8 (Spring 1977):234–249.

Jacoby, N. "The Conglomerate Corporation." *Center Magazine* 2 (July 1969).

Kinney, William R., Jr. "Predicting Earnings: Entity versus Subentity Data." *Journal of Accounting Research* 9 (Spring 1971):127–136.

Kochanek, Richard Frank. "Segmental Financial Disclosure by Diversified Firms and Security Prices." *Accounting Review* 49 (April 1974): 245–258.

Langetieg, T.C. "An Application of a Three-Factor Performance Index to Measure Stockholder Gains from Mergers." *Journal of Financial Economics* 6 (1978):365–383.

Levy, H., and M. Sarnat. "Diversification, Portfolio Analysis, and the Uneasy Case for Conglomerate Mergers." *Journal of Finance,* 25 (September 1970):745–802.

Lewellen, W. "A Pure Financial Rationale for the Conglomerate Merger." *Journal of Finance* 26 (May 1971):521–537.

Lintner, John. "Expectations Mergers and Equilibrium in the Purely Competitive Securities Markets." *American Economic Review, Papers and Proceedings* 61 (May 1971):101–111.

Mandelker, G. "Risk and Return: The Case of Merging Firms." *Journal of Financial Economics* 1 (December 1974):303–335.

Manne, H.G. "Mergers in the Market for Corporate Control." *Journal of Political Economy* 73 (1965):110–120.

Mautz, Robert K. *Financial Reporting by Diversified Companies.* New York: Financial Executives Research Foundation, 1968.

Mueller, D.C. "A Theory of Conglomerate Mergers." *Quarterly Journal of Economics* 83 (August 1969):643–659.

Ronen, Joshua. "The Dual Role of Accounting: A Financial Economic Perspective." in *Handbook of Financial Economics,* edicted by J.L. Bicksler. Amsterdam: North Holland Publishing Company, 1979.

Ronen, Joshua, and J. Livnat. "Incentives for Segment Reporting." *Journal of Accounting Research* (in press).

Sinrich, N. "Tax Incentives and the Conglomerate Merger: An Introduction." *St. John's Law Review* 44 (special ed.) (Spring 1970).

Stallman, James C. "Toward Experimental Criteria for Judging Disclosure Improvement." *Empirical Research in Accounting: Selected Studies 1969,* supplement to *Journal of Accounting Research* 7 (1969): 29–43.

Steiner, P.O. *Mergers.* Ann Arbor: University of Michigan Press, 1975.

Stevens, D.L. "Financial Characteristics of Merged Firms: A Multivariate Analysis." *Journal of Financial and Quantitative Analysis* 8 (March 1973):149–158.

Appendix 4A

Individual 1 has at $t = 0$ the following probabilities:

$$P(S = 1) = .4 \qquad P(S = 2) = .3 \qquad P(S = 3) = .3$$

He also assesses the probability of using X at $P(X) = .4$ and of using Y at $P(Y) = .6$.

The signal prior to $t = 1$ is $A = 0$, $B = 1$. The probability that state 1 prevails can be computed as follows:

$$P(S = 1 | A = 0, B = 1)$$

$$= \frac{P(S = 1, A = 0, B = 1)}{P(A = 0, B = 1)}$$

$$= \frac{P(S = 1) P(A = 0, B = 1 | S = 1)}{\sum_{i=1}^{3} P(S = i)[P(A = 0, B = 1 | S = i)]} . \qquad (4A.1)$$

We now assume that the only dependence between the signals regarding A and B occurs through the segment's use of accounting method X or Y. (Both segments apply the same accounting method.) Under these assumptions, equation 4A.1 becomes

$$\frac{P(S=1)[P(A=0,B=1|S=1,X)P(X)+P(A=0,B=1|S=1,Y)P(Y)]}{\sum_{i=1}^{3} P(S=i)[P(A=0,B=1|S=i,X)P(X) + P(A=0,B=1|S=i,Y)P(Y)]}$$

$$= \frac{P(S=1)[P(A=0|S=1,X)P(B=1|S=1,X)P(X) + P(A=0|S=1,Y)}{\sum_{i=1}^{3} P(S=i)[P(A=0|S=i,X)P(B=1|S=i,X)P(X)+P(A=0|S=i,Y)}$$

$$\frac{P(B=1|S=1,Y)P(Y)]}{P(B=1|S=i,Y)P(Y)]}$$

$$= \frac{.4(.2 \times .3 \times .4 \times + .25 \times .2 \times .6)}{.4(.2 \times .3 \times .4 + .25 \times .2 \times .6) + .3(.1 \times .2 \times .4 + .22 \times .1 \times .6)}$$

$$+ .3(.05 \times .2 \times .4 + .25 \times .3 \times .6)$$

$$= .51. \tag{4A.2}$$

The probabilities of the other states are similarly computed. As for the nonsegment case, observing the signal $C = 1$, we have

$$P(C=1) = P(A=-1, B=2) + P(A=0, B=1) + P(A=1, B=0) + P(A=2,$$

$$B=4).$$

We revise the probability of the states conditional on $C = 1$ in the same fashion, except that we now consider four signals in the squared bracket of equation 4A.2 instead of the single one we had before.

Appendix 4B:
The Ronen and Livnat Model for Testing Voluntary Disclosure

The usual setting of the CAPM is assumed with one modification: Individuals agree not only in their assessments of the distributions of the end-of-period values of firms but also on the reports to be published by those firms. These assessments are characterized by a multivariate normal distribution given by

$$\begin{pmatrix} V \\ S \end{pmatrix} \sim N \left[\begin{pmatrix} \bar{V} \\ \bar{S} \end{pmatrix}, \begin{pmatrix} C_v & C_{vs} \\ C_{sv} & C_s \end{pmatrix} \right], \tag{4B.1}$$

where V is an $(n \times 1)$ vector of end-of-period values of the n firms. $\bar{V}$ is its expected value. S is an $(n \times 1)$ vector of signals (reports). $\bar{S}$ is its expected value. C_v, C_{vs}, and C_s are the $(n \times n)$ covariance matrixes corresponding to these vectors.

Once the reports are issued, market participants use the revised probabilities given by

$$\begin{pmatrix} V \\ S \end{pmatrix} \sim N \{ [\bar{V} + C_{vs} C_s^{-1} (S - \bar{S})], (C_v - C_{vs} C_s^{-1} C_{sv}) \} \tag{4B.2}$$

Prices in the CAPM are established according to:

$$P = \frac{1}{r} (\bar{V} - m C_v U), \tag{4B.3}$$

where P is an $(n \times 1)$ vector of current market prices. r is the risk-free interest rate. m is the market price of risk and U is an $(n \times 1)$ unity vector.

Upon disclosure of the reports, market participants substitute the posterior parameters of equation 4B.2 in equation 4B.3 to obtain the new vector of prices P'. Subtracting P from P', one obtains

$$P' - P = \frac{1}{r} C_{vs} C_s^{-1} (S - \bar{S} + m C_{sv} U). \tag{4B.4}$$

In regression form, for a given security j, equation 4B.4 takes the form:

$$p_j' - p_j = a_0 + a_1 (s_j - \bar{s}_j) + a_2 (s_m - \bar{s}_m), \tag{4B.5}$$

where a_0, a_1, and a_2 are regression coefficients resulting from the covariance matrixes in equation 4B.4. s_j is the earnings report of firm j. s_j is its expected

63

value. s_m is a weighted average of earnings reports of all firms in the market. The weighting scheme is determined by the covariance structure in equation 4B.4. $\bar{s}_m$ is its expected value. Equation 4B.5 is used to assess the expected price changes if firm j provides only consolidated-based reports.

Suppose now that firm j provides segment information as well. Rather than having to consider n firms in the economy, market participants should consider the previous $n - 1$ firms plus the $(k + 1)$ additional segments that firm j consists of. Thus, the market equilibrium will price $(n + k)$ assets or earnings streams and set the equilibrium price of firm j equal to the sum of the individual prices of its segments. Following the analysis outlined by equations 4B.1 through 4B.4, one can show that the price changes of firm j will be

$$p'_j - p_j = a_0 + \sum_{i=1}^{k+1} a_i(s_{ij} - \bar{s_{ij}}) + a_{k+2}(s'_m - \bar{s'}_m), \quad (4B.6)$$

where a_0 through a_{k+2} are regression coefficients. s_{ij} is the ith segment-earnings report of firm j. $\bar{s_{ij}}$ is its expected value. s'_m is a weighted average of the earnings reports of other firms in the economy. (It is different from the respective term in equation 4B.5 because the weighting scheme will be different.) $\bar{s'}_m$ is its expected value.

Equation 4B.6 can be used to assess the predicted price changes in cases of segment reporting. It is hypothesized that segment earnings will be voluntarily disclosed when the predicted price changes under equation 4B.6 are more favorable than the respective price changes of equation 4B.5.

**Part II
Social and Legal Issues**

5

The Social and Political Consequences of Conglomerate Mergers

John J. Siegfried and
M. Jane Barr Sweeney

Conglomerate mergers may have significant economic, political, and social consequences. In order to gain some appreciation for the welfare effects of conglomerate mergers, the Bureau of Economics of the Federal Trade Commission published major reports in 1969 and 1980. The underlying theme of *Economic Report on Corporate Mergers,* published in 1969, was that conglomerate firms reduce economic efficiency by hampering competition through engaging in reciprocal dealing with their customers, reducing potential entry, and cross-subsidizing predatory efforts that increase market concentration in the long run.[1] These hypotheses were debated extensively during the 1970s.[2] The recently published volume, *The Economics of Firm Size, Market Structure and Social Performance,* explores how the economic characteristics of conglomerates affect the income distribution, worker satisfaction, political power, and welfare of local communities.[3] The themes of the book are that social goals other than efficiency also matter and that economists have useful insights to contribute to debates about them.

In this chapter we attempt to summarize the contributions of economists regarding the effects of conglomerates on the nonefficiency dimensions of performance. We review the hypotheses relating the fundamental economic characteristics of conglomerates (market concentration, large size, and product and geographic dispersion) to various nonefficiency social goals. Then we briefly summarize the available empirical evidence on the hypotheses.

The issues surveyed in this chapter are of considerable significance for public policy. The vast majority of testimony at the Spring 1979 hearings on S. 600, the Small and Independent Business Protection Act of 1979, spon-

Portions of this chapter appeared: John J. Siegfried, "The Effects of Conglomerate Mergers on Political Power: A Survey," in *The Conglomerate Corporation: A Public Policy Problem,* edited by Roger D. Blair and Robert Lanzillotti (Cambridge, Mass.: Oelgeschlager, Gunn and Hain, 1981). Reprinted with permission. The authors thank Katherine E. Maddox, George H. Sweeney, and Lawrence White for comments on an earlier draft of this chapter.

sored by Senator Edward Kennedy, concentrated on the effects that conglomerate mergers may have on social goals other than economic
efficiency.[4] In addition, there have been many specific proposals to limit the
discretion of firms to move or close plants and to control the extent of business influence on the political process.

The concept of social property rights may help to explain the rising
interest in nonefficiency goals of the economy. If individuals or firms
believe that they deserve some right to constancy of the rules that define
behavior, changes in such rules are likely to arouse resistance since they
would effectively constitute redistributions of wealth. Both individuals and
firms may feel threatened by changes in social property rights. People who
have moved into a community, voted in elections, and gone to work for a
small firm that contributed generously to local charities may feel that they
have been treated unjustly if the firm grows large, discontinues its contributions to local charities, contributes heavily to local political campaigns,
or perhaps, ultimately moves to another location.

Business firms depend on social property rights as well. If, for example,
it becomes very difficult for companies to reverse decisions (for example,
about where to locate production facilities), then the expected returns from
investments will decline (since a negative return stream cannot be truncated)
and certain investments may never be undertaken in the first place.
Businesses often make decisions under the belief that they can change them
in the future if things do not work out as planned. They may feel that they
have been treated unjustly if they later discover that their decisions are irre-
vocable because the social property rights of consumers, employees, or local
community residents are invoked.

Presumably such conflicts over social property rights might be handled
efficiently by private transactions. There are some examples of employees'
purchasing plants or exerting such social pressure on firms that the firms
find it preferable to remain with their initial plant locations or policies. In
cases in which transactions costs are very high, however, private markets do
not function well. In such cases we may depend on the judicial system to
resolve the conflict. Unfortunately, courts are not well equipped to weigh
the values of competing claims. They have no method of determining the
true values adversaries place on different states of nature since the adver-
sary system creates incentives to exaggerate values and the participants do
not have to stand behind their claims with a willingness and ability to pay.

The problem of valuing social property rights is particularly acute in the
areas of political power, local community welfare, income redistribution,
and worker welfare because individuals' values depend on their *perceptions*
of reality, which may deviate significantly from reality itself. If business size
really has no effect on political power, yet people continue to think that it
does, and if people value dispersion of power greatly, how should we value

their dissatisfaction? Shall it be valued at zero because, in fact, we know that there is no influence of business on political outcomes? Or should we recognize the value of reducing perceived business political power, even though in reality actual business political power is unaffected?

The valuation problem reduces to the issue of consumer sovereignty in social issues. Should we respect people's views regardless of how wrongheaded we think they are? If one argues that advertising should not be regulated since consumers are intelligent enough to understand their values and are in the best position to know what is best for themselves, are we not obliged also to accept the notion that people are intelligent enough and understand their values enough so that if they want to dismantle corporate giants for factually unsound reasons, we should urge them to do so?

The main difference between these noneconomic social goals and economic efficiency is that there is no consensus regarding the value of the noneconomic goals analogous to the general agreement that more efficiency is always preferred to less efficiency (if there are no associated negative by-products in achieving it). Whether more business political power is better or worse depends on the view one has of how social values should be determined. Whether a redistribution of wealth is desirable or not depends on who is identified as more deserving and one's view of the effect that redistributive policies have on the total output of goods and services available for redistribution. Whether workers should enjoy their job more or less depends on how individuals value the monetary and nonmonetary elements of compensation packages and whether one believes that wages should be or actually are adjusted to reflect different characteristics of jobs. Whether a plant should be moved from one community to another is likely to depend on the residence of workers who are asked.

There is, no doubt, an optimal level of such things as political power of business firms, dissatisfaction from working in large, impersonal firms, income redistribution, and local community welfare. However, the values placed on the marginal benefits and the marginal costs of various levels of achievement of these goals determine whether or not the effects that accompany conglomeration move us toward this optimal level. To value such things as an increased or diminished quantity of business political power requires knowledge of a social-demand curve that is very elusive. Because considerable disagreement exists regarding the value of such things, it is difficult to determine if more or less political power, worker dissatisfaction with job conditions, income redistribution, or welfare of certain communities are net benefits or costs to society. In this chapter we do not attempt to deal with such issues. Indeed, they seem to us to be solidly grounded in value judgments. Our purpose in this chapter is simply to chronicle the effects of conglomeration on various types of noneconomic social goals without passing judgment on the net welfare implications of these effects.

Effects on Political Democracy

There is no shortage of proclamations regarding the importance of the connection between economic structure and the political influence of business. Unfortunately, careful theoretical and empirical analyses of the intertwined relationships between business and politics are in short supply. The greatest confusion probably arises from the failure to distinguish among the multiplicity of attributes possessed by conglomerate firms, each of which may affect the firms' intensity of effort and effectiveness in influencing policy. The essential structural characteristics of conglomerates are: (1) market concentration, (2) firm size, (3) product diversification, and (4) geographic dispersion. It has been argued that each of these elements of market structure is a characteristic of conglomerates.[5]

For business successfully to influence political outcomes, there must be sufficient incentives to make such efforts, adequate resources to mount the effort, enough knowledge of the production process for political influence to apply those resources to the objectives effectively, and finally, a response from the political decision makers that achieves the desired goals. We believe that much of the ignorance surrounding the debate on political influence of conglomerate firms emanates from the failure to recognize that individual market-structure elements (for example, market concentration) principally determine the incentives to influence government policy, while firm-size characteristics primarily dictate the efficiency with which such efforts are transformed into results—that is, the theoretical reasons to expect firms in more concentrated industries to have a greater effect on political decisions arise from the larger effort that firms in concentrated industries are likely to muster. The reasons to expect large firms to have more effect on political outcomes are based on the greater efficiency with which they apply their resources to achieving the objectives, holding constant the intensity of their effort.[6] If this characterization of the political-influence process is accurate, measures of market concentration should be most successful in explaining the intensity of efforts to influence policy—for example, lobbying efforts and campaign contributions. Absolute firm size should be most successful in explaining differences in political outcomes holding the effort variables constant.

Market Concentration

Market concentration affects the incentives of individual firms to contribute to group efforts designed to influence industrywide political decisions. The nature of the political decision-making process creates a divergence between firm and industry incentives to invest in these activities. Because the costs of excluding noncontributors from the benefits are prohibitive, each individual firm in a competitive industry will reap some of the benefits of any successful efforts to influence policy regardless of whether it assumes part of the costs. Indeed, in order to collect sufficiently broad support for a policy initiative or position, proponents will likely find it in their interest to broaden their appeal beyond a single firm to an industry or sector of the economy. This increases the opportunity for free riders.

The standard theory of collective action yields the prediction that, as a public good, political influence will be supplied at less than the efficient level.[7] Olson identified the number and size distribution of individuals (here, firms) constituting a group (here, industry) as the primary factor determining the effectiveness of group efforts to produce public goods.[8] There are several reasons for this logic. First, the fewer the firms in an industry, the better is the chance that their values and objectives will coincide, thus reducing the bargaining and organizational costs of forming a collective-action group. Second, the fewer the firms in an industry, the greater will be the relative share of benefits accruing to each individual firm (other things, such as size distribution, held constant). This increases the expected dollar value of benefits to a firm undertaking the investment on its own. Third, the fewer the firms in an industry, the easier it is for the collective-action group to enforce any voluntary agreements among the firms. For example, because the impact of noncompliance by one firm on the remaining firms increases inversely with the number of firms, it is easier for three firms, each of which has pledged $10,000 to a certain lobbying effort, to evaluate compliance with the pledge than it is for each of 100 firms pledging $300 each to determine the level of compliance with their agreement. Finally, as the size distribution of firms becomes more unequal, the chance of any one firm's finding it in its interest to pursue the public policy alone increases because the share of benefits from a successful effort to influence policy accruing to the largest firm usually rises with its relative share of the market. Since these factors minimize the possibility that any one firm will attempt to be a free rider if the market is more concentrated, we expect efforts at political influence to increase with market concentration. If results are related to efforts, we should observe that the achievement of political goals is more frequent in more concentrated industries than in competitive industries.

If industry profits and market concentration are positively related, there may be another reason to expect greater political efforts from concentrated industries. On the one hand, if economic rents accrue to firms with market power, they may be used to further political objectives. On the other hand, if investments in political influence were better than the alternative investment opportunities of a firm, why would they have to be financed out of economic rents? One answer is that it may be difficult to obtain a bank loan to finance political activities. In that case, capital-market imperfections create an advantage for firms that can finance such investments out of retained earnings.

The impact of market concentration on political influence might be negative if the visibility that usually accompanies high levels of market concentration tends to attract adverse public attention and to increase opposition to political efforts by firms in highly concentrated industries. If opposing efforts are encouraged, the projected marginal benefit of investments in political influence would fall, thus reducing the optimal level of such efforts.

A major problem with the interpretation of statistical results correlating political outcomes with market concentration is that the direction of causation is not clear. Perhaps certain political outcomes affect concentration. For example, tariffs and tax reductions increase the after-tax profitability of domestic producers, thereby tending to increase the number of firms and decrease the level of concentration. For this reason, a negative correlation might be observed even though concentration is causing more political influence.

Firm Size

The relationship between absolute firm size and political power seems to be the basis for much of the U.S. concern about conglomerates and aggregate concentration. Presumably the hypothesis is that one large firm would have more political influence than ten firms, each one-tenth of the size of the larger firms. Thus, aggregation of economic power yields disproportionately greater political power.

The reasons for expecting absolute firm size to create disproportionate amounts of political power fall into three main categories. First, large firms have a greater incentive to participate in politics because larger firms usually (although certainly not always) have greater market shares. Thus, even if other firms in their industry choose to ride free, large firms would be more likely to enjoy benefits from their efforts that exceed the expected costs. This argument for expecting more concentrated industries to participate more intensively in political influence is similar to that based on collective-choice theory.

Second, larger firms may have greater access to the critical resources necessary for producing political influence because they are more likely to have acquired these resources already for their production of nonpolitical goods and services. There may be important elements of joint cost in performing economic and political activities. For example, the larger firms already have the public-relations experts, attorneys, Washington law firms, and executives with personal contacts throughout the political system needed to make a political-influence effort possible at reasonable marginal cost.

Third, what makes the absolute size of available resources, and, hence, firm size so important politically is the fact that political involvement has certain fixed costs associated with it. The larger firms will be better able to reach the minimum initial resource constraint necessary to attain a profitable level of influence production. The heavy fixed-cost nature of the inputs to political influence means that the average cost of influencing policy by large firms will be lower than for small firms. Since small firms can rarely reach the minimum size to participate efficiently in the political process, they must rely on group participation—with all of the intraorganizational differences, lack of control, and consequent weakening of influence that go with it.

However, just as in the case of firms in more concentrated industries, the greater visibility of large firms increases the likelihood of attracting opposition to their political efforts and raises the cost of successfully influencing policy. If large firm size discourages efforts to influence political outcomes, the effect of firm size on political outcomes would be negative.

Legal constraints might also disadvantage larger firms. For example, firms may establish as many political-action committees as they wish, but they are limited by law (the Federal Election Campaign Act Amendments of 1976) to a single $5,000 contribution per candidate for each election. By merging, two firms will effectively reduce their combined contribution limit from $10,000 to $5,000.

Geographic Dispersion

The effect of the greater geographic diversity of conglomerates upon their ability to influence public policy is not clear. If each member of Congress has many constituent groups competing for his attention, and if he allocates his time to their requests in proportion to their likely impact on his reelection, then it follows that an industry must be sufficiently large in any congressional district to pass the minimum threshold to gain recognition. Consequently, for a given industry size, industries with firms located in fewer different geographic areas will be more likely to capture the attention of their representatives and to achieve their political-influence goals. In other words, there are economies of scale in obtaining a hearing for one's views so that a larger single presence in congressional districts produces advantages.

In addition, conflicts of interest between political group members are less likely to occur within specific regions than if the firms have diverse locations. For example, sun-belt versus snow-belt issues may hinder the formation of an interest group. Therefore, geographic concentration may increase the prospect for successful collective action and subsequent political influence.

While geographic concentration may improve the chances for obtaining the attention and support of a sponsor for certain legislation, industries that are highly concentrated geographically may lack the broad-based political support necessary to pass legislation and to have it implemented. The optimal geographic dispersion may be a few areas in which the industry is highly concentrated and clearly significant to the political representatives, with the rest of the industry spread over at least one-half of the districts, so that a majority voting for special legislation favoring the industry can claim a victory for some constituency.

Dispersion might also be inversely related to political efforts and successful outcomes because it may increase the communications and organizational costs of forming an effective political-action group. Thus, the net effect of the greater geographic dispersion of conglomerates upon their ability to influence public policy is ambiguous.

Product Diversification

Product diversification is another attribute of conglomerates that may create greater incentives for or efficiency in influencing public policies through the political apparatus. First, diversified firms might find that the cultivation of political gardens for one purpose is also profitable for their other interests. When special problems arise, a diversified firm is more likely to have dealt with them at one time or another in some part of its total operation. Furthermore, diversified firms can mobilize support for their efforts to influence policy from a wider range of sources and are more likely to find support from some important constituencies.

More diversified firms tend to have varied interests that may be affected in contrary ways by a specific policy. For example, if a firm is both an exporter and an importer, which position should it take on tariffs? The importance of this fact for political influence is ambiguous. A conglomerate merger between two firms that previously had produced political influence in opposition to each other might lead to a resolution of the conflict within the firm and a single focused effort at influencing policy. Consequently, conglomerate mergers may increase political power. However, the internal organizational characteristics of firms might inhibit a strict profit-maximizing approach in favor of some negotiated settlement among disputants within a firm. Such settlements might take the form of agnosticism toward controversial issues, thereby eliminating any net effect the competing efforts might have made and, consequently, reducing political influence.

Finally, it has also been argued that diversified firms cannot press as hard on any one issue as a single-purpose organization because they are more likely to jeopardize their success in another area. Therefore, diversified firms might be less successful in influencing policy on any one issue.

Empirical Evidence

The systematic empirical studies of the political influence of business fall into two categories: (1) investigations of the effect of economic variables on political instruments such as campaign contributions or lobbying efforts and (2) studies that relate economic variables directly to political outcomes. Studies of political instruments should be most useful in assessing the validity of the free-rider theory, which predicts greater political involvement by firms in more-concentrated industries. The political-outcome studies are more difficult to interpret since a correlation between economic variables and political results could be the consequence either of greater efforts by firms to influence policy or greater effectiveness in using a given amount of resources to achieve their goals.

Four empirical studies look at political instruments. Pittman's two studies and the study by Marx examine the determinants of campaign contributions.[9,10] Mann and McCormick investigate the relationship between firm attributes and lobbying efforts in California.[11] Eight empirical studies devoted to political outcomes relate the economic environment directly to policy results from three substantive areas: regulation, tariff protection, and tax burdens.[12]

The empirical studies report varied and conflicting results. On the one hand, the studies of political instruments (campaign contributions and lobbying expenditures) agree on the positive effect of market concentration on efforts to influence policy. These results are consistent with the theory of private versus group incentives from which we derive the proposition that effort to influence policy should be determined by the divergence of individual and group interests.

On the other hand, the studies of political outcomes reveal quite diverse results. The three studies of tariff protection report a negative, neutral, and positive effect, respectively, of market concentration on effective rates of protection. Siegfried's study of corporation income-tax rates finds a negative effect of concentration on political influence, but Stigler finds that occupations with local markets, in which market concentration is higher, obtained entry regulation sooner than other occupations. Overall, the tests seem to favor the free-rider hypothesis.

The evidence on firm size is also mixed. Mann and McCormick find that larger firms spend more on lobbying, but not as much more as one would expect on the basis of their size. Salamon and Siegfried find that larger firms have greater success in obtaining special tax favors, but neither Coolidge and Tullock nor Marx find any evidence to support such a conclusion. If larger firms actually devote proportionately less to political lobbying, as Mann and McCormick find, and yet are more successful in achieving their goals, as Salamon and Siegfried find, their relative efficiency advantage in producing political influence (the economies-of-scale argument) can be inferred to be quite large.

Geographic concentration does not appear to matter. Pincus finds that geographically concentrated industries were more effective in obtaining protective tariffs in 1824. This is consistent with the dependence of communications costs on physical proximity at that time. However, the studies that have examined the effect of geographic concentration on contemporary policy have failed to find any systematic relationship between it and political influence. The three studies that looked explicitly at product diversification, the most apparent characteristic of conglomerates, found no net impact on political influence, with the exception of Marx's positive relationship between conglomeration and campaign contributions.

Effects on Worker Satisfaction

A conglomerate merger may affect a worker's satisfaction by altering his employment, wages, or the quality of his work environment. A worker's satisfaction will be reduced if his job is lost, real wage falls, or his work environment deteriorates, ceteris paribus. In addition, the satisfaction of an employed worker may decline if his real wage falls more than the increase in the implicit value of his job amenities or if his real wage rises less than the decrease in the implicit value of amenities attributable to the merger. Thus, in order to gauge the impact of a conglomerate merger upon a worker's satisfaction, we must consider its impact upon the probability of employment and upon the wages and amenities enjoyed by workers who remain employed after the merger.

Employment

The level and composition of a firm's employment may be affected by a conglomerate merger for several reasons. In a world of imperfect capital markets, internal financing is normally cheaper than external borrowing. By increasing the size of the internal capital market and/or by increasing stockholders' estimates of the firm's profitability and cyclical stability, the firm's access to capital may be improved and interest costs reduced by a merger. As interest rates decline, the cost of capital goods falls, and producers may be encouraged to substitute capital for labor in the production process. At the same time, the reduced cost of financing will encourage the producer to expand output and to employ more of both capital and labor. The net effect upon employment will depend upon the relative size of these two effects. Workers who are less easily replaced by (or are complementary to) capital will experience a smaller decrease or greater increase in employment. Thus, if skilled workers are complementary to capital, as the capital-skill-complementarity hypothesis suggests, conglomerate mergers may increase the employment of skilled labor relative to unskilled labor.[13] However, if a conglomerate merger improves allocative efficiency sufficiently, employment of both skilled and unskilled labor may increase.

Second, through its effect on total firm size, a conglomerate merger may allow a firm to exploit certain economies of scale in the provision of nonproduction services like marketing, distribution, personnel services, management, and advertising. The actual effect of these economies on the firm's employment will, however, be ambiguous. If employees were underemployed prior to the merger, consolidation of services may result in some reduction in employment; but if the merger improves efficiency and increases output, employment in these services may increase. In addition, the reduction in the cost of providing nonproduction services may encourage firms to perform internally those services that had previously been provided by external consultants. Thus, a firm that had previously employed an outside legal firm may now find it less costly to hire its own legal staff. Of course, even though the firm's employment may increase, the net effect on total employment of such a transfer of services may be zero or even negative.

Third, a conglomerate merger may increase a firm's product and input market power. Increased industrial concentration may encourage employers to reduce output and, consequently, employment. In addition, a merger may increase a firm's input market power. If industrial concentration is increased, the number of purchasers of certain specialized types of labor may be reduced. Further, a conglomerate merger may reduce union bargaining power. Because of the greater diversity of its product line, a conglomerate may be more able to withstand an industrywide strike and, therefore, may be less willing to accede to union demands. Offsetting this, however, is the possibility that greater firm size and visibility may encourage unions to organize and/or support a strike by employees of a newly consolidated firm, but if the firm's monopsony power is increased by the merger, employment and/or wages may decline.

Thus, the net effect of a conglomerate merger on firm employment is unclear. If the merger improves efficiency, output and employment may increase. If capital costs decline, the firm may be encouraged to substitute capital for labor, and employment, particularly employment of unskilled labor, may decline. If the firm's product and/or input market power increases, employment may decline as well.

Wages and the Work Environment of Employed Workers

Empirical studies of firm and industrial wage differentials suggest that average wages are higher in larger firms and in more concentrated industries.[14] These studies suggest that a conglomerate merger may increase (or at least not reduce) an employee's wages. In order to understand the effects of higher wages on a worker's satisfaction, it is important to consider why conglomerates might offer higher average wages than other firms. If the wage is increased to compensate for a decrease in the quality of the employee's work environment, the effect on a worker's satisfaction will be very different than if the wage is increased with no change in the work environment.

Opponents of conglomerate mergers have expressed concern that the higher wages are at the expense of various job- and firm-specific amenities. Their concern is based upon the theory of equalizing differences. In a world of perfect information and complete factor mobility, competitive factor market equilibrium requires that the satisfaction of the marginal worker be equal across firms. Any firm that offers a higher wage must be offering less of some amenities or the market would not be in equilibrium.

A number of features of conglomerate firms suggest that a worker may, on the one hand, indeed enjoy a less satisfactory working environment after a merger. In particular, the high fixed, low variable costs of capital may encourage a conglomerate with higher capital-labor ratios and higher capital-labor complementary to increase work effort, decrease the flexibility in hours worked, and increase job specialization with a resulting increase in job pressure and tedium. In addition, the larger work-group size may require that an individual worker compromise more to conform to common group work rules. Finally, greater geographic distance between top management and labor may lead to a feeling of worker alienation.

On the other hand, a conglomerate merger may increase a worker's satisfaction by decreasing the riskiness of a particular job and by increasing the worker's sphere of promotion. Any time an employee accepts a particular job, there is the possibility that the job will be terminated. Because of its greater product and/or geographic diversity, a conglomerate offers greater cyclical stability in employment. In addition, an employee may be more protected from structural unemployment by the possibility of transferring to a new job or new plant within the same firm should his current job become obsolete. Similarly, larger firm size increases the number of job openings potentially available to a worker interested in promotion within the firm.[15]

Empirical efforts to assess the impact of conglomerate mergers upon job satisfaction are practically nonexistent. Dunn found that satisfaction with work environment increased with firm size, holding plant size constant. She also found that satisfaction decreased with plant size—a result that indicates the potential difficulty in extrapolating the results of the more numerous plant studies to conglomerates.[16] Unfortunately, the limited nature of her sample makes any conclusions tenuous. All that can be said is that her results do not appear to support the view that a conglomerate merger will reduce a worker's satisfaction with his work environment.

Is it possible that a conglomerate merger could lead to an increase in a firm's average wage without reducing the job- and firm-specific amenities enjoyed by its workers by an equivalent amount, as Dunn's empirical results suggest? There are several reasons why this might occur.

First, the higher firm wage may simply be a statistical aberration. If a conglomerate merger increases the ratio of skilled to unskilled workers and if skilled workers are paid more than unskilled workers, then the average wage paid by the firm would tend to be higher after the merger even if the merger had no effect upon the wages of skilled and unskilled workers. In this case, average firm wages could increase without affecting an employed worker's satisfaction in any way.[17]

Second, large conglomerates may be more easily organized than smaller firms. If unions push for higher wages, the higher wages may reflect a reduction in the employer's monopsony power. Offsetting this, however, is the fact that a merger may increase an employer's bargaining power with industrial unions as discussed previously.[18]

Third, a conglomerate may find that labor costs may actually be reduced by paying employees a wage greater than the current market-clearing wage. When information in imperfect and factor mobility is limited, wages are not the only cost of employment. Higher wages may reduce recruiting costs by improving a firm's relative market attractiveness. If there are significant diseconomies of scale in hiring at the going wage, a large firm, with a higher absolute number of new hires per period, may choose to raise wages in order to economize on hiring costs.[19]

Higher wages may also reduce turnover costs. An employee will be less likely to leave when alternative market opportunities are not as good as his current job. If labor is more complementary to capital in a conglomerate, firm-specific investment in labor may be higher, and turnover costs may be very large. The conglomerate may choose to pay higher wages in order to protect past investment in labor.[20]

Higher wages may also enable a firm to increase the quality of its employees.[21] For the same amount of recruiting effort, the employer should receive more applications for employment after the wage increase. If the employer's screening system does not decrease in accuracy, labor quality will improve as the number of applicants increases. A conglomerate may be more concerned about labor quality than a single-plant or -product firm since increased work-group size, greater specialization of labor, and geographic diversity may increase labor force complementarity, the importance of the internal labor market as a source of promotion, and the distance between management and labor. Improved labor force quality will reduce the possibility that a single worker will slow the entire production process, improve the quality of workers subject to promotion, and decrease the need for close supervision of workers by management.

In addition, higher wages may allow an employer to forestall the introduction of unions. Since its larger size and greater product and/or geographic visibility may make a conglomerate a more likely target for unionization by unions with a broad industrial base, a conglomerate may choose to offer higher current wages in order to reduce a union's bargaining power and to restrain future labor costs.

If, by offering higher current wages, a firm can reduce total labor costs, such behavior can increase the satisfaction of both stockholders and workers. A compensatory decrease in job amenities would simply reduce the firm's labor market advantage and increase labor costs.

Finally, after a merger, a firm may simply be in a better position to offer higher wages to its employees. If firms are utility- rather than profit-maximizing entities, managers may choose to please employees by offering higher wages than ordinary profit maximization would allow.[22] If a merger improves a firm's profits, the manager's ability to raise wages without incurring the stockholders' wrath is increased. Some evidence suggests that firms in more concentrated industries do share monopoly profits with employees.[23]

Thus, conglomerates may lead to an increase in average firm wages with little or no reduction in job satisfaction. Higher average wages may reflect a difference in labor quality, in the degree of unionization, in hiring or turnover costs, or in ability to offer higher wages as well as a difference in firm- or job-specific amenities. It is not proper to conclude that, because conglomerates offer higher wages, the quality of the work environment must be lower. Further studies of employee's actual perceptions of the work environment are necessary before any statement of the impact of conglomerate mergers on total worker satisfaction may be made.

Effects on the Distribution of Income

Even if the distribution of rewards does not influence allocative efficiency, the effect of conglomerate mergers upon the distribution of income may be important from a policy standpoint.[24] If an equitable distribution of income is viewed as a good by the majority of the community, if the transactions costs of redistributing income are large, and if conglomerate mergers increase the inequity of the income distribution, then controls on conglomerate mergers might be warranted even if these mergers increase allocative efficiency.

Through its effects on factor payments and charitable contributions, a conglomerate merger can be expected to affect the nominal-income distribution. Through its effects on product prices, the real-income distribution will be affected as well. The character of these effects, however, is far from clear.

In most cases, a merger is undertaken to increase firm profitability.[25] On the one hand, improved capital markets, reduced transactions costs, increased ability to exploit available scale economies in nonproduction services, and added protection from cyclical fluctuations should decrease costs, raise output and factor payments, and reduce final product prices— that is, by increasing allocative efficiency, the merger may increase everyone's nominal and real income. Some parties may, however, gain more than others. The exact effect upon any one individual will depend upon the character of the firm's production function, the nature of the input supply and product demand curves, and the composition of the individual's consumption and input market baskets.

On the other hand, a conglomerate merger may increase firm profits by increasing the firm's product or input market power. If this increased power reduces allocative efficiency, the profit increase will occur at the expense of consumers who are forced to pay higher prices for final products and owners of factors of production who experience a decrease in factor demand. In this case, someone must lose both absolutely and relatively. Thus, the effect of a conglomerate merger upon the level and distribution of income will depend critically upon the source of the improved profitability.

Factor Payments

Payments to Stockholders. As noted in the previous section, conglomerate mergers are expected to increase firm profitability. As long as potential extra profits are not dissipated in consummating the merger, passed on to factor owners and consumers in the form of higher factor prices and/or lower final good prices, or given away through charity or taxes, stock prices and firm dividends should increase.[26]

The effect upon the distribution of income of this increased return to stockholders will, however, depend upon the distribution of stock ownership. While it is true that within the United States the median income of stockholders exceeds the median income of all individuals,[27] stock ownership is not confined, exclusively, to upper-income groups. Significant numbers of lower-income retirees and middle-income workers, who exercised employee stock options, receive income from dividends. Since a $1 increase in dividend income will have a greater relative effect upon the income of low-income stockholders than that of high-income stockholders, an increase in dividend payments will possibly decrease income inequality.

A simple example illustrates this point. Suppose that four people live in the community with pre-merger incomes as indicated in table 5-1. Each individual owns the indicated number of shares of stock in one of the firms that is merging. After the merger, dividends increase by 10¢ a share, and post-merger incomes of all stockholders are as indicated [for example, 100 + 50(.10) = 105]. In this case, income inequality, as measured by either the coefficient of variation or the Gini coefficient, will decrease after the merger. Obviously, a conglomerate merger will be more likely to reduce income inequality via stock price increases if low-income people hold a large share of the merging firms' stocks.

Payments to Factor Owners other than Stockholders. The effect of a merger on payments to factors other than capital is far from clear. It will depend upon how employment and factor prices are affected.

If the merger reduces interest costs, fixed inputs may be substituted for variable inputs in the production process. Thus, more capital goods and skilled labor may be employed while less unskilled labor may be used. At least in the short run, the price of capital goods and skilled labor will increase, reflecting their relatively inelastic supply. Employment of these inputs will increase slightly. The effect upon the price and employment of unskilled labor will depend upon the elasticity of supply of unskilled labor and upon the relative size of the output and substitution effects of the reduced capital costs. Since we expect that the supply curve for unskilled labor is relatively elastic, much of the change in factor payments will reflect employment rather than price changes.

Thus, if a merger reduces output, we would expect to observe a reduction in the employment of unskilled labor with only a moderate reduction in wages. Employment of skilled labor and capital goods will be less affected. The effect on factor prices will depend upon the relative size of the output and substitution effects. If the demand for skilled labor and/or capital goods increases (decreases), prices may increase (decrease) substantially.

The effect upon the distribution of income will depend upon the availability of alternative employment and upon the distribution of factor ownership across income groups. If there is already an excess supply of unskilled labor, the merger may increase the number of unemployed and thus low-income families. The effect upon the rest of the income distribution is less clear. It may become more or less dispersed depending upon the size of the substitution and output effects and the pattern of factor ownership across income groups.

Table 5-1
Hypothetical Effects of Merger on Income Distribution

Person	Premerger Income of Individual	Stockholding in Shares	Postmerger Income of Individual
1	100	50	105
2	50	30	53
3	10	0	10
4	5	20	7
Mean income	41.25		43.75
Coefficient of variation	.925		.909
Gini coefficient	.492		.481

The results of a simulation study by Lankford and Stewart of the effects of a reduction in monopoly power upon the distribution of income within the United States suggest that the effect of a conglomerate merger upon the distribution of income may be rather small.[28] If conglomerates reduce output, average households with incomes greater than $30,000 would appear to benefit at the expense of lower-income households. However, because of differences in households' factor shares within income classes, the impact upon households in the same income bracket may vary greatly. Their results suggest that any increase in monopoly distortion will have only a moderate impact on the inequality of the income distribution—that is, a relatively small number of households will experience substantial gains, but most households will experience a moderate decrease in factor income.

Charitable Contributions

Through their effects upon firm contributions to charity, conglomerate mergers may also affect the income distribution. If conglomerates give more money to organizations that aid lower-income groups than other firms, then the income distribution may be made more equal by allowing a merger to be consummated. However, corporate contributions may represent a transfer of gift giving from stockholders whose dividend may decline, from government whose tax revenue is reduced, or from factor owners whose income may fall. A complete analysis of the effect of the gift-giving behavior of conglomerates upon the character of the income distribution would require knowledge of the gift-giving behavior of stockholders, factor owners, consumers, and the government, as well as that of the firm. We only consider the effect of a merger upon the size and distribution of the firm's charitable gifts.

A conglomerate merger may lead to an increase or a decrease in total corporate giving.[29] Due to the mildly progressive nature of the corporate tax structure, the marginal cost of charitable giving will be smaller for firms with higher absolute profits. This suggests that the marginal cost of gift giving may decline after a merger, which should induce a firm to increase charitable giving. Since the last increase in marginal tax rates occurs at an income of $50,000, however, this price effect will only influence the gift-giving behavior of very small firms. Further, if firms undertake charitable giving for the goodwill it creates and if there are significant economies of scale in generating such goodwill, a conglomerate, with its higher absolute earnings, may be in a better position to exploit these economies and, thus, may be more interested in charitable giving. Therefore, while several small firms might not be willing to donate individually in order to have their name appear on the symphony program, they might together be willing to donate a large amount to have their corporate name appear on symphony hall. In addition, if consumers' images of all firms in an industry are affected by their image of one firm so that all firms share the benefits of one firm's attempt to increase its goodwill, firms will have an incentive to underinvest in charitable giving. If conglomerate mergers increase industrial concentration, the importance of this free-rider problem will be reduced. Finally, firms may undertake charitable giving out of purely philanthropic motives. If conglomerate mergers increase total firm earnings, funds available for satisfying these motives will increase.

Conversely, a conglomerate merger may lead to a reduction in total firm giving for several reasons. For example, charitable giving may represent the utility-maximizing behavior of managers or stockholders. If the managers or stockholders of the merging firms have similar philanthropic interests, total giving may decline. One gift by the conglomerate may provide as much satisfaction as two equal-sized gifts by the separate firms had provided prior to the merger. If the managers or stockholders have different philanthropic interests, the lack of agreement may also lead to a reduction in total giving. Rather than promote discord within the firm, giving to groups in dispute may be curtailed. In addition, charitable giving may be regarded as a job amenity by employees. By giving to charities of interest to their employees, employers may be able to reduce wages. If larger work-group size makes agreement on desirable places to give more difficult, the amenity value of and thus the total amount of gift giving may decline. Finally, corporate goodwill need not be confined to a particular product or area. By merging, a firm may be able to capitalize upon the acquiring firm's good name and reduce its investment in charitable giving with no reduction in product demand. A reduction in giving would be particularly likely if there is a limit to how much goodwill can be generated through charitable giving so that the marginal benefit of contributions declines rapidly.

Empirical results indicate that larger firms may give more than smaller firms, but a positive elasticity of giving with respect to income is not sufficient to insure that a merger will increase total corporate giving. If the income of the conglomerate is not significantly larger than the total income that the merged firms would have earned independently, then the income elasticity must be close to or greater than one to insure an increase in total corporate contributions. Various estimates of the income elasticity have been made, with the results ranging from .5 to 1, but limitations of each study make definitive conclusions suspect.[30]

In order to measure the effect of increased industrial concentration upon charitable giving, Nelson and Whitehead both considered the effect of the number of firms in an industry upon charitable giving.[31] Whitehead's results supported the view that industrial concentration would increase charitable giving; Nelson's did not. Given the difficulty with using numbers of firms as a measure of concentration, the difference in results may not be surprising. Using four firm seller concentration ratios as a measure of market power, Maddox and Siegfried found that market power had a positive impact on charitable giving.[32]

Finally, a study by the Business Committee of the Arts of corporate arts supporters suggests that firms with local rather than national product markets may tend to contribute more to artistic groups.[33] Thus, if the product markets of a conglomerate have a broader geographic scope than the product markets of the merging firms, total contributions to the arts and, perhaps, to charities, as a whole, might decline after a merger. However, the committee's results need not imply that total contributions will decline. For reasons discussed later, conglomerates may choose to contribute less to the arts and more to other groups.

The interim results of a direct-interview study by Maddox and Siegfried of corporate-giving behavior suggests that total corporate giving may increase after a merger.[34] Of the eighty firms interviewed, five had recently moved their headquarters and fifty-one had either made an acquisition or had been acquired within the last few years. Twenty-four firms felt that contributions to local charities had increased after corporate headquarters were moved out of a community, ten felt they declined, and eighteen reported no change (four could not answer). Thus, over twice as many firms reported an increase in giving in the community that lost headquarters as reported a decrease. Since most firms give more to charities in headquarters cities than in cities with branch plants, this suggests that total gift giving may have increased. Of course, it may be possible that firms are temporarily giving to charities in cities that contain recently acquired firms in order to compensate for disruptions caused by the merger or to increase firm recognition. Further study is required to determine if total firm contributions will increase over the long term.

Conglomerate mergers may affect the choice of organizations that will receive charitable gifts as well as the size of total corporate gifts. As discussed previously, larger work-group size makes gift giving to groups of interest to particular employees less appealing to producers. Similarly, an increase in the number of stockholders and/or managers increases the likelihood that some individual will be opposed to supporting a particular charity. Thus, contributions to religious organizations and political campaigns are likely to be reduced. In addition, the greater a product and geographic market diversity of conglomerates might lead to greater interest in gift giving to organizations with a broader national appeal than to local or special-interest groups. Thus, the results of the Business Committee of the Arts study of corporate arts supporters may reflect the fact that contributions to local art galleries and symphonies are less appealing to firms with national markets.[35]

The effect of such shifts in the targets of charitable giving upon the character of the income distribution will depend upon the chosen charities. If a firm gave to the local art gallery prior to the merger but gives to the United Way after the merger, income inequality might be reduced. However, if prior to the merger the firm gave to the local day-care center, income inequality might be increased if contributions now are given to public television. Further study of the targets of charitable giving is necessary before any statement may be made about the effect of conglomerate mergers on this aspect of the income distribution.

Product Prices

If a conglomerate merger leads to an increase in industrial concentration, product price may increase. If a product's price increases, the real income of any individual who would have bought this product prior to the price increase will be reduced. In addition, if producers pass along to consumers at least some part of an increase in input prices, the real income of any individual consuming a good derived from this product will decline as well. The effect on individuals who do not buy this product or any product derived from it is less clear. At least in the short run, prices of goods and inputs complementary to it will fall, while prices of substitutes will increase. The effect on consumers will depend upon the composition of their premerger market basket and the size of these secondary price changes. Some individuals may, conceivably, experience an increase in real income.

Even if everyone's real income falls, the effect on the distribution of real income will depend critically upon the character of the product-demand function. As long as the good is a normal good, higher-income purchasers will experience a larger absolute loss in real income. Since their real income is larger, though, the effect on their real income relative to that of lower-income families is ambiguous. An increase in the price of a normal good may increase or decrease the dispersion in real income. The results of a study by Maddox, Siegfried, and Sweeney of the incidence of product price changes suggest that the real-income distribution effects of product price increases vary greatly across products.[36] Their results suggest that mergers that result in an increase in the price of wine and liquor, furniture, or musical instruments would reduce income inequality, while mergers that result in an increase in the price of cigarettes, drugs, or utilities would increase income inequality. Thus, in order to gauge the impact of a conglomerate merger upon the real-income distribution, particular care must be given to measuring the probable impact of that merger on product prices and to determining the income levels of consumers ultimately affected by the price changes.

A conglomerate merger may increase or decrease the inequality in the nominal- and/or real-income distributions. The effects on payments to factors, charitable gifts, and product price changes are ambiguous. Only careful study of firm's production process, input and product markets, and decision-making behavior can determine the likely impact of a firm's merger upon the distribution of income.

Effect on Community Welfare

Critics of conglomerate mergers have expressed concern that a merger may reduce the quality of life in the community in which the acquired firm is located. Some people feel that this area will become vulnerable to the somewhat arbitrary behavior of a group of managers that has little interest in the community's welfare because of its geographic distance from it. Fear is expressed that plants will be closed, employment growth will be curtailed, and/or that the community that once depended upon the corporate managers for community guidance will now be subjected to the whims of a politically more powerful force that threatens job loss and shows no interest in the external costs of its behavior.[37]

Are these concerns justified? Are conglomerates likely to close plants previously operated by a recently acquired firm? Would these plants have closed anyway, or does their closure represent the arbitrary whim of disinterested managers? Do conglomerates prey upon a community's fear of plant closure, justified or not, in order to exploit their own interests to the possible detriment of the community?

The effects of a conglomerate merger upon plant closures are not clear.[38] Several factors suggest that a conglomerate may be willing to relocate plants in areas outside of the acquired firm's home community, but other factors suggest that conglomerates may be unlikely to terminate a division entirely.

   As noted previously, conglomerate mergers may allow firms to exploit certain economies of scale in research and development, advertising, inventory control, and so forth. If these scale economies are more easily exploited when plants are in close proximity, a conglomerate may tend to consolidate plants in one central location. In many cases, however, a firm might simply move corporate activities to the headquarters city while still maintaining the previous plant for actual production. Nevertheless, if significant complementarities exist between production processes, and if one of the acquiring firm's plants has substantial excess capacity, fixed costs might be significantly reduced by consolidating production within that plant. Thus, if joint production is possible, the risk of plant relocation may increase after a merger.

   Because of their greater geographic and product diversity, conglomerates may also have greater incentives to close a particular plant. The greater geographic diversity of a conglomerate may reduce the cost of acquiring information concerning resource costs and the location of product markets outside of the acquired firm's immediate area. Thus, a conglomerate may be better able to determine the optimal location for the acquired firm's plant. If the cost of relocation is less than the expected profit gain, relocation might be justified. Further, the greater physical distance between top management and employees may reduce the importance placed upon the disruption of the employees' lives in the plant's location or termination decision; but even if management does have concern for the acquired firm's employees, the greater possibility of internal placement of employees displaced may make it easier for top management to discontinue a division's operation. In addition, the greater the firm's product diversity, the more unlikely it is that the closure of a division will pose a threat to the firm's continuity. Therefore, owners and managers of conglomerate firms may be more willing to close a division currently earning less-than-normal profits. Excess funds that had previously been invested in submarginal enterprises may be invested in activities with higher returns. The closure of the Youngstown Sheet and Tube steel plants may be an example of such behavior.[39]

   Merger may also be an important way to insure a firm's continued operation. Improvements in efficiency due to better access to capital or other scarce resources (for example, research-and-development personnel or superior management) or greater ability to exploit available scale economies may reduce costs enough to turn profitable unit firms into profitable divisions of the conglomerate. Further, where bankruptcy is an imminent possibility, cross-subsidization may allow the more diversified conglomerate to maintain employment temporarily. Greater reserves make it easier to withstand cyclical instability and give the firm added time to turn the business around.

In addition, complementarities between products may encourage conglomerates to maintain unprofitable divisions. The cost of terminating a plant or business will depend upon its relationship to the rest of the firm. Abandoning a business whose product is complementary to others sold by the firm or that shares some distribution channels may involve a potential loss in profits greater than the loss in earnings from the exited business. Similarly, despite a persistent loss, a firm might choose to remain in an industry rather than incur the wrath of a union that also covers members of other more profitable divisions. Thus, once a business has been assimilated into the firm, jointness of costs may make it less easy for a conglomerate to close unprofitable divisions.

Finally, management of conglomerate firms is more highly visible than management of smaller concerns. If there is a stigma attached to closing a plant and admitting a lapse in good business vision, managers of conglomerates may be less inclined to close a plant. This will obviously require that stockholders be sufficiently disinterested in total firm profits so that management can exercise some discretion in plant closings.

In a study of plant closings in rural Iowa, Barkley and Paulsen found that multiplant firms, including conglomerates, were less likely to close plants due to bankruptcy than were single-plant firms.[40] The reasons for this are not clear. On the one hand, conglomerates may have avoided bankruptcy because of greater efficiency or improved cyclical stability. On the other hand, conglomerates may have judiciously avoided acquiring firms headed for bankruptcy. Some evidence suggests that acquired firms may be at least as well managed and profitable as acquiring firms.[41]

In the same study, Barkley and Paulsen found that branch plants of multiplant firms, including conglomerates, were considerably more geographically mobile than single-plant firms. Further, plant closings by multiplant firms were more closely tied to variations in the business cycle than were closings of single-unit plants.[42] This is consistent with the hypothesis that managers of conglomerates are more aware of and responsive to changes in product demand or resource cost.

Thus, a conglomerate may be more willing than a single-product or -plant firm to close a viable local plant; but if this closing improves allocative efficiency, the net social benefit may be positive. While employees and property owners in the original city will suffer, employees and property owners in the new location will benefit. It is quite conceivable that the increase in benefits to the new city and to consumers of the firm's products will exceed the loss to the old community. Thus, legislation to control plant closings or limit conglomerate mergers could reduce total welfare while protecting obsolete plants from closure.[43]

In addition, it should be pointed out that any effort to limit merger possibilities reduces the potential profits and/or increases the risk of starting a new business. By reducing the potential salvage value of a firm, limitations on mergers may reduce the growth of single-unit firms as well. Thus, if conglomerate mergers had been banned at the time these plants were opened, some plants acquired by conglomerates might never have existed.

Even if conglomerates are not more likely to close plants than single-product firms, the ability of conglomerate firms to make communities feel hostage may have important welfare effects. Communities may be more willing to make concessions to conglomerates in the form of reduced taxes, looser pollution-control requirements, greater subsidization of plant or road-construction costs, and so forth. To the extent that these concessions reduce funds for investment in local public goods or lead to an increase in negative externalities, community welfare may be reduced. Some evidence suggests that such concessions are made to large firms with greater geographic scope and are not made to smaller local plants.[44] However, this may depend critically upon the extent of the local firm's buying market power. Small firms in one-employer towns may be just as likely to exploit their market power and cause a less-than-optimal investment in social overhead capital.

In addition, it is felt that because of their greater geographic distance from the community, top management will be less interested in the social affairs of the community in which the acquired firm is based. It is feared that the greater geographic diversity of conglomerates will increase the geographic mobility of middle managers. Increased mobility may reduce the managers' long-term interest in community development and reduce their willingness to assume a leadership role in the community.[45] Whether this fear is justified or not is hard to say. Since input and product markets may be broadened by a merger, charitable and other social contributions on the local level may be less important to continued firm viability. However, the greater size and diversity of conglomerates may increase firm visibility in any market. Failure to continue contributions begun by an acquired firm may have strong negative effects on product demand for all of the firm's products. Further, the level and composition of contributions depends somewhat upon the tastes and preferences of management and stockholders. Quite possibly, owners and managers of the conglomerate may be more rather than less charitably and socially inclined than the original owners and managers of the acquired firm. The interim results of the study by Maddox and Siegfried of corporate giving behavior suggests that charities in the acquired firm's community do not suffer after a merger.[46]

While no doubt exists that a corporate merger may have significant effects on community welfare, it is not clear whether the net effect will be positive or negative. A merger may breed new life into a less-than-viable local plant or lead to a transfer of the local firm's resources to other divisions of the conglomerates, but even if the merger reduces employment in and/or social commitment to the acquired firm's community, the net social benefit may be positive. In assessing the welfare effects of conglomerate mergers, concerns of parochial interest groups must be distinguished from true net social costs.

Conclusions

This chapter has reviewed the (mostly ad hoc) theories relating the characteristics of conglomerate firms (large size, market concentration, product diversity, and geographic dispersion) to four social goals: political democracy, worker satisfaction, income distribution, and local community welfare. In each case, we found reasons why conglomeration might increase or decrease the social goal. Consequently, the net impact of conglomeration on these important issues becomes an empirical question. Unfortunately, the empirical evidence on these issues is limited and suffers from severe measurement problems. In view of the myriad of hypotheses concerning conglomerates and the high emotional content of the issues raised in this chapter, more systematic theoretical and empirical research should be of paramount interest to the Washington policymakers.

Notes

1. Federal Trade Commission, *Economic Report on Corporate Mergers* (Washington, D.C., 1969).

2. For an exhaustive review of the literature, see Dennis C. Mueller, "The Effects of Conglomerate Mergers: A Survey of The Empirical Evidence," *Journal of Banking and Finance* (1977):315-347.

3. John J. Siegfried, ed., *The Economics of Firm Size, Market Structure and Social Performance,* Federal Trade Commission, Bureau of Economics, 1980.

4. U.S., Congress, Senate, Hearings before the Subcommittee on Antitrust, Monopoly, and Business Rights of the Committee on the Judiciary, 96th Cong., 1st Sess. on S.600, The Small and Independent Business Protection Act of 1979, Part 2, (Washington, D.C.: U.S. Government Printing Office, 1979).

5. The arguments that conglomerate firms are larger, more geographically dispersed, and have greater product diversification are straightforward. The link between conglomerates and market concentration is less obvious. The case for such a link is made in *Economic Report on Corporate Mergers,* pp. 230-235.

6. Large firm size should also affect the incentives to influence policy since larger firms stand to gain a greater share of whatever benefits are produced. This role of firm size—namely, its impact on the size distribution of firms—is included in the market-concentration argument. Firm size is considered with other things, in particular the size distribution of firms, held constant.

7. See, for example, James M. Buchanan, *The Demand and Supply of Public Goods* (Chicago: Rand McNally, 1968), chapter 5; Anthony Downs, *The Economics of Democracy* (New York: Harper and Row, 1957); and Mancur Olson, *The Logic of Collective Action* (Cambridge, Mass.: Harvard University Press, 1965).

8. Olson, *Logic of Collective Action.*

9. Russell Pittman, "The Effects of Industry Concentration and Regulation on Contributions in Three 1972 U.S. Senate Campaigns," *Public Choice* 27 (Fall 1976):71–80; and Pittman, "Market Structure and Campaign Contributions," *Public Choice* 31 (Fall 1977):37–52.

10. Thomas G. Marx, "Political Consequences of Conglomerate Mergers," *Atlantic Economic Journal* 8 (March 1980):62–63. For more details, see Marx, "Political Consequences of Conglomerate Mergers" (unpublished paper, General Motors Corporation, January 1980).

11. Michael Mann and Karen McCormick, "Firm Attributes and the Propensity to Influence the Political System," in Siegfried, *Economics of Firm Size.*

12. George J. Stigler, "The Theory of Economic Regulation,"*Bell Journal of Economics and Management Science* 2 (Spring 1981):3–21; John J. Siegfried, "The Relationship between Economic Structure and the Effect of Political Influence: Empirical Evidence from the Federal Corporation Income Tax Program" (Ph.D. dissertation, University of Wisconsin, 1972); Charles P. McPherson, "Tariff Structures and Political Exchange" (Ph.D. dissertation, University of Chicago, 1972); Lester M. Salamon and John J. Siegfried, "Economic Power and Political Influence: The Impact of Industry Structure on Public Policy," *American Political Science Review* 71 (September 1977):1026–1043; Cathleen Coolidge and Gorden Tullock, "Firm Size and Political Power," in Siegfried, *Economics of Firm Size;* Jonathan J. Pincus, *Pressure Groups and Politics in Antebellum Tariffs* (New York: Columbia University Press, 1977); Richard E. Caves, "Economic Models of Political Choice: Canada's Tariff Structure," *Canadian Journal of Economics* 9 (May 1976):278–300; and Marx, "Political Consequences."

13. The capital-skill complementarity hypothesis states that the elasticity of substitution of capital for unskilled labor is greater than the elasticity of substitution of capital for skilled labor. See Z. Griliches, "Capital-Skill Complementarity," *Review of Economics and Statistics* (1969), pp. 465–468; and Robert D. Brogan and Edward W. Erickson, "Capital-

Skill Complementarity and Labor Earnings," *Southern Economic Journal* 42 (July 1975):83–88.

14. See, for example, Lucia F. Dunn, "The Effects of Firm and Plant Size on Employee Well-Being," in Siegfried, *Economics and Firm Size;* Leonard W. Weiss, "Concentration and Labor Earnings," *American Economic Review* 56 (March 1966):96–117.

15. See Frank P. Stafford, "Firm Size, Workplace Public Goods, and Worker Welfare," in Siegfried, *Economics of Firm Size,* for a discussion of the workplace costs and benefits of large firm size.

16. Dunn, "Effects of Firm and Plant Size." The results of plant studies are mixed, but most suggest a negative association between plant size and satisfaction. See L. Porter and E. Lawler, "Properties of Organizational Structure in Relation to Job Attitudes and Job Behavior," *Psychological Bulletin* (1965), pp. 23–51; F.M. Scherer, "Industrial Structure, Scale Economies, and Worker Alienation," in *Essays on Industrial Organization in Honor of Joe S. Bain,* edited by R. Masson and D. Qualls (Cambridge, Mass.: Ballinger, 1976); and John E. Kwoka, Jr., "Established Size, Wages, and Job Satisfaction: The Trade-offs," in Siegfried, *Economics of Firm Size.*

17. See Brogan and Erickson, "Capital-Skill Complementarity," for use of this argument to explain the relationship between industrial concentration and wages.

18. Harold M. Levinson, "Unionism, Concentration, and Wage Changes: Toward a Unified Theory," *Industrial and Labor Relations Review,* January 1967, pp. 198–205; and Martin Segal, "The Relation between Union Wage Impact and Market Structure," *Quarterly Journal of Economics,* February 1964, pp. 96–114.

19. J.C. Ullman, "Interfirm Differences in the Cost of Search for Clerical Workers," *Journal of Business* 41 (1968):153–165.

20. G.S. Becker, *Human Capital,* 2d ed. (New York: Columbia University Press, 1975); Stephen A. Ross and Michael Wachter, "Wage Determination, Inflation, and the Industrial Structure," *American Economic Review* 63 (September 1973):675–692; and Wachter, "Cyclical Variation in the Interindustry Wage Structure," *American Economic Review* 60 (March 1970):75–84.

21. Albert Rees and George P. Schultz, *Workers and Wages in an Urban Labor Market* (Chicago: University of Chicago Press, 1970), p. 219.

22. Armen A. Alchain and Reuben A. Kessel, "Competition, Monopoly, and Pursuit of Pecuniary Gain," in *Aspects of Labor Economics* (Princeton: National Bureau of Economic Research, 1962).

23. See the empirical results of James A. Dalton and E.J. Ford, Jr., "Concentration and Labor Earnings in Manufacturing and Utilities," *Industrial and Labor Relations Review* 31 (October 1977):45–60; and Dal-

ton and Ford, "Concentration and Professional Earnings in Manufacturing," *Industrial and Labor Relations Review* 31 (April 1978):379–384 for possible support for this view. See also Weiss, "Concentration and Labor Earnings," for a contrary view.

24. See Robert Smiley, "Firm Size, Market Power, and the Distribution of Income and Wealth: A Survey"; and F.M. Scherer, "Commentary," in Siegfried, *Economics of Firm Size,* for a discussion of the literature linking the distribution of rewards to allocative efficiency.

25. This may not always be the case. See F.M. Scherer, *Industrial Market Structure and Economic Performance,* 2d ed. (Chicago: Rand McNally, 1980), pp. 127–138, for a discussion of firm motives for merging. However, even if mergers are not undertaken to increase profits, profits may be increased by the merger.

26. See ibid., pp. 138–141; and George Benston, "Conglomerate Mergers: Causes, Consequences and Remedies," in U.S., Congress, Senate, Hearings before the Subcommittee on Antitrust, Monopoly, and Business Rights of the Committee on the Judiciary, 96th Cong., 1st Sess. on S.600, The Small and Independent Business Protection Act of 1979, Part 2 (Washington, D.C.: U.S. Government Printing Office, 1979), pp. 215–228, for a discussion of the financial consequences of mergers.

27. The New York Stock Exchange, *Fact Sheet: 1975 Shareowner Census at a Glance,* News Release, 9 December 1975.

28. Ralph Lankford and John F. Stewart, "A General Equilibrium Analysis of Monopoly Power and the Distribution of Income," in Siegfried, *Economics of Firm Size.*

29. The following discussion relies heavily on Katherine E. Maddox and John J. Siegfried, "The Effect of Economic Structure on Corporate Philanthropy," in Siegfried, *Economics of Firm Size.*

30. For a review of the literature on the income elasticity of charitable giving, see Katherine E. Maddox, "Review of the Literature on Corporate Philanthropy" (unpublished manuscript, Vanderbilt University, August 1980). See also Ralph L. Nelson, *Economic Factors in the Growth of Corporation Giving,* Occasional Paper 111, (New York: National Bureau of Economic Research, 1970); Ralph A. Schwartz, "Private Philanthropic Contributions: An Economic Analysis," (Ph.D. dissertation, Columbia University, 1966); and Paul J. Whitehead, "Some Economic Aspects of Corporate Giving" (Ph.D. dissertation, Virginia Polytechnic Institute and State University, 1976).

31. Nelson, *Economic Factors,* p. 61; and Whitehead, "Some Economic Experts."

32. Maddox and Siegfried, "Effect of Economic Structure."

33. Marion R. Fremont-Smith, *Philanthropy and the Business Corporation* (New York: Russell Sage Foundation, 1972), pp. 42–44.

34. Katherine E. Maddox and John J. Siegfried, "The Effect of Market Structure on Corporate Philanthropy: Interim Report on Interview Results" (unpublished manuscript, Vanderbilt University, October 1980).

35. Fremont-Smith, *Philanthropy and the Business Corporation,* pp. 42–44.

36. Katherine E. Maddox; John J. Siegfried; and George H. Sweeney, "The Incidence of Price Changes in the U.S. Economy" (unpublished manuscript, Vanderbilt University, October 1980).

37. See, for example, the testimonies of Douglas Johnson and Martin Yenawine in U.S. Small Business Administration, Office of Advocacy, "Public Hearings on Proposed Take-Over of Carrier Corporation by United Technologies Corporation," Syracuse, N.Y., 2 November 1979, pp. 31–36 and 165–168.

38. Much of the following discussion is based upon Richard E. Caves and Michael E. Porter, "Barriers to Exit," in Masson and Qualls, *Essays on Industrial Organization,* pp. 39–70.

39. Opinions on the reason for the closure differ. See Benston, "Conglomerate Mergers," pp. 241–242. For a different view, see F.M. Scherer, "Prepared Statement of F.M. Scherer," p. 138 in the same volume.

40. David L. Barkley and Arnold Paulsen, *Patterns in the Openings and Closings of Manufacturing Plants in Rural Areas of Iowa* (Ames: Iowa State University, North Central Regional Center for Rural Development, May 1979).

41. For a review of the literature on the financial aspects of mergers, see Scherer, *Industrial Market Structure,* pp. 138–141; and Benston, "Conglomerate Mergers."

42. Barkley and Paulsen, *Patterns in Openings and Closings.*

43. See Richard A. Posner, "Prepared Statement of Richard A. Posner," in U.S. Congress, Senate, Hearings before the Subcommittee on Monopoly and Business Rights of the Committee on the Judiciary, 96th Cong., 1st Sess. on S.600, The Small and Independent Business Protection Act of 1979, Part 2, (Washington, D.C.: U.S. Government Printing Office, 1979), p. 11; and Richard B. McKenzie, *Restrictions on Business Mobility* (Washington, D.C.: American Enterprise Institute, 1979).

44. Roger W. Schmenner, "How Corporations Select Communities for New Manufacturing Plants," in Siegfried, *Economics of Firm Size.*

45. See testimony of Martin Yenawine, in "Public Hearings"; and Bureau of National Affairs, "Conglomerate Mergers: A Study of Competition, Power, and Philosophy" (Washington, D.C.: Bureau of National Affairs, 1980).

46. Maddox and Siegfried, "Effect of Market Structure."

6 Mergers and Aggregate Concentration

Lawrence J. White

The Celler-Kefauver Amendments to Section 7 of the Clayton Act in 1950 effectively put an end to mergers that might have serious economic consequences for competitive markets. The Justice Department Antitrust Division and the Federal Trade Commission have had an enviable legal record in challenging mergers that might have competitive consequences (and, of course, in discouraging a much larger number of mergers that are never even proposed). As Justice Potter Stewart complained in a dissent to a Supreme Court majority decision forbidding yet another merger, "The sole consistency that I can find is that in litigation under Section 7, the government always wins."[1]

The mergers that remain untouched by the act are conglomerate mergers—those with no direct competitive consequences. Though some critics of conglomerate mergers still try to find competitive consequences,[2] the stories that can be told are weak, and the evidence that can be marshalled to support those stories is weaker still.[3]

A quite different critique of conglomerate mergers focuses on a social-political concern with bigness—namely, mergers among large firms will increase those firms' absolute and relative size. The prospect of a small group of very large companies' dominating the U.S. economic landscape and wielding substantial social and political power because of their relative size is not a pleasant one for many, if not most, Americans. The Jeffersonian tradition favoring small over large is still a strong one in the U.S. polity. The U.S. economy went through a major merger wave in the late 1960s and again in the late 1970s. Each time, a genuine political concern arose about apparent trends toward bigness that were allegedly being exacerbated by the merger waves.[4]

Efforts to measure the relative importance of large firms have usually used data on aggregate concentration—the percentage of some national aggregate economic measure (for example, assets, employment, sales) that is concentrated in the hands of the largest corporations (for example, the largest 100, 200, and so on). Unfortunately, these aggregate concentration

The research for this chapter was supported in part by a grant to New York University by the Sloan Foundation.

calculations have usually been done badly in the past. Misleading or incomplete information has been marshalled, and an excessive emphasis has been placed on the manufacturing sector.[5]

This chapter provides the proper measures of aggregate concentration. Along the way, we put the merger wave of the late 1970s in proper perspective and discuss the pitfalls and problems of the proper measurement of aggregate concentration. The results of this chapter indicate that, despite the merger waves, aggregate concentration has not been increasing in the United States. These results, of course, indicate nothing about the absolute problem—that is, whether the relative size of large firms is already too great. The results simply say that, whatever the nature of the absolute problem, it does not seem to be getting any worse and may even be getting slightly better. Since there seem to be widespread perceptions that the contrary is the case, we believe these results are important.

In the second, we briefly review the evidence on mergers. In the third section, we discuss the difficulties of computing aggregate-concentration measures. The fourth section contains the measures of aggregate concentration we have computed, and the last section provides a brief conclusion.

Merger Statistics

The available merger data are summarized in table 6–1. The first column is drawn from FTC data representing most mergers and acquisitions in the U.S. economy.[6] The column provides only the number of mergers. Using a more inclusive set of criteria, W.T. Grimm has compiled a second merger series, shown in the second column. Using a more stringent set of criteria, the journal *Mergers and Acquisitions* has also compiled a merger series, shown in the third column; again, only the number of mergers is provided. The last two columns refer to relatively large mergers in the mining and manufacturing sectors compiled by the FTC; both the number of mergers and the assets of the acquired firms are provided.

All of these series clearly indicate that the U.S. economy went through a merger wave in the late 1960s and again in the late 1970s. Apparently, however, the wave of the 1970s was smaller than that of the 1960s. This is certainly true for the absolute numbers of mergers and, at least through 1978, true for the absolute value of assets involved in large mergers in mining and manufacturing. In relative terms, the wave of the late 1970s was even smaller. In 1965, shortly before the first merger wave, the U.S. Internal Revenue Service (IRS) reported tax returns from 11.4 million firms; a decade later, in 1975, the number of firms was up to 14 million.[7] In the earlier year, the IRS listed assets in mining and manufacturing corporations at $388.1 billion, and a decade later, assets in mining and manufacturing corporations were \$1,009.1 billion.[8] Thus, in relative value terms, the later merger wave was less than half as important as the earlier wave.

These data are obviously sketchy and deficient. An obvious lack is the absence of the value of assets for the overall merger series. Also, the overall FTC series does not cover mergers in which the acquired firm is outside the FTC's regulatory jurisdiction, such as banks, airlines, and railroads. And it would be useful to have a series on the numbers of spin-offs and divestitures and the assets involved, but to this author's knowledge, no such series exists.

We return to these merger data in our discussion of aggregate concentration in the manufacturing sector. We first turn, however, to a discussion of the problems of measuring aggregate concentration.

Table 6-1
Mergers and Acquisitions

Year	FTC: Number of Completed Mergers and Acquisitions	W.T. Grimm Number of Mergers	Mergers & Acquisitions (Journal): Number of Mergers	FTC: Mergers in Manufacturing and Mining Involving Firms with Assets of \$10 Million or More	
				Number	Assets of Acquired Firm
1960	1,345	—	—	51	\$1.5 billion
1961	1,724	—	—	46	2
1962	1,667	—	—	65	2.3
1963	1,479	—	—	54	2.5
1964	1,797	—	—	73	2.3
1965	1,893	2,125	—	64	3.3
1966	1,746	2,377	—	76	3.3
1967	2,384	2,975	1,354	138	8.3
1968	3,932	4,462	1,829	174	12.6
1969	4,542	6,107	1,712	138	11
1970	3,089	5,152	1,318	91	5.9
1971	2,633	4,608	1,237	59	2.5
1972	2,839	4,801	1,263	60	1.9
1973	2,359	4,040	1,064	64	3.1
1974	1,474	2,861	825	62	4.5
1975	1,047	2,297	859	59	5
1976	1,171	2,276	1,058	81	6.3
1977	1,183	2,244	1,139	100	9
1978	1,245	2,106	1,346	110	10.7
1979	—	—	1,420	—	—

Source: U.S. Federal Trade Commission, *Statistical Report on Mergers and Acquisitions,* various years; *Mergers and Acquisitions,* various issues; and Joseph M. Sheer, "Divestitures and Spin-offs," Master's thesis, New York University, 1978.

Problems of Measuring Aggregate Concentration

A number of measurement bases exist that might be used for aggregate concentration calculations—for example, sales, assets, profits, employees, and value added. Unfortunately, theory provides little guidance for choice among these measures. Unlike the problem of measuring concentration ratios in individual markets—in which case oligopoly theory clearly points toward using sales as the measurement base—no strong theory surrounds the social-political consequences of size that could guide our choice.

Each of the measurement bases has its advantages and disadvantages for use in calculating economywide aggregate concentration ratios. We shall discuss each measure in turn. (Implicitly, we shall be using value added as our standard of comparison.)

Sales

Sales-revenue data are readily available from the profit-and-loss statements of virtually every large company in the economy. Aggregate sales data are available for most sectors of the economy from Department of Commerce data sources and, in the case of regulated industries, from the relevant regulatory agencies. The IRS publishes (albeit, with a four- or five-year delay) aggregate sales data derived from income-tax returns.

However, sales data have some very serious drawbacks. First, they probably overstate the relative importance of firms that buy raw materials, apply only a small amount of processing to them, and then resell them (for example, finishers, wholesalers, retailers)—that is, they overstate the relative importance of firms for which the value-added-to-sales ratio is relatively low. Second, sales measures involve obvious problems of double counting; the aggregate of sales by all companies in the economy far exceeds GNP. Third, sales-revenue measures used in the financial sector are much closer to the value-added measures and not readily comparable to the sales revenue of other industries. For example, a stock brokerage firm reports as sales revenues the commissions earned on transactions but not the gross value of the flows of transactions; a normal retailer (for example, a supermarket) reports as sales revenues the gross value of sales flows and not just his commission (markup). Finally, many large firms have overseas operations and report their sales on a consolidated basis. Sometimes U.S.-based operations are reported separately; sometimes not. An aggregate concentration ratio that included large firms' overseas operations in the numerator but only domestic aggregates in the denominator would overstate the relative importance of large firms at any point in time. Also, more seriously, comparisons over time may be biased if the overseas operations of large firms are expanding at a different rate than their domestic operations. (Even if foreign operations could be properly included in an aggregate-concentration ratio—say, by including foreign operations in both the numerator and the denominator of the ratio—there is a serious question as to whether the overseas operations should or should not be included in a measure that is attempting to capture *domestic* social-political consequences; again, the absence of theory is a handicap here).

Assets

Like sales, assets are readily available from the balance sheets of virtually all companies. Aggregate asset data are available for regulated sectors of the economy from the relevant regulatory agencies and for the entire corporate sector from IRS income-tax data.

Again, however, there are serious drawbacks. First, because large firms tend to be more capital intensive than small firms, an assets measure probably overstates the true relative importance of large firms. Second, inclusion of the financial sector introduces serious double counting. Many of the assets of the financial sector represent the liabilities of other sectors, which in turn have bought assets with the cash generated from issuing the liabilities. Thus, aggregate concentration measures based on assets must deal with the nonfinancial and financial sectors separately; an economywide measure would not be appropriate or meaningful. Finally, like sales, most companies report assets on a consolidated worldwide bases, and the same biases that plague sales measures would also affect assets measures.

Profits

Again, profits data are available for virtually all large firms. The national income accounts provide aggregate data on corporate profits. However, since large firms tend to be relatively capital intensive and the absolute size of profits tends to be related (roughly) to the level of assets, a profits measure will also overstate the relative importance of large firms (the double-counting problem disappears, however). The worldwide versus domestic problem also remains.

Employment

Most companies' annual reports list their employees, and the Bureau of Labor Statistics provides aggregate private-sector-employment data. The reverse aspect of the capital intensity of large firms is that small firms tend to be relatively labor intensive; hence, an employee measure will probably understate the true relative importance of large business. Again, because companies may report employees only on a worldwide basis, the worldwide versus domestic problems are present.

Value Added

Economists usually prefer the use of value added for measuring the economic activity or contribution of firms. Value added would also appear to be the proper measure for aggregate concentration calculations. The social-political consequences of size are probably best represented by the contributions that a firm makes to economic activity. Further, value added avoids the double counting and biases of other measures, and it can be applied to all sectors.

The major drawback is a practical one: Value-added concentration measures are regularly collected only for the manufacturing sector. It is very difficult or impossible to calculate value added from most profit-and-loss statements (and overseas elements would also enter into most attempts). Thus, given the current state of data collection, value-added measures must be restricted to the manufacturing sector.

In the end, any presentation of aggregate concentration ratios must be a compromise between suitability and availability. As we see in the next section, the data presented in this chapter are no exception.

Data on Aggregate Concentration

Broad Sectors

Let us begin with manufacturing, but we do not stop there as do many other investigators. It is important to realize that manufacturing has been falling in relative importance and now accounts for less than 25 percent of the U.S. GNP. Table 6-2 provides data on the current relative importance of the broad sectors in the U.S. economy.

Table 6-3 provides a number of measures of aggregate concentration in the manufacturing sector. The first part of the table is drawn from the U.S. Bureau of the Census' *Census of Manufactures* (supplemented by the *Annual Survey of Manufactures*). This is the cleanest data that can be found in the entire area of aggregate concentration calculations; it is value-added data, and both numerators and denominators of the ratios refer only to domestic operations.

Table 6–2
GNP and Employment Originating in Various Sectors of the U.S. Economy, 1978
(percentage)

Sector	GNP	GNP (excluding government)	Employment	Employment (excluding government)
Agriculture, forestry, fisheries	3.0	3.5	3.5	4.2
Mining	2.6	3.0	0.9	1.0
Construction	4.7	5.3	4.4	5.2
Manufacturing	24.2	27.6	21.2	25.2
Transportation	3.7	4.2	3.0	3.5
Communication	2.6	3.0	1.3	1.5
Electric, gas, sanitary services	2.5	2.8	0.8	1.0
Wholesale trade	17.2	19.6	5.1	6.1
Retail trade			15.1	18.0
Finance, insurance, real estate	13.8	15.7	4.9	5.8
Service	12.5	14.2	11.7	19.9
Government and government enterprises	12.1	—	16.1	—
Rest of world	1.0	1.1	—	—
Self-employed and family workers, nonagricultural	—	—	7.1	8.4

Source: U.S. Department of Commerce, Bureau of the Census, *Statistical Abstract of the United States, 1979* (Washington, D.C.), pp. 403, 410–412, 439.

As can be seen, the share of the value added in manufacturing accounted for by the largest firms has risen in the past thirty years. However, virtually all of this increase took place by 1963, before the merger wave of the late 1960s. These increases were not primarily due to mergers but rather to rapid internal growth by large firms that happened to be in rapidly growing industries in the postwar period—for example, motor vehicles, rubber, petroleum, aircraft construction, defense, chemical, and electrical equipment. Despite the merger wave of the late 1960s, virtually no increase occurred in aggregate concentration in manufacturing. It seems unlikely that the aggregate concentration data in manufacturing for the late 1970s, when they are compiled, will show any increase despite this latest merger wave.

If one had seen only these census data (the census employment data support the census value-added data), one might wonder why so much concern arose about mergers and aggregate concentration. The remaining data in table 6–3 indicate why. They appear to show a rise in aggregate concentration in the 1960s. But the data are seriously flawed because they include overseas operations. In the FTC data, overseas operations were included in

Table 6-3
Aggregate Concentration Ratios in the Manufacturing Sector
(percentage)

	1947	1950	1954	1955	1958	1960	1963	1965	1967	1968	1969	1970	1971	1972	1973	1974	1975	1976	1977	1978
							Census of Manufactures Data[a]													
Share of value added																				
Largest 50	17	—	23	—	23	—	25	—	25	—	—	—	—	25	—	—	—	24	24	—
Largest 100	23	—	30	—	30	—	33	—	33	—	—	—	—	33	—	—	—	34	33	—
Largest 200	30	—	37	—	38	—	41	—	42	—	—	—	—	43	—	—	—	44	44	—
Share of employment																				
Largest 50	—	—	—	—	—	—	19	—	20	—	—	—	—	17	—	—	—	18	—	—
Largest 100	—	—	—	—	—	—	25	—	26	—	—	—	—	23	—	—	—	24	—	—
Largest 200	—	—	—	—	—	—	32	—	34	—	—	—	—	31	—	—	—	32	—	—
							Federal Trade Commission[b]													
Share of assets																				
Largest 100	—	37.7	—	44.3	—	46.4	—	46.5	48.2	49.1	48.2	48.5	48.9	47.6	44.7[d]	44.4[d]	45.0[d]	45.4[d]	45.9[d]	45.5[d]
Largest 200	—	42.7	—	53.1	—	56.3	—	56.7	59.4	60.8	60.1	60.4	61.0	60.0	56.9[d]	56.7[d]	57.5[d]	58.0[d]	58.5[d]	58.3[d]

W.N. Leonard's Data[c]

Largest 200 firms											
Share of sales	—	—	47.7	—	—	50.5	—	—	—	—	62.5	—
Share of assets	—	—	53.0	—	—	57.0	—	—	—	—	66.8	—
Share of net income after taxes	—	—	63.6	—	—	60.4	—	—	—	—	62.1	—
Share of employment	—	—	39.5	—	—	48.4	—	—	—	—	60.7	—

[a]U.S. Bureau of the Census, *Census of Manufactures* and *Annual Survey of Manufactures* (Washington, D.C., various years).

[b]U.S. Department of Commerce, *Statistical Abstract* (Washington, D.C., various years).

[c]W.N. Leonard, "Mergers, Industrial Concentration, and Antitrust Policy," *Journal of Economic Issues* 10 (June 1976):354–382.

[d]Data before 1973 include worldwide operations; data for 1973 and after include only domestic operations.

both the numerator and denominators of the ratios prior to 1973. Though this was better than just including them in the numerator, the FTC measure still overstates the relative domestic importance of large firms because only large firms tend to establish overseas operations. Leonard's data are even more flawed because he included overseas operations only in the numerators of the ratios. Also, because it was larger firms that tended to expand their operations overseas in the 1950s and 1960s, both sets of data seriously overstate the trend in aggregate concentration in domestic manufacturing during these decades.

Once we move away from manufacturing, we must unfortunately abandon value added. Table 6-4 provides a variety of aggregate concentration measures for five other sectors of the economy. Becuase the sectors are fairly well defined, some of the criticisms of these measurement bases, when used for the entire economy, apply with less force to these individual sectors. Also, the data apply only to domestic operations, except for transportation, which includes the international operations of airlines and steamship companies.

As can be seen, the spotty data for the 1960s show a mixed pattern. In banking and life insurance, the relative importance of large firms declined; in utilities, retail trade, and transportation, the opposite was true. In the 1970s, however, in virtually all sectors for all measures, the share of activity accounted for by the largest firms was either constant or falling. The only exception to this pattern was in the category of transportation sales revenues; in this last case, internal growth by airlines and railroad mergers has meant a relative increase in sales by the largest firms.

Entire Private Sector

We now turn to economywide measures. These have been compiled from the *Fortune* lists of the 1,000 largest manufacturing firms and the 50 largest banks, insurance companies, diversified financial companies, retailing companies, transportation companies, and public utilities, respectively. The lists for all 1,300 largest firms only extend back to 1972, so our measures cover only the 1970s.[9]

Value-added measures are not available, so we have chosen the two major components of value added—employment and profits—which are provided by the *Fortune* lists. Bureau of Labor Statistics data are used for aggregate nonagricultural private-sector employment; Department of Commerce data are used for aggregate corporate profits.

Our estimates of aggregate concentration ratios for the entire private sector are provided in table 6-5. Employment concentration appears to have declined substantially during the 1970s, regardless of whether one looks at the largest 100, 200, or 1,300 companies. If we had used total employment (for the public and private sectors combined) as the base, the decline in the concentration ratios would have been even greater, since public-sector employment has been expanding more rapidly than private-sector employment. Profit concentration has also declined for the largest 100, 200, and 1300 companies.

These data have one problem: the numerators of the ratios include consolidated worldwide operations for the individual companies. Accordingly, the reported ratios definitely overstate the true domestic ratios. The more important question, though, for comparisons over time is whether the overseas operations of the large companies expanded at a different rate than their domestic operations. Between 1972 and 1977, the value of U.S. direct investment abroad increased by 65.5 percent;[10] mostly large firms operate abroad. During the same period, the value of the assets of the 1,150 largest nonfinancial companies on the *Fortune* lists increased by a somewhat smaller amount, 60.6 prcent. This latter increase is a weighted average of domestic and foreign operations. Accordingly, the purely domestic increase was probably smaller than this last figure. If these relative rates of increases in assets are indicative of the rates of increases of the general operations of large companies at home and abroad in the 1970s, then the trends in the data in table 6-5 have an upward bias as compared to the true (but unobservable) domestic ratios. Thus, our finding of a downward trend in aggregate concentration is a yet stronger and more remarkable result.

Aggregate concentration in the 1970s, then, clearly has not increased and has very likely decreased. The merger wave of the late 1970s, even through 1979, has not meant any worsening of the problem of aggregate concentration.   •

These data are consistent with another comprehensive series compiled by the FTC's Bureau of Economics. That series computes aggregate concentration ratios using the domestic assets of all nonfinancial corporations. As can be seen in table 6-6, those data indicate a modest decrease in aggregate concentration between 1958 and 1975. Our data in table 6-5 indicate that this trend probably continued through to the end of the 1970s.

Conclusions

Has aggregate concentration in the U.S. economy increased in the 1960s and the 1970s? The answer, very clearly, is no. Opponents to large conglomerate mergers will have to find some other grounds for their opposi-

Table 6–4
Aggregate Concentration Ratios in Nonmanufacturing Sectors
(*percentage*)

	1955	1960	1965	1966	1967	1968	1969	1970	1971	1972	1973	1974	1975	1976	1977	1978	1979
Banking: Largest 50[a]																	
Share of assets	—	39.1	39.4	—	—	—	—	34.3	—	—	—	37.3	35.7	35.3	35.5	35.2	—
Share of deposits	—	38.5	38.4	—	—	—	—	32.2	—	—	—	35.4	33.5	32.0	31.9	31.8	—
Life Insurance: Largest 50[b]																	
Share of assets	—	87.7	85.5	84.8	84.4	83.9	83.4	82.9	82.4	81.9	81.1	80.7	79.9	79.1	78.2	77.8	—
Share of insurance in force	—	83.1	77.4	72.2	75.5	74.7	74.3	73.5	72.8	72.2	71.7	70.8	70.9	71.0	71.0	70.4	69.7
Electric and Gas Utilities: Largest 40[c]																	
Share of assets	—	—	—	57.4	58.1	58.7	59.4	60.3	—	61.2	—	—	60.4	60.1	59.8	59.9	—
Share of net income after taxes	—	—	—	53.8	54.0	54.6	53.9	54.6	—	54.7	—	—	52.9	52.2	53.4	52.4	—

Retail Trade: Largest 50[d]

Share of sales revenues	13.9	16.3	17.2	—	18.8	—	—	19.8	19.6	20.0	20.0	20.9	21.0	20.6	20.5	20.2	19.8
Share of employment	—	—	17.1	—	18.4	—	—	21.4	20.9	21.0	21.8	21.6	21.0	20.8	20.1	19.7	20.0

Transportation: Largest 50[e]

Share of sales revenues	—	53.2	55.5	—	59.7	—	—	58.1	57.1	56.7	58.4	60.2	66.0	61.6	62.3	—	—
Share of employment	—	—	—	—	35.0	—	—	35.3	—	33.3	33.6	33.1	37.2	35.9	35.0	35.1	33.7

[a]U.S. Federal Deposit Insurance Corp., *Assets and Liabilities: Commercial and Mutual Savings Banks* and *Annual Report*, various years.

[b]American Council of Life Insurance, *Life Insurance Fact Book*, various years; *Fortune; Statistical Abstracts*, various years.

[c]*Statistical Abstract*, various years; American Gas Association, *Historical Statistics of the Gas Utility Industry, 1966–1975* (Arlington, Va.), 1977.

[d]*Fortune; Statistical Abstract*, various years.

[e]*Fortune; Statistical Abstract*, various years.

Table 6-5
Aggregate Concentration Ratios in the Entire Private Sector
(percentage)

	1972	1973	1974	1975	1976	1977	1978	1979
Share of Nonagricultural Private-sector employment								
Largest 100	18.2	—	—	—	—	17.3	—	16.7
Largest 200	23.9	—	—	—	—	22.7	—	22.6
Largest 1,300ᵃ	37.3	37.4	37.0	36.5	36.1	35.5	34.7	34.2
Share of corporate net income after taxes								
Largest 100	43.3	—	—	—	—	39.8	—	39.4
Largest 200	55.4	—	—	—	—	50.2	—	49.9
Largest 1,300ᵃ	76.6	75.1	72.6	71.4	73.8	71.4	70.4	71.1

Sources: *Fortune,* various years; U.S. Department of Commerce, *Survey of Current Business,* various years; U.S. Department of Labor, *Employment and Earnings,* various years.
ᵃSee note 9.

Table 6-6
Aggregate Concentration Ratios for Assets of Largest 200 Nonfinancial Corporations
(percentage)

	1958	1963	1967	1972	1975
Largest 50	24.4	24.4	24.5	23.4	23.3
Largest 100	32.1	31.7	32.0	30.7	30.6
Largest 150	37.4	36.7	37.0	35.9	35.6
Largest 200	41.1	40.5	41.2	39.9	39.5

Source: U.S. Federal Trade Commission data, cited by D. Schwartzman, "Prepared Statement," in U.S., Senate, Subcommittee on Antitrust, Monopoly, and Business Rights, *Mergers and Economic Concentration: Hearings on S.600,* 96th Cong. 1st Sess. (26 April 1979), p. 600.

tion. The available data, when properly compiled, will simply not support any assertions that aggregate concentration is increasing; if anything, the trends appear to be in the opposite direction.

Notes

1. *United States* v. *Von's Grocery Company,* 384 U.S. 270 (1966).
2. See Federal Trade Commission, *Economic Report on Corporate Mergers* (Washington, D.C., 1969).

3. For a critique, see G.J. Benston, *Conglomerate Mergers: Causes, Consequences, and Remedies* (Washington, D.C.: American Enterprise Institute, 1980).

4. See FTC, *Economic Report;* U.S., Congress, Senate, Subcommittee on Antitrust, Monopoly, and Business Rights, *Mergers and Economic Concentration: Hearings on S.600,* 96th Cong., 1st Sess. (1979); and J.H. Shenefield, *Report of the Attorney General Pursuant to Section 10(c) of the Small Business Act, as Amended: Conglomerate Mergers, Small Business, and the Scope of Existing Anti-Merger Statutes* (Washington, D.C.: U.S. Department of Justice, 20 June 1979).

5. For a further critique, see Benston, *Conglomerate Mergers,* chapter 3; and L.J. White, "What Has Been Happening to Aggregate Concentration in the United States?" *Journal of Industrial Economics,* March 1981.

6. For further details on coverage, see Federal Trade Commission, *Statistical Report on Mergers and Acquisitions* (Washington, D.C., November 1978).

7. U.S. Internal Revenue Service, *Statistics of Income,* (Washington, D.C., various years).

8. Ibid.

9. The ratios computed for the full 1,300 firms use as their numerators simply the relevant sum of the 1,300 firms in the *Fortune* lists. Thus, technically, these are not the 1,300 largest firms since a few firms below the cut-off points on some of the lists are larger than a few firms on other lists. Thus, the ratios for the 1,300 are slight understatements of the true ratios for the largest 1,300, but it is unlikely that this would bias the trends. Also, the figures in table 6-5 are different from those found in White, "What Has Been Happening" because of revisions in the national income accounts data for corporate profits.

10. See U.S., Department of Commerce, Bureau of the Census, *Statistical Abstract of the United States, 1979* (Washington, D.C.: U.S. Government Printing Office, 1979), p. 850, and comparable tables in earlier editions.

7

Chiarella and Rule 14e-3: Theory and Practice

W. Scott Cooper,
John J. Huber, and
Benjamin M. Vandegrift

For nearly four decades, the federal courts have used the open-ended language of Section 10(b) of the Securities Exchange Act of 1934 (the Exchange Act) and the rules thereunder to construct a framework in which to regulate broadly varied conduct relating to securities transactions.[1] The Securities and Exchange Commission's Rule 10b-5,[2] the language of which is even more open ended than the statute under which it is promulgated, has served as the cornerstone of a sophisticated federalized corporate law.[3] Two other developments have lent support to the construction of this framework. First, the creation of the principle by the judiciary, in *Kardon v. National Gypsum Co.,* that Rule 10b-5 gave rise to a private right of action ensured frequent litigation regarding the scope of the rule.[4] Second, the amendment, in 1966, of Rule 23 of the Federal Rules of Civil Procedure made it worthwhile for an entrepreneurial attorney to litigate the language of Rule 10b-5 on behalf of a large number of injured plaintiffs.[5]

As section 10(b) and Rule 10b-5 were held, during the late 1960s and early 1970s, to reach more and different transactions, commentators struggled to gain some sense of the scheme of regulation that the federal courts were imposing on the U.S. corporate system. Although certain commentators urged the courts to look to common-law policies,[6] the fact that few cases were litigated to judgment enabled the courts to avoid imposing vast, almost unlimited, damage verdicts and to deal instead with the more theoretical issues of materiality, scienter (foreknowledge), and standing

It was not surprising that the courts would have so much difficulty in finding the limits of Rule 10b-5. So many situations seemed to fit easily within the rule's penumbra. If an insider or an outsider told another that a particular company would earn $2 per share when that person knew the company would earn $1 per share, that conduct—that is, a misrepresenta-

The authors gratefully acknowledge the contribution of Donald C. Langevoort in the preparation of this chapter. As a matter of policy, the Securities and Exchange Commission disclaims responsibility for any private publication of any of its employees. The views expressed herein are those of the authors and do not necessarily represent the views of the commission or its staff.

tion—violated clause (b) of Rule 10b–5. And, if an insider with knowledge of a nonpublic, material fact about the issuer traded, that conduct violated Rule 10b–5 even though the insider traded into an anonymous market and had no idea with whom he transacted. However, insider trading was not specifically covered by Rule 10b–5 because the rule does not refer to silence. The decision in *Texas Gulf Sulphur* indicated under what circumstances a person would violate Rule 10b–5 by trading in the absence of any misrepresentations or omissions to state facts necessary to make statements that have been made not misleading. The Second Circuit held that "anyone in possession of material inside information must either disclose it to the investing public, or, if he is disabled from disclosing in order to protect a corporate confidence, or he chooses not to do so, must abstain from trading or recommending the securities concerned while such information remains undisclosed."[7] Since *Texas Gulf Sulphur,* the courts have been faced with questions as to the limits of the *Texas Gulf Sulphur* disclose-or-abstain-from-trading rule.

One especially troublesome problem involved purchases based on non-public knowledge of, or about, a cash tender offer. Both prospective offerors and persons who, through some association with a prospective offeror, learned of its plans often purchased subject-company securities prior to the public announcement of the tender offer. Early commentators suggested that such conduct might violate Rule 10b–5.[8]

To some extent, at least with respect to purchases by the prospective offeror, the passage of the Williams Act in 1968 mooted this question.[9] That act added, among others, Subsections 13(d), 14(d), and 14(e) to the Exchange Act. Section 13(d) requires any person who, as a result of an acquisition, becomes the beneficial owner of more than 5 percent[10] of a class of registered[11] equity securities to file with the Commission and to send to the issuer and exchanges where the security is traded a statement disclosing certain information about the purchaser and the acquisition within ten days of the acquisition. Section 14(d)(1) requires any person who makes a tender offer that, upon consummation, would result in the beneficial ownership of more than 5 percent[12] of the shares of a class of registered equity securities to file with the Commission and make certain disclosure on the date the offer is first published or sent or given to security holders and thereafter. By requiring disclosure of equity acquisition at a relatively low percentage, Sections 13(d) and 14(d) appeared to put congressional imprimatur on purchases below that level.[13]

Though the Williams Act appeared to solve one problem, however, it created others. Partly as a result of the passage of the Williams Act, the number of tender offers increased.[14] As it did, so did the instance of trading on the information that a tender offer was about to occur.[15]

It was not until the Supreme Court's decision in *United States* v.

Chiarella that the application of Section 10(b) to purchases unaccompanied by disclosure of information concerning a potential tender offer became clear.[16] *Chiarella,* of course, involved an anonymous transaction in the marketplace motivated by what Professor Brudney has called an "unerodable informational advantage."[17] The defendant was a "mark-up" man in the composing room of a financial printer in New York. He was assigned, among other duties, the task of preparing various announcements of tender offers planned by corporate entities with which he had no other relationship. Needless to say, the printer had no relationship with the subjects of these potential tender offers.

Although the names of the tender-offer subjects were encoded throughout the materials, the printer was able to decipher the identity of the target company and, thus, to place orders with his broker prior to the public announcement of the tender offer. Chiarella was convicted and appealed. The Second Circuit affirmed, holding that Chiarella, positioned as he was in a financial printshop, was a market insider—that is, one who regularly received material information relating to a securities transactions. Had the Second Circuit's decision stood, one more piece would have been fitted into the vast Section 10(b) puzzle. To use Professor Brudney's terms, anyone positioned so as to become a regular recipient of information who gained an unerodable informational advantage as a result of that position would violate Rule 10b-5 if he traded prior to the public disclosure of the information. The Second Circuit's decision represented a major step toward the long-awaited parity-of-information rule.[18]

Even Professor Brudney had not called for a rule of parity, however. Indeed, Brudney argued forcefully that there were unerodable informational advantages that, while perceptible as forms of unfairness, did not outweigh the benefits of informational discovery.[19] Indeed, Brudney sharply criticized a then outstanding SEC rule proposal that would have required the bidder in a tender offer, once it has determined to make a tender offer, to abstain from further purchases until after public disclosure of its intention to make the tender offer.[20]

In any event, the Supreme Court reversed Chiarella's conviction. The Court held that Section 10(b) and thus Rule 10b-5 simply did not reach anonymous transactions in the marketplace unless the transactor's position or action caused him to act in breach of fiduciary duty. In this rather general statement, the Supreme Court affirmed much of the federal common law of insider trading. Significantly, the Court described the commission's decision *In the Matter of Cady, Roberts*[21] as "an important step in the development of Section 10(b) when the commission held that a broker-dealer and his firm violated that section by selling securities on the basis of undisclosed information obtained from a director of the issuer corporation who was also a registered representative of the brokerage firm."[22] The

Cady, Roberts decision imposed, administratively, in the context of transactions in the anonymous marketplace, the disclose-or-abstain-from-trading rule later adopted by the Second Circuit in *SEC* v. *Texas Gulf Sulphur*. Approving the disclosure-or-abstain rule, the Court linked this obligation to

> [A]n affirmative duty to disclose material information [which] has been traditionally imposed on corporate "insiders," particularly officers, directors, or controlling stockholders. We, and the courts, have consistently held that insiders must disclose material facts which are known to them by virtue of their position but which are not known to persons with whom they deal and which, if known, would affect their investment judgment.[23]

However, the Court went on to point out that, while not a novel twist in the law, this disclosure-triggering duty did not arise from just any relationship but only from those in which the potential transactional victim was "entitled to know [the information] because of a fiduciary or similar relation of trust and confidence between [the insider and the victim]."[24] In the case of a corporate insider, such a relationship is not difficult to find. The common law has long held that a fiduciary relationship encompassing trust and confidence arises, in the corporate context, out of the management-investor relationship. Indeed, as the law has developed, when any person positioned so as to receive information that may affect the value of the interests in the entity over which he holds the trusteeship, he abuses that trust if he uses the information for his own advantage.[25]

Perhaps the reason Chiarella's conviction could not stand was because his informational advantage was gained as a result of his employment in the print shop and not as a result of his relationship to the issuer. If, however, the statement is true, the language of the opinion may mean that the relationship, and not the type of information, is paramount in creating the duty to disclose or abstain from trading—that is, if the president of the subject company had come into possession of the same information that Chiarella had gained as a result of his employment in the print shop, then under the Supreme Court's analysis, the subject company's president would have violated Rule 10b-5 if he had traded or tipped prior to disclosing this information.[26] Under this analysis, *Chiarella* would represent something of an extension of Rule 10b-5 since, in the past, insiders who traded while possessed of market information about the issuer's stock were at least arguably outside the reach of Rule 10b-5.[27]

The tone of the *Chiarella* opinion does not, however, bear out that analysis. Enough language in the opinion links the receipt of the information with the relationship to render questionable any conclusion other than that the Supreme Court meant to restrict Rule 10b-5 to situations in which the receipt of the information *resulted from* or *arose out of* the fiduciary relationship.[28] Thus, situations in which the insider receives information concerning his corporation fortuitously, from a source outside the corporation, or in any other way not resulting from his occupying a position of trust and confidence, may be outside the ambit of Rule 10b–5 because, in the Supreme Court's view, trades resulting from the receipt of such information do not involve an abuse of trust.

Chiarella should, however, not be read too broadly. It applies, as a practical matter, only to anonymous transactions in the market—those that are inevitably accompanied by the silence of the initiating transactor. Assuming one of the parties makes a material misrepresentation or omits to state a material fact, face-to-face transactions remain actionable under Rule 10b–5 regardless of prior relationships. Active market manipulations continue to be actionable.[29] Moreover, fiduciaries (not necessarily corporate insiders) who trade with their beneficiaries on the basis of an informational advantage will violate Rule 10b–5.[30] Schemes to defraud still fall within the ambit of Rule 10b–5 so long as they are "in connection with" the purchase or sale of a security.[31]

Obviously, the problem the commission faced, after *Chiarella,* was how to prohibit misuse of material, nonpublic information relating to a tender offer in anonymous transactions in the market. At the time of the *Chiarella* decision, the commission had outstanding a rule proposal under Section 14(e) of the Exchange Act that was designed to accomplish that end outside the vehicle of Rule 10b–5.[32] It is this proposal, ultimately adopted as Rule 14e–3,[33] that forms the focus of the remainder of this article.[34]

Rule 14e–3

In this section, we analyze the scope of Rule 14e–3 and the authority of the SEC to adopt a rule in the face of a Supreme Court decision that left a closely related section of the Exchange Act inapplicable to the very conduct that Rule 14e–3 seeks to proscribe. The analysis of the rule's scope proceeds by an examination of the language of Section 14(e), the section's legislative history, and the judicial decisions interpreting Section 14(e). We conclude that, while none of these provides a sharply drawn parameter for the rule, when taken together with rulemaking authority lodged elsewhere in the Exchange Act, they do provide sufficient support for the broad approach the commission has taken.

With respect to the authority of the commission to adopt Rule 14e–3, we analyze the function of agency rulemaking where the rulemaking power is couched in terms of authority to define fraud and to prescribe means reasonably designed to prevent such fraudulent conduct. We conclude that such language contains positive rulemaking authority that extends beyond the authority granted to the SEC by Section 10(b) of the Exchange Act. Moreover, Section 23(a) of the Exchange Act provides separate authority for the adoption of the rule.[35]

Scope of Section 14(e)

One of the central theses of this chapter is that Section 14(e) applies to activity conducted during the entire process of any tender offer and not merely to the period from the commencement to the expiration of a formal offer. This thesis is based, in part, on the language of the statute itself. Section 14(e) consists of two sentences. The first is a self-operative, antifraud provision that was enacted as part of the Williams Act in 1968; the second sets forth the commission's rulemaking authority and was added by the 1970 amendments to the Williams Act. In full text, Section 14(e) states

> It shall be unlawful for any person to make any untrue statement of a material fact or omit to state any material fact necessary in order to make the statements made, in light of the circumstances under which they are made, not misleading, or to engage in any fraudulent, deceptive, or manipulative acts or practices, in connection with any tender offer or request or invitation for tenders, or any solicitation of security holders in opposition to or in favor of any such offer, request, or invitation. The commission shall, for purposes of this subsection, by rules and regulations define and prescribe means reasonably designed to prevent such acts and practices as are fraudulent, deceptive, or manipulative.

The critical language of the statute regarding its scope of application is the phrase *in connection with any tender offer*.[36] On its face, this language appears to mean that, assuming a transaction is a tender offer,[37] and that the conduct at issue is a result of or in some way relates to that tender offer, Section 14(e) is applicable.[38] Despite the breadth of the previous statement, for the rule to be workable there must be some attempt at limit setting. At some point, the tender-offer process begins and ends. In this search for limits, we put to one side those difficult questions of what constitutes a tender offer. Indeed, while Rule 14e-3 may apply to an unconventional tender offer, for the most part it appears to have been drawn with the conventional tender offer in mind. Thus, our focus, in the main, will be on the tender offer that is characterized by a public announcement by the bidder.

Although Section 14(e) applies to any tender offer and would apply at least from the time a tender offer is first published or sent or given to security holders—that is, the tender offer's commencement—through its consummation or withdrawal, it is not clear at what stage prior to commencement Section 14(e) becomes applicable.[39] Also, if Rule 14e-3 were construed not to apply until commencement, then the printer's conduct and, more importantly, transactions in subject-company stock by insiders of the bidder would not be proscribed.

In this regard, the statute itself offers some guidance. Note that the first sentence of Section 14(e) links the phrase "in connection with" with the phrase "any solicitation of security holders in opposition to or in favor of any [tender offer]." The term "solicitation" appears elsewhere in the Exchange Act. Under Section 14(a), which relates to the solicitation of proxies, that term has been broadly defined. As the Second Circuit stated in *Studebaker Corp* v. *Gittlin*,[40] "a letter which did not request the giving of any authorization was subject to the Proxy Rules if it was part of 'a continuous plan' intended to end in a solicitation and to prepare the way for success.[41] To hold otherwise would mean, as Learned Hand said in *SEC* v. *Okin*,[42] that "one need only spread the misinformation adequately before beginning to solicit and the commission would be powerless to protect shareholders."[43]

Although obvious differences exist between proxy solicitations and tender offers, to a large extent and particularly in relation to early solicitations they are analogous. For example, a potential offeror's management often solicits known subject-company shareholders to gauge the possibility of success of the potential tender offer.

In adopting the Williams Act, Congress was certainly aware of the close analogy between proxy solicitations and tender offers.[44] Indeed, it appears that Congress may have deliberately patterned the Williams Act on the proxy-solicitation provisions it felt had successfully been used by the commission in regulating proxy contests for corporate control. In this sense, then, Section 14(e)'s applicability and thus the scope of Rule 14e-3 would reach conduct committed substantially in advance of the commencement of a tender offer.[45]

However, no analysis of the scope of Section 14(e) would be complete without a comparison of its language to that of Rule 10b-5. The operative language of the section and of the rule is identical except that Rule 10b-5 is applicable "in connection with the purchase or sale of any security," while Section 14(e) applies "in connection with any tender offer." While these phrases have typically been compared for standing purposes, they may also be compared on the issue of scope of application. Indeed, one court construing Section 14(e) has relied on a line of cases holding that, for a fraud to be actionable under Rule 10b-5, it must have occurred prior to or contemporaneous with the sale of securities.[46]

Cross application of this concept from Rule 10b-5 to Section 14(e) leads to the conclusion that the "in connection with" phrase would include actions prior to or contemporaneous with the tender offer. The comparison with both Section 14(e) and Rule 10b-5, therefore, suggests that Section 14(e) applies prior to the commencement of the tender offer.

The legislative history of the Williams Act supports this view. Both the Senate and House Reports state that Section 14(e):

> Would affirm the fact that persons engaged in making or opposing tenders
> or otherwise seeking to influence the decision of investors or the outcome
> of the tender offer are under an obligation to make full disclosure of
> material information to those with whom they deal.[47]

The use of the phrase "making tender offers" appears to recognize that
tender offers do not occur overnight, that they involve a process of extensive planning and execution, and that commencement is only one stage of
that process.[48]

Moreover, the legislative history also recognizes that a subject-company shareholder has, with respect to the offer, three choices: (1) to tender to the instant or a competing bidder, (2) to hold the securities being
sought, or (3) to sell the securities into the market.[49] Note, however, that
during the precommencement period, alternatives (2) and (3) are available
to the subject-company shareholders. If Section 14(e) only applied to the
post commencement period, bidders and others could make misstatements,
omissions, and half-truths with relative impunity, causing market disruption and investment decisions to be made because a tender offer had not yet
commenced. Avoidance of this anomaly and implementation of congressional intent of providing investor protection to shareholders in the context
of tender offers render a restrictive reading of the legislative history of the
Section 14(e) inappropriate.

Despite the volume of tender-offer litigation, very few courts have
addressed the scope of Section 14(e).[50] The earliest lower-court decision was
Levine v. *Seilon Inc.,*[51] in which a former preferred shareholder brought a
damage action under Sections 10(b) and 14(e) alleging that the issuer never
intended to make a previously announced issuer exchange offer in which
preferred stockholders would exchange their stock for common shares of
the issuer. In dismissing the complaint, the district court stated that Section
14(e) only applied to tender offers that are "actually made."[52] The Second
Circuit affirmed on other grounds and, although not reaching the Section
14(e) issue, noted that "we are not sure we would agree with the district
court's rather restrictive reading of [Section 14(e)]."[53]

ICM Realty v. *Cabot, Cabot & Forbes Land Trust* represents a broad
judicial construction of Section 14(e).[54] In an injunctive action, plaintiff
(the subject company) alleged that defendant (the offeror) had an overall
plan to make a tender offer, had entered into contracts with five banks that
agreed to exchange securities for those of the defendant, and had filed a
Schedule 13D (but not a registration statement) that indicated that an exchange offer might be made in the future. On a motion to dismiss, the court
held that plaintiff had stated a cause of action under Section 14(e) "since
the alleged misrepresentations are alleged to have been made in connection
with the overall plan."[55]

Cases since 1974 have not followed either the restrictive view of *Levine*

or the broad interpretation of *ICM. Anaconda Co.* v. *Crane Co.* involved
the application of Sections 14(e) and 14(d) to statements by a subject company during the precommencement period.[56] Crane, the offeror, first made
a public announcement of its intention to make an exchange offer and
Anaconda, the subject company, then made a public announcement of its
possible opposition to the offer. Although both announcements preceded
Crane's filing of its registration statement, the court found that Sections
14(e) and 14(d) were applicable to Anaconda's press release, the communication at issue in the case.

The *Levine* argument that Sections 14(d) and 14(e) do not apply until an
exchange offer is actually commenced was used by the defendant subject
company, without success, in *Applied Digital Data Systems, Inc.* v. *Milgo
Electronic Corp.*[57] There, a bidder that had publicly announced the terms of
its exchange offer brought an action under Sections 14(d) and 14(e) to en-
join the subject company from selling a substantial amount of authorized,
but unissued, stock to a third corporation. In rejecting the company's
"overly strict and literal reading of the statute,"[58] Judge Weinberg reasoned that:

> [T]here is no apparent reason why any given action may not be taken "in
> connection with" a development reasonably certain to take place in the
> future or why a recommendation to reject a proposed tender offer is not
> also a recommendation to "reject a tender offer."[59]

Since the dangers the Williams Act was intended to guard against are present from the time of the public announcement of the proposed offer, Judge
Weinberg concluded that those remedial purposes would be frustrated if the
act's disclosure and fair-play provisions were confined to the period after an
offer had been formally made.[60]

The rationale of *Applied Digital* was used in *Reserve Management* v.
Anchor Daily Income Fund, in which an investment adviser made two proposals for a merger to an investment company.[61] The court found no claim
for injunctive relief since the investment adviser did not make a public
announcement of a proposed tender offer nor did it engage in any other
conduct sufficient to establish a "clear and definite intent to make a tender
offer as contemplated in *Applied Digital.*"[62] Although the decision has been
viewed as narrowing *Applied Digital,*[63] the facts of the case indicate that the
investment adviser only proposed a merger, not a tender offer.[64] Moreover,
the alternatives of no public announcement or no intent to make a tender
offer appear to be at least as broad, if not broader, than *Applied Digital.*

While *Applied Digital* was an injunctive action that focused on precommencement announcements that were followed by the commencement of a
tender offer, three recent cases—*Berman* v. *Gerber Products Co.,*[65] *Lewis*

v. *McGraw*,[66] and *Panter* v. *Marshall Field & Co.*[67]—were damage actions that concerned announcements that were not followed by the commencement of tender offers. *Berman* and *Marshall Field* distinguished between the pariticipation in a tender offer that never takes place and the investment decision to sell into the market after announcement of a proposed tender offer; *Lewis* only considered the issue of deception that prevents a tender offer from commencing.

The *Berman* case arose from the opposition of Gerber's management to an announced tender offer by Anderson, Clayton & Co. In seeking in excess of $100 million in damages, the Gerber shareholders alleged that management's efforts to arrange a friendly merger and disclosure with respect to the Anderson, Clayton offer, which was subsequently withdrawn, violated Section 14(e).

While deciding that management's actions were not connected in any substantial fashion with Anderson, Clayton's offer, Judge Fox recognized

> That statements made by either the offeror or the target company prior to the actual effective date of a tender offer but after the announcement of the offer and the preliminary filings fall within the purview of 14(e). . . . During this interim period, the policies behind Section 14(e) apply with as much force as they do following the effective date of the offer.[68]

The alleged misrepresentations and omissions during the precommencement period were considered with respect to the shareholder's decision to sell in a rising market or to retain their shares rather than the decision to tender *vel non*. The court viewed causation in fact as an essential element of a private action under Section 14(e) but explained that the requisite causation would exist to the extent that the nonselling plaintiff-shareholders were misled into retaining, rather than selling, their Gerber stock.[69] Judge Fox found support for this conclusion in the legislative history of the Williams Act, which

> Indicates that the legislation was intended to reach such transactions as well as those involving the actual tender of a stockholder's shares.[70]

After examining the disclosures that were material to the investment decision to sell or hold, the court concluded that no misrepresentations occurred and that the omissions were not material. Under either level of the analysis in *Berman*, Section 14(e) is applicable during the precommencement period and, even though a proposed tender offer is withdrawn, two aspects of the investment decision (for example, to sell or hold) are operative during the precommencement period.

Unlike *Berman*, the damage action in *Lewis* concentrated on the efforts and disclosures by the management of McGraw-Hill, Inc., which allegedly denied the plaintiff-shareholders the opportunity to sell their stock to American Express Company, the prospective bidder, in a tender offer that never occurred. In its *per curiam* opinion, the Second Circuit affirmed the dismissal of the shareholders' damage action.[71] The opinion is based on the absence of reliance, a necessary element in a private action for damages under Section 14(e).[72] Since no offer was ever made, the court reasoned, the shareholders could not have relied on the subject company's statements concerning the proposed tender offer.

The Second Circuit's opinion may be read as resting on an analysis of reliance and causation in that particular case.[73] The closing note of the Second Circuit's opinion casts a shadow on limiting the reliance/causation rationale to the facts of that case. The court notes that precommencement statements will still be actionable under Section 14(e): (1) for damages, if an offer is ultimately made and reliance can be demonstrated or presumed; and (2) for injunctive relief where an offer appears to be likely and reliance on the statements is possible.[74] Although this note can be read to preclude any damage action where a tender offer is never made, a better approach would be to follow the *Berman* two-prong analysis. Alternatively, one might separate the violation of Section 14(e) from the issue of damages. Thus, there may be a violation of the statute, but no damages would result because of the lack of reliance. Either of these approaches would better comport with the purpose of the Williams Act and avoid the possibility of subject companies' being able to thwart prospective tender offers without the risk of a damage action.

Unfortunately, *Lewis* was not limited to its facts by the Seventh Circuit in *Marshall Field*,[75] which involved the takeover attempt by Carter Hawley Hale (CHH) of Marshall Field & Co. that began as a merger proposal and that, in the final stages, before being withdrawn, took the form of a proposed exchange offer. In an action for damages, the plaintiff-shareholders alleged that Marshall Field violated Section 14(e) by denial of the opportunity to tender their shares to CHH[76] and by causing them not to dispose of their shares in the rising market. In a split decision, the majority affirmed the district court's grant of a directed verdict on both Section 14(e) claims.

With respect to the first theory, the majority found *Lewis* to be directly on point and held that because the requisite element of reliance was absent, since the shareholders never had the opportunity to tender, Section 14(e) was not violated. The court also rejected two arguments against applying *Lewis:* (1) it benefits a subject company that, through deception, is able to thwart a tender offer, and (2) statements in the precommencement period can affect investment decisions during the offer. The court found the first claim to be irrelevant since the offer was withdrawn by CHH because of Marshall Field's conduct—that is, acquisitions and expansion plans that posed antitrust questions—which were matters for state law and not federal securities law.[77] The second claim was inapt since the offer never materialized.[78]

With respect to the second theory, the majority found that Section 14(e) was intended to apply only during an actual tender offer and therefore held that Section 14(e) does not provide a damages remedy for alleged misrepresentations or omissions of material fact when the proposed tender offer never becomes effective.[79] The holding disregards the court's prior recognition that, upon announcement of a proposed tender offer, the investment decision is threefold: to tender, to sell into the rising market, or to retain the shares being sought.[80] Although the court analyzed the lost tender-offer opportunity separately from the decision not to sell into the market, it failed to distinguish them and to recognize, as the *Berman* court did, that Section 14(e) applies during the precommencement period, whether or not an offer is made, with respect to the decision to sell into the market or hold.

These and other errors in the majority's reasoning are the subject of Judge Cudahy's opinion that dissented from the majority's second Section 14(e) holding.[81] The dissent viewed the majority decision as providing a major loophole to incumbent management through which to force withdrawal of unwanted tender offers and Section 14(e) liability, thereby frustrating the remedial purposes of the Williams Act.[82] The dissent concludes that Section 14(e) is applicable in the precommencement period,[83] that *Lewis* should not be construed to the contrary, and that the distinction between the lost tender-offer opportunity and the decision to sell into the market is "clear and realistic."[84]

Admittedly, the decisions discussed here have focused on the first publicly announced indications of the tender offer by either the bidder or the subject company as the trigger for the application of Section 14(e).[85] Usually, they have dealt with deception during the period from the public announcement of a proposed tender offer to the commencement or withdrawal of that offer. With the exception of *ICM*, the cases have not analyzed a fact pattern in which no public announcement by press release occurred. The overall-plan approach of the *ICM* decision is, however, consistent with the triggering mechanism of Rule 14e-3—that is, that the bidder has taken a substantial step or steps to commence or has commenced a tender offer.[86] Given that the principal abuse in the tender-offer context has been insider trading in the precommencement period, it would indeed be anomalous if courts were to limit Section 14(e) (and, thus, the operation of Rule 14e-3) to the period subsequent to the public announcement of an intention to make a tender offer. Since the bidder is typically in control of when the public announcement will be made, Rule 14e-3 could be circumvented, and the investor protection it provides would be lost if the public announcement benchmark was applied mechanically in a case under Rule 14e-3. For Rule 14e-3 to be fully effective, therefore, the "in connection with" phrase in Section 14(e) should be construed broadly. The "substantial step or steps to commence" standard of Rule 14e-3 is a reasonable approach to address the abuse of insider trading and comports with both the language of Section 14(e) and its legislative history.

Authority under Section 14(e)

We now turn to the question of the commission's authority to adopt rules like Rule 14e-3. This authority is lodged, as stated earlier, in the second sentence of Section 14(e). That sentence is couched in terms of authority to define and to prescribe means reasonably designed to prevent fraudulent practices taken in connection with a tender offer. Our thesis is that the language of the second sentence of Section 14(e) provides the commission with the authority to reach conduct that may not be, in and of itself, fraudulent. We base this conclusion on our assessment that Congress, during the legislative process, focused on abusive tender-offer-trading practices by insiders and from our comparison of the rulemaking authority in Section 14(e) with rulemaking authority lodged elsewhere in the Exchange Act.

Legislative History. In both the Senate and House hearings on the legislation that became the Williams Act, extensive testimony was introduced relating to the adverse effects of leaks and rumors of impending tender offers on the marketplace.[87] Although this testimony focused on the relationship of leaks to a proposed precommencement bidder-filing requirement,[88] it highlighted the market disruption and abusive practices associated with leaks of proposed tender offers. As one New York Stock Exchange official testified

> [C]urrently to ensure secrecy and to avoid leaks and rumors . . . tender offers are normally made to stockholders immediately after a decision to make the offer is reached and a price has been determined. In spite of all precautions, there have been cases where tender offers have been preceded by leaks and rumors which caused abnormal market problems.[89]

In addition, Senator Bennett expressed concern about insider trading prior to the commencement of a tender offer:

> I am concerned with the situation which makes it possible for insiders to take advantage of their knowledge that the pending offer is coming and therefore get a quick profit by buying stock with the sure knowledge that they are going to have a market for it.[90]

As passed in 1968, the William Act did not expressly prohibit trading based on an informational advantage gained as a result of a relationship with a bidder. Nor did it grant rulemaking power to the commission under Section 14(e) to proscribe such practices. Not until later did the commission decide to make its own bid for such authority.

In March 1969, Chairman Budge appeared before the Senate Subcommittee on Securities to present his views on the problems facing the securities industry.[91] In reviewing tender offers, Chairman Budge made several suggestions for revising the Williams Act, one of which requested that Section 14(e) be amended "to grant the commission rulemaking authority over purchases by a potential tender offeror and his associates comparable to that provided in Section 13(e) for purchases by the issuer."[92] Chairman Budge's suggestions were incorporated in S.3431, which became the 1970 Williams Act amendments.

In introducing S.3431, Senator Harrison A. Williams described the proposed grant of rulemaking authority to the commission as being of "utmost necessity."[93] He explained

> [T]he techniques used in corporate takeovers and tender offers have become increasingly sophisticated and change rapidly. This is particularly true in situations where the takeover is resisted by incumbent management—industrial warfare develops. Claims and counterclaims, charges and countercharges are hurled back and forth. Efforts are made to influence the price of the securities involved. The commission must be given full rulemaking powers in order to deal with these rapidly changing problems.[94]

Also, in the Senate hearings, Senator Williams added that "the bill before us would add to the commission's rulemaking power and enable it to deal promptly and with flexibility with this rapidly changing problem.[95]

Chairman Budge described the language of the amendment as being identical to that contained in Section 15(c)(2) of the Exchange Act, which grants the commission rulemaking power with respect to fraudulent, deceptive, or manipulative practices by brokers and dealers in transactions in the over-the-counter markets.[96] In response to Senator Williams's request for examples of the fraudulent, deceptive, or manipulative practices used in tender offers that the proposed rulemaking powers could be employed to prevent, the commission's Division of Corporation Finance submitted a memorandum that listed as one of the areas to be covered by rulemaking the situation in which "a person who has become aware that a tender offer is to be made or has reason to believe that such bid will be made, may fail to disclose material facts with respect thereto to persons who sell to him securities for which the tender bid is to be made."[97]

Thus, insider trading and leaks of information relating to a tender offer were highlighted to Congress at the time of the original passage of the Williams Act. Moreover, when rulemaking authority was added to Section 14(e) in 1970, trading in subject-company securities by persons in possession of material, nonpublic information relating to a prospective tender offer was one of the examples furnished to Congress of the fraudulent, deceptive, or manipulative practices that the new authority would address. It appears, then, reasonably clear that Congress believed it had delegated to the commission rulemaking power designed to deal with this problem. The remaining issue is, of course, how much authority Congress actually delegated.

Section 14(e)'s Rulemaking Language. As stated earlier, Section 14(e) grants to the commission for purposes of that subsection the authority both to "define" and to "prescribe means reasonably designed to prevent" such acts and practices as are fraudulent, deceptive, or manipulative. The definitional power enables the commission to define an act or practice as being fraudulent, deceptive, or manipulative even though it was not so at common law and, indeed, may not have been unlawful prior to the adoption of the definition.[98] For example, prior to the adoption of Rule 14e-3, warehousing[99] was prohibited neither by common law nor by Rule 10b-5.[100] With the adoption of Rule 14e-3(a), warehousing is now defined as a fraudulent, deceptive, or manipulative act or practice (and thus proscribed). This definitional power is also consistent with Congress's intent that the rulemaking authority enable the commission to react quickly and flexibly to the constantly changing tender-offer environment.[101]

The second facet of the commission's rulemaking authority under Section 14(e) is the power to prescribe means reasonably designed to prevent fraudulent, manipulative, or deceptive acts or practices. This authority is potentially more significant than the power to define in that it enables the commission to regulate conduct that in and of itself is neither fraudulent, deceptive, nor manipulative in order to prevent conduct that is. The only limit appears to be that the means—that is, the rulemaking—is reasonably designed to yield prevention. Presumably, there must be a nexus between the rule and the abuse it is designed to reach. Rule 14e-3(d) is an example of this type of rulemaking. It proscribes both deliberate tips of material, nonpublic information, as well as inadvertent leaks of such information where it is reasonably likely that the tippee will either trade on the information or tip someone else who might do so. Inadvertent tipping unaccompanied by knowledge or recklessness would ordinarily not be considered fraudulent, deceptive, or manipulative. Because of the adverse effects of insider trading on tender offers and the consequent undermining of the purposes of the Williams Act,[102] proscribing tipping directly is a means reasonably designed to prevent the trading on the basis of such material, nonpublic information. Thus, in our view, this rulemaking power enables the commission to adopt prophylactic measures to address abusive practices.[103]

The breadth of this rulemaking power can be seen by comparing it to the power delegated to the commission in Section 15(c)(2) of the Exchange Act on which it is based.[104] As originally enacted in 1934,[105] Section 15(c) provided only definitional power to the commission.[106] The addition of the proscriptive power to the definitional power by the 1938 amendment that created Section 15(c)(2)[107] was explained by the House Report as being intended to clarify and broaden the commission's rulemaking power to prevent fraudulent, manipulative, and deceptive acts and practices.[108] Thus, Congress envisioned the prescriptive power as encompassing the prevention of fraud and as being broader than the original delegation—that of defining fraud. In light of Chairman Budge's testimony in 1969,[109] the commission apparently views the language of Section 14(e) in a similar manner. Not only does the commission have the power to define otherwise permissible conduct as fraudulent but also it has the power to design rules that reasonably will prevent that conduct. Moreover, such rulemaking authority enables the commission to define fraud to include silence in the absence of a duty to speak recognized at common law and to proscribe such conduct.

Policy behind Section 14(e) Rulemaking Authority. In addition to the language of Section 14(e), its legislative history, and a comparison to other sections of the Exchange Act, its broad rulemaking authority is based on the policy considerations. By passing the Williams Act, Congress closed a significant disclosure gap in the federal securities laws and enacted comprehensive regulation of tender offers. Enactment of Section 14(e) demonstrates Congress's belief that a specific antifraud provision was needed in the tender-offer area, one that would grant the commission the flexibility to deal with the dynamic nature of tender-offer practice and the needs for investor protection in contests for corporate control. Although it draws on other sections, Section 14(e) is different in language and more important in application. These differences, particularly that of subject matter, set Section 14(e) apart from other antifraud provisions. Therefore, Section 14(e) should not be viewed merely as a tender-offer analogy to either Section 10(b) or Section 14(a). The separate and independent nature of Section 14(e) can be seen in the rulemaking thereunder. Specifically, Rule 14e-3 was proposed and adopted pursuant to Section 14(e), not Section 10(b). Rather than an inadvertence, this action appears to be a recognition by the commission that, with respect to insider trading in tender offers, Section 14(e), rather than Section 10(b), is the appropriate and sufficient authority for rulemaking.

Operation of Rule 14e-3

Stated generally, Rule 14e-3 posits two operative duties. First, the rule imposes a duty to "disclose or abstain from trading" on any person in possession of material, nonpublic information relating to a tender offer, which information was acquired from the bidder or from the subject company.[110] Second, the rule establishes a duty—or, more correctly, a prohibition— against tipping material, nonpublic information relating to a tender offer.

Although the duty to "disclose or abstain" is stated in absolute terms, Rule 14e-3 does contain a series of exceptions. Principal among these is an exception for the multiservice financial institution that, in its capacity as an investment banker, gains access to material, nonpublic information that it is prohibited from using. At the same time, it may be conducting a retail securities business as a part of which it may be recommending the security in a manner consistent or inconsistent with the information. This exception is designed to ameliorate what, at first glance, appears to be an almost unsolvable problem in this day of highly diversified securities firms.[111]

The rule also provides exceptions for purchases, pursuant to the tender offer, of the target's securities, by brokers or other agents of the tender offeror and for sales of subject-company securities by any person to an offering person. As becomes clearer later in the discussion, these exceptions, while not related to conduct that would ordinarily be thought of as unlawful, are necessary because of the broad reach of Rule 14e-3's obligation to disclose or refrain from trading.

The cases that have been litigated under Section 14(e) have, for the most part, involved its scope rather than its application to particular kinds of conduct. For that reason and for the further reason that the analytic framework of Rule 14e-3 is drawn from Rule 10b-5, most of the discussion that follows will be closely compared with the application of Rule 10b-5 to similar situations.[112]

The Duty to Disclose or Abstain from Trading

Unlike Rule 10b-5's duty to disclose or abstain, which is expressed only in the common law of Section 10(b), that duty is explicit in Rule 14e-3. Under subsection (a) of the rule, the prohibition is triggered once a person has commenced, or has taken substantial steps to commence, a tender offer.[113] After that point, anyone in possession of material information relating to the offer—information that person knows or has reason to know is nonpublic and was acquired, directly or indirectly, from the offering person, the subject company, or any of either's affiliates—may not purchase or sell the securities (or cause others to purchase or sell the securities) sought pursuant to the offer unless the information is publicly disclosed within a reasonable time prior to the purchase or sale.

Analytically, this rather simple rule requires that two questions be answered. First, when and under what circumstances will the duty imposed by Rule 14e-3(a) arise? Second, assuming the existence and application of a duty under Rule 14e-3(a), what does fulfillment of the duty require?

When Does the Duty to Disclose or Abstain from Trading Arise? As a general matter, the common law of Rule 10b-5 imposes a duty on an insider to disclose or refrain from trading if a reasonable expectation exists on the part of the issuer (or other source of information) that the insider will not trade. Thus, if the insider trades, the breach of his common-law duty to the source (not to the other transacting party) is the basis of his liability under Rule 10b-5. This is the theory that underpins the commission's decision in the *Cady, Roberts*[114] proceeding as well as the Second Circuit's benchmark decision in *Texas Gulf Sulphur*. *Chiarella* did no more than confirm that such a breach of duty was a necessary element of a Rule 10b-5 violation.

In contrast, under Rule 14e-3(a), the duty to disclose or abstain from trading will arise because a person, other than the person making the tender offer, is in possession of material information relating to a tender offer— information he knows or has reason to know has been acquired from the offering person, the issuer of the securities sought or to be sought in the tender offer, or any officer, director, partner, or any other person acting on behalf of the offering person or such issuer. No requirement of preexisting relationship is present in Rule 14e-3.

The significance of the absence of the need to show a fiduciary like relationship should be apparent. The irrelevance of that element of proof of a violation invests Rule 14e-3 with a far broader scope, in the context of a tender offer, than that of Rule 10b-5. Instead of a limit linked to common-law concepts, Rule 14e-3's impact broadcasts whenever, and no matter how tangentially, the focused-upon conduct is involved. Thus, the printer in the Supreme Court's *Chiarella* decision would have been subject to this duty and in violation thereof when he traded.

Materiality. Both Rule 10b-5 and Rule 14e-3 explicitly relate their information trigger to the concept of materiality. Although described by various courts and commentators as elusive and incapable of definition, in practice the courts seem to have little difficulty in deciding whether a bit of information is material. The basic test of materiality seems to be the one set forth in *TSC Industries, Inc.* v. *Northway, Inc.*[115]:

> An omitted fact is material if there is a substantial likelihood that a reasonable shareholder would consider it important in deciding how to [act]. . . . Put another way, there must be a substantial likelihood that the disclosure of the omitted fact would have been viewed by the reasonable investor as having significantly altered the "total mix" of information made available.[116]

Northway, of course, involved a violation of Rule 14a-9 (17 CFR 240.14a-9) in the context of a proxy contest, rather than a question of insider trading under Rule 10b-5. It has been suggested that the standard of materiality is somehow different depending on the context.[117] Indeed, the American Law Institute's proposed federal-securities code would require proof that a "fact of special significance" caused the transaction before liability can be assessed against an insider.[118]

Nevertheless, it would appear that the courts are tending toward wholesale adoption of the *Northway* test in both Rule 10b-5 insider-trading cases[119] and in cases under Section 14(e).[120] Given this trend, it is virtually certain that the courts will use the *Northway* test under Rule 14e-3.

Realistically, of course, there should be even less difficulty in deciding whether information is material under Rule 14e-3. For one thing, the context is far narrower—that is, the information universe relates only to a tender offer rather than to any information about an issuer. For the most part, the information will be that there is about to be a tender offer. What the courts will have to decide is whether that raw information alone is material.

Obviously, the narrow tender-offer context is the key to any decision involving materiality. In the first place, the information must originate directly or indirectly either with the issuer or the subject company. If the information originates with someone who, in the normal course of either company's internal communication channels, would ordinarily receive or have access to that information, then a court should hold that information to be material. This would, of course, include all directors and senior management. It would also include personnel of a more ministerial nature such as the company secretary and even clerical personnel who ordinarily attend board meetings. More difficult to analyze are situations in which the decision to make a tender offer has not congealed. The so-called bear-hug letter is an example. Company C, considering making a tender offer for the stock of Company Y, sends a confidential letter to the latter suggesting a friendly merger but also indicating the possibility of a tender offer if the merger suggestion is refused. May a director of Company X buy Company Y stock? May a director of Company Y?

The answer would seem to be that neither should be able to buy. From the point of view of the marketplace, both knew exactly the same information and came to this information through the normal channels of corporate communication. Thus, although in a larger Rule 10b-5 informational context neither might be said to have material information[121] in the narrower tender-offer context, neither may trade without disclosing or violating Rule 14e-3(a).

There appears to be no "bright line" test for determining when material information is created. A great deal of planning goes into a tender offer long before it is presented to the board. It would be indefensible to argue that any time senior management entertains the possibility of making a tender offer, material information is created. Nevertheless, at some point in the planning process, the decision to go ahead begins to congeal. Unlike typical insider-trading cases, it will be of little use to analyze the information in terms of objectivity, specificity, or to contrast it to information already outstanding in the market. For the most part, the terms and other details will have little effect on the materiality of tender-offer information; the major interest in the market is that there is about to be a tender offer. Thus, it is submitted that the appropriate method of analysis is to review the chronology of planning until the point is reached when all prior substantial conditions to the offer have fallen away. At that point, if a person receives or acquires material information relating to a tender offer, such person must, under Rule 14e-3(a), disclose that information or refrain from trading.

Substantial Steps. Closely tied to the question of materiality and, indeed, in support of the previous analysis is the initiating point in the duty-imposition process. Under Rule 14e-3(a), the duty is not triggered until someone has taken a substantial step to commence a tender offer. At that point it becomes unlawful for any other person to use material, nonpublic information relating to that tender offer to buy or sell subject-company securities.

There is no requirement in the rule that the information be material at the time the substantial step is taken. Apparently, the information may become material before or after (or even simultaneously with) the taking of the substantial step.

There is also nothing in the rule itself that even indicates what is meant by a substantial step. Release No. 34-17120 does not indicate that the SEC realizes that a substantial-step test is not entirely an objective one. It also indicates that substantial steps include (but are not limited to) voting on a resolution relating to the tender offer by the offering person's board of directors, the formulation of a plan or proposal to make a tender offer, or activities that substantially facilitate the tender offer such as arranging financing for a tender offer; preparing, directing, or authorizing the preparation of tender-offer materials; or authorizing negotiations.

Thus, Rule 14e-3 apparently contemplates two different judicial findings. The first would relate to defining the taking of a substantial step; the second relates to whether (and when) the information became material. These findings are not mutually exclusive. The only required relationship is that the materiality finding must obtain at a time subsequent to the finding of the taking of a substantial step.[122]

Another difference under Rule 14e-3 from the typical antifraud case brought under Rule 10b-5 is the lack of a need to relate the information used to the breach of common-law relationships. Since *Chiarella,* of course, nondisclosure cases under Rule 10b-5 have been pegged to the fiduciary relationship between the person trading and the source of the information. Under Rule 14e-3 the relationship is irrelevant; the duty to disclose or abstain is triggered by information acquisition alone. Nevertheless, not all material information is covered; only that information relating to a tender offer. Thus, if X, who has no preexisting relationship to Company A, trades upon the receipt of material information about A that did not relate to a tender offer, no violation of either Rule 10b-5 or of Rule 14e-3 will occur. X will not have violated Rule 10b-5 because of the manner in which he received the information, and he will not have violated Rule 14e-3 because of the type of information involved.

Along the same line, the duty to disclose or abstain from trading under Rule 10b-5 is usually triggered because the source of the information is the issuer itself. [123] However, this is not a condition to the same duty under Rule 14e-3. The source of the information that triggers the obligations of Rule 14e-3(a) can be an offering person, an issuer of the securities sought or to be sought in the tender offer, or any person acting on behalf of either of them. In order for Rule 14e-3's duty to be triggered, the information must have been acquired, directly or indirectly, from such enumerated persons. Release No. 34-17120[124] (the release in which Rule 14e-3 was adopted) indicates that the term "acquired" replaced the term "received" in the rule as earlier proposed to indicate that information obtained by conversion, misappropriation, or other means is subject to the duties imposed by Rule 14e-3(a).[125]

That the commission imposed the duty to disclose or abstain on persons who received tender-offer information from the bidder is not terribly surprising. After all, it is within that company that the information about the tender offer originates and the opportunity for creating unerodable information advantages exists. However, the duty will also attach to persons who receive tender-offer information from the subject company. The commission's November 1979 proposal did not include this aspect of the rule. Rather, it focused solely on information received directly or indirectly from the bidder. In a footnote to Release No. 34-17120, the commission points out that "this revision [to include information emanating from the target] responds to concerns of the commentators that the . . . [November proposal] did not address adequately material, nonpublic information emanating from the subject company."[126] In particular, the commission was concerned about a bidder hoping to facilitate the tender offer by alerting subject companies in advance of the tender offer followed by subject-company insider purchases. As adopted, Rule 14e-3 imposes a duty on a subject-company insider—indeed, on the subject company itself—to cease making purchases of subject-company securities until subsequent to a public announcement of the tender offer.

Interestingly, the imposition by Rule 14e-3 of the duty to disclose or abstain on those who receive nonpublic tender-offer information from the subject company creates overlapping liability under Rule 10b-5. Note that once the subject company receives the information, such information becomes, like any other information that may affect the price of a company's securities, inside information that may not, under Rule 10b-5, be used for anyone's personal benefit. Thus, purchases by subject-company insiders based on that information would violate Rule 10b-5 as well as Rule 14e-3.

The standard of knowledge required to violate Rule 14e-3 may prove to be one of its more complex attributes. As the adopting release points out, "the information which will trigger the operation of the rule (1) must be material, (2) must relate to a tender offer, (3) must be nonpublic, and (4) must have been acquired directly or indirectly from the offering person, from the issuer, or from another specified person."[127] For the last two requisites, there is a knows-or-has-reason-to-know standard applicable to the person who has gained possession of the information. For the first two requisites—materiality and relation to a tender offer—there is no knows-or-has-reason-to-know standard.

Ordinarily, these differing standards should not cause any particular difficulty. When, as will probably be the case, the information also involves the question of whether there is to be a tender offer, it will be difficult, if not impossible, for a defendant to argue that (1) it did not relate to a tender offer and (2) in that context it was not material.

The knowledge standard, then, is designed to distinguish between situations in which the information received came into the possession of the recipient as the result of a rumor or other triggering source and situations in which the information is received as the result of a leak or selective communication originating with one of the enumerated persons. If, for example, Company A tells broker-dealer X that it is about to make a tender offer for the securities of Company B and asks if it will serve as dealer manager for the offer, and if X tells Y about the approach, Y would violate Rule 14e-3(a) if he purchased subject-company securities.[128]

What Does the Duty Require? Under Rule 14e-3(a), as under Rule 10b-5, the person subject to the duty imposed by that rule must disclose within a reasonable time prior to a purchase or sale, by press release or otherwise, the information received and its source. Release No. 34-17120 states that the disclosure must be made in a manner that will fully disseminate the information.[129] The release also sets forth various, nonexclusive methods of disclosure. Disclosure to a national securities exchange on which the subject security is listed would probably serve to lift the trading prohibition. Disclosure to the National Association of Securities Dealers, Inc., if such security is authorized for trading in the NASDAQ interdealer quotation system, would probably serve the same purpose. A daily newspaper with a national circulation or a national news service might be other vehicles of disclosure.[130]

Thus, both Rule 10b-5 and Rule 14e-3 require disclosure to the marketplace. Neither, however, appears to require duplicative disclosure of information already publicly disclosed. Indeed, subsequent to its disclosure, the information by definition loses its character as nonpublic, and the duty to disclose or abstain evaporates.

As a practical matter, of course, persons who possess material, inside information do not reveal it publicly. Either they are under a charge not to reveal it or they hope to use it, unrevealed, to their own advantage. In general, then, the only disclosure problems that will arise are the type that arose in *Texas Gulf Sulphur,* where a number of insiders attempted to beat the gun by trading subsequent to disclosure but before the market has had an opportunity to digest the information.

Not surprisingly, the commission and the courts have previously addressed, in the context of Rule 10b-5, the question of when information becomes public. *In the Matter of Investors Management Co., Inc.,* the commission held that "information is nonpublic when it has not been disseminated in a manner making it available to investors generally."[131] In *Texas Gulf Sulphur,* the Second Circuit indicated that, "before insiders may act upon material information, such information must have been effectively disclosed in a manner sufficient to insure its availability to the investing public."[132] Finally, in the *Cady, Roberts* case, the commission instructed insiders to "keep out of the market until the established procedures for public release of the information are carried out instead of hastening to execute transactions in advance of, and in frustration of, the objectives of the release."[133]

Prior to the decision in *Ernst & Ernst* v. *Hochfelder,* [134] these cases carried the implication that there is imposed on an insider in possession of material inside information, some duty of inquiry into the degree to which the information is nonpublic.[135] Where violations of Rule 14e-3 are at issue and where questions of scienter under *Hochfelder* are irrelevant, the argument is compelling that one who seeks to trade based on information he knows or has reason to know has originated with either the bidder or the target must inquire into whether the information has become public.[136]

This analysis indicates that the central concepts of Rule 14e-3 are based in the common law of Rule 10b-5. However, Rule 14e-3, while to a certain extent overlapping, is comparable to Rule 10b-5 only by analogy. In the first place, Rule 14e-3 addresses, unlike Rule 10b-5, a particular kind of problem in the securities markets.[137] Rule 14e-3 is a severely limited antifraud rule in that it operates only in the area of tender offers; but for that very reason, it does not require the safeguards against a flood of litigation that the Supreme Court apparently requires of Rule 10b–5. There would be no docket-clearing purpose in holding that Rule 14e–3(a)'s duty to abstain or disclose attached only, for example, where the initiating transactor acted with scienter. The number of tender offers are finite, and they, as a rule, move through the courts rather quickly. Thus, the basic prohibition in Rule 14e–3(a) to disclose or abstain from trading has, unlike Rule 10b–5, its own built-in parameters.

Despite these useful parameters, the prohibition on trading is, within the context of a tender offer, a rather broad one. For that reason, and for the more important reason that the securities industry has become the creature of large full-service firms, the felt need was for an exception to the duty that would accommodate industry developments. We turn now to that exception.

Rule 14e-3 and the Multiservice Brokerage Firm

Generally. As the adopting release makes clear, "the abuse which Rule 14e–3(a) is directed at is the actual misuse of material, nonpublic information in connection with a sale or purchase."[138] The commission recognized, however, that this prohibition was capable of application to a nonnatural person—that is, a multiservice financial institution—even though the individuals making the investment decision on behalf of the institution or firm did not actually know the nonpublic information or even that such information was known to others employed by the firm. For that reason, Rule 14e–3 provides a significant exception to the prohibition in Rule 14e–3(a) for a firm engaged in several aspects of the securities business that can show that the individual decision makers did not know the material, nonpublic information at the time of the purchase or sale and that the firm had implemented one or a combination of reasonable procedures to ensure that such individuals would not violate Rule 14e–3(a). The commission apparently believed that Rule 14e–3(a) should not be adopted without taking into consideration existing practices in the banking, insurance, investment management, and brokerage businesses. The provisions of paragraph (b)(2) of the rule thus permit so-called Chinese walls, restricted lists, and other reasonable procedures that insulate one function of the firm from another.[139] The rule is not designed to promote or condone lax or ineffective procedures, since the exemption would not in any event apply if the individual making or causing a purchase or sale knew the material, nonpublic information. Indeed, a defendant in an action under the rule would have to establish, in proving its entitlement to the exemption in Rule 14e–3(b)(1), that the individual investment decision maker did not possess the information.

Rule 14e-3(b)(2) does not specify particular procedures to be employed in implementing a Chinese wall or a restricted list, nor does the rule distinguish between different functions or prefer one method of control over the other. Instead, in light of evolving concepts and competitive considerations between and among the banking, insurance, and brokerage industries, the rule leaves detailed implementation of procedures to the private sector. If the private sector fails to initiate or for some reason does not continue to design and maintain adequate procedures, the commission will no doubt wish to revisit this issue.[140] This chapter addresses the viability of a Chinese wall as a defense to trading on material, nonpublic information. The analysis of restricted lists and other procedures is left for another time.

Scope of the Exception. Questions involving the duties of multiservice securities firms with respect to the inevitable conflict-of-interest situation in which they find themselves have troubled the securities industry for some time.[141] The exception provided by Rule 14e-3(b) will resolve some, but by no means all, of those questions. The principal reason that Rule 14e-3(b) does not resolve all of the questions is that the exception applies only to the prohibition contained in Rule 14e-3(a). It does not apply to Rule 14e-3(d) or, for that matter, to any other obligation the firm may have under the federal securities laws or at common law. The discussion that follows, then, is an exploration of these other obligations with a view toward ascertaining their impact subsequent to the adoption of Rule 14e-3.

Duty to Maintain Confidences. Regardless of the existence of Rule 14e-3(a), multiservice securities firms have a duty to the source to prevent inside information about an issuer or a transaction that is obtained by one department of the firm from being spread to and misused by another department of the firm.[142] Less clear, however, is how this duty[143] is to be carried out in light of the coexisting duty of fair treatment that a multiservice securities firm owes to its retail clients.[144]

This duty of a broker to its customers was underscored in a common-law fraud context in *Black* v. *Shearson Hammill & Co.*[145] There a brokerage firm was held liable for recommending a security without disclosing adverse information that was in the firm's possession but that, because of its confidential nature, could not be publicly disclosed. In *Black,* the recommending account executive actually knew the undisclosed information—indeed, he was simultaneously liquidating his own positions in the security—and yet continued to recommend the stock. The court recognized the conflicting duties that brokerage firms face as a result of legitimate financial activities but stated that "brokerage customers should not be deprived of the 'traditional fraud standard' because [the broker] has chosen to occupy the dual role."

Black by no means answers the question of liability where the recommending broker does not, because of a Chinese wall or otherwise, know the information in question, at which point a very different set of issues arises. Indeed, the conduct of the broker in that case—making buy recommendations while at the same time selling for his own account—was willfully and egregiously contrary to his customer's interest. Acceptance of the result in *Black* as correct, then, has little bearing on the Chinese wall problem.

The issue was, however, posed directly in *Slade* v. *Shearson Hammill & Co.,*[146] where the plaintiffs alleged that Shearson, Hammill & Co. (Shearson) received, in its capacity as investment banker to Tidal Marine International (Tidal Marine), adverse nonpublic information about Tidal Marine, yet nonetheless allowed its salesmen to continue to promote the sale of Tidal Marine stock to its retail brokerage customers. In its motion for summary judgment, Shearson contended that its internal policies and procedures prohibited that firm's investment-banking department from releasing, or even discussing, any information about one of its investment-banking clients to members of the retail-sales organization and/or to the firm's public customers prior to public disclosure of the information.[147] Shearson also contended that, as a matter of law, the firm was precluded from using information obtained by its investment-banking department to prevent the solicitation of purchases by its retail-sales personnel until the information was made public.

In its opinion denying Shearson's motion, the district court quoted the Second Circuit's opinion in *Texas Gulf Sulphur* to the effect that:

> Anyone in possession of material inside information must either disclose it to the investing public, or, if he is disabled from disclosing it in order to protect a corporate confidence, or he chooses not to do so, must abstain from trading in or *recommending* the securities concerned while such inside information remains undisclosed.[148] [emphasis added by court]

The essence of the *Slade* decision, then, is that mere proof of the existence a Chinese wall, albeit effective, is insufficient to relieve a multiservice securities firm from liability under Rule 10b–5 to its retail customers for transactions that were solicited by the firm's retail-sales organization on the basis of information that the firm, as an institution, knew was incorrect.

The *Slade* district court decision was certified to the Second Circuit for review of the question of whether or not a brokerage firm that receives adverse material, nonpublic information about an investment-banking client is permitted to disregard that information and continue to recommend the securities of such client on the basis of public information.[149] The commission, in its *amicus* brief to the Second Circuit, took the position that, if a firm creates an effective Chinese wall that insulates the brokerage department from the special knowledge of the investment-banking department, the firm may, without violating Rule 10b-5, continue to effect retail-securities transactions in securities of the investment-banking client.[150] The brief also stated, however, that in those instances where the retail side of the securities firm is, or at least has been, making recommendations relating to the investment-banking client's securities, the Chinese wall must be supplemented with a restricted list.[151] The brief emphasized the need to implement the list in a manner that does not itself convey material information. To do this, the commission suggested that a security be placed on the list as soon as the investment banker entered into the arrangement with its client—and before any material information is received. Such a procedure would prevent the very act of adding the security to the list from becoming a tip.

Despite the commission's suggestion in its *Slade* brief that a restricted list was, or should be, required where the firm was recommending a security, it does not appear that the adoption of Rule 14e-3(b)(2) represents a retrenchment by the commission.[152] This is so because the issue presented in *Slade* v. *Shearson Hammill & Co.* was very different from one that would usually be posed under Rule 14e-3.

Unlike the situation in *Slade,* in the tender-offer context the critical information is the identity of the subject company. The subject company would not usually be the source of the information to the firm.[153] The placing of the subject company's name on a restricted list could not occur prior to the receipt of any material information. Placement of a nonclient's name on the list can therefore not be accomplished in the neutral fashion contemplated in the *Slade* brief. Sophisticated market watchers will not take long to deduce the reason for the addition of the subject company's name to the firm's restricted list. Thus, the placement of the subject company's name on the restricted list may very well run counter to the commission's admonition in its *Slade* brief that the list should not serve as a signal to the market that a tender offer is about to occur.[154]

Duties to Disclose. To understand further the nature of a broker-dealer's obligations in the Chinese-wall context, it is important to recognize the basis on which the courts and the commission have imposed upon broker-dealers certain affirmative duties of disclosure to investors. Under the so-called shingle theory, a broker-dealer implicitly represents that he will deal fairly with his customers in accordance with the standards and practices of the profession.[155] The broker-dealer's failure to live up to this implied representation constitutes a violation of Rule 10b-5 and, possibly, other antifraud provisions of the federal securities laws. Apart from, but related to, the shingle theory, broker-dealers under certain circumstances have fiduciary obligations to customers, and failure to disclose the abuse of these obligations may give rise to Rule 10b-5 liability.[156]

Both the shingle theory and the fiduciary theory have been applied in a number of different contexts to impose liability on a securities professional.[157] In addition to these obligations, broker-dealers, in recommending securities, implicitly represent that they have adequately and reasonably investigated the particular securities and must disclose facts they know and those that are reasonably ascertainable.[158] Also, under the suitability doctrine, a broker-dealer may recommend only those securities transactions that it reasonably believes are suitable in light of the customer's financial situation and needs.[159]

None of these various obligations, however, appears to give rise to any duty on the part of a broker to disclose to his customer material, nonpublic information known to investment bankers within his firm, on the other side of a properly constituted Chinese wall. Although there appears to be no judicial authority directly on point, the commission has rejected claims, asserted by a broker[160] and by investment advisers,[161] in defense to charges that they violated the antifraud provisions of the securities laws by selling securities for their clients on the basis of adverse, nonpublic information; that their fiduciary obligations to their clients required them to take such action; and that the failure to have taken such action would have subjected them to liability for breach of those obligations. This follows logically from the fact that the shingle theory permits the customer to demand only what he is reasonably entitled to expect.

In *Cady, Roberts,* the commission stated that, while the broker occupied a fiduciary relationship to his customers, "this relationship could not justify any actions by him contrary to law. Even if we assume the existence of conflicting fiduciary obligations, there can be no doubt which is primary here. On these facts, clients may not expect of a broker the benefits of his inside information at the expense of the public generally.[162] In *Investors Management,* the commission emphasized that "the obligations of a fiduciary do not include performing an illegal act. . . ."[163]

To be sure, a number of cases have imposed a heavy obligation on a brokerage firm to have a reasonable basis for its recommendations and to disclose to the customer who receives a recommendation any adverse information known to the firm.[164] Even here, however, there is little support for the no-recommendation policy advocated by the commission in *Slade.* In the best known of these cases, *Hanly* v. *SEC,*[165] the individuals making the recommendations were aware of adverse information they had withheld from their customers. More importantly, however, they were also aware that the information could have lawfully been disclosed.

In the final analysis, this question of obligation under Rule 10b–5 and its shingle-theory subset becomes one of reasonable expectation. A retail customer of a multiservice brokerage firm does not (or at least in contemplation of law should not) have an expectation that his brokerage firm will violate its legal obligation not to tip material, nonpublic information in order to meet his usual or general broker's obligation to his customer. The shingle theory's requirements that a broker make a reasonable investigation does not extend to breaching the Chinese wall.[166]

We are not aware of any commission actions against a broker-dealer that has obtained nonpublic information as a result of usual investment-banking activities and that has restricted the availability of that information while continuing to conduct investment-management or retail-brokerage activities. Where a Chinese wall is established, therefore, a broker should owe no duty to his customers to disclose nonpublic information known to the investment bankers on the other side of the wall. The disclosure of such information would be an illegal act that would benefit the customer at the expense of the public generally.[167] In terms of the customer's reasonable expectations, the shingle theory reasonably requires the broker to act only on the basis of all material information lawfully available to him—but not to gain access to information that need not otherwise be disclosed and is being entrusted confidentially to another part of the firm under a separate, equally compelling fiduciary relationship. The law can hardly be read to deem the broker to be representing to the client something he cannot legally deliver. Under a Chinese wall, the customer will be treated like the customers of firms without the separate insider contact as if that separate relationship were being carried out in a wholly different enterprise—and not be advantaged by the happenstance of access elsewhere in the firm to the private information. Neither theory nor practicality could suggest that a broker's implied representation of diligence and fair dealing demands any more than this.[168] Consequently, neither the shingle theory nor any of its variations provides a basis for attacking the legal viability of the Chinese wall.

Duties at Common Law. While the Chinese wall problem has not been directly faced outside the securities context, substantial underlying support for the views expressed in the previous section can be derived from fiduciary-law constructs in other fields. In agency and trust law, there has naturally been much discussion of the fiduciary's obligation of full disclosure and diligence in protecting the interests of his beneficiary. It is commonly said, for example, that an agent or trustee must use due care to ensure that his principal or beneficiary obtains the advantage of all material information reasonably available to him. Thus, in *Hazzard* v. *Chase National Banks* [287 N.Y.S. 2d 541 (Sup. Ct. 1936)] the court held that a bank trust department, which had substituted certain collateral held in trust, was liable for its breach when the substituted securities turned out to be worthless. The court found that one of the bank's commercial-department officers, who was on the board of directors of the debtor, knew that the securities were worthless and that, even though no communication had occurred between him and the trust department and he was not aware of the substitution, his knowledge was imputed to the bank as trustee.

At the same time, the law has established clearly articulated limits on this general fiduciary principle, limits that are of major significance to the Chinese wall problem. Section 381 of the *Restatement (Second) of Agency* recognizes the prevailing rule that:

> [U]nless otherwise agreed, an agent is subject to a duty to use reasonable efforts to give his principal information which is relevant to affairs entrusted to him and which, as the agent has notice, the principal would desire to have *and which can be communicated* without violating a superior duty to a third person. [emphasis added]

Comment (e) on the *Restatement* makes clear that "it is normally understood that [the agent] is not to communicate to the principal any information which he already has, or which he acquires during the performance of the agency, the disclosure of which to the principal would be a breach of duty to a third person, as when an attorney, having acquired confidential information from a client, is subsequently employed by another client to conduct a transaction in which the information is relevant."[169] This rule is the converse of the equally well-settled principle (codified in Section 395) that:

> [U]nless otherwise agreed, an agent is subject to a duty to the principal not to use or to communicate information confidentially given him by the principal or acquired by him during the course of or on account of his agency or in violation of his duties as agent, in competition with or to the injury of the principal, on his account or on behalf of another, although such information does not relate to the transaction in which he is then employed, unless the information is a matter of general knowledge.

Read together, then, Sections 381 and 395 reflect the widely held recognition by the courts that, as a practical matter, agents often serve multiple principals, and that the agent's duty to any one of those principals cannot extend so far as to require a breach of the duty of confidentiality owed to another. Nor, in the absence of an actual conflict of interest, is he required to refrain from acting on behalf of one principal or the other. Notably, the *Hazzard* case involved no claim that the information regarding the worthless securities was confidential; indeed, the court seemed to assume that the information was the sort that reasonably should have been available to the bank as trustee for the debtor's debenture holders.

These same principles carry over into the question of imputation of knowledge received by an agent. Section 281 of the *Restatement* provides:

> A principal is not affected by the knowledge of an agent who is privileged not to disclose or act upon it and who does not disclose or act upon it.

This reflects the universal agreement to the effect that "where an agent's duties to others prevent him from disclosing facts to the principal, the latter is not bound because of the agent's knowledge."[170]

The basic concept expressed in Sections 281, 381, and 395 and in the underlying case law shed some significant light on the proper scope of the fiduciary obligation in the Chinese wall situation. While most of the cases noted here deal with imputation of knowledge from agent to principal, the same rule logically applies to imputation of notice within a multiservice fiduciary entity. As we have seen, the principle rests on the idea that there ought be no obligation to convey information received in a separate confidential capacity, even if it would plainly be material to the beneficiary. It would be wholly inconsistent with this purpose to impute knowledge throughout the fiduciary entity—assuming the existence of a wall and no knowledge on the part of the trading or recommending person—when the imputed knowledge is of the sort to which the beneficiary is plainly not entitled. Consequently, these common-law principles, though never really reaching the difficult problems posed by the Chinese wall, by no means cast doubt on the legal efficacy of the wall. To the contrary, they suggest that a wall is a wholly proper way of separating the competing duties owed to differing clients in a multiservice situation.[171]

Summary. In sum, the policies and procedures exemplified by Chinese walls and restricted lists represented a practical business response to the potential liability of institutional trading while in possession of material, nonpublic information. Rule 14e–3(b) is based on this practical response and the case law under Rule 10b–5 and recognizes that, where properly implemented, these policies and procedures do not pose the abuse that Rule 14e–3(a) was intended to reach.

Other Exceptions

Rule 14e–3 provides two additional exceptions to the disclose-or-abstain-from-trading duty of Rule 14e–3(a). The first exception, Rule 14e–3(c)(1), recognizes that an offering person usually employs other persons, such as a dealer manager, to assist in the successful completion of a tender offer and that such other persons should not be liable for violations of Rule 14e–3(a) for actions in the course of their employment. The second exception, Rule 14e–3(c)(2), is designed to permit certain transactions, without triggering a violation of Rule 14e–3(a), in circumstances in which the potential for misuse of material, nonpublic information relating to a tender offer is negligible.

Rule 14e–3(c)(1) permits a person employed by the offering person to purchase securities of the subject company on behalf of the offering person without violating Rule 14e-3(a), even if the offering person has communicated material, nonpublic information relating to the tender offer to such person. The adopting release makes clear that this exception is intended to provide relief solely for an agent of, or other person employed by, the offering person for purchases in the course of his agency or employment on behalf of the offering person and does not alter any other provision of the federal securities laws affecting the ability of the offering person to make acquisitions of the securities of the subject company.[172] Hence, this exception should not be viewed as a method by which an offering person could consumate otherwise unlawful acquisitions.

Rule 14e-3(c)(2) provides that a sale of subject-company securities to the offering person by any person will not violate the duty imposed by Rule 14e-3(a), even if the selling person possesses material, nonpublic information relating to a tender offer. The adopting release indicates that this exception is intended to permit sales of subject-company securities to the offering person by certain insiders prior to the commencement of a tender offer and by persons who acquire material, nonpublic information during the course of a tender offer.[173]

*Prohibition on the Selective Communication of
Material, Nonpublic Information*

How Does the Duty Arise? Rule 14e-3(d) prohibits the practice of selective communication of material, nonpublic information relating to a tender offer. This practice is, of course, the analogue to the tipping of insider information under Rule 10b-5, a practice long held "equally reprehensible" to trading on the basis of material, inside information.[174] Under Rule 14e-3(d), it is unlawful for certain persons to communicate material, nonpublic information relating to a tender offer to any other person under circumstances in which it is reasonably foreseeable that such communication is likely to result in a violation of Rule 14e-3. The persons subject to the proscription on communication are the offering person; the issuer; an officer, director, partner, employee, or any other person acting on behalf of the offering person or the issuer; or any person who is a tippee of one of these persons enumerated.

A violation of Rule 14e-3(d) requires two elements. First, the person must possess material, nonpublic information relating to a tender offer. Such information can be created by that person—for example, the offering person or the issuer—or it may have been acquired from the offering person or the issuer or from a person who is in the informational chain stretching from the offering person or the issuer.[175] Second, the person tips the information to another person. Under Rule 14e-3(d), tipping occurs when a person selectively communicates the material, nonpublic information under circumstances where it is reasonably foreseeable that the communication is likely to result in a violation of Rule 14e-3.[176] In this manner, Rule 14e-3(d) reaches intermediate tippees, regardless of whether they trade on the basis of the information, if such intermediate tippee knows or has reason to know the information is nonpublic and knows or has reason to know the information has been acquired directly or indirectly from the offering person, the issuer, or any director, officer, partner, employee, or any other person acting on behalf of either of them.

Under Rule 10b-5, a corporate insider can be held liable for a violation of Rule 10b-5 for communicating material, inside information to persons who then traded.[177] Moreover, persons with a duty to speak or to abstain from trading on material, inside information will be held liable for violating Rule 10b-5, regardless of whether such persons trade on the information, if they divulge confidential, material, inside information to other persons who then trade on the information.[178] In addition to the circumstances that inside information has been revealed to someone who takes advantage of this superior knowledge by trading in the company's stock, the prerequisites of tipping liability are that the tipped information must be material and that the tipper must have acted with scienter.[179]

With respect to tipping liability under Rule 10b-5, materiality has usually been assessed under the standard set forth by the Supreme Court in *Northway*.[180] Several courts also have found a lack of materiality in the reaction of those who were exposed to the inside information.[181]

The prohibition in Rule 14e-3(d) is, of course, similar to Rule 10b-5's common-law proscription on tipping. Since the standard of materiality in *Northway* has been applied in a number of Section 14(e) cases, it seems probable that this standard would be applied for tipping liability under both Rule 14e-3(d) and Rule 10b-5. The proscription on selective communication under Rule 14e-3(d) and Rule 10b-5 is also similar in that it must be reasonably foreseeable that the person who receives the information will use it to his advantage.

There are, however, at least two significant differences between Rule 14e-3(d) and Rule 10b-5. First, Rule 14e-3(d) is somewhat broader than Rule 10b-5. It does not, for example, require, as does Rule 10b-5, that the tippee actually trade on the information. All that is necessary to incur liability under Rule 14e-3(d) is that the tip be made under circumstances in which it is reasonably foreseeable that it (the communication) is likely to result in a violation of Rule 14e-3. Also, of course, the violation can occur in the form of either a trade or a secondary tip by the tippee. Second, Rule 14e-3(d) does not impose a scienter requirement as does Rule 10b-5. A tipper need not know that the tippee will use the information to his advantage. The only necessary test under Rule 14e-3(d) is reasonable foreseeability under the circumstances.

Defenses. Under Rule 14e-3(d), the proscription on selective communication will not apply to communications by any offering person, issuer, or person acting on either's behalf made in good faith to persons involved in the planning, financing, preparation, or execution of the tender offer or to any person pursuant to a requirement of any statute or rule or regulation promulgated thereunder.[183] The adopting release states that this exception was provided in order that Rule 14e-3(d) would not hinder tender-offer practice or expose the offering person and the issuer to an unwarranted litigation hazard.[184] The release also states that the good-faith standard is critical to the exception and that the person seeking the availability of the exception must establish good faith.[185]

Again, comparison with Rule 10b-5 puts those defenses into better perspective. Under Rule 10b-5, a defense to tipping liability is usually directed to the lack of materiality of the information conveyed[186] or the absence of scienter on the part of the tipper.[187] The existence of an arguably valid business purpose for disclosure will usually be deemed by courts to be strong evidence that the tipper did not act with scienter[188]; however, it has been suggested that even a disclosure for a corporate purpose could amount to illegal tipping if the person knows that the recipient will use the information for personal purposes in the market.[189]

Conclusion

Chiarella and Rule 14e-3 represent different approaches to the same problem—that is, trading while in possession of material, nonpublic information relating to a tender offer. While *Chiarella* represents an unsuccessful attempt to extend the reach of a general rule under a catchall antifraud section, Rule 14e-3 is a provision predicated on an antifraud provision, directed only to tender offers, that specifically creates a duty with respect to material, nonpublic information.

The specificity in the duties enumerated by Rule 14e-3(a) and (d) necessitated specific exceptions under rule 14e-3(b), (c), and (d) in order that the proscribed conduct would embrace only abusive conduct in tender-offer practice. Such specificity in an antifraud rule constitutes a new rulemaking approach, one that is designed to provide clarity to an area that was uncertain, while promoting investor protection where abuses were ongoing and increasing.

The future of this specific response will be determined both by judicial interpretation and by the response of the investment community. Judicial interpretation is particularly needed with respect to the application of both Section 14(e) and Rule 14e-3 to the precommencement period. The response of the investment community with respect to the creation and maintenance of policies and procedures such as Chinese walls and restricted lists will determine whether Rule 14e-3 is a sufficient response or merely the first step in addressing the problem of insider trading in the context of tender offers.

Notes

1. Section 10(b) of the Securities Exchange Act of 1934 reads as follows:

> It shall be unlawful for any person, directly or indirectly, by the use of any means or instrumentality of interstate commerce or of the mails, or of any facility of any national securities exchange
>
> (b) To use or employ, in connection with the purchase or sale of any security registered on a national securities exchange or any security not so registered, any manipulative or deceptive device or contrivance in contravention of such rules and regulations as the commission may prescribe as necessary or appropriate in the public interest or for the protection of investors.

2. Rule 10b-5 (17 CFR 240.10b-5), adopted by the commission in 1942, states that it shall be unlawful for any person, directly or indirectly, by the use of any means or instrumentality or interstate commerce, or of the mails, or of any facility of any national securities exchange, (a) to employ any device, scheme, or artifice to defraud; (b) to make any untrue statement of a material fact or to omit to state a material fact necessary in order to make the statements made, in light of the circumstances under which they were made, not misleading; or (c) to engage in any act, practice, or course of business which operates or would operate as a fraud or deceit upon any person, in connection with the purchase or sale of any security. Rule 10b-5 is unusual among the 10b series of rules. Except for Rule 10b-5, the 10b series is quite narrow, dealing, for example, with highly technical securities-market matters such as short tendering (Rule 10b-4) or stabilization during a public offering (Rule 10b-7). Rule 10b-5 is so general that it has been difficult to articulate its outer parameters. Indeed, until 1975, it often seemed even at the Supreme Court level that there were none. See, for example, *Superintendent of Insurance of the State of New York* v. *Bankers Life & Casualty Co.,* 404 U.S. 6 (1971). Beginning, however, with the Court's decision in *Blue Chip Stamps* v. *Manor Drug Stores,* 421 U.S. 723 (1975), the Court, in a series of cases, has delineated a less-expansive scope to Rule 10b-5. See also *Ernst & Ernst* v. *Hochfelder,* 425 U.S. 185 (1976); and *Santa Fe Industries, Inc.* v. *Green,* 430 U.S. 462 (1977).

3. The theory of the federal securities laws in general and Section

10(b) in particular is disclosure. However, disclosure is a powerful tool that, more often than not, is designed to have an effect on normative conduct. Thus, the disclose-or-abstain-from-trading rule enunciated by the Second Circuit in *SEC* v. *Texas Gulf Sulphur Co.,* 401 F.2d 833 (2d Cir. 1968), *cert. denied sub nom. Coates* v. *SEC,* 394 U.S. 976 (1969), is designed not so much to produce disclosure as it is to deter trading by insiders. At one point in its development, Rule 10b-5 was considered to cover even failures to disclose overreaching and breach of the duty of loyalty by corporate management. *Green* v. *Santa Fe Industries, Inc.,* 533 F.2d 1283 (2d Cir. 1976), *reversed,* 430 U.S. 462 (1977).

4. 69 F. Supp. 512 (E.D. Pa. 1946). Recent Supreme Court cases, for the most part, have denied the existence of private rights of action. See, for example, *Touche Ross & Co.* v. *Redington,* 442 U.S. 560 (1979). It is interesting to consider how the jurisprudence of Rule 10b-5 would have developed had the issue of whether Section 10(b) contained a private right of action been decided in the negative.

5. In 1966, Rule 23 of the Federal Rules was amended to include an opt-out provision, which precluded any member of the judicially designated class from litigating his own claim outside the class action unless he affirmatively notified the court of his intention to opt out of the proceeding. For background on the 1966 amendments, see Advisory Committee on Civil Rules, Proposed Rules of Civil Procedure, 39 F.R. D. 69, 95–107 (1966). Recent cases have, by imposing substantial individual notice requirements, rendered federal class actions far less useful to plaintiffs than they once were. See *Coopers & Lybrand* v. *Livesay,* 437 U.S. 463 (1978); *Oppenheimer Fund, Inc.* v. *Sanders,* 437 U.S. 340 (1978); *Eisen* v. *Carlisle & Jacqueline,* 417 U.S. 156 (1974).

6. See, for example, Ruder, *Current Problems in Corporate Disclosure,* 30 Bus. Law 1081 (1975); Bromberg, *Are There Limits to Rule 10b-5,* 29 Bus. Law 167 (1974).

7. *Texas Gulf Sulphur,* 401 F.2d at 848.

8. See, for example, Mundheim & Fleischer, *Corporate Acquisition by Tender Offer,* 115 U. Pa. L. Rev. 317 (1967).

9. Pub. L. No. 90–439, 82 Stat. 455 (1968).

10. As originally enacted, the Williams Act had a 10 percent beneficial-ownership threshold. The threshold was reduced to 5 percent by Pub. L. No. 91–567, §3, 84 Stat. 1497 (1970).

11. See *infra* note 39.

12. See *supra* note 10.

13. See Rule 14d-3 (17 CFR 240.14d-3).

14. See Leiman, *Recent Developments in Takeovers,* in PLI, Eighth Annual Institute on Securities Regulation 207 (Mundheim, Fleischer, and Vandegrift, eds. 1977).

15. See "SEC Cracking Down on Trading by Insiders," *The New York Times,* 7 March 1980, p. D-1.

16. 445 U.S. 222 (1980).

17. Brudney, *Insiders, Outsiders, and Informational Advantages under the Federal Securities Laws,* 93 Harv. L. Rev. 323, 354 (1979). Professor Brudney has developed the theory that the essential "element which makes an informational advantage [that is, material, nonpublic information] unusable by those who possess it in dealing with those who do not is the inability of the latter to overcome it lawfully, no matter how great may be their diligence or large their resources."

18. A parity-of-information rule would require that *all* material information, corporate or market, inside or outside, be disclosed prior to any purchase or sale of a security. No court has ever held that such a rule is required. One commentator has come close to saying so. See Bauman, *Rule 10b-5 and the Corporation's Affirmative Duty to Disclose,* 67 Geo. L. J. 935 (1979).

19. Brudney, *supra* note 17 at 361-363.

20. In February 1979, the commission proposed, as its answer to pre-tender-offer trading, Rule 14e-2. If adopted, that proposed rule would have required a bidder that had determined to make a tender offer and any person who learned, directly or indirectly from the bidder, of that determination to disclose that information prior to accomplishing any trading in the target company's stock. See Release No. 34-15548 (15 February 1979) (44 FR 9956).

21. 40 S.E.C. 907 (1961).

22. 445 U.S. at 227.

23. *Id.* at 227, quoting *Cady, Roberts,* 40 S.E.C. at 911.

24. 445 U.S. at 228, citing Restatement (Second) of Torts §551(2)(a) (1976).

25. This point is true whether the insider buys (from an existing shareholder) or sells (to a nonshareholder). Either way, the abuse of the duty created by the existence of the relationship is clear. Interpositioning of a corporate entity does not dilute; rather, it serves to enhance the existence of this duty. See Fleischer, Mundheim, and Murphy, *An Initial Inquiry into the Obligation to Disclose Market Information,* 121 U. Pa. L. Rev. 798 (1973). For a discussion of the U.S. common-law cases, see Cary and Eisenberg, *Cases and Materials on Corporations,* 714 (1980).

26. Compare *SEC* v. *Hall,* No. 80-0504, filed 22 February 1980 (D.D.C.), Lit. Rel. No. 9013.

27. Compare *Frigitemp Corp.* v. *Financial Dynamics Fund, Inc.,* 524 F.2d 275 (2d Cir. 1975); *Mills* v. *Sarjem Corp.,* 133 F. Supp. 753 (D.N.J. 1955).

28. "[T]he duty arose from . . . the existence of a relationship afford-

ing access to inside information intended to be available only for a corporate purpose." 445 U.S. at 227.

29. *Zweig* v. *Hearst Corp.,* 594 F.2d 1261 (9th Cir. 1979).

30. See *Chasins* v. *Smith Barney & Co.,* 438 F.2d 1167 (2d Cir. 1970); *Charles Hughes & Co., Inc.* v. *SEC,* 139 F.2d 434 (2d Cir. 1943); *Arleen W. Hughes,* 27 S.E.C. 629 (1948). See also Release No. 34–13662 (23 June 1977) (42 FR 31810); Wolfson; Phillips; and Russo, *Regulation of Brokers, Dealers and Securities Markets,* §2.03 (1977).

31. *Affiliated Ute Citizens* v. *U.S.,* 406 U.S. 128 (1972).

32. The rule proposal outstanding at the time of the *Chiarella* decision was actually the second proposal dealing with the use of material, nonpublic information relating to a tender offer. In February 1979, the commission had proposed a somewhat different rule in conjunction with a whole series of tender-offer-disclosure rules. See *supra* note 20. See also Release No. 34–15584 (the February proposal). This February proposal would have applied to any person in possession of nonpublic information, received directly or indirectly from a bidder, that the bidder would make a tender offer for the securities of another company. The proposed rule would have proscribed any purchase of subject-company securities unless prior to purchase the purchaser publicly announced the information received and its source. It would also have required a bidder who knew or had violated, or was about to violate, the rule promptly to make an appropriate public announcement of the information.

33. Rule 14e–3 (17 CFR 240.14e–3) provides:

(a) If any person has taken a substantial step or steps to commence, or has commenced, a tender offer (the "offering person"), it shall constitute a fraudulent, deceptive, or manipulative act or practice within the meaning of section 14(e) of the Act for any other person who is in possession of material information relating to such tender offer, which information he knows or has reason to know is nonpublic and which he knows or has reason to know has been acquired directly or indirectly from (1) the offering person, (2) the issuer of the securities sought or to be sought by such tender offer, or (3) any officer, director, partner or employee or any other person acting on behalf of the offering person or such issuer, to purchase or sell or cause to be purchased or sold any of such securities or any securities convertible into or exchangeable for any such securities or any option or right to obtain or to dispose of any of the foregoing securities, unless within a reasonable time prior to any purchase or sale such information and its source are publicly disclosed by press release or otherwise.

(b) A person other than a natural person shall not violate paragraph (a) of this section if such person shows that:

(1) The individual(s) making the investment decision on behalf of such person to purchase or sell any security described in paragraph (a) or to cause any such security to be purchased or

sold by or on behalf of others who did not know the material, nonpublic information; and

(2) Such person had implemented one or a combination of policies and procedures, reasonable under the circumstances, taking into consideration the nature of the person's business, to ensure that individual(s) making investment decision(s) would not violate paragraph (a), which policies and procedures may include, but are not limited to, (i) those which restrict any purchase, sale and causing any purchase and sale of any such security or (ii) those which prevent such individual(s) from knowing such information.

(c) Notwithstanding anything in paragraph (a) to the contrary, the following transactions shall be violations of paragraph (a) of this section:

(1) Purchase(s) of any security described in paragraph (a) by a broker or by another agent on behalf of an offering person; or

(2) Sale(s) by any person of any security described in paragraph (a) to the offering person.

(d) (1) As a means reasonably designed to prevent fraudulent, deceptive, or manipulative acts or practices within the meaning of Section 14(e) of the Act, it shall be unlawful for any person described in paragraph (d)(2) of this section to communicate material, nonpublic information relating to a tender offer to any other person under circumstances in which it is reasonably foreseeable that such communication is likely to result in a violation of this section *except* that this paragraph shall not apply to communication made in good faith,

(i) To the officers, directors, partners, or employees of the offering person, to its advisors or to other persons involved in the planning, financing, preparation, or execution of such tender offer;

(ii) To the issuer whose securities are sought or to be sought by such tender offer, to its officers, directors, partners, employees, or advisors or to other persons involved in the planning, financing, preparation, or execution of the activities of the issuer with respect to such tender offer; or

(iii) To any person pursuant to a requirement of any statute or rule or regulation promulgated thereunder.

(d)(2) The persons referred to in paragraph (d)(1) of this section are:

(i) The offering person or its officers, directors, partners, employees, or advisors;

(ii) The issuer of the securities sought or to be sought by such tender offer or its officers, directors, partners, employees, or advisors;

(iii) Anyone acting on behalf of the persons in paragraph (d)(2)(i) or the issuer or persons in paragraph (d)(2)(ii); and

(iv) Any person in possession of material information relating to a tender offer, which information he knows or has reason to know is nonpublic and which he knows or has reason to know has been acquired directly or indirectly from any of the above.

34. There also remains the intriguing question of the so-called lost theory of *Chiarella*. In both the Second Circuit and the Supreme Court, the government argued that the printshop worker had "breached a duty to the acquiring corporation when he acted upon information that he obtained by virtue of his position as an employee of a printer employed by the corporation." The government urged that such a breach of duty would support a finding that Rule 10b-5 had been violated. The Supreme Court did not disagree. Justice Powell's majority opinion simply refused to consider this "misappropriation theory." In the majority's view, the district court had failed to submit this issue to the jury.

Thus, the question of whether a breach by misappropriation is actionable under Rule 10b-5 remains extant even under present law. If the American Law Institute's Federal Securities Code is enacted, the commission will have the authority to proscribe such conduct, even by outsiders. ALI Fed. Sec. Code §1602. In the meantime, however, any proscription relating to informational advantages gained, in the context of a tender offer, by a non-insider of the subject company must rest on the commission's recently adopted Rule 14e-3, if the non-insider was not the tippee of the insider and had no other fiduciary duty to disclose the information. See *United States* v. *Newman*, [CURRENT BINDER] (CCH) *Fed. Sec. L. Rep.* ¶98,332 (2d Cir. 30 October 1981).

35. Rule 14e-3 was proposed and adopted pursuant to Section 23(a) as well as Section 14(e). See, respectively, Release No. 34-16385 (29 November 1979) (44 FR 70349) and 324-17120 (4 September 1980) (45 FR 60410). Section 23(a)(1) authorizes the commission "to make such rules and regulations as may be necessary or appropriate to implement the provisions of this title for which [it is] responsible or for the execution of the functions vested in [it] by this title. . . ." The commission is granted similar rulemaking powers in each of other federal securities laws. See, for example, Section 19 of the Securities Act of 1933; Section 20 of the Public Utility Holding Company Act of 1935; Section 319 of the Trust Indenture Act of 1939; Section 38 of the Investment Company Act of 1940; and Section 211 of the Investment Advisers Act of 1940. In construing a statute similar to Section 23(a), the Supreme Court stated that a duly promulgated agency regulation will be sustained as long as it is "reasonably related to the purposes of the enabling legislation." *Mourning* v. *Family Publications Services, Inc.*, 411 U.S. 356 (1973), quoting from *Thorpe* v. *Housing Authority of the City of Durham*, 393 U.S. 269, 280-281 (1969). While Section 23(a) would allow the commission to adopt rules where no express statutory authority exists, it

has been used to bolster rule making that is also promulgated pursuant to specific statutory authority. See, for example, Rules 13e-3 and 13e-4, and Release Nos. 34-16075 (8 August 1979) (44 FR 46736) and 34-16112 (22 August 1979) (44 FR 48406). In upholding the validity of Rule 2(e) promulgated pursuant to Section 23(a), the Second Circuit in *Touche Ross & Co.* v. *SEC,* 609 F.2d 570 (2d Cir. 1979) followed the analysis in *Mourning.* Apparently, the commission believes that Section 23(a) is separate and that specific grants are not subsumed within or rendered redundant by the general provisions of Section 23(a)(1).

36. While this phrase has been viewed by courts—see, for example, *Electronic Specialty Co.* v. *International Controls Corp.,* 409 F.2d 937 (2d Cir. 1969)—and commentators—see, for example, Aranow & Einhorn, *Tender Offers for Corporate Control,* 117-121, (1973)—as broadening standing in tender offers beyond that provided in Section 10(b) of the Exchange Act, it also pertains to the existence of a right of action. The issue of standing is sometimes merged with the analysis of the existence of a cause of action. See *Applied Digital Data Systems* v. *Milgo Electronics,* 425 F. Supp. 1153 n.20 (S.D.N.Y. 1977).

37. While the term *tender offer* is not defined in the Williams Act, its legislative history, or any adopted rule thereunder, courts have formulated definitions that apply to unconventional as well as conventional offers—see, for example, *Wellman* v. *Dickinson,* 475 F. Supp. 783 (S.D.N.Y. 1979) and *The Hoover Co.* v. *Fuqua Ind. Inc.,* [1979-1980 Transfer Binder] Fed. Sec. L. Rep. (CCH) ¶97, 107 (N.D. Ohio 1979)—and the commission has proposed a definition of the term that, if adopted, would be applicable to the Williams Act and to Regulations 14D and 14E thereunder (Release No. 34-16385).

38. Although Section 14(e) does not specify jurisdictional means—for example, mails or the means or instrumentalities of interstate commerce or the facilities of a national securities exchange—see, for example, Bromberg, *The Securities Law of Tender Offers,* 15 N.Y.L.F. 459, 474 (1969)—the commission's position is the jurisdiction means are implicit in the statute. See Memorandum of Law of the Securities Exchange Commission, *amicus curiae, Brascan Limited* v. *Edper Equities Ltd.,* 477 F. Supp. 733 (S.D.N.Y. 1979). Any difficulty may be overcome by an allegation and proof of the use of the mails or interstate facilities or registration of subject-company securities. See Bromberg, *supra* at 474, n. 72, citing 6 Loss, *Securities Regulation* 3661 (2d ed. 1961).

39. Section 14(e) has been applied to third-party tender offers, not subject to regulation by Section 14(d). See, for example, *Butler Aviation Int'l. Inc.* v. *Comprehensive Designers Inc.,* 307 F. Supp. 910 (S.D.N.Y. 1969) affirmed, 425 F.2d 842 (2d Cir. 1970) [cause of action under Section 14(e) in an exchange offer although such offers were exempt at that time

from Section 14(d)(1)]; *Jack Smith* v. *The Newport National Bank,* 326 F.
Supp. 874 (D.R.I. 1971) (tender offer for securities of a national bank);
Weeks Dredging & Contracting Inc. v. *American Dredging Co.,* 451 F.
Supp. 469 (E.D. Pa. 1978); *A & K Railroad Materials Inc.* v. *Green Bay and
Western Railroad,* 437 F. Supp. 636 (E.D. Wis. 1977) [classes of securities
were not registered pursuant to Section 12 nor were the issuers subject to the
periodic reporting requirements of Section 15(d)]. Section 14(e) applies to
issuer offers as well as to third-party offers. See, for example, *Bertozzi* v.
King Louie International, 420 F. Supp. 1166 (D.R.I. 1976). While Section
14(d)(1) sets forth a 5 percent amount, Section 14(e) has no percentage
figure. One commentator has conjectured that the difference between Sections 14(d) and 14(e) may be attributable simply to Congress's recognition
of commission's workload and its traditional preoccupation among issuers
with those listed on exchanges or traded over the counter. Bromberg, *supra*
note 20 at 536. See also Section 14(d)(8), which exempts certain tender offers from Section 14(d) and provides exemptive authority to the commission.

40. 360 F.2d 692 (2d Cir. 1966), citing *SEC* v. *Okin,* 132 F.2d 784 (2d
Cir. 1943).

41. *SEC* v. *Okin,* 132 F.2d at 786.

42. 132 F.2d at 786.

43. *Id.*

44. See, for example, 113 Cong. Rec. 24664 (1967); H.R. Rep. No.
1711, 90th Cong., 2d Sess. 3 (1968). As Chairman Cohen explained in the
Senate Hearings on the bill that became the Williams Act:

> [T]he procedures provided by the bill in the case of contested tender offers are
> analogous to those now followed when contending factions solicit proxies under the
> commission's proxy rules.

Senate Committee on Banking and Currency, Hearings before the Subcommittee on Securities on S.510, 90th Cong., 1st Sess. 20–21 (1967). See also
Senate Hearings at 30 and 178.

45. But compare *Piper* v. *Chris-Craft,* 430 U.S. 1 (1977) (Court rejected analogy to standing in proxies in holding that defeated bidder did not
have standing in a damage action).

46. *Applied Digital,* 425 F. Supp at 1153, citing *Kogan* v. *National
Bank of North America,* 402 F. Supp. 359, 361 (E.D.N.Y. 1975); *Pepsico
Inc.* v. *W.R. Grace & Co.,* 307 F. Supp. 713, 720 (S.D.N.Y. 1960).

47. S. Rep. No. 550, 90th Cong., 1st Sess. 10–11 (1967); H.R. Rep.
No. 1711, *supra* note at 11.

48. See Senate Hearings, *supra* note 44 at 12 *et passim* (testimony of
Manual F. Cohen).

49. S. Rep. No. 550, 90th Cong., 1st Sess. 2 (1967); H.R. Rep. No.
1711, *supra* note 44 at 2.

50. The Supreme Court has only spoken in general terms. In *Piper* v.

Chris-Craft, the Court stated that "the sole purpose of the Williams Act was the protection of investors who are confronted with a tender offer." 430 U.S. at 35. However, *Piper* was not involved with precommencement activities but rather the standing of a defeated bidder in a damage action against the subject company and others for their activities during the postcommencement period. In *Rondeau* v. *Mosinee Paper Corp.,* 422 U.S. 49 (1975), a case involving the beneficial ownership filing requirements of Section 13(d), the Court viewed the purpose of the Williams Act as ensuring "that public shareholders who are confronted by a cash tender offer for their stock will not be required to respond without adequate information." *Id.* at 58. But again, *Rondeau* did not involve the precommencement period of a tender offer.

51. 69 Civ. 209 (S.D.N.Y. 29 December 1969).

52. *Id.* at 4.

53. *Levine* v. *Seilon, Inc.,* 439 F.2d 328, 335 (2d Cir. 1971).

54. [1973-1974 Transfer Binder] Fed. Sec. L. Rep. (CCH) ¶94,585 (S.D.N.Y. 1974).

55. *Id.* at 96,048.

56. 411 F. Supp. 1208 (S.D.N.Y. 1975).

57. 425 F. Supp. 1145 (S.D.N.Y. 1977).

58. *Id.* at 1154.

59. *Id.* at 1153.

60. *Id.* at 1154.

61. 459 F. Supp. 597 (S.D.N.Y. 1978).

62. *Id.* at 608.

63. *Lewis* v. *McGraw,* 495 F. Supp. 27, 30 (S.D.N.Y. 1979).

64. See Release No. 34-16385 (44 FR 70349) in which the commission, in proposing a definition of the term *tender offer,* states that mergers are not tender offers within the meaning of the proposed definition. 44 FR at 70352.

65. 454 F. Supp. 1310 (W.D. Mich. 1978).

66. 495 F. Supp. 27 (S.D.N.Y. 1979), *affirmed per curiam* 619 F.2d 192 (2d Cir. 1980), *cert. denied,* 101 S. Ct. 354 (1980).

67. [1979-1980 Transfer Binder] Fed. Sec. L. Rep. (CCH) ¶97,299 (N.D. Ill. 1980), *affirmed,* Nos. 80-1375, 80-1389 (7th Cir. 2 April 1981).

68. 454 F. Supp. at 1318 (citations omitted).

69. The court analyzed causation in terms of materiality or reliance:

The inquiry as to materiality in the tender-offer context is whether there exists a substantial likelihood that a reasonable shareholder would consider a particular fact important in deciding what to do with his stock. . . . The element of reliance essentially concerns whether the misrepresentation or omission actually induced the plaintiff himself to act differently than he would have acted in his investment decision.

Id. at 1324.

70. *Id.* at 1325 (citations omitted).

71. 619 F.2d 192 (2d Cir. 1980).

72. *Id.* at 195.

73. While the district court had dismissed on these grounds, it had first held that the complaint sufficiently alleged deception "in connection with a tender offer" because "the prospective offeror had made a public announcement of a proposed tender offer and [plaintiff had alleged] a clear and definite intent to make a tender offer." *Lewis* v. *McGraw,* 495 F. Supp at 30. Moreover, the district court refused to limit Section 14(e) to only injunctive actions or to preclude damage action for pre-tender-offer violations where no tender offer ever occurs. Such a limitation on damage actions would effectively safe-harbor incumbent managment that successfully thwarts unwanted tender offers by deception. *Id.*

74. *Lewis* v. *McGraw,* 619 F.2d at 195.

75. Nos. 80–1375 and 80–1389 (7th Cir. 2 April 1981).

76. Under this theory, damages would have exceeded $200 million. *Id.* at 14.

77. *Id.* at 17, citing *Santa Fe Industries* v. *Green,* 430 U.S. 462 (1977).

78. *Id.*

79. *Id.* at 20.

80. *Id.* at 14.

81. *Id.* at 67–71.

82. *Id.* at 68.

83. As the dissent states:

A shareholder, who in the face of a proposed tender offer elects not to sell into the market in reliance on managment's misleading statements, is in a position similar to that of a shareholder who elects not to tender to the bidder in reliance upon such statements. Congress clearly protected the latter as well as, I believe, the former.

Id. at 70–71.

84. *Id.* at 70.

85. The holding in *Marshall Field,* which expands *Lewis* to apply to the decision to sell into the market, poses troublesome questions concerning the scope of Section 14(e). In the authors' view, the holding is inconsistent with prior case law, particularly *Applied Digital* and *Berman;* does not reflect the economic realities of the tender offer process, which is a continuum of events not limited by the formal commencement of a tender offer; and is contrary to the investor protection purposes of the Williams Act.

86. See Release No. 34–17120, 45 FR at 60413, n. 33, for a discussion of the phrase "substantial step or steps to commence a tender offer."

87. See, for example, Senate Hearings, *supra* note 44 at 69 *et passim;* Hearings on H.R. 14475 and S.510 before the Subcommittee on Commerce and Finance of the House Committee on Interstate and Foreign Commerce, 90th Cong., 2d Sess. 43 *et passim* (1968).

88. Section 2(2) of S.510 as introduced in the Senate on 18 January 1967 contained a five-day advance-filing requirement for any person making a tender offer subject to that subsection. The requirement was not included in the Williams Act. See S. Rep. No. 550, *supra* note 47 at 4.

89. Senate Hearings, *supra* note 44 at 72.

90. Senate Hearings, *supra* note 44 at 74.

91. Senate Committee on Banking and Currency, Hearing before the Subcommittee on Securities, "Problems in the Securities Industry," 91st Cong., 1st Sess. (1969).

92. *Id.* at 15.

93. 116 Cong. Rec. 3034 (1970).

94. *Id.*

95. Hearings on S.3431 before the Subcommittee on Securities of the Senate Committee on Banking and Currency, 91st Cong., 2d Sess. 2 (1970).

96. *Id.* at 10.

97. *Id.* at 12.

98. Similar definitional power has been used in other areas to proscribe conduct that was not violative of the common law. See, for example, Rules 10b-6 and 10b-13, which were promulgated pursuant to Section 10(b) of the Exchange Act.

99. Warehousing is the practice of a bidder informing institutional investors of material, nonpublic information relating to a tender offer, such as the bidder's intention to make the offer. The institutions are able to take positions in the subject company's securities in return for the assurance to the bidder that they will tender to the bidder in the forthcoming tender offer. The institutions benefit in that they are able to purchase securities at the lower market price, as yet unaffected by the impending offer, and the bidder benefits by assuring itself that large quantities of the securities to be sought will be held in friendly hands until commencement and will be tendered to the bidder.

100. *Institutional Investor Study Report of the Securities and Exchange Commission,* H.R. Doc. No. 92-64, 92nd Cong., 1st Sess. XXXIII (Comm. Print 1971). The study concluded that warehousing should be dealt with by new rules rather than under Rule 10b-5.

101. See *supra* notes 94 and 95 and accompanying text.

102. These effects include disparities in market information and market disruption. Moreover, leaks may lead to the same stampede effect the Williams Act was designed to avert in the context of tender offers. *Rondeau* v. *Mosinee Paper Co.,* 422 U.S. at 58 n. 8; See Release No. 34-17120, 45 FR at 60412; 34-15548, 45 FR at 9977.

103. See Release No. 34-16385, 44 FR at 70354.

104. See *infra* notes 107-108 and accompanying text.

105. Pub. L. No. 719, §15, 48 Stat. 895 (1934).

106. The former provision of Section 15(c) became Section 15(c)(1) under the 1938 amendments. See H.R. Rep. No. 2307, 75th Cong., 3d Sess. 10 (1938).

107. Section 15(c)(2) of the Exchange Act states

> No broker or dealer shall make use of the mails or any means or instrumentality of interstate commerce to effect any transaction in, or to induce or attempt to induce the purchase or sale of, any security (other than an exempted security or commercial paper, bankers' acceptances, or commercial bills) otherwise than on a national securities exchange of which it is a member, in connection with which such broker or dealer engages in any fraudulent, deceptive, or manipulative act or practice, or makes any fictitious quotation, and no municipal securities dealer shall make use of the mails or any means or instrumentality of interstate commerce to effect any transaction in, or to induce or attempt to induce the purchase or sale of, any municipal security in connection with which such municipal securities dealer engages in any fraudulent, deceptive, or manipulative act or practice, or makes any fictitious quotation. The commission shall, for the purposes of this paragraph, by rules and regulations define, and prescribe means reasonably designed to prevent, such acts and practices as are fraudulent, deceptive, or manipulative and such quotations as are fictitious.

108. H.R. Rep. No. 2307, *supra* note 106 at 11.

109. See *supra* note 91.

110. Rule 14e-3(a).

111. See discussion *infra* at 136.

112. The discussion of the case law under Section 10(b) and Rule 10b-5 is not intended to be a comprehensive examination of insider trading and tipping under Section 10(b) and Rule 10b-5 but is set forth solely for comparison purposes. For a more comprehensive analysis of the case law under Section 10(b) and Rule 10b-5, see Bauman, *supra* note 18; Brudney, *supra* note 17; Fleisher; Mundheim; and Murphy, *supra* note 18.

113. The rule refers to such person as an "offering person" and this chapter uses that term to refer to such person.

114. 40 S.E.C. at 912-917.

115. 426 U.S. 438 (1976).

116. *Id.* at 449.

117. American Law Institute, Proposed Federal Securities Code, §202(56), Comment 1 (1980).

118. *Id.*, §1603(a). Other tests have been enumerated in insider-trading cases. The best known among these are the probability-magnitude and market-impact tests. The probability-magnitude test weighs the likelihood

that an event will occur against the magnitude of its impact if it should occur. The market-impact test weighs the actual impact on the market of disclosure of the information in question. But, as the SEC itself said in a recent
administrative proceeding "these test are . . . merely serviceable, objective
methods for making the factual determination mandated by *Northway,* and
they have been regularly employed since *Texas Gulf Sulphur. Northway* did
not disapprove these tests, and courts have continued to use them." *In the
Matter of Raymond L. Dirks,* 21 SEC Docket 1401, 1408 n. 32 (22 January
1981), *citing SEC* v. *Mize,* 615 F.2d 1046, 1051, 1053 (5th Cir. 1980), *cert.
denied,* 101 S. Ct. 271 (1980); *Lilly* v. *State Teachers Retirement System,*
608 F.2d 55, 59 (2d Cir. 1979), *cert. denied,* 100 S. Ct. 2159 (1980); *Harkavy*
v. *Apparel Industry, Inc.,* 571 F.2d 737, 741-742 (2d Cir. 1978); *SEC* v.
Bausch & Lomb, Inc., 565 F.2d 8, 17-18 (2d Cir. 1977); *SEC* v. *Parklane
Hosiery Co., Inc.,* 422 F. Supp. 477, 485 (S.D.N.Y. 1976), *affirmed,* 558
F.2d 1083, 1089 (2d Cir. 1977).

    119. See, for example, *ITT* v. *Cornfeld,* 619 F.2d 909 (2d Cir. 1980);
Healey v. *Catalyst Recovery of Pennsylvania, Inc.,* 616 F.2d 641 (3rd Cir.
1980); *Kidwell* ex. rel. *Penfold* v. *Miekle,* 597 F.2d 1273 (9th Cir. 1979);
Holmes v. *Bateson,* 583 F.2d 542 (1st Cir. 1978); *SEC* v. *Savoy Industry,
Inc.,* 587 F.2d 1149 (D.C. Cir. 1978); *SEC* v. *Bausch and Lomb, Inc.*

    120. Judge Friendly, in *Electronic Specialty Co.* v. *International Con-
trols Corp.,* 409 F.2d 937 (2d Cir. 1969), reaffirmed a test for materiality in
the context of a tender-offer case decided prior to the enactment of the
Williams Act. He stated that materiality was based on whether any of the
stockholders would probably not have tendered their shares if the alleged
violations had not occurred. Since the Supreme Court decision in *Northway,* however, the courts have applied the latter decision's much narrower standard of materiality. Little distinction has been made between
which antifraud section is involved. Justice Blackmun, in his opinion con-
curring in the judgment of *Piper* v. *Chris-Craft Industries,* stated that the
term "material" was recently defined by the Supreme Court in *Northway*
and did not refer to the fact that *Piper* was an action involving Section 14(e)
while *Northway* was an action involving Rule 14a-9. 430 U.S. at 50. Since
Piper, several other cases have utilized the *Northway* standard in cases involving Section 14(e) claims. See *Seaboard World Airlines, Inc.* v. *Tiger International, Inc.,* 600 F.2d 355 (2d Cir. 1979); *Prudent Real Estate Trust* v.
Johncamp Realty, Inc., 599 F.2d 1140 (2d Cir. 1979); *Raybestos-Manhat-
tan, Inc.* v. *Hi-Shear Industries,* 503 F. Supp. 1122 (E.D.N.Y. 1980); *SEC*
v. *Texas International Co.,* 498 F. Supp. 1231 (N.D. Ill. 1980); *Greenfield*
v. *Flying Diamond Oil Corp.,* [1979-1980 Transfer Binder] (CCH) Fed.
Sec. L. Rep. ¶97,298 (S.D.N.Y. 1980); *SEC v. Wills,* 472 F. Supp. 1250
(D.D.C. 1978); *Flynn* v. *Bass Brothers Enterprises, Inc.,* 456 F. Supp. 484
(E.D.Pa. 1978); *Berman* v. *Gerber Products Company; Weeks Dredging &*

Contracting v. *American Dredging; Morgan* v. *Prudential Funds, Inc.,* 446 F. Supp. 628 (S.D.N.Y. 1978).

121. On the other hand, if the Company Y director knows or has reason to know that Company Y would be receptive to an acquisition by Company X, he may violate Rule 10b–5 by purchasing Company Y shares. *SEC* v. *Geon Industries, Inc.,* 531 F.2d 39, 47–48 (2d Cir. 1976).

122. The other side of the determination of when the duty will arise is the determination of who has standing to sue for violations of a duty to disclose or abstain from trading under Rule 10b–5. In order to have standing to sue under Rule 10b–5, the plaintiff must be a seller or purchaser of securities. *Blue Chip Stamps* v. *Manor Drug Stores.* See also the discussion beginning at *supra* note 39 and accompanying text regarding the application of Rule 14e–3 to transactions and activities prior to the commencement of the tender offer.

123. See, for example, *Texas Gulf Sulphur Co.; Investors Management Inc.,* 44 S.E.C. 633 (1971). See *supra* note 27.

124. (4 September 1980) (45 FR 60410).

125. 45 FR at 60413 n.37. Thus, if X, an employee of a financial printer, learns from confidential tender-offer materials furnished to the printer by Company A that Company A has resolved to make a tender offer for Company B, then X will be subject to a duty under Rule 14e–3(a) to disclose the information or abstain from trading in Company B's stock. See also the discussion *supra* at note 34.

126. 45 FR at 60413 n.37.

127. Release No. 34-17120, 45 FR at 60413.

128. Assuming that X was encouraging Y to buy subject-company securities and that such a purchase was reasonably foreseeable to X, the communication of X to Y would violate Rule 14e–3(d). See *infra* at 144.

129. 45 FR at 60414.

130. *Id.*

131. 44 S.E.C. 633, 643 (1971). This formulation would appear to be applicable with respect to information under Rule 14e–3(a), when compared with the disclosure duty to avoid the prohibition on trading under Rule 14e–3(a).

132. 401 F.2d at 854.

133. 40 S.E.C. at 915.

134. 425 U.S. 185 (1976).

135. With the advent of the theory, in *Ernst* v. *Hochfelder* and *Aaron* v. *SEC,* 100 S. Ct. 1945 (1980) that scienter is an element of a Rule 10b–5 violation, it is unlikely that any previous decision that held irrelevant a defendant's good-faith belief that the information was public are any longer viable authority. Thus, the Second Circuit's holding that the beliefs of certain defendants in the *Texas Gulf Sulphur* case, where they honestly believed that the news of a mammoth ore strike had become public when

they placed their orders, were to no avail is probably no longer correct. Under present law, this part of the case should have been remanded to permit the defendants to show that, at most, they had negligently failed to pursue their duty of inquiry with respect to the public nature of the information about the ore strike.

136. Presumably, the commission will require that the information be publicly disclosed first. Thus, even if the market for the subject company's stock begins to move upon the basis of leaks or rumors relating to a tender offer, a person possessed of material information relating to the tender offer may not trade and later argue that the information was in fact public. Not until information is disclosed in a public manner will the prohibition against trading be lifted.

137. The perceived need to address trading on the basis of nonpublic information relating to a tender offer has been felt outside the United States. In Britain, for example, the 1980 Companies Act established prohibitions on insider trading during takeover offers. Section 68(4) provides that where an individual is contemplating, or has contemplated, making a takeover offer for a company in a particular capacity, that an individual shall not deal on a recognized stock exchange in securities of that company if he knows that information that the offer is contemplated or no longer contemplated is unpublished price-sensitive information in relation to those securities. Section 68(5) extends the same prohibition to an individual who has knowingly obtained (directly or indirectly), from an individual to whom subsection (4) applies, information that the offer referred to in subsection (4) is being contemplated or is no longer contemplated, if he knows the information is unpublished price-sensitive information in relation to those securities. Section 73(2) defines unpublished price-sensitive information as information that (i) relates to specific matters relating or of concern (directly or indirectly) to that company—that is, is not of a general nature relating or of concern to that company—and (ii) is not generally known to those persons who are accustomed or would be likely to deal in those securities but that, if it were generally known to them, to be likely materially to affect the price. With respect to exceptions to liability, Section 68(8) would permit a transaction where the individual did not use the information, good-faith transactions by an individual in functions as a liquidator, receivor, or trustee in bankruptcy or a jobber (specialist) to deal in the securities if the information was obtained by him in his business as a jobber and was of a description that would be reasonable to expect him to obtain in the ordinary course of business and he deals in good faith in the course of that business. In addition to Section 68(8), Section 68(10) would permit the individual to deal or do any particular thing in the securities, even if he has information relating to any particular transaction, if he does that thing to facilitate the completion or carrying out of the transaction.

138. Release No. 34–17120, 45 FR at 60414.

139. Assume Company A is planning a tender offer for Company B and asks Company X, a multiservice securities firm to act as dealer-manager for the offer. X's retail-sales department has an outstanding sell recommendation for the Company B stock but has constructed a Chinese wall between its investment-banking and retail-sales departments. Because of Rule 14e-3(b) (and assuming the Chinese wall is effective), X will not violate Rule 14e-3(a) if it continues to recommend the Company B stock.

140. In Release No. 34-17120, the commission stated that it "expected that present practices [adopted to prevent the use of material, nonpublic information] would continue and may, in certain instances, be strengthened to ensure the availability of this exception to liability. The commission will carefully monitor and review the impact that Rule 14e-3(b) has on present practices." (footnote omitted) 45 FR at 60416.

141. See cases and articles cited at *infra* notes 143 and 144.

142. This duty finds its source in the common law. For example, the Restatement of Agency, discussed in more detail, *infra,* states

> Unless otherwise agreed, an agent is subject to a duty to the principal not to use or to communicate information confidentially given him by the principal or acquired by him during the course or on account of his agency . . . unless the information is a matter of general knowledge.

Restatement (Second) of Agency, §395 (1958). It is reasonably well settled that a securities firm owes a duty to its investment-banking clients not to disclose confidential information divulged to the firm by the client in, or as a result of, the investment-banking relationship. See *Schein* v. *Chasen,* 478 F.2d 817 (2d Cir. 1973), *vacated and remanded on other grounds sub nom. Lehman Bros.* v. *Schein,* 416 U.S. 386 (1974); but see *Schein* v. *Chasen,* 313 So.2d 739 (Fla. 1975).

143. This chapter discusses the problem of the Chinese wall only as it relates to the multiservice securities firm. The somewhat different problems the commercial-banking industry has in this area are discussed in a number of articles. See, for example, Lybecker, *Regulation of Bank Trust Department Investment Activities: Seven Gaps, Eight Remedies,* 90 Banking L.J. 914 (1973) (Part I), 91 Banking L.J. 6 (1974) (Part II); Herzel and Colling, *The Chinese Wall and Conflict of Interest in Banks,* 34 Bus. Law. 73 (1978); Huck, *The Fatal Lure of the "Impermeable Chinese Wall,"* 94 Banking L.J. 100 (1977).

144. See *Shapiro* v. *Merrill Lynch, Pierce, Fenner & Smith,* 495 F.2d 228 (2d Cir. 1974); *In the Matter of Investors Management; Merrill Lynch, Pierce, Fenner & Smith, Inc.,* Securities Exchange Act Release No. 8459 (25 November 1968).

145. 72 Cal. Reptr. 157 (Ct. App. 1968).

146. [1973-1974 Transfer Binder] Fed. Sec. L. Rep. (CCH) ¶94,439 (S.D.N.Y. 1974), *remanded,* 517 F.2d 398 (2d Cir. 1974).

147. This argument, although not mentioned in the district court opinion, is noted in the Second Circuit's opinion remanding the case. 517 F.2d at 401.

148. ¶94,329 at 95, 132, citing *Texas Gulf Sulphur Co.,* 401 F.2d at 848.

149. *Slade* v. *Shearson, Hammill & Co.. [1973*-1974), *remanded* 517 F.2d 398 (2d Cir. 1974). After receiving briefs and hearing argument, the Second Circuit decided that it had improvidently granted certification.

150. Brief for the SEC, *amicus curiae* at 9, *Slade* v. *Shearson, Hammill,* 517 F.2d 398 (2d Cir. 1974).

151. It is part of the oral history of the commission that this position, limiting the use of the restricted list to those instances where the retail side of a multiservice securities firm was recommending the security to customers, was taken in order to permit bank trust departments that buy and sell securities only for managed accounts to continue, so long as an effective Chinese wall was in place, to operate normally during those periods when the commercial side of the bank is in possession of material, nonpublic information. See Lipton, *Rule 10b-5: The End of Isolation,* in PLI, *Sixth Annual Institute on Securities Regulation* 397, 407 (1975) (remarks of Harvey Pitt).

152. The *Slade* court itself, in its opinion certifying the question to the Second Circuit, seemed to question its earlier rationale. A prerequisite for certification under 28 U.S.C. §1292 was a conclusion that a "substantial ground for difference of opinion existed as to the legal question at issue." As to this requirement, the court noted that *Slade* presented an issue of first impression and then stated

> Neither the case on which the court principally relied in disposing of the summary judgment motion, *SEC* v. *Texas Gulf Sulphur* [citations omitted], nor any other case cited by the plaintiffs involved in the same combination of investment-banking and brokerage functions as does the case at bar. Nor does any case cited by the parties concern a broker who advised its customers to take action *inconsistent* with the inside information it possesses. . . . Thus, the January 2 opinion constituted an application of the principle enunciated in *Texas Gulf Sulphur* to a situation which another court might find to be so different as to render the principle inapposite. [emphasis added by court]

Slade v. *Shearson, Hammill & Co.,* [1973-1974 Transfer Binder] Fed. Sec. L. Rep. (CCH) ¶94,439, at 95, 531-532 (S.D.N.Y. 1974).

153. It is possible to have such a result, however, if, for example, the subject company receives notice from the bidder and then hires the firm to

evaluate the contemplated bid. But in this case the brokerage firm would acquire the information indirectly from the bidder by means of the subject company.

154. For other discussion by the commission that consider or at least refer to the use of Chinese walls and other procedures to guard against the abuse of inside information, see Reports of Bank Securities Activities of the Securities and Exchange Commission, 95th Cong., 1st Sess. 509–510, 529 (Comm. Print 1977), Statement of the Securities Markets 18 (1972); Institutional Investors Study Report of the Securities and Exchange Commission 5, p. 2539 (1971); Report of the Special Study of Securities Markets of the Securities and Exchange Commission, 88th Cong., 1st Sess., Part I, 438–440 (1963).

155. See, for example, *Charles Hughes & Co., 139 F.2d at 437; Duker & Duker,* 6 S.E.C. 386, 388–389 (1939); Loss, *Securities Regulation,* 1482–1493 (1961).

156. See, for example, *Chasins* v. *Smith, Barney & Co.,* 305 F. Supp. at 495–496 (failure to disclose market-making capacity); *Arleen Hughes* v. *Securities and Exchange Commission,* 174 F.2d 969 (D.C. Cir. 1949) *affirming, Arleen W. Hughes,* 27 S.E.C. 629 (1948) (trading as principal without disclosing best price at which customers could purchase securities in open market).

157. See, for example, *J. Logan & Co.,* 41 S.E.C. 88 (1962), *affirmed per curiam sub nom. Hersch* v. *SEC,* 325 F.2d 147 (9th Cir. 1963), *cert. denied,* 377 U.S. 937 (1964) (churning violates shingle theory); *Kavil* v. *A.L. Stamm & Co.,* [1966-1967 Transfer Binder] Fed. Sec. L. Rep. (CCH) ¶91,915 (S.D.N.Y. 1967) (trading in excess of authority violates Rule 10b-5 since broker implicitly represents that he will adhere to scope of agency); *Opper* v. *Hancock Securities Corp.,* 250 F. Supp. 668 (S.D.N.Y. 1966), *affirmed per curiam,* 367 F.2d 157 (2d Cir. 1966) (failure to sell customer's stock pursuant to order while selling same stock from own account violates fiduciary obligations and Rule 10b-5).

158. See, for example, *Hiller* v. *SEC,* 429 F.2d 856, 857–858 (2d Cir. 1970); *Hanly* v. *SEC* F.2d 589, 597 (2d Cir. 1969), *affirming, Richard J. Buck & Co.,* Securities Exchange Act Release No. 8482 (31 December 1968).

159. See Roach, *Suitability Obligations of Brokers: Present Law and Proposed Federal Securities Code,* 29 Hastings L.J. 1067 (1978); Mundheim, Professional Responsibility of Broker-Dealers: The Suitability Doctrine, 1965 Duke L.J. 445 (1965).

160. *Cady, Roberts & Co.,* 40 S.E.C. at 916.

161. *Investors Management Co.,* 44 S.E.C. at 647.

16.2 40 S.E.C. at 916.

163. 44 S.E.C. at 647.

164. 415 F.2d 589 (2d Cir. 1969).

165. To the same effect is the holding in *Black* v. *Shearson, Hammill & Co.,* 266 Cal. App. 2d 362, 72 Cal. Rptr. 157 (1968).

166. The commission has continued to bring actions against broker-dealers that have recommended securities on the basis of inadequate information or have recommended securities with the use of false and misleading information. *In the Matter of Merrill Lynch, Pierce, Fenner and Smith,* Securities Exchange Act Release No. 14149 (9 November 1977). Those actions frequently rely upon the principles recited in *Hanly.* As stated in the text, however, the *Hanly* cases are not true inside-information cases but appear to involve broker-dealers that have either made deliberate misrepresentations, have simply failed to investigate an issuer diligently, or have ignored adverse information available through normal research channels. See also *Nassar & Co., Inc.* v. *SEC* [1977–1978 Transfer Binder] Fed. Sec. L. Rep. (CCH) ¶96,185 (D.C. Cir. 1977).

167. *Van Alstyne, Noel & Co.,* 33 S.E.C. 311, 321 (1952), *modified on other grounds,* 34 S.E.C. 593 (1953), is not to the contrary, as asserted by one commentator. See M. Lipton, *The Chinese Wall Solution to the Conflict Problems of Securities Firms,* 50 N.Y.U.L. Rev. 459, 476 (1975). In *Van Alstyne,* the commission upheld the imposition of sanctions against a broker-dealer whose partners, while in possession of adverse, nonpublic information, made favorable statements that they knew were false and misleading with respect to an issuer's financial condition and prospects. The commission rejected respondent's contention that its obligations to the issuer precluded it from disclosing the adverse information to the public, stating that regardless of any such duty, when the broker-dealer "disseminated favorable and optimistic information with respect to [the issuer's] condition and prospects, it made itself subject to an overriding duty of disclosure to its customers. Registrants should have appreciated that giving to a customer favorable or optimistic information and withholding unfavorable information which it considered confidential would be misleading and unfair to the customer. Having chosen to continue to effect transactions in [the issuer's] stock, registrant should have refrained from making any statements which would be rendered misleading by the failure to disclose such financial misinformation." 33 S.E.C. at 321. *Van Alstyne* thus does not stand for the proposition that the broker-dealer's duty to disclose material information to his clients always supercedes his duty to the issuer not to disseminate inside information. Rather, it holds that a broker may not continue to make favorable recommendations concerning a security once it discovers information, either public or nonpublic, that renders those recommendations false and misleading. The whole purpose behind the Chinese wall, of course, is to shield the brokerage department of a firm from acquiring material, nonpublic information from the investment-banking department, and thereby to prevent this conflict from arising. Nothing in

Van Alstyne indicates that a broker could be held liable for failure to disclose information of which he is unaware but that is in the possession of an investment banker on the other side of the wall.

To make this clear to the customer, it may well be advisable for the broker to disclose at the commencement of his relationship with his customer the existence of the wall along with a disclaimer that any recommendations will be the product of information available on a lawful basis to the trading or research departments. See Note, *The Conflicting Duties of Brokerage Firms,* 88 Harv. L. Rev. 396 (1974).

169. See *Imperial Finance Corp.* v. *Finance Factors Ltd.,* 490 P.2d 662 (Hawaii 1971), holding no breach of care for failing to convey confidential information within departments of a finance company, where plaintiff understood that information would be kept confidential, citing Section 381 and comment (e).

170. (Reporter's comments to Section 281); *accord, Ross* v. *Mayflower Drug Stores,* 12 A.2d 569 (Pa. 1940); *Charleston Library Society* v. *Citizens & Southern Bank,* 23 S.E.2d 623 (S.C. 1942).

171. See Recent Cases, 27 Vand. L. Rev. 815, 823 and n.27 (1974); Note, *Conflicting Duties of Brokerage Firms, supra* at 411–412 and n.94 ("It is unclear, however, what policy is served by imputation of knowledge in [the *Slade*] context. Such imputation may go beyond prevailing agency doctrine, and moreover, even if agency doctrine would ordinarily lead to that result, the troubling conflict of duties facing brokers argues for some relaxation of strict common-law rules.")

172. Release No. 34-17120, 45 FR at 60416. The commission specifically notes that if Rule 10b-13 (17 CFR 240.10b-13) would prohibit an offering person from purchasing or arranging for the purchase of subject-company securities, then the transaction would not occur, notwithstanding the fact that the provisions of Rule 14e-3(a) were rendered inapplicable by operation of Rule 14e-3(c)(1).

173. Release No. 34-17120, 45 FR at 60416.

174. *Texas Gulf Sulphur,* 401 F.2d at 820.

175. If X, a member of the board of directors of Company A, tells Y that Company A has resolved to make a tender offer for Company B and that Y could make a killing if he bought Company B stock before commencement of the tender offer, then X would in all probability have violated Rule 14e-3(d). If Y purchased Company B stock prior to any disclosure, the Y would have violated Rule 14e-3(a). Moreover, if Y conveyed to Z the same information that Y had been given by X so that Z could get in on the profits, then Y would in all probability have violated 14e-3(d).

176. Release No. 34-17120 indicates that this standard was not intended to have an impact on casual and innocently motivated social discourse. Moreover, the release states that the standard of reasonably

foreseeable would take into account the identity, position, reputation, or prior actions of the participants and other relevant factors. 45 FR at 60417.

177. *Texas Gulf Sulphur Co.*, 401 F.2d at 852; *SEC* v. *Lum's, Inc.*, 356 F. Supp. 1046, 1056 (S.D.N.Y. 1973)

178. *Shapiro* v. *Merrill Lynch,* 495 F.2d at 237 (underwriter who disclosed nonpublic information to brokerage customers).

179. *Elkind* v. *Liggett & Myers, Inc.*, 635 F.2d 156, 166 (2d Cir. 1980).

180. *Elkind,* 635 F.2d at 166; *duPont Clore Forgan, Inc.* v. *Arnold Bernhard & Co., Inc.*, [1978 Transfer Binder] Fed. Sec. L. Rep. (CCH) ¶96,346, at 93,176 (S.D.N.Y. 1978); *SEC* v. *Bausch & Lomb, Inc.*, [1976–1977 Transfer Binder] Fed. Sec. L. Rep. (CCH) ¶95,722, at 90,504–509 n.2 (S.D.N.Y. 1976).

181. *Elkind,* 635 F.2d at 166. See also *Lilly* v. *State Teachers Retirement System,* 608 F.2d at 58; *SEC* v. *Shapiro* 494 F.2d 1301, 1307 (2d Cir. 1974).

182. See *supra* note 120.

183. If Company A tells X, a broker-dealer, that it is about to make a tender offer for the securities of Company B and asks if X will serve as dealer-manager for the offer, will Company A have violated Rule 14e-3(d) even if X trades on the information or passes the information to its customers? Probably not, unless Company A did not make the communication in good faith. However, if X were in fact to trade based on the information or to communicate the information to customers, then X will have violated Rule 14e-3(a) and probably Rule 14e-3(d).

184. Release No. 34-17120, 45 FR at 60417.

185. *Id.*

186. *Elkind,* 435 F.2d at 166; *SEC* v. *Monarch Fund,* 608 F.2d 938, 942 (2d Cir. 1979).

187. *SEC* v. *Bausch & Lomb,* 420 F. Supp. 1226 (S.D.N.Y. 1976), *affirmed,* 565 F.2d 8 (2d Cir. 1977).

188. 2 Bromberg & Lowenfels, *Securities Fraud and Commodities Fraud* §7.5 (3) (d).

189. The need for a complementary provision concerning the communication of material, nonpublic information as well as prohibition on trading on the basis of material, nonpublic information was also seen in the British system discussed in *supra* note 137. Section 68(6) provides that an individual who is prohibited from dealing on a recognized stock exchange in any securities shall not counsel or procure any other person to deal in those securities, knowing or having reasonable cause to believe that that person would deal in them on a recognized stock exchange. Section 68(7) provides that an individual who is prohibited from dealing on a recognized stock exchange by reason of his having information shall not communicate that information to any other person if he knows or has reasonable cause to

believe that that or some other person will make use of the information for the purpose of dealing, or of counseling or procuring any other person to deal, on a recognized stock exchange in those securities. The exceptions under Section 68(8) and 68(10) described in note 137, *supra,* are equally applicable to Sections 68(5) and 68(6).

8

Do We Want a
New, Tough
Antimerger Law?

Dennis C. Mueller

Congress has on three occasions tried to deter the growth of corporate size and power: in 1890 with the passage of the Sherman Act, in 1914 with the passage of the Clayton Act, and in 1950 with the Celler-Kefauver Amendment to Section 7 of the Clayton Act. Today it finds itself once again confronted with the issue of whether new legislation is needed to retard corporate growth.

The Sherman Act was passed in the midst of what is probably still today the greatest merger wave in this country's history. Although not directed solely at mergers, one of the goals of Section 2 was to stop the creation of monopolies via merger, as was occurring in numerous industries at the time. In this objective it was successful as *Northern Securities* (1904) and other cases were soon to prove, but the act could not prevent mergers bringing together companies of less than monopolistic dimensions. Recognition of this contributed to the impetus behind the second major effort to curtail corporate power in 1914.

The Clayton Act differs from its predecessor by trying to halt and constrain monopoly power "in its incipiency" rather than dealing with it in its fully developed state as the Sherman Act does. Section 7 directly prohibits mergers that would "substantially lessen competition" or "tend to create" a monopoly.

A cavernous loophole in the antimerger section of the 1914 statute and restrictive judicial interpretations made it an ineffective constraint on corporate mergers. A second great merger wave took place in the 1920s in spite of the apparent attempt by Congress in 1914 to put an end to such waves.

In the late 1940s, the Federal Trade Commission presented evidence suggesting that a new merger wave was in process. This and other events of the day led to the Celler-Kefauver Amendment to Section 7 of the Clayton Act closing the act's loophole. Subsequent enforcement and judicial interpretations have produced a dramatic reduction in the number and significance of horizontal and vertical acquisitions.[1] Nevertheless, starting in the

1950s and cresting in the late 1960s, the United States experienced its third great merger wave. Although large horizontal and vertical acquisitions could be and were successfully challenged under the Celler-Kefauver Amendment, most conglomerate mergers appear to be beyond this statute's reach, and it was these that made up the bulk of the third great wave.

· Figure 8-1 presents data on the number of acquisitions and volume of assets acquired by year since 1950. The precipitous drop in merger activity following 1968 coincides with the collapse of the 1960s bull market and the onset of the recession induced by the first Nixon administration. This pro-cyclical pattern has characterized all three major merger waves.

In recent years merger activity has again started upward. This is even more apparent in figure 8-2, which includes data for 1978. (Data in figures 8-1 and 8-2 are from different sources and are not directly comparable.) In 1978, the total value of all major corporate mergers was $34.2 billion, up 64 percent from 1977's $22 billion. It is this recent surge of merger activity that has ignited interest in new antimerger legislation.

There is little doubt that the first two large merger waves led to

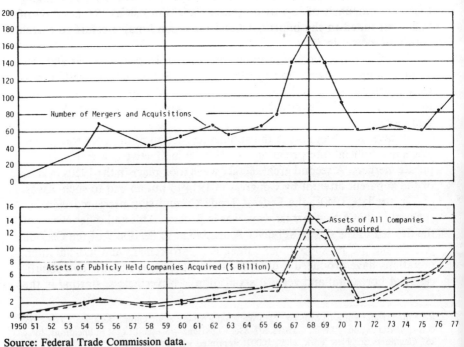

Source: Federal Trade Commission data.

Figure 8-1. Mergers and Acquisitions of Manufacturing and Mining Firms of Over $10 Million in Assets, 1950-1977

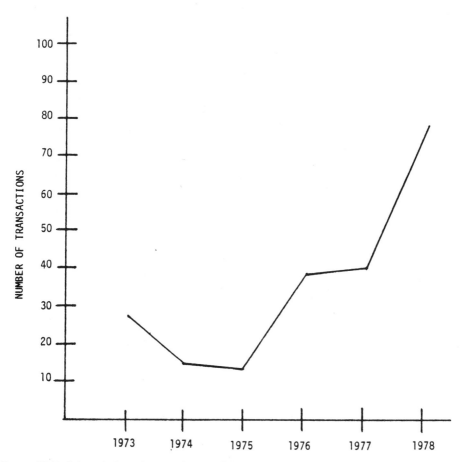

Source: W.T. Grimm & Co. (1978 data is unpublished). Used with permission.
Note: Data include transactions announced during year stated but canceled after end of the calendar year.
Figure 8-2. Number of Corporate Mergers and Acquisitions Valued at $100 Million
       or More

increases in both overall and industry concentration levels. Since the 1950
amendment horizontal merger activity has been inconsequential, and industry concentration levels have exhibited no pattern of change that seems to be
merger related.[2]

Overall concentration has continued to creep upward, however. Table
8-1 presents some figures.[3] The 200 largest mining and manufacturing firms
now control in excess of 60 percent of all mining and manufacturing assets.
McGowen's investigation of the role of mergers in explaining overall

Table 8-1
Overall Concentration and Mergers

Year	Total Assets, Manufacturing	Manufacturing and Mining Assets Acquired by 200 Largest Manufacturing Companies (as of 1975)	Manufacturing and Mining Assets Acquired as a Percentage of Total Manufacturing Assets	Percentage of Manufacturing Assets Held by 200 Largest Manufacturing Companies
1959	252,134	687.9	0.3	55.4
1960	262,308	789.4	0.3	55.3
1961	275,964	1480.7	0.5	55.8
1962	292,640	1205.6	0.4	55.5
1963	310,207	1871.7	0.6	55.2
1964	335,190	1075.7	0.3	54.8
1965	371,524	1815.7	0.5	54.8
1966	405,967	1929.5	0.5	56.3
1967	448,026	5252.8	1.2	57.3
1968	500,564	7717.1	1.5	58.5
1969	572,127	6054.5	1.1	56.6
1970	612,913	3260.2	0.5	56.7
1971	646,646	930.6	0.1	57.3
1972	698,660	739.1	0.1	56.5
1973	786,163	1767.0	0.2	56.1
1974	885,823	1874.6	0.2	57.5
1975	944,582	2592.0	0.3	57.3
1976	1,029,744[a]	2809.1	0.3	58.0
1977	1,124,808[a]	5236.9[b]	0.5	58.7

Sources: Total assets are as reported by IRS. Assets acquired are from the FTC *Statistical Report on Mergers,* various years. Assets held by 200 largest are for the 200 largest manufacturing firms as reported by Standard and Poor's COMPUSTAT, as supplemented by the *Fortune* 500 listing.

Note: Since numbers are from different sources, they are not all strictly comparable to the last decimal. But the orders of magnitude and general movement of values should be comparable.

[a]Approximated using figures in the *Statistical Abstract.*

[b]Preliminary.

concentration increases suggests that mergers accounted for some 2/3 of the increase between 1950 and 1960.[4] His analysis indicated, further, that overall concentration would begin to fall in the absence of mergers. Similar conclusions have been obtained by Hannah and Kay for the UK.[5]

The data in the final two columns of the table indicate that the level of overall concentration remained virtually unchanged between 1958 and 1966. During this period the top 200 acquired around a half of one percent of manufacturing and mining assets per annum. Thus, without these acquisitions, and without offsetting internal growth increases, overall concentration might have been expected to decline by about a half of a percent per annum. In 1967 and 1968 the amount of assets acquired by the top 200 increased considerably, and here we witness the only significant increase in overall concentration of the decade. It seems hard to believe that the two are unrelated.

In the period since the end of World War II, the economy has expanded nearly threefold, and yet the top 200 firms grew even faster. This is remarkable, because one would expect such a long period of economic prosperity to have produced a *reduction* in overall concentration. Sustained prosperity is known to foster the birth and rapid growth of new firms. Such a reduction in overall concentration did occur during the one period of sustained growth this economy experienced in the last century, which was not accompanied by substantial merger activity, the period between the depression low point in 1933 and the end of World War II.[6] That overall concentration has not gone down since the end of World War II seems largely the result of the immense number of mergers that has taken place over this period.

The suspected role of mergers in increasing or preserving present concentration levels, and the recent rise in merger activity, combine to explain current interest in antimerger legislation. Were the upward trend in merger activity to continue, or the stock market and economy to revive to the 1960s level, a merger wave of unsurpassed dimensions might be unleashed, pushing levels of overall concentration up to new heights.

To many observers, the level of overall concentration is a matter of some indifference. Little progress has been made in the development of hypotheses that link overall concentration levels to anticompetitive behavior. The costs of rising (or not falling) overall concentration levels would appear to be more closely related to sociological or political objectives than traditional economic welfare indicators. Those who find these objectives too nebulous to warrant government interference with "the market for corporate control," reject out of hand all proposals to curb merger activity significantly.

But to those who favor, *ceteris paribus,* decentralized decisionmaking structures over centralized decisionmaking, and dispersed political power over concentrated political power, the possibility of further increases in overall concentration carries with it some real, if unmeasurable costs. These observers will favor new legislation curbing merger activity, if it does not come at too high of a cost. The question then is what would be the cost of new, tough antimerger legislation?

To answer this question we must know what causes mergers to take place, what their economic effects are, and how the proposed legislation would alter the status quo. We address each of these issues in turn.

The Determinants of Mergers

The number of hypotheses about the causes of mergers is almost as large as the number of mergers itself. Several explanations do not posit allocative efficiency changes, however, e.g., mergers to realize tax savings, mergers due to differences in the evaluations of the acquired firm's shares, mergers due to differences between the merging companies' P/E ratios.[7] Since no efficiency gains have been hypothesized for these mergers, none should be lost by prohibiting them. In discussing the desirability of new antimerger legislation, we shall focuş, therefore, on only those theories that do posit allocative efficiency effects. These can be grouped into three categories: mergers that increase market power, mergers that improve efficiency, and mergers that worsen efficiency as a side effect to the pursuit of some non-profit maximizing goal. We examine each in turn.

The Celler-Kefauver Amendment seems to have eliminated the possibility of any substantial increase in market power from a horizontal or vertical acquisition. New legislation, if it is needed at all to curb market power increases, is needed in the conglomerate merger area.

Conglomerate mergers have been accused of advancing market power through the elimination of potential entrants and rivals. Examples of both types of mergers can be found, most readily, perhaps, in the judicial record of successfully prosecuted Section 7 cases. Indeed, a review of key decisions suggests that most, if not all instances of the likely creation of reciprocal buying power, or the elimination of potential entrants via a merger can be prevented under existing law.[8] A detailed case study of nine leading conglomerates by the FTC[9] concluded that the mergers of these firms, which presumably were not in violation of Section 7, lent "little support for any hypothesis of predatory expansion of market positions through use of 'conglomerate power.' From a competitive standpoint, the effects of conglomerate diversification . . . appear to be largely *neutral*."[10]

Of the many possible efficiencies, which have been cited in relation to conglomerate mergers, three appear to be most worthy of additional examination: (1) financial economies, (2) the redeployment of capital, and (3) the replacement of inefficient managers.

A merger between companies with imperfectly correlated profit streams can improve the risk/return position of a holder of either company's shares.[11] But a stockholder can always achieve the same risk-spreading position by creating a portfolio of both, and the transaction costs of achieving risk reduction in this way are usually less than those of consummating a merger. Also, the option of buying mutual funds greatly enhances the opportunity set of the shareholder, even if he normally holds but a few different stocks. Nor is there much evidence that mergers do reduce the riskiness of the merging companies' shares.[12]

Conglomerates have also been said to be more efficient than the external capital market in some respects in reallocating capital from low to high marginal returns areas.[13] The first cost of using the capital market is taxes. If funds are to flow through the capital market from company *C* with low investment opportunities to company A with high opportunities, C must first pay them out as dividends or interest. These funds are then taxed as ordinary income prior to their transfer to and reinvestment by A. If A is a subdivision of C, the funds can be transferred directly. No taxes are paid at the time of transfer, and those that are paid are at the lower capital gains rate and only upon the stockholder's sale of the shares in the conglomerate C.

The transfer of capital via internal capital markets may also economize on search costs. If capital is to flow from C to A through the capital market, each share- and bondholder of C must investigate the investment opportunities available. When A is a division of C a single search is made by the managers. Since information gathering exhibits strong economies of scale, centralized gathering of information can be more efficient.

Last of all, if A must compete with other firms for capital it has to reveal information about its investment plans to the market. Due to the difficulties in appropriating the value of information, this may reduce the value of the information about investment opportunities A possesses. If A is part of a large diversified company, however, A can compete for capital with the other divisions without the parent company's relinquishing possession of the information to the market, with the accompanying negative effects on the creation of new investment opportunities.[14]

The case histories of many of the conglomerates of the 1960s are consistent with the capital redeployment thesis. Weston and Mansinghka's sample of 63 conglomerates started the decade with profit rates significantly below a nonmerging control group.[15] After the merger wave was completed, this sample of conglomerates had profit levels equal to those of the control group. The companies the conglomerates acquired had higher profit rates than they themselves.[16] They may, therefore, also have had higher marginal returns on investment. Whether they did, and whether the conglomerates' acquisitions led to a reallocation of capital superior to that achievable by the external capital market cannot be discerned from Weston and Mansinghka's results. The acquisition of firms with higher profit rates could account for the rise in the conglomerates' profit rates without any capital market efficiencies having arisen. The FTC case study of nine conglomerates found no systematic evidence of capital shifting into the R and D, advertising and investment areas. Indeed, what evidence of changed capital flows there was suggested movement *out of* the acquired companies.[17] Although this too could be consistent with a capital redeployment hypothesis, it is not the hypothesis Weston and Mansinghka put forward, or the one that typically seems to be implied.

The third efficiency related hypothesis to consider is that mergers are designed to achieve the replacement of managers who do not achieve the maximum performance levels possible for their companies. Manne[18] developed this hypothesis with respect to replacing incompetent managers, but it is also consistent with the Marris[19] thesis that overzealous pursuit of growth or other nonstockholder-welfare-related goals will result in an outside take-over.

While the logic underlying the "market for corporate control" thesis is simple and compelling, evidence in its support is complex and self-contra-dictory. Several studies have found the companies acquired by the conglom-erates not to differ in profitability from other firms of similar size within the same industries that were not acquired.[20] Lynch's investigation of 28 conglomerates led him to conclude that they tried to acquire "successful, profitable companies" with "capable management that can be retained."[21] On the other hand, both Mandelker[22] and Smiley[23] found that acquired companies experienced less than average rates of return on their common shares in the months prior to their acquisition. These results may differ from the others due to sample differences. An alternative explanation rests on the procyclical nature of merger activity. Stevens[24] presents evidence sug-gesting that acquired companies are "conservatively" managed, i.e., have low leverage ratios, high liquidity and dividend payouts, and lower price/earning ratios. In a period of rising stock prices, the share price of these companies may rise less rapidly than those of more aggressively man-aged firms yielding the results Mandelker and Smiley found. Although this explanation could explain the Mandelker-Smiley results, it would not seem to suggest that the managers of these firms were either incompetent or growth maximizers. But the hypothesis needs to be directly tested.

To add to the confusion, the FTC case study of the acquisitions of nine conglomerates found that the firms these nine acquired were earning some-what lower profits than their base industries, but that their profit rates did not tend to improve following the mergers.[25] This study also tried to estab-lish whether the managers of acquired firms tended to be replaced following the acquisition. In a quarter of the cases all three top managers were gone three years after the acquisition, and in a quarter they were still there. In the other cases some were gone and some were there.[26] The study concluded that "the evidence does not suggest dramatic changes in top management of firms after they are acquired by conglomerates."[27]

Growth is the most obvious nonstockholder-welfare-related goal to be satisfied by mergers. Casual observation suggests and statistical analysis confirms that acquiring firms grow faster than those that abstain.[28] Since there are both pecuniary and nonpecuniary advantages to managing large, growing companies, the pursuit of growth *per se,* regardless of the efficien-cies or market power a merger may generate, seems difficult to reject on a priori grounds as a motive behind many mergers.[29] It is worth noting that the managerial thesis does not imply that managers pass up opportunities that would increase market power or efficiency. Thus, the managerial hypothesis is consistent with *some* mergers being profitable. The hypothesis simply states that mergers will occur even in the absence of such possibilities and, therefore, that many mergers might be unprofitable.

One major advantage the managerial hypothesis has over the neoclassical view—that all mergers must either increase market power or improve efficiencies—is that the managerial thesis is consistent with the procyclical nature of merger activity. There is no obvious reason why the incompetencies of managers should be more apparent at a time when business performance in general is good and stock market values are on an upswing. Similarly, it is not clear why the long run advantages from redeploying capital or spreading risks should be so much more apparent in times of prosperity than in normal times or a recession. Thus, there seems to be no particular reason, based on the neoclassical theories of the motives for mergers, to expect a procyclical merger pattern. The close association between merger activity and stock market values that has characterized the merger history of this country seems incapable of explanation within the realm of the neoclassical theories.[30]

The managerial theories argue that managers pursue growth via acquisition beyond the point that maximizes stockholder welfare. Their discretion to do so is bounded by the threat of takeover should managerial pursuit of growth drive the price of the firm's stock down too far. Their capacity to do so is limited by their ability to finance new acquisitions out of new equity and debt issues and the internal fund flows of the company. In a period of boom and economic upswing both the freedom and the resources to pursue growth should increase. With rising stock prices and profits, stockholders should be more content with the performance of their companies' managers, even though these performances remain below their maximum value. The markets for both equity and debt should be receptive to new issues during a market boom, and cash flows are up also. Acquisitions will appear "cheap," and can be expected to occur in greater frequency. The managerial theory thus predicts a procyclical merger pattern.

The managerial thesis can also account for an otherwise inexplicable difference between the current acceleration of merger activity and the wave of the 1960s. Although the bulk of mergers in the 1960s were financed by new debt and equity issues, the most recent mergers have been financed more commonly by cash.[31] This is precisely what one would expect under the managerial thesis. The economy has been relatively healthy in recent years, and many firms find themselves with large accumulations of cash. But the stock market has remained in the doldrums. Thus, internal cash flows are "cheap" relative to external capital as compared at least to the 1960s. This is not what the neoclassical theory would predict. One of the cornerstones of this theory is the Miller-Modigliani theorem that the cost of capital is independent of the source of finance.[32] At any point in time all sources of capital should be equally cheap or expensive. If the transaction costs of using one form of capital versus another made external finance a more attractive source of capital to finance mergers in the 1960s, there is no reason why it should not be relatively more attractive today. The evidence that it is not runs counter to the neoclassical thesis.

Although the evidence we have on merger patterns does not appear to be consistent with the neoclassical theories of why mergers occur, it is not sufficient to reject these theories outright. To shed further light on the relative merits of each hypothesis, the effects of mergers must be examined. If mergers increase profitability to an appreciable extent, one or more market power or efficiency hypothesis must be valid, and any restrictions placed on mergers must be judged accordingly. If mergers are only mildly profitable or not at all, managerial motives must be considered of importance, and the significance of market power or efficiency gains can be discounted.

The Effects of Mergers

Thomas Hogarty undertook a survey of the empirical literature on the first two merger waves in this country and concluded that:

> Undoubtedly the most significant result of this research has been that no one who has undertaken a major empirical study of mergers has concluded that mergers are profitable, i.e., profitable in the sense of being more profitable than alternative forms of investment. A host of researchers, working at different points of time and utilizing different analytic techniques and data, have but one major difference: whether mergers have a neutral or negative impact on profitability.[33]

Unfortunately, the empirical literature on the most recent merger history has not reached such uniformity in its conclusions. Nevertheless, a careful examination of this literature reveals conclusions consistent with those Hogarty reached regarding the earlier literature.

Those studies, which have concluded that mergers do increase corporate profitability, have focused on the time period up to but ending with the stock market boom, or have placed heavy weight on the gains achieved by the stockholders of the acquired companies at the time they sold out to the acquiring firms.[34] If the performance of the acquiring companies is measured both over the period of stock market rise and economic boom, and stock market fall and recession, the acquiring companies do no better or worse than nonacquiring control group companies.[35] The only long run winners from mergers, other than perhaps the managers, appear to be the stockholders of the acquired firms, based on their gains when they sold out. Stockholders of the acquiring companies may come out ahead if they sell out when the mergers are consummated or at the market's peak, but their gains are fully offset by the losses of those to whom they sell, who hold the shares into the post-merger/market-decline period.

These conclusions follow from an examination of some three dozen studies of mergers in the United States, where the dominant form of merger is a variant on the conglomerate merger. Surprisingly, the same results seem to hold in Europe, where the predominant form of merger is horizontal. Geoffrey Meeks undertook a detailed analysis of more than 1,000 mergers in the UK over the post–World War II period, and concluded that the mergers probably led to a deterioration in the profitability of merging companies, and certainly did not result in any increase.[36] Cowling and his colleagues conducted exhaustive case studies of nine British firms engaging in substantial merger activity.[37] Again the conclusion is reached that the mergers on average did not improve efficiency.

Less work has been done on mergers in other European countries. One study just reaching conclusion has tested in parallel a set of hypotheses concerning the determinants and effects of mergers with data from Belgium, France, West Germany, the Netherlands, and Sweden, as well as the UK and US. In only one country, the UK, was a slight increase in profits detected in the three to five years following a merger. An examination of rates of return on acquiring company shares revealed that these returns were either less than or at best equal to the rates of return earned on the shares of similar companies not engaging in acquisitions over the same time periods, in six of the seven countries. A mixed pattern developed in Belgium, where stockholders of acquiring firms did slightly better than one control group and worse than another.[38]

All in all, there appears to be little evidence in Europe or the United States of efficiency gains having been either realized or expected as a result of mergers. Given the different nature of mergers in Europe and the US, this is a remarkable result. Horizontal mergers are the most likely means of obtaining economies of scale in production and distribution, and these are the most significant forms of economies a firm might be expected to achieve. Similarly, if replacement of bad managers were a typical reason behind mergers, horizontal mergers should be the most likely form of merger for achieving this objective since managers in the same industry should be in the best position to spot and improve on a given management's failings. Yet little evidence has been found suggesting improvement in operating performance as a consequence of horizontal mergers in those countries where they are allowed, and considerable evidence exists implying no improvement in efficiency and even possibly some decline following these mergers. Note, too, that horizontal mergers are the most likely of all forms of mergers to result in market power increases. If some of them did, then the evidence indicating no increase or even a decline in profitability from horizontal mergers would imply that whatever market-power-related profit increases occurred, they were fully offset by complementary efficiency declines. Such an interpretation of the European results on horizontal mergers would imply that they unambiguously resulted in social welfare losses.

Policy Implications

Several economists have concluded,[39] on the basis of the negative evidence on efficiency effects they assembled, that new and stringent restrictions on mergers should be instituted. If the purpose behind most mergers is to obtain growth or some other managerial goal, and their effect is to worsen efficiency or at best leave it unchanged, then a total ban on mergers would, if anything, increase economic efficiency. In addition, mergers may substitute for more socially beneficial expenditures to produce growth, such as capital investment and R and D.

A more conservative interpretation of the existing empirical evidence is that mergers neither increase nor decrease economic efficiency on average. If this interpretation were accepted, why not allow mergers to take place in the absence of evidence that they increase market power? Why not continue with the present antimerger policy?

Such a position is in the spirit of our traditional *laissez faire* attitude toward business behavior. But such a position would run counter to another traditional ideal in this country—our Jeffersonian preference for deconcentrated and decentralized economic and political power. As noted earlier, mergers have been a major contributor to the creation and preservation of existing levels of overall concentration. A policy of treating conglomerate mergers with indifference can be expected to perpetuate or worsen this country's present levels of overall concentration. Thus, if we assume that mergers have a neutral effect on economic efficiency, the choice is between the largely ideological goals of a hands-off policy toward the market for corporate control, and a reduction in future levels of overall concentration.

Such a choice can only be made on ideological grounds. Since the hands-off policy is the status quo, the burden of proof that society would not be made worse off by some form of ban on mergers must fall on the proponents of such a ban. Can one really be safe in concluding from the above literature, that a merger ban would have no net economic costs? Is it possible that a ban would produce economic inefficiencies that are not reflected in the performance histories of the firms actually engaged in mergers? Suppose, for example, that many mergers do come about because managers pursue growth rather than profits. Now it is not necessary for managers to pursue growth via the merger route, unless their options to pursue growth through internal expansion are limited, as when a firm is in a mature industry. Prohibiting mergers by such a company could improve economic efficiency, if it then returned its excess cash flows to the capital market. If these funds were ploughed back into its internal growth opportunities instead, the outcome might be inferior to allowing the company to merge. Thus, mergers to redeploy capital may be optimal, in a second best sense, if firms will not voluntarily and cannot be forced involuntarily to transfer internal fund flows through the external capital market.

An important constraint on managerial pursuit of nonprofit goals is the threat of outside takeover. Restrictions on mergers could weaken this constraint and allow even greater latitude to pursue nonprofit-oriented goals, although obviously not by mergers.

Thus, thwarting a (second best) redeployment of capital, and blunting the efficiency effects of the threat of takeover can be costs of restricting merger activity even if we assume that managers pursue growth and existing mergers are only break-even transactions. In addition, *some* mergers do definitely improve economic efficiency by allowing a more efficient allocation of capital or replacing bad managers, even if all mergers on average do not. Thus, any form of total ban on mergers, even if its *net* effect on economic efficiency were neutral, would be inferior to a partial ban that somehow let the mergers promising the greatest efficiencies through. In examining the various antimerger proposals that have been made, therefore, we shall pay particular attention to their impact on the markets for corporate control and the allocation of capital, and will judge them according to the contribution they make to the performance of these markets.

The Antimerger Options

Several different types of statutes to reduce the number of large, conglomerate mergers have been proposed in recent years. Variants on these are being discussed and drafted by the Senate Antitrust and Monopoly Subcommittee, the Justice Department and the FTC. Since these are currently in the drafting stage, and will undoubtedly undergo revision in Congress, we shall not focus on the details of the different proposals here. Instead, we shall examine a few hypothetical proposals, which contain the salient features of the different alternatives.

Proposal 1: An outright ban of all acquisitions by the X largest companies, where X is probably 100 or 200.

This is a simple and effective way of halting mergers by the country's biggest companies. Concentration increases at the level of the X largest would cease or reverse. Acquisitions by companies below the top X would presumably continue unabated, however. Indeed, since the threat of takeover by one of the X largest would be removed, managers of smaller firms would have even more discretion to pursue growth via merger. The percentage of assets held by the X largest would decline, while the percentage held by, say, the $X + 1$ to 500th largest would very likely increase, perhaps dramatically. The extent to which such a ban would effectively reduce the significance of overall concentration would depend largely on one's cutoff for measuring overall concentration. If one wished to stop increasing concentration only within the top X, the ban would be effective. If however, one was also troubled by rising control of economic activity by firms in the size groups just below X, but had chosen X as a political compromise, then the ban would have but a partial or mixed impact on reducing overall concentration. Concentration among the top 500 might continue at present levels or even increase, while the distribution of concentration within the top 500 shifted downward.

The second proposal would avoid this difficulty, and would also attempt to allow those mergers by members of the X largest that were most likely to improve economic efficiency.

Proposal 2: All acquisitions by the X largest firms are banned, subject to an efficiencies defense, i.e., one of the X largest can undertake an acquisition if it can demonstrate either before a regulatory agency like the FTC or in court that the merger is reasonably likely to result in a substantial improvement in economic efficiency. X is some number between 100 and 500.

Proposal 2 switches the burden of proof in justifying a merger to the acquiring firm. In principle, any real efficiencies that could be substantiated might qualify to justify a merger. In practice, fairly narrow definitions of the allowable efficiencies under the statute would probably have to be established to reduce the costs of administering the law.

Given the evidence indicating that most mergers today do not *ex post* improve economic efficiency, most mergers, presumably, could not *ex ante* pass an effectively administered efficiencies defense. Thus, Proposal 2 should achieve the major objective of new antimerger legislation, a significant reduction in the level of concentration-increasing merger activity. At the same time, however, it would allow those mergers to take place that are most likely to improve economic efficiency. This latter feature of the proposal would also allow the cutoff size of company to be covered by the legislation to be placed further down on the largest company list.

The chief uncertainty with Proposal 2 is what its administrative costs would be. Antitrust legislation has traditionally been written with a broad brush, and the details have been filled in by administrative and judicial interpretation. So would it likely be with new legislation. If, in the early cases litigated under such a rule, agreement was reached on the criteria for establishing an efficiencies defense in the few areas where it seems most applicable, an effective screen could evolve that would not prove to be an administrative nightmare. Replacement of incompetent managers and redeployment of capital appear the most likely areas where efficiencies might be reasonably argued. The first should not be that difficult to establish. Data on the profitability of the merger target, the recent returns on its common shares, and similar statistics can be cheaply assembled. Presumably the potential acquirer would gather these in any event. Evidence that the acquirer had successfully improved the performance of previous acquisitions would also be relevant.

The potential benefits from capital redeployment should also not be difficult to establish. If the target company has limited investment opportunities this should be reflected in low investment returns relative to cash flows, and low stock price/earnings ratios. The acquirer should exhibit the reverse characteristics. Note, here, however, an overlap between the redeployment of capital and bad-managers hypotheses. If the managers of the company with limited investment opportunities are maximizing stockholder welfare, dividend payments and/or stock repurchases should be high. This company's capital is already being returned to the market, and there is no *excess* capital to redeploy. To assume there is, is to assume that the target company's managers are not maximizing stockholder welfare.

If the acquiring company has excess capital, then it is its managers who would overinvest internally were mergers prohibited. Here we have a possible difficulty in allowing an efficiencies defense. To use it some managers may have to reveal that they would overinvest in internal growth, if denied the option to rechannel their internal fund flows into the more promising investment opportunities of the company they seek to acquire. But if they would overinvest on internal expansion in the absence of merger opportunities, what is to prevent them from overinvesting on external expansion by acquiring more firms than they can efficiently manage? The use of data on the successfulness of past acquisitions to justify future acquisitions is again advised.

While Proposal 2 appears capable of achieving its twin goals, many fear that the administrative costs of an efficiencies defense would be too high. This has led to variants on Proposal 3.

Proposal 3: Any firm within the X largest can acquire any other so long as its spins off at the time of acquisition another independent company with assets at least as large as those of the acquired company. X is some number between 100 and 500.

Proposal 3 ensures that there are no direct, immediate increases in overall concentration as a result of mergers, thus achieving the major objective of new legislation. At the same time, it allows companies to undertake any acquisition promising to be profitable, and should work to restrict companies' acquisitions to the profitable set by thwarting the most important size effect of mergers through the spin-off requirement. What is more, all of this could be accomplished without bringing the government and courts into detailed examinations of individual mergers. Each company decides for itself when a merger promises sufficient gains to justify spinning off an equivalent amount of assets.

While Proposal 3 seems to involve considerably lower administrative costs than Proposal 2 it is not without some potential headaches. The acquirer has an incentive to inflate the book values of the assets it spins off, and some surveillance by the government authorities would be necessary to ensure that the newly created firm had assets of economic value equal to those of the acquired company. The acquirer may also have inadequate incentives to create a viable, independent company, since viability might require giving up managerial talent, cash reserves, or physical assets that it can well use itself. It might, therefore, choose to set up companies, which met the asset size requirement, but which two, three, or five years following the merger drift into bankrupty. To avoid this the regulatory authorities will have to evaluate the survival chances of the spin-off firm at the time of spin-off, a task of considerable, potential complexity. Alternatively, the Justice Department and FTC will have to be prepared to endure the embarrassment of witnessing subsequent bankruptcies of the companies created under the new law, and undoubtedly pressures to have companies reacquired by either the former parents or other large firms under a failing firm defense. Either way administrative costs are going to be involved.

Both of these difficulties could be avoided by measuring the size of both the acquired company and the spin-off firm by the market values of the debt and equity purchased and created through the transaction.[40] Using market values gives one an easy-to-measure and uncontroversial index of company size. If the spun-off firm seemed to be in danger of bankruptcy, the capital market would place low values on its debt and equity and the acquiring firm would have trouble matching the size of the company it acquired. The acquirer would then be faced with a trade-off between spinning off a physically small firm with a bright future, or a larger company with dimmer prospects.[41] In either case, the intent of the spin-off provision would be satisfied.

Most of the companies that would be affected by legislation resembling Proposal 3 are already diversified. Setting up one or more divisions as separate corporations should not be difficult. Some corporations might be large, yet perhaps vertically integrated in such a way that no spin off could occur without incurring significant transaction costs or inefficiencies. If such a company had an opportunity to make an acquisition with substantial, potential efficiencies, one might wish to allow the merger without requiring a spin off. This possibility suggests combining Proposals 2 and 3.

Proposal 4: Any firm within the X largest can acquire any other so long as it creates another independent company with market value at least as great as that of the acquired firm, or demonstrates that no such spin offs are possible without incurring substantial inefficiencies and the merger is likely to result in a substantial improvement in economic efficiency. X is some number between 100 and 500.

With both options available, each can be interpreted stringently. The size of spin offs can be measured in market values; a narrow interpretation of efficiency defenses can be employed.

The bill introduced in the Senate on March 8, 1979, S. 600, is a combination of Proposals 1 and 4. It includes a flat ban on the acquisition of any firm with sales or assets of $2 billion or above by any other firm of this size (128 companies had sales above $2 billion in 1978 according to *Fortune*). It allows *either* an efficiencies defense or a spin off of comparable size for acquisitions of $350 million sales or assets and above by firms of this size not covered by the flat ban (502 companies had sales above $350 million in 1978 according to *Fortune*). Thus, the provisions of the bill are restricted to acquisitions of Fortune 500 firms by Fortune 500 firms. As drafted it is likely to reduce the number of mergers of this dimension drastically. Its effect on total merger activity and overall concentration is less clear. To the extent mergers are merely a means to the pursuit of growth, the new law, if passed, might simply divert large firms from acquiring other large firms to acquiring companies below the two cutoffs; just as the Celler-Kefauver Amendment does not seem to have reduced the amount of merger activity, but merely diverted it from horizontal and vertical acquisitions. The number of "small" companies (below the top 502) disappearing due to mergers could increase dramatically, since it takes ten $200 million acquisitions to equal one $2 billion one. This is ironic since the bill is entitled the "Small and Independent Business Protection Act of 1979." But the bill is in its early stages and is unlikely to pass in its present form (or perhaps with its present name).

Let us turn to some complementary reforms that should be contemplated along with the present legislation.

Complementary Reforms

Tough, comprehensive antimerger legislation along the lines discussed in the previous section might still have some adverse effects on the market for corporate control and/or the flow of capital across firms even with spin-off and efficiency defense provisions. To avoid these, additional reforms could be undertaken.

The effect of the reduction in the number of bidders for badly managed firms on the market for corporate control could be offset by removing some of the legal stratagems available to incumbent managers to enable them to avoid unfriendly takeover attempts. With these legal barriers lowered, more bidders could enter the market supplanting the largest companies that might be inhibited from competing under new legislation.

The role mergers now play in the market for corporate control could be preserved entirely, without incurring the permanent effect on overall concentration mergers now have, by instituting the following policy.

Proposal 5: Any firm within the X largest can acquire any other so long as it spins off the selfsame company as an independent and viable entity within Y years. X is some number between 100 and 500; Y is a number between 3 and 5.

Proposal 5 would allow any acquisition to remove bad management, but forces a return to the status quo after the managers have been removed. The acquirer can claim the entrepreneurial reward from finding and removing bad managers, but that is all. Coupling Proposal 5 with a weakening of the defensive maneuvers available to incumbent managers would make the market for corporate control a more effective disciplinary force on managerial behavior than it is today, while at the same time halting the use of acquisitions to achieve growth.

The most obvious reform to encourage greater use of the external capital market is to end the discriminatory tax treatment of dividends and capital gains. Public finance reformers have for a long time argued in favor of treating capital gains as regular income and taxing them as such. Alternatively, if macro-investment considerations dominate, both dividends and capital gains could be taxed at some lower rate, like the present rate on capital gains. If dividends and capital gains were equally taxed, and managers maximized stockholder welfare, pursuit of the latter goal would ensure the socially optimal allocation of capital. Any restrictions on merger activity would reduce economic efficiency, and a new antimerger law would force a trade-off between the sociopolitical objectives underlying the desire to reduce overall concentration and economic efficiency. But if managers maximize growth, as the existing evidence suggests they do, a new antimerger law would prohibit some mergers that did not promise returns equal to or greater than the market rate of interest. Whether such an antimerger law would thereby improve economic efficiency would hinge on what managers did with their internal fund flows in the absence of merger opportunities. If they persisted to pursue growth even if forced to do so by internal expansion, and even if dividends and capital gains were equally taxed, a new antimerger law could still have some negative efficiency effects. To avoid these, managers would have to be forced to use the external capital market. This could be accomplished by placing a heavy tax on all undistributed profits.[42]

The latter would be a radical step—indeed, more radical than any of the antimerger proposals. Before such a step could be taken, exhaustive analysis and debate would be needed. But the option does indicate that there are alternatives to a second-best mechanism for allocating capital via mergers, just as there are alternatives to the present use of mergers to discipline managers. If mergers are thought to play an important role in either of these areas today, then appropriate complementary reforms should be contemplated when considering any new antimerger legislation.

It should be reemphasized, however, that the existing evidence does not suggest that mergers do on average lead to significant improvements in economic efficiency of any kind. From what we now know it seems likely that a flat ban on mergers by the largest X firms would result in *no net loss* in economic efficiency, and could produce a gain. Thus, if an antimerger statute with either an efficiencies defense or spin-off provision were passed, there would be little chance of a deterioration in economic efficiency over the present situation, even if the new law did not prove to be a perfect screen for separating efficiency improving mergers from the rest. The sociopolitical gains from stopping or reversing the upward rise in aggregate concentration that has characterized this century appear obtainable without any cost in lost economic efficiency. The answer to the question posed in the title of this chapter must be—yes!

Notes

1. For a review of merger legislation, see F.M. Scherer, *Industrial Market Structure and Economic Performance* (Rand McNally: Chicago, 1971), pp. 473–490.

2. W.F. Mueller and L.G. Hamm, "Trends in Industrial Market Concentration, 1947 to 1970," *Review of Economics and Statistics,* 56, November 1974, pp. 511–520.

3. Estimating trends and levels of overall concentration is difficult. Company data invariably include foreign and nonmanufacturing assets. Thus, there is some tendency to inflate both the level and upward trend of

overall concentration within manufacturing as such. The key proposition of this discussion, that mergers are the major contributor to those increases that do occur or preventative of overall concentration declines, remains valid, however.

4. J.J. McGowan, "The Effect of Alternative Antimerger Policies on the Size Distribution of Firms," *Yale Economic Essays,* 5, Fall 1965, pp. 423–474.

5. L. Hannah and J.A. Kay, *Concentration in Modern Industry* (Macmillan: London, 1977).

6. See M.A. Adelman, "The Measurement of Industrial Concentration," *Review of Economics and Statistics,* 33, November 1951, pp. 269–296; and Scherer, *Industrial Market Structure,* pp. 41–44. Hannah and Kay find a decline in overall concentration in the UK over roughly the same period of time, a period also characterized by relatively little merger activity in the UK, ibid., pp. 72–82.

7. See R. Sherman, "How Tax Policy Induces Conglomerate Mergers," *National Tax Journal,* 25, December 1972, pp. 521–529; M. Gort, "An Economic Disturbance Theory of Mergers," *Quarterly Journal of Economics,* 83, November 1969, pp. 624–642; and W.J. Mead, "Instantaneous Merger Profit as a Conglomerate Merger Motive," *Western Economic Journal,* 7, December 1969, pp. 295–306.

8. See P.O. Steiner, *Mergers* (University of Michigan Press: Ann Arbor, 1975), pp. 218–287.

9. Federal Trade Commission, *Conglomerate Merger Performance: An Empirical Analysis of Nine Corporations* (Government Printing Office: Washington, D.C., 1972).

10. Ibid., p. 86, italics in original.

11. See J. Lintner, "Expectations, Mergers and Equilibrium in Purely Competitive Securities Markets," *American Economic Review,* 61, May 1971, pp. 101–111.

12. See D.C. Mueller, "The Effects of Conglomerate Mergers: A Survey of the Empirical Evidence," *Journal of Banking and Finance,* 1, December 1977, pp. 315–342.

13. J.F. Weston, "The Nature and Significance of Conglomerate Firms," *St. John's Law Review,* special edition 44, Spring 1970, pp. 66–80; and O.E. Williamson, *Corporate Control and Business Behavior: An Inquiry into the Effects of Organization Form on Enterprise Behavior* (Prentice-Hall: New York, 1970).

14. Williamson, *Corporate Control.*

15. J.F. Weston and S.K. Mansinghka, "Tests of the Efficiency Performance in Conglomerate Firms," *Journal of Finance,* 26, September 1971, pp. 919–936.

16. R.M. Melicher and D.F. Rush, "Evidence on the Acquisition-

Related Performance of Conglomerate Firms," *Journal of Finance,* 29, March 1974, pp. 141-149.

17. FTC, *Conglomerate Merger Performance,* pp. 49-52.

18. H. Manne, "Mergers and the Market for Corporate Control," *Journal of Political Economy,* 73, April 1965, pp. 110-120.

19. R. Marris, *The Economic Theory of Managerial Capitalism* (Free Press: Glencoe, Ill., 1964).

20. S.E. Boyle, "Pre-Merger Growth and Profit Characteristics of Large Conglomerate Mergers in the United States 1948-68," *St. John's Law Review,* special edition 44, Spring 1970, pp. 152-170; R.L. Conn, "Performance of Conglomerate Firms: Comment," *Journal of Finance,* 28, June 1973, pp. 154-159; D.L. Stevens, "Financial Characteristics of Merged Firms: A Multivariate Analysis," *Journal of Financial and Quantitative Analysis,* 8, March 1973, pp. 149-158; Melicher and Rush, "Evidence on Acquisition-Related Performance"; and D.C. Mueller, ed., *The Determinants and Effects of Mergers: An International Comparison,* mimeo, Berlin, 1979.

21. H.H. Lynch, *Financial Performance of Conglomerates* (Harvard Business School: Boston, 1971).

22. G. Mandelker, "Risk and Return: The Case of Merging Firms," *Journal of Financial Economics,* 1, December 1974, pp. 303-335.

23. R. Smiley, "Tender Offers, Transactions Costs and the Firm," *Review of Economics and Statistics,* 58, February 1976, pp. 22-32.

24. Stevens, "Financial Characteristics."

25. FTC, *Conglomerate Merger Performance,* pp. 55-58.

26. Ibid., p. 42-46.

27. Ibid., p. 47.

28. S.R. Reid, *Mergers, Managers and the Economy* (McGraw-Hill: New York, 1968); Weston and Mansinghka, "Tests of Efficiency Performance"; Melicher and Rush, "Evidence on Acquisition-Related Performance."

29. See Marris, *Economic Theory;* and D.C. Mueller, "A Theory of Conglomerate Mergers," *Quarterly Journal of Economics,* 83, November 1969, pp. 643-659.

30. On the relationship between stock market and merger activity, see R.L. Nelson, *Merger Movements in American Industry 1895-1956* (Princeton University Press: Princeton, N.J., 1959); and "Business Cycle Factors in the Choice Between Internal and External Growth," in W. Alberts and J. Segall, eds., *The Corporate Merger* (University of Chicago Press: Chicago, 1966).

31. A.F. Ehrbar, "Corporate Takeovers Are Here to Stay," *Fortune,* 3 May 1978.

32. M.H. Miller and F. Modigliani, "The Cost of Capital, Corporate

Finance and the Theory of Investment," *American Economic Review,* 48, June 1958, pp. 261-287.

33. T.F. Hogarty, "Profits from Mergers: The Evidence of Fifty Years," *St. John's Law Review,* special edition 44, Spring 1970, p. 389.

34. For a discussion and references, see Mueller, "The Effects of Conglomerate Mergers."

35. Ibid. and Mueller, *Determinants and Effects of Mergers.*

36. G. Meeks, *Disappointing Marriage: A Study of the Gains from Merger,* Cambridge University Press: Cambridge, 1977.

37. K. Cowling, P. Stoneman, J. Cubbin, J. Cable, G. Hall, S. Domberger, and P. Dutton, *Mergers and Economic Performance,* Cambridge University Press: Cambridge, 1979, forthcoming.

38. Mueller, *Determinants and Effects of Mergers.*

39. See, for example, Meeks, *Disappointing Marriage;* and Mueller, *Determinants and Effects of Mergers.*

40. The FTC has proposed that market value be used to measure the size of spin off.

41. If the prospects were so dim that bankruptcy seemed imminent, the market value of the firm would be near zero, and the spin-off provision would not be satisfied except for a very small acquisition.

42. This proposal was made by Milton Friedman to get rid of the corporate income tax [*Capitalism and Freedom* (University of Chicago Press: Chicago, 1962), pp. 130-133]. H.G. Grabowski and D.C. Mueller discuss it in the general context of managerial overinvestment ("Life-Cycle Effects on Corporate Returns on Retentions," *Review of Economics and Statistics,* 57, November 1975, pp. 400-409). Alan Fisher of the FTC has proposed it as a substitute for antimerger legislation.

Comment

Kenneth M. Davidson

We in the Office of Special Projects in the Federal Trade Commission's Bureau of Competition have looked at many of these issues. My comments reflect my personal views and not necessarily those of the FTC or any of its commissioners.

In general, I agree with Professors White and Siegfried that (1) aggregate concentration has not increased and (2) that measurement of specific variables shows that "good corporate behavior" sometimes is associated with larger firm size and sometimes with smaller firm size. Indeed, I would be hard pressed to dispute the general thrust of either of these conclusions because both could trace their origins to the FTC. At *Hearings on S.600, The Small and Independent Business Protection Act of 1979,* FTC Chairman Michael Pertschuk and his Bureau of Competition Director Alfred F. Dougherty, Jr. and Bureau of Economics Director William S. Comanor each based his testimony on the proposition that, although some sectors of the economy had experienced increased concentration (most notably the manufacturing sector), overall aggregate concentration has remained relatively stable for at least thirty years.[1] In fact, the evidence White has developed and assembled relies, in part, on a table prepared by the FTC tracing the share of nonfinancial assets held by the 400 largest corporations and was included in Dougherty's testimony.[2] Siegfried's excellent review of the state of economists' knowledge is based on an FTC symposium whose proceedings he has ably edited.[3]

However, I would add a few observations to this agreement. First, although the level of aggregate concentration has not increased, it is nevertheless very high. The 400 largest nonfinancial corporations own about one-half of all nonfinancial corporate assets. Second, as Comanor pointed out in his testimony on S.600, one would have expected concentration to have decreased between 1950 and 1980 as a result of the economy's enormous expansion.[4] Several economic studies have attributed the failure of concentration to decline to mergers and acquisitions by the nation's largest firms.[5] Third, because the economy has grown and concentration has not declined, the largest firms have greatly increased their size, whether measured by annual sales, assets, or number of employees.

The growth in the absolute size of the nation's largest firms changes many things. Decisions by the managers of a single firm now affect many more people—more employees, more consumers, and more investors.

Accordingly, the consequences of decisions by corporate managers are magnified. Discriminatory (and nondiscriminatory) hiring practices have a broader impact; decisions to support a direction or level of research take on new significance when they involve hundreds of millions of dollars. The experience of Chrysler Corporation shows that an impending bankruptcy can be transformed from a series of personal tragedies to a public problem if the firm is large enough. Large firm size promotes visibility, and it also provokes reactions to unwanted visible effects (such as plant closings, pollution, and product defects). It promotes internal planning systems and self-conscious interactions with other large private and public organizations. Large firm size promotes government regulation by reducing the self-correcting tendencies of diversity and by making regulation easier because of private bureaucratic structures. Thus, I think we can say that mergers and resultant growth in firm size promote social change, even if the consequences for specific variables are equivocal in the measurable short run. In addition, the merger process absorbs the time and attention of chief executive officers (CEOs), time that might otherwise be turned to issues of capital investment, research, productivity, and innovation.

I think we must examine the dimensions and causes of current merger activity. We are in the midst of a merger wave that is characterized by very large acquisitions. According to W.T. Grimm & Co., 80 acquisitions of firms valued at over $100 million occurred in 1978—almost twice the number that occurred in 1977 and more than five times as many as in 1975. Despite a stagnant stock market, despite gyrating interest rates that have twice exceeded 20 percent, and despite the 1980 recession, the number of $100 million mergers has continued unabated—there were 83 in 1979 and 94 in 1980.

What drives these mergers? Let me suggest four motives:

1. Good business sense,
2. Managerial or personal motives,
3. Predispositions to grow,
4. Advice to merge.

As to the first, there is a general assertion, notably by Franco Modigliani, that the stock market is undervalued.[6] Even if this analysis were rejected, surely there are transactions for which an acquisition makes sense because of business synergies or because a company is a good buy. At the FTC we have looked at some of these economic reasons.

The admittedly incomplete evidence we have seen does not support a conclusion that these mergers are dictated solely by economic factors. For example, in examining the large acquisitions of 1978, we found no support for the thesis that target firms were poorly run. We found that the average return on equity of the target firms was significantly higher than the return realized by the firms listed in the *1978 Fortune Double 500 Directory*.[7] A study recently completed for the FTC by researchers at the University of North Carolina also found no support for the financial-fit hypothesis—that is, the target firms in the 1970s, at least, do not appear to have been underleveraged.[8]

However, many other business reasons for mergers exist that have not been examined fully. Another recently completed study sponsored by the FTC reviewed over thirty merger motives using an in-depth interview process.[9] Professor Boucher ranked those motives using the views of fourteen leading participants in the merger process, including my fellow panelist Martin Lipton, other attorneys, investment bankers, CEOs, accountants, and business consultants. On the one hand, these merger experts noted the importance of noneconomic factors but ranked only economic factors among the top eight motives. On the other hand, these same experts conceded that the postmerger record of acquiring firms does not demonstrate that mergers have, on average, helped firms achieve economic objectives. Overall measures of corporate performance after mergers are very complex, and I defer here as I have done elsewhere, to Dennis Mueller, who is more qualified to explain why he believes that (1) there is, on average, no economic benefit flowing from mergers and (2) that most acquiring firms have not benefited from mergers.[10]

Since the publication of the Berle and Means's work in the 1930s, it has been widely accepted that the personal preferences of CEOs and the economic interests of managers influence corporate decision making.[11] Baumol has suggested, and the Boucher interviews confirm, that personal prestige is more a function of sales volume than rate of profit.[12] And Marris has shown that executive salaries correlate more closely with sales volume than profit rate.[13] Even if it is clear that the interests of firms and their managers sometimes diverge, however, the impact of this divergence on merger decisions remains unclear.

The Boucher study also suggests that the business community has a bias in favor of growth, by merger or otherwise. Growth in size, market share, sales volume, or profits is seen as a sign of health or vitality. I would be troubled if this organic metaphor was taken too literally. As Richard Berendzen, president of American University, said in a different context, "Growth for its own sake is the ideology of the cancer cell."[14]

Finally, we have the advice of business consultants: Firms ought to merge to take advantage of more profitable investment opportunities afforded by the diversified firm.[15] The business buzz words of the 1970s encouraged mergers—namely, the Boston Consulting Group model, quarterly return-on-investment objectives, PIMS data, the experience curve, profit centers, and portfolio management of corporate assets. All of these contribute to the confidence that diversification will add to profitability and that diversified firms are manageable. Recent articles in business journals have questioned this advice. These newer articles suggest greater profit and growth opportunities for firms with small market shares and for larger firms in mature markets.[16] They also suggest that assumptions about the interchangeability of managers and the effectiveness of quarterly-performance targets are misplaced.[17]

I think this questioning is vital and long overdue. We are entering the fourth year of a merger boom that is engaging the time, talent, and capital resources of the nation's largest firms. Given faltering increases in domestic productivity and stiff competition from abroad, we cannot afford a repetition of what is now accepted to have been a sterile rearrangement of corporate ownership during the conglomerate merger boom of 1960s.

The consequences of mergers can have a profound impact on individual firms and the nation's economy. We at the FTC take enforcement action only against a small proportion of firms that are considered to be anticompetitive. The business community must take sole responsibility for judging the benefits of most merger transactions—and on that judgment rests the nation's social and economic future. Thus, it is important that business executives carefully examine the gilded advice of business consultants, that they resist imperial delusions, and that they not confuse growth in firm size with business vitality.

Notes

1. U.S., Senate, "Hearings on S.600, The Small and Independent Business Protection Act of 1960," before the Subcommittee on Antitrust, Monopoly and Business Rights of the Committee on the Judiciary, 96th Cong., 1st Sess., Part 1 (1979).

2. Ibid., p. 146, table I.

3. J.S. Siegfried, ed., *The Economics of Firm Size, Market Structure and Social Performance,* Proceedings of a Conference Sponsored by the Bureau of Economics (Washington, D.C.: Federal Trade Commission, July 1980).

4. U.S., Hearings on S.600," p. 18.

5. See, for example, J.J. McGowan, "The Effects of Alternative Antimerger Policies on the Size Distribution of Firms," *Yale Economic Essays,* Fall 1969, p. 423.

6. S. Rose, "The Stock Market Should be Twice as High as It Is," *Fortune,* 12 March 1979, p. 138.

7. See A Dougherty and K.M. Davidson, "Limitation without Regulation: The FTC's Bureau of Competition Approach to Conglomerate Mergers," *Utah Law Review,* 1980, p. 106.

8. W.T. Carlton; R.S. Harris; and J.F. Stewart, "An Empirical Study of Merger Motives" (Prepared for the Bureau of Competition, Federal Trade Commission and the Office of Economic Research, Office of Advocacy, Small Business Administration, Washington, D.C., December 1980).

9. W. Boucher, "The Process of Conglomerate Mergers" (Prepared for the Bureau of Competition, Federal Trade Commission, Washington, D.C., June 1980).

10. See, for example, D.C. Mueller, "The Effects of Conglomerate Mergers" *Journal of Banking and Finance,* 1977, p. 315.

11. A.A. Berle and G.C. Means, *The Modern Corporation and Private Property* (1932).

12. W.J. Baumol, *Business Behavior, Value and Growth* (1959).

13. R. Marris, *The Economic Theory of "Managerial" Capitalism* (1964).

14. "Cabbage with a College Education," Keynote address, Gettysburg College, 1 September 1978.

15. See, for example, B.D. Henderson, *Henderson on Corporate Strategy* (Cambridge, Mass.: AGY, 1979).

16. See, for example, R.G. Hamermesh; M.J. Anderson; and J.E. Harris, "Strategies for Low Market Share Businesses," *Harvard Business Review,* May/June 1978, p. 95; W.K. Hall, "Survival Strategies in a Hostile Environment," *Harvard Business Review,* September/October 1980, p. 75.

17. R.H. Hayes and W.J. Abernathy, "Managing our Way to Economic Decline," *Harvard Business Review,* July/August 1980, p. 67.

Comment: The Legal, Social, and Economic Environment for Mergers: Industrialization to Reindustrialization

Eleanor M. Fox

One hundred years ago, the United States experienced the Industrial Revolution. Enterprising industrialists rapidly expanded capacity, fell into cutthroat competition with competitors, and settled their economic battles by combination in the form of the now legendary trust. The trusts abused virtually all segments of society—farmers, shippers, small sellers, small buyers, and the general population.[1] In 1890, Congress passed a law against the trusts—the Sherman Antitrust Act.[2]

Confronted by this new antitrust law, industrialists sought a new form of combination. At the turn of the century, they devised the holding company. The holding company perpetuated the old abuses,[3] and in 1914, the people got a law against holding companies that threatened competition.[4]

Industrialists sought a new loophole. They found they could escape the technicalities of the new law by acquiring assets instead of stock. The asset acquisitions were upheld as legitimate,[5] and at the same time, the Supreme Court dealt permissively even with stock acquisitions.[6]

The late 1940s were marked by both a merger movement and World War II. Senator Kefauver and Congressman Celler, with others, looked with despair on the cartels in Germany and their prominent role in catapulting Hitler to power. They wanted to preserve, in the United States, a structure of business and society that would never, that could never, produce another Hitler. Fearing that mergers would create a society in which fewer and fewer people would control most of the industrial assets of the country, and fearing, too, that such concentrations of power would trigger a need for more and excessive government to regulate the now bigger business, Kefauver and Celler became the principal spokesmen for a merger law that would plug the assets loophole and stop the rising tide of industrial concentration.[7] Thus emerged the Celler-Kefauver Amendment of 1950.[8]

The Celler-Kefauver Amendment, and interpretations of it by the Warren Court in the 1960s, prodded risk-averse firms to look away from acquisitions of competitors and toward other acquisition targets.[9] In the same "go-go years" of the 1960s, firms and their managers, seeking growth, empire-building, and lucrative opportunities, discovered good fortunes that lay in the pursuit of undervalued assets and the acquisition of internal sources of capital. Thus arose the drive toward conglomeration.[10]

In the late 1960s and early 1970s, serious questions arose as to whether even large conglomerate mergers would lessen competition and thus run afoul of the law. For every merger case that reached the Supreme Court before the mid-1970s, the Supreme Court found a theory for illegality. If the merger eliminated substantial potential competition from a concentrated market,[11] or if it created a significant probability of reciprocity that gave a merger partner preferred access to a substantial share of a market,[12] the merger was probably illegal. As highly diversified conglomerates acquired major firms in new markets, at least one of the prohibited effects was likely to occur.

Some observers were convinced that by the early 1970s the Warren Court was ready to condemn consolidations of enormous companies, or acquisitions by the largest firms of leading firms in concentrated markets, either on grounds that the merger law barred substantial increases in aggregate concentration for social and political reasons or on the theory that such large combinations had an inherent probability of lessening competition in some of the many markets in which the combined firms operated.[13] However, the government's controversial settlement in 1972 of the cases challenging ITT's acquisitions of Hartford Fire, Grinnell, and Canteen assured that the Warren Court would never hear such a case.[14]

Meanwhile, in 1969, President Nixon appointed Warren E. Burger chief justice of the Supreme Court, and through various ensuing retirements and appointments the balance and ideology of the Supreme Court changed.[15] The Court of the 1980s, in matters of antitrust, focuses on market impact and the preservation of opportunities and incentives for lowering costs and increasing inventiveness. Overruling a Warren Court precedent in 1977, the Burger Court declared that noneconomic social values have no place in antitrust analysis.[16] The Burger Court holds the government, as antitrust plaintiff, to rigorous burdens and standards even in cases of mergers of competitors;[17] and in potential competition cases it has laid down standards for success so strict that the government never wins.[18]

While the legal climate for mergers has become more permissive, so too has the legislative and overall political environment. Moreover, business strategists are teaching theory, which has achieved some acceptance, that very large market share will produce firm efficiencies and strengthen U.S. firms in their efforts to compete successfully with the now strong German and Japanese producers and Japanese trading companies.

The new climate is hospitable to larger corporate size and may condone or even promote both loose- and tight-knit combinations. On the legislative front, the bills of the 1970s for the break-up of leading firms in concentrated industries, prohibitions of very large conglomerate mergers, and prohibition of large acquisitions by integrated oil companies have been drained of impetus. Legislative concern about corporate bigness has been replaced with concern about the performance of U.S. firms in international markets. S.300 and S.600 (the conglomerate- and oil-merger bills) have been replaced, on the agendas of senators, with S.144, the Export Trading Company Bill, which would immunize even unreasonable restraints of trade at home on the theory that such restraints may be necessary to improve the U.S. trade position abroad.[19]

Free-market economists, business strategists, and trade advocates are preaching the doctrines of permissiveness. Free-market economists propose that mergers, even of competitors, pose little or no public policy challenge unless, perhaps, as a result of merger, only three or four competitors remain in a high-barrier market and thus present the danger of successful collusion.[20] Business strategists propose that costs decline as experience accumulates; thus, the bigger, the more efficient.[21] Trade advocates urge that business combination and relaxation of antitrust is necessary to restore the U.S. comparative advantage abroad.[22]

The course of merger policy and strategy provokes new questions for the 1980s, and it provokes old questions within a new frame. Given the new progressiveness of U.S. trading partners, hard competition by lower-cost producers abroad, and expansive, worldwide distribution networks of foreign combinations, what is and should be the merger policy of the United States?

Are the premises of the new permissiveness right or wrong? Is large size (by merger or otherwise) necessary or important to realize economies or muscle to increase consumer satisfaction at home or competitive advantage abroad? Is growth of muscle for countervailing power abroad productive or counterproductive to U.S. political and economic interests? Even if advocates prove the benefits of yet greater size, how broadly do the principles apply, and what and how weighty are the hidden costs? If we should bundle all our strength into one great U.S. producer of, for example, automobiles or steel, on the theories that combination produces economies and strength, that markets are worldwide, and that the pressures of the numerous foreign competitors will cause the U.S. participant in the worldwide race constantly to seek lower costs and better performance, will we have confronted ourselves with a pocket of power greater than the government itself? Will this new enterprise on which we have placed all our bets have gained the power to keep cheap foreign steel or autos out of the country? And, when the U.S. competitor lags behind, will higher tariffs not be compelling public policy in order to protect U.S. steelworkers, autoworkers, local communities, and the ability of the U.S. firm to regain its strength?

As policymakers rush to the aid of big but laggard U.S. firms, these must not be the forgotten questions of the 1980s.

Notes

1. See H. Thorelli, *The Federal Antitrust Policy* (Baltimore: Johns Hopkins University Press, 1955).

2. The Sherman Antitrust Act, 26 Stat. 209 (1890).

3. See *Standard Oil Company of N.J.* v. *United States,* 221 U.S. 1 (1911).

4. The Clayton Act, 38 Stat. 730 (1914).

5. See *Thatcher Mfg. Co.* v. *FTC,* 272 U.S. 554 (1926).

6. For example, *United States* v. *Columbia Steel Co.,* 334 U.S. 495 (1948).

7. See S. Rep. No. 1775, 81st Cong., 2d Sess. (1950); H.R. Rep. No. 1191, 81st Cong., 1st Sess. (1949).

8. The Celler-Kefauver Amendment to the Clayton Act, 64 Stat. 1125 (1950).

9. For example, *United States* v. *Von's Grocery Co.,* 384 U.S. 270 (1966); *Brown Shoe Co.* v. *United States,* 370 U.S. 294 (1962).

10. See, for example, J. Dean, "Causes and Consequences of Growth by Conglomerate Merger: An Introduction," *St. John's Law Review* (special edition 44) 15 (1970).

11. *FTC* v. *Proctor & Gamble Co.,* 386 U.S. 568 (1967).

12. *FTC* v. *Consolidated Foods Corp.,* 380 U.S. 592 (1965).

13. Compare B. Fox and E.M. Fox, *Corporate Acquisitions and Mergers* §14.02 (New York: Matthew Bender, 1981).

14. See E.M. Fox, "The ITT Antimerger Cases: The Anatomy of Three Consent Judgments," Conference Board Record, June 1972, p. 34.

15. See E.M. Fox, "Antitrust, Mergers, and the Supreme Court: The Politics of Section 7 of the Clayton Act," *Mercer Law Review* 26 (1975): 389.

16. *Continental T.V., Inc.* v. *GTE Sylvania Inc.,* 433 U.S. 36 (1977).

17. For example, *United States* v. *General Dynamics Corp.,* 415 U.S. 486 (1974).

18. *United States* v. *Marine Bancorporation,* 418 U.S. 602 (1974).

19. See S. Lohr, "Antitrust: Big Business Breathes Easier," *The New York Times,* 15 February 1981, p. 1, col. 2.

20. See, for example, R.H. Bork, *The Antitrust Paradox* (New York: Bain, 1978), pp. 221–222.

21. See R.B. Shapiro, "Corporate Strategy and Antitrust Policy: The Experience Curve Model," in *Shifting Boundaries between Regulation and*

Competition, Conference Board Info. Bull. no. 77, p. 11 (1980). But compare R. Craswell, "Antitrust Policy Issues Raised by Some Business Strategy Models," in *Papers on Business Strategy and Antitrust,* FTC Office of Policy Planning, Washington, D.C., 1980, pp. 23–28.

22. See H.R. Rep. No. 96-1151 on the Export Trading Company Act of 1980, 96th Cong., 2d Sess. (1980).

Part III
Empirical Studies
of the Determinants
# of Mergers

9 Financial Motives in Conglomerate Mergers: An Empirical Test

Ivan E. Brick,
Lawrence J. Haber, and
Daniel Weaver

The relation between diversification and merger benefits has been the subject of theoretical debate in recent years. In this chapter, our aim is to test empirically some of the hypotheses generated in that literature. To isolate diversification effects from other possible motives for merger (such as operational synergies) we confine our attention to conglomerate mergers. Using the cumulative residual approach, we have obtained the merger premium for 114 companies (57 conglomerate mergers). The regressions performed indicate that significant positive correlation exists between the merger premium and leverage and between the merger premium and the diversification measure. These results corroborate the view of Scott (1977) that diversification, especially in the presence of high levels of debt, provides a powerful stimulus for merger.

The earliest approaches to conglomerate merger [for example, Adelman (1961), Alberts (1960), Renshaw (1968), and Smith and Schreiner (1969)] viewed corporate acquisition in the context of the Markowitz (1952; 1959) theory of asset selection. They emphasized the diversification effects of the acquisition of assets (firms) whose returns were not highly correlated with the returns of the acquiring company as a major motive in conglomerate merger. However, Levy and Sarnat (1973) questioned the importance of this motive. They showed that such diversification is valueless in a world of perfect capital markets because individual investors may achieve the same results through homemade diversification—that is, diversifying their own portfolio. Moreover, even when there is a constraint on the number of securities an investor may own, the effect of this sort of corporate growth on an investor's welfare is ambiguous. Though the standard deviation of a firm's returns may be reduced by corporate acquisition (perhaps with no reduction in the acquiring firm's expected rate of return), the number of securities available to the investor may also be reduced, which lowers his latitude for choice between risk and expected rate of return. Finally, Levy and Sarnat noted that, in the presence of the bankruptcy costs—or any sort of capital-cost economy of scale—the argument for conglomerate merger becomes stronger. The merged firm has more stable cash flows, and hence the probability of incurring bankruptcy costs is reduced.

This last observation was the departure point for several acticles [for example, Lewellen (1971), Higgins and Schall (1975), and more recently, Scott (1977)]. They were concerned with the effect of market imperfections—taxes and bankruptcy costs—on the stock, debt, and total values of the merging firms. The major thrust of this literature is that, in the absence of economies of scale for bankruptcy costs, there are few incentives for merger. However, our tax structure does encourage mergers to some degree. The losses of a potentially bankrupt partner can be used as a tax deduction for a profitable enterprise; if the firm were allowed to go bankrupt, the deduction would be lost. Gains of this sort are due to the coinsurance effect.

The empirical literature does not deal with conglomerate mergers explicitly but groups them with all other mergers. Most of the articles, at least incidentally, are concerned with the existence of above normal returns for the acquiring and acquired firm as a result of merger. If such excess returns exist, their timing and distribution reflect the structure and efficiency of the market for mergers. Mandelker (1974) was the first researcher explicitly to use the Capital Asset Pricing Model (CAPM) in determining residual (excess) returns. He found, on the one hand, that stockholders of the acquiring firm earned normal returns during the pre- and postmerger periods. On the other hand, stockholders of the acquired firm earned significant abnormal returns in the seven months preceding the completion of mergers. These results are consistent with the hypothesis of a perfectly competitive efficient market (on the demand side) for acquisitions.

Dodd and Ruback (1977) contended that Mandelker's use of the completion date of merger in a test of market efficiency was inappropriate since notice of the merger usually comes prior to the completion date. They suggested using instead the date of public announcement of the merger. In a study of tender offers, they found that target firms earned significant abnormal returns in the month in which the offer was announced, regardless of whether the offer was accepted. Also, they reported that stockholders of successful bidding firms earned a small abnormal return in the month of announcement.

The finding that acquiring firms earn excess returns corroborated an earlier finding. Halpern (1973), using a variant of the method employed by both Mandelker and Dodd and Ruback, found that when he adjusted for general market factors (using an industry index) and for the relative size of the acquiring and acquired firms, the gains of the merger were equally distributed among the participants. Halpern concluded that the market for mergers is efficient but noncompetitive (both the acquired and acquiring firms are uniquely suited to one another in some way).

Ellert (1976), in a study of the effects of antitrust actions on the performance of the merger partners, used methods similar to Mandelker's. He noted, however, that, while acquiring firms have positive excess returns prior to merger, these returns occur long before they could be attributable to any merger activity. Also, while acquired firms experience marked positive returns in the seven months prior to merger anouncement, they have significant negative returns in the period before merger completion. Possibly, this might indicate that prior management was inefficient. The main result of Ellert's study was that antimerger action by the government had little effect upon merger gains and, hence, was not likely to affect concentration of monopoly power.

Finally, Langetieg (1978) compared the performance of merged firms to a control group of firms of the same industry that did not merge. Furthermore, Langetieg used a two-factor model (market and industry factors) to describe the stochastic-return process in the capital markets. He found that the abnormal returns to the acquiring firms in the postmerger period were not significantly positive. However, the premerger returns for both parties were small but significant. Consistent with previous studies, the acquired firms seemed to register greater excess rates of return than the acquiring firms.

A Model of Diversification Benefits

In this section we present a model similar to those of Scott (1977) and Kim and McConnell (1977) that demonstrates the role of leverage and diversification in the determination of the total merger premium. In a single-period framework, consider two firms, A and B, that are possible merger partners and define:

X_i = The operating earnings of firm i.

R_i = Total cash flow to bondholders of firm i. We assume for simplicity that these payments are entirely tax deductible.

B_i = The bankruptcy cost for firm i. These costs might be a function of a cash shortfall—that is, $R_i - X_i$.

CF_i = The total cash flow of firm i.

t = The corporate income-tax rate.

Then the cash flow of firm A can be defined in two distinct states: solvency $(X_A \geq R_A)$ and bankruptcy $(X_A < R_A)$. More formally:

$$CF_A = \begin{cases} (1 - t)X_A + tR_A & X_A \geq R_A \\ \\ X_A - B_A & B_A \leq X_A < R_A. \end{cases}$$

If the firm's operating earnings exceed its fixed payments, then the cash flow of the firm is one minus the tax rate times its taxable income ($X_A - R_A$), which represents payments to the stockholders of firm A plus R_A, which represents the payments to bondholders. However, in the event that operating earnings are less than R_A, the firm is insolvent and its entire earnings less bankruptcy costs are paid to the bondholders of the firm. The cash flows for firm B may be represented in the same way.

Now, if we assume the firms merge, the cash flows of the merged firm may be defined as:

$$CF_M = \begin{cases} (1 - t)(X_A + X_B) + t(R_A + R_B) & X_A + X_B \geq R_A + R_B \\ \\ (X_A + X_B) - B_M & B_M < X_A + X_B < R_A + R_B. \end{cases}$$

The interpretation of these outcomes is the same as that of the single firms except that both the operating earnings and the fixed payments are summed. But bankruptcy costs of the merged firm are not necessarily the sum of those of the individual firms. If the bankruptcy costs of the merged firm are less than sum of the bankruptcy costs of the constituent firms, there are economies of scale in bankruptcy. However, the existence of such economies is debatable. In fact, one may argue that the larger the assets of the bankrupt firm, the (proportionately) more difficult the reorganization becomes upon insolvency, so that there would be diseconomies of scale in bankruptcy – that is, $B_M > B_A + B_B$.

In this one-period framework, the benefits of merger $[CF_M - (CF_A + CF_B)]$ may be defined as the difference between the cash flows of the merged firm and the sum of the cash flows of the individual firms. Thus,

$$CF_M - (CF_A + CF_B) =$$

1. 0 $X_A > R_A, X_B > R_B$; $X_A + X_B > R_A + R_B$

2. $t(R_B - X_B) + B_B$ $X_A > R_A, X_B < R_B$; $X_A + X_B > R_A + R_B$

3. $t(R_A - X_A) + B_A$ $X_A < R_A, X_B > R_B$; $X_A + X_B > R_A + R_B$

4. $t(X_A - R_A) + B_B - B_M$ $X_A > R_A, X_B < R_B$ $X_A + X_B < R_A + R_B$

5. $t(X_B - R_B) + B_A - B_M$ $X_A < R_A, X_B > R_B$ $X_A + X_B < R_A + R_B$

6. $B_A + B_B - B_M$ $X_A < R_A, X_B < R_B$; $X_A + X_B < R_A + R_B$

This relationship represents a contingency table of the gains or losses of merger abstracting from the type of coinsurance effects analyzed by Kim and McConnell (1977) and Higgins and Schall (1975). We do this by assuming that stockholders receive side payments from bondholders or recall all bonds prior to the merger and reissue debt after merger so that no wealth transfer from stockholders to bondholders occurs.

While the interpretation of each term in the contingency table would be cumbersome, we may note the following: (1) If the state of the world is such that both firms remain solvent, there is no financial benefit from merger. (2) If both firms individually would have gone bankrupt, there is no benefit from merger unless economies of scale exist in bankruptcy costs – that is, $B_M < B_A + B_B$. (3) If one firm is solvent and one is insolvent and the merged firm would be solvent, then there would be a tax savings [for example, $t(R_B - X_B)$ in line 2] and a saving on bankruptcy costs (B_B in line 2). Thus, there is a positive benefit from merger in this case. Here, the tax savings result because the merged firm is able to take advantage of the tax losses of the otherwise insolvent firm. (4) If one firm is solvent and the other insolvent and the merged firm would be insolvent, then there would be a tax benefit [for example, $t(X_A - R_A)$ in line 4] but an increase in bankruptcy costs ($B_B - B_M$ in line 4). Here, these effects are offsetting so that in general the benefits of merger are unclear. If we assume, however, that bankruptcy costs are a monotonically increasing function of the cash shortfall, then there will always be a decrease in bankruptcy costs (for example, $B_B - B_M > 0$ in line 4), and hence there is a positive benefit of merger. Finally, in this case, the tax benefit occurs because the income of the solvent partner is no longer taxable.

Although we may make no conclusive case for conglomerate merger in this example, we may use it to illustrate several hypotheses that we test later. First, if financial benefits are to be derived from conglomerate merger, then these benefits must result from diversification unless there are economies of scale in bankruptcy. Consider the case in which the cash flows of the constituent firms are correlated, in the sense that whenever $X_A > R_A$, then $X_B > R_B$, and whenever $X_A < R_A$, then $X_B < R_B$. Abstracting from economies of bankruptcy costs, there would be no benefit to a merger. Thus, our hypothesis suggests that the prime financial motive for merger is diversification—that is, the greater the degree of diversification, the smaller the likelihood of default of the merged firm. Consequently, this would imply lower expected bankruptcy costs and smaller likelihood of forfeiture of tax credits. Second, we may note that if there is no debt in this example, then no possibility of bankruptcy exists for any of the firms. Therefore, there is again no benefit to merger (as the line 1 case will apply). Hence, the second hypothesis is that, for a given degree of diversification, the greater is the leverage, the greater are the benefits to merger.

In summary, the hypothesis we test is that positive correlation exists between the merger premium and some measure of diversification and between the merger premium and the debt-equity ratios of both firms.

Data and Methodology

As discussed in the previous section, we must measure diversification and the merger premium. An appropriate measurement of diversification measures the degree to which merger would decrease the variability of cash flows and hence reduce the probability of default. Accordingly, we use the correlation of the net incomes of the two merger partners, CORRNI. The sample correlation obtained from the *Moody's Industrial Manual* for the period $y - 10$ to $y - 1$, where y is the year of the merger. A low CORRNI would indicate a high degree of diversification between the two firms. Hence, we would expect a negative relationship between CORRNI and the merger premium.

To measure the merger premium, we used the familiar cumulative residual technique first developed by FAMA et al. (1969). We employ the market model to obtain the cumulative average residual. The market model can be expressed as

$$R_i = \alpha_i + \beta_i R_M + E_i,$$

where R_i is the rate of return of security i and R_M is the rate of return of the market portfolio. The parameter estimates $\hat{\alpha}$ and $\hat{\beta}$ were calculated using monthly return data from the CRSP files for the period $t - 96$ to $t - 12$, where t is the announcement date of the merger. As Halpern (1973) demonstrates, there is an effect on stock prices prior to the announcement of the merger due to the leaking of information about the impendeing merger. In order to minimize the possibility of this information effect's biasing our estimators, $t - 12$ was chosen as the end month of estimation. Employing the parameter estimates, the market model was used to estimate the cumulative residual of each firm for the period $Z - 12$ to Z, where Z is the completion date of the merger. We assume that markets are efficient so that any information regarding the value of the merger is fully assessed by the market by the completion date [see Mandelker (1974), Ellert (1976), and Langetieg (1978)]. Thus, this cumulative residual is the merger premium.

We regress the merger premium of the acquiring company, CUM1; the acquired company, CUM2; and the weighted-average merger premium of the two components, CUMD, against the debt-equity ratio of the acquiring company, DE1; the debt-equity ratio of the acquired company, DE2; and CORRNI. The weights employed to estimate CUMD were based on the book value of assets of each company for the fiscal year prior to the merger.

As we argued in the previous section, the existence of a high degree of diversification without a significant degree of leverage would not have as great an effect on the merger premium as the existence of a significant degree of both leverage and diversification. To measure this interaction between leverage and diversification, we use the dummy variable, DUM-CORR, which is defined as follows:

$$
\text{DUMMCOR} = \begin{cases} 1 & \text{if } DE1 > DE2, DE1 > .87, \text{ and } CORRNI < \\ & .385 \\ & \text{or} \\ & \text{if } DE2 > DE1, DE2 > .31, \text{ and } CORRNI < \\ & .385 ; \\ 0 & \text{otherwise.} \end{cases}
$$

(The sample means of DE1, DE2, and CORRNI are .87, .31, and .385 respectively.) We expect a positive relationship between CUM and DUM-CORR.

Finally, to account for any tax consequences resulting from the method of acquisition—that is, cash or stock—a dummy variable, DUMSTK, was included and is defined as follows:

$$
\text{DUMSTK} = \begin{cases} 0 & \text{if acquisition is by stock,} \\ 1 & \text{if acquisition is by cash.} \end{cases}
$$

We also used the geometric mean of 1 plus the residual error for the period Z-12 to Z as a second measure of the merger premium. This geometric mean was approximated by taking the natural logarithm of 1 plus the residual error for each month between Z-12 to Z and obtaining the average of these logarithms. We then regress this new measure of the merger premium against our independent variables as described previously, where LCUM1, LCUM2, and LUMCD are the merger premiums of the acquiring company, the acquired company, and the weighted-average merger premium of the two companies respectively.

The sample consists of 57 conglomerate mergers (a total of 114 companies) occurring between March 1957 and March 1976. These mergers were selected on the basis of Federal Trade Commission classification as pure conglomerate (category number 5). Also, both partners were required to be listed on the New York Stock Exchange. The debt-equity ratios, the book value of assets, and net-income figures were obtained from *Moody's Industrial Manual*. Finally, Fisher's value-weighted market index was used as a proxy for the return of the market portfolio.

Recently, several studies [for example, Bey and Pinches (1980), Brenner and Smidt (1977), Brown (1977), and Morgan (1976)] suggest that the market model suffers from heteroscedasticity. In the presence of heteroscedasticity, the ordinary least squares estimators are unbiased and consistent but are not efficient. Therefore, we expect our estimates of the merger premium to be also unbiased, and we feel justified in our use of the ordinary least squares model.

Finally, it is possible that residuals from different securities at the same calendar month are correlated and therefore we should use a portfolio residual technique. However, as Brenner (1979) notes, this is a problem in studies in which each relative month is also the same calendar month for many securities. However, since the mergers studied here are not usually contemporaneous, this problem is negligible (see table 9-1).

Results

The sample mean, the standard deviation, and the standard error of the mean of the various characteristics of our sample are given in table 9-2. The cumulative average residual of the acquiring and acquired company for the period Z-12 to Z are, respectively, .096 and .237. This is consistent with estimates obtained in other studies [see, for example, Dodd and Ruback (1977)]. The acquiring companies are on average much larger than the acquired company (see table 9-2 where ASSETS1 and ASSETS2 are the book value of the assets of the acquiring and acquired firm respectively for the fiscal year prior to the completion of the merger). Furthermore, they are on average more highly levered than the acquired companies.

The regression model used for our analysis is

$$CUM = \gamma_0 + \gamma_1(DE1) + \gamma_2(DE2) + \gamma_3(DUMSTK) + \gamma_4(DUMCORR)$$
$$+ \gamma_5(CORRNI) + e_i.$$

The dependent variables are CUMD, LCUMD, CUM1, LCUM1, CUM2, or LCUM2, respectively, for alternative runs. According to our model, we would expect to find that γ_5 is significantly negative and that γ_4 is significantly positive. In addition, because an incentive or disincentive to merge is magnified by the amount of debt, we cannot predict *a priori* the signs of γ_1 and γ_2. However, under the assumption that a firm chooses its merger partner on a rational basis, we would expect that highly levered firms would only merge with partners that offer significant bankruptcy-cost savings due to diversification. Therefore, γ_1 and γ_2 should be significantly positive. Finally, because of the tax consequences of merger acquisition via cash, we added the dummy variable DUMSTK. Since rational managers would select the method of acquisition that is optimum, we would then expect that, for a cross-sectional sample, $\gamma_3 = 0$.

Table 9–1
The Pattern of Merger Announcements and Completions

Announcement Month	Number of Merger Announcements	Completion Month	Number of Merger Completions
1	1	7	1
11	1	13	1
21	1	25	1
22	1	30	1
25	1	32	1
29	1	39	1
47	1	51	2
48	1	52	1
51	1	59	1
59	1	81	1
74	1	87	1
86	1	99	1
95	1	101	1
97	1	102	1
98	1	108	1
104	1	119	1
113	1	122	1
117	1	123	1
118	1	124	1
123	1	125	1
125	1	130	1
126	1	133	1
128	1	134	1
131	2	135	2
132	1	136	2
133	1	137	1
134	2	138	1
135	4	139	4
136	2	140	1
139	2	141	2
140	1	142	1
141	1	144	1
143	1	147	1
146	1	151	1
147	1	158	1
152	1	159	2
157	1	171	1
165	1	173	1
172	1	174	1
184	1	190	1
188	1	192	1
205	1	206	1
210	1	214	1
215	2	220	1
225	3	226	3
227	1	229	1

Table 9–2
Sample Values

Variable	Mean	Standard Deviation	Standard Error of Mean
CUMD	.129	.295	.039
CUM1	.096	.339	.045
CUM2	.237	.364	.048
ASSETS1	$771.5 million	$845.4 million	$112.0 million
ASSETS2	$202.5 million	$232.6 million	$31.1 million
DE1	.871	2.183	.289
DE2	.312	.316	.042
CORRNI	.385	.462	.062

As summarized by table 9–3 and 9–4, the results essentially support the model. In particular, γ_4 is significantly positive for dependent variables CUMD, LCUMD, CUM1, or LCUM1.[1] Similarly, at least one leverage variable is significantly positive for all of the dependent variables except for CUM2 and LCUM2. However, γ_5 is not significantly different from zero, and there is no strong relationship between our independent variables and the merger premium for the acquired company—that is, CUM2 and LCUM2. These results suggest that the interaction between diversification and leverage is the significant factor and not diversification by itself. Further, although previous studies have indicated that an acquiring firm purchases another firm for the latter's relatively lower degree of leverage [see, for example, Melicher and Rush (1974)], the model and the results presented here indicate that the merger premium of the acquiring company increases with leverage of the acquired firm.

We also tested our model with an alternative specification of DUM-CORR, now defined as:

$$\text{DUMCORR} = \begin{cases} 1 & \begin{array}{l} \text{if DE1} > \text{DE2, DE1} < .87, \text{ and CORRNI} > .385. \\ \text{or} \\ \text{if DE2} > \text{DE1, DE2} < .31, \text{ and CORRNI} > .385;} \end{array} \\ 0 & \text{otherwise.} \end{cases}$$

In this case, our interaction variable identifies the merger in which a significant degree of leverage and very little diversificatin exist. We would therefore expect a negative relationship between DUMCORR and the merger-premium variable. The results as summarized by tables 9–5 and 9–6 confirm our previous findings. γ_3 is not significantly different from zero. The leverage variables are more significant under the new specification of our

Table 9-3
Initial Specification of DUMCORR, Regression Results, Natural Dependent Variable

Dependent Variable	Intercept	DE1	DE2	DUMSTK	DUMCORR	CORRNI	PROB > F	R²
CUMD	-.0614 (-.8232)	.0259*** (1.5177)	.2104** (1.7496)	.0311 (.3980)	.1850** (1.8282)	.0992 (1.0843)	.0756	.1796
CUMD	-.0517 (-.7395)	.0253*** (1.5033)	.2163** (1.8278)	—	.1928** (1.9585)	.0995 (1.0972)	.0417	.1769
CUM1	-.1019 (-1.1617)	.0293*** (1.4657)	.2065*** (1.4611)	-.0124 (-.1352)	.2353** (1.9788)	.1345 (1.2508)	.1085	.1636
CUM1	-.1058 (-1.2892)	.0296*** (1.4961)	.2042*** (1.4701)	—	.2322** (2.0102)	.1343 (1.2621)	.0589	.1633
CUM2	.2161** (2.1163)	.0011 (.0495)	-.1921 (-1.1676)	.0304 (.2843)	.1142 (.8257)	.0844 (.6745)	.8384	.0403
CUM2	.2256** (2.3603)	.0006 (.0270)	-.1863 (-1.1519)	—	.1219 (.9062)	.0847 (.6834)	.7332	.0387

Note: The numbers within the parentheses are the t statistics.

**Significant at 5 percent level.
***Significant at 10 percent level.

Table 9–4
Initial Specification of DUMCORR, Regression Results, Logarithmic Dependent Variable

Dependent Variable	Intercept	DE1	DE2	DUMSTK	DUMCORR	CORRNI	PROB > F	R^2
LCUMD	−.0049	.0008	.0222**	.0031	.0150**	.0068	.0262	.2228
	(−.9102)	(.6675)	(2.5314)	(.5499)	(2.0332)	(1.0189)		
LCUMD	−.0039	.0007	.0228**	—	.0158**	.0068	.0138	.2180
	(−.7782)	(.6297)	(2.6374)		(2.1965)	(1.0311)		
LCUM1	−.0075	.0009	.0204***	−.0016	.0242**	.0087	.0482	.1985
	(−1.0882)	(.6333)	(1.8433)	(−.2230)	(2.5961)	(1.0353)		
LCUM1	−.0080	.0010	.0201**	—	.0238**	.0087	.0241	.1977
	(−1.2409)	(.6596)	(1.8475)		(2.6273)	(1.0433)		
LCUM2	.0114***	−.0001	−.0066	.0100	.0040	.0040	.7086	.0567
	(1.7666)	(−.0979)	(−.6356)	(1.4748)	(.4634)	(.5018)		
LCUM2	.0146**	−.0003	−.0047	—	.0066	.0041	.9438	.0148
	(2.3535)	(−.2146)	(−.4523)		(.7550)	(.5091)		

Note: The numbers within the parentheses are the t statistics.

**Significant at 5 percent level.

***Significant at 10 percent level.

Table 9–5
Regression Results, Alternative Specification of DUMCORR, Natural Dependent Variable

Dependent Variable	Intercept	DE1	DE2	DUMSTK	DUMCORR	CORRNI	PROB > F	R^2
CUMD	-.0382	.0379**	.3965*	.0770	-.2109**	.1051	.0661	.1853
	(-.5423)	(2.1475)	(2.7084)	(.9976)	(-1.9266)	(1.1464)		
CUMD	-.0063	.0362**	.4035*	—	-.1976**	.0927	.0513	.1688
	(-.1008)	(2.0598)	(2.7598)		(-1.8191)	(1.0213)		
CUM1	-.0650	.0422**	.4009**	.0411	-.2138**	.1210	.1663	.1436
	(-.7739)	(2.0026)	(2.2952)	(.4469)	(-1.6369)	(1.1061)		
CUM1	-.0480	.0413**	.4047**	—	-.2067***	.1144	.1034	.1401
	(-.6961)	(1.9843)	(2.3381)		(-1.6074)	(1.0641)		
CUM2	.2126**	.0147	.0263	.0701	-.2637**	.1395	.4651	.0873
	(2.2548)	(.6222)	(.1347)	(.6793)	(-1.8002)	(1.1368)		
CUM2	.2417*	.0131	.0327	—	-.2517**	.1282	.3821	.0787
	(2.8913)	(.5613)	(.1684)		(-1.7400)	(1.0606)		

*Significant at 1 percent level.
**Significant at 5 percent level.
***Significant at 10 percent level.

Table 9-6
Regression Results, Alternative Specification of DUMCORR, Logarithmic Dependent Variable

Dependent Variable	Intercept	DE1	DE2	DUMSTK	DUMCORR	CORRNI	PROB > F	R^2
LCUMD	-.0017 (-.3356)	.0013 (1.0261)	.0298* (2.6998)	.0060 (1.0354)	-.0075 (-.9105)	.0035 (.5177)	.0915	.1712
LCUMD	.0007 (.1502)	.0012 (.9285)	.0304 (2.7506)	—	-.0064 (-.7901)	.0026 (.3814)	.0758	.1531
LCUM1	-.0022 (-.3332)	.0018 (1.0667)	.0323** (2.2633)	.0030 (.3999)	-.0115 (-1.0787)	.0033 (.3692)	.3212	.1094
LCUM1	-.0010 (-.1718)	.0017 (1.0413)	.0326** (2.3046)	—	-.0110 (-1.0467)	.0028 (.3209)	.2192	.1065
LCUM2	.0112*** (1.8491)	.0003 (.2397)	.0016 (.1277)	.0115*** (1.7259)	-.0100 (-1.0581)	.0062 (.7809)	.5693	.0737
LCUM2	.0160* (2.8962)	.0001 (.0696)	.0026 (.2067)	—	-.0080 (-.8386)	.0043 (.5428)	.9255	.0174

*Significant at 1 percent level.

**Significant at 5 percent level.

***Significant at 10 percent level.

dummy variable, DUMCORR. γ_4 is significantly negative for the dependent variables, CUMD and CUM1. However, as before, γ_5 is not significantly positive, and there is no strong relationship between the dependent variables and the merger premium for the acquired firm.

In order to test for multicollinearity, we examined the eigenvalues (λ_i) of the correlation matrix for regressor (non dummy) variables. For orthogonal data, $\lambda_i = 1$ for all i, and $\Sigma 1/\lambda_i = 3$ (the number of regressors). In this case, $\Sigma 1/\lambda_i = 3.12$, which demonstrates that the ordinary least squares estimates do not have a high mean square error.

Conclusions

The empirical results are supportive overall of the diversification motive for conglomerate merger. However, we feel that the work in this area is far from completed. In particular, our model assumes that the conflict of interest between bondholders and stockholders in the face of the coinsurance effect is resolved either by returning all debt prior to the merger announcement or by side payments from the bondholders to the stockholders [see, for example, Scott (1977) and Kim and McConnell (1977)]. An empirical model should be developed that will indicate, from the financial characteristics of the merging firm, which class of creditors will benefit most from the coinsurance effect. For example, if one of the merger partners is failing financially, we might expect that the stockholders of this firm will benefit at the expense of the stockholders of the other. However, it is also possible that the financially superior firm is in a better bargaining position to extract a greater percentage of the total merger premium. This might explain the weak results we obtained for the acquired companies in our empirical model. Future research in this area is planned by the authors.

Note

1. Whenever directionality is assumed, then a single-tailed test is performed. Otherwise, a two-tailed test is used.

References

M.A. Adelman. "The Anti-Merger Act, 1950–1960." *American Economic Review, Proceedings,* May 1961, pp. 236–244.

W.W. Alberts. "The Profitability of Growth by Merger." In *The Corporate Merger,* edited by Alberts and J.E. Segall. Chicago and London, 1966, pp. 235–287.

R.P. Bey and G.E. Pinches. "Additional Evidence of Heteroscedasticity in the Market Model." *Journal of Financial and Quantitative Analysis,* June 1980, pp. 299–322.

M. Brenner. "The Sensitivity of the Efficient Market Hypothesis to Alternative Specifications of the Market Model." *Journal of Finance,* September 1979, pp. 915–929.

M. Brenner and S. Smidt. "A Simple Model of Non-Stationarity of Systematic Risk." *Journal of Finance,* September 1977, pp. 1081–1092.

S.J. Brown. "Heteroscedasticity in the Market Model: A Comment." *Journal of Business,* January 1977, pp. 80–83.

P. Dodd and R. Ruback. "Tender Offers and Stockholder Returns: An Empirical Analysis." *Journal of Financial Economics,* December 1977, pp. 351–374.

J.C. Ellert. "Mergers, Antitrust Law Enforcement, and Stochastic Returns." *Journal of Finance,* May 1976, pp. 715–732.

E. Fama; L. Fisher; M. Jensen; and R. Roll. "The Adjustment of Stock Prices for New Information." *International Economic Review,* February 1969, pp. 1–21.

P. Halpern. "Empirical Estimates of the Amount and Distribution of Gains to Companies in Merger." *Journal of Business,* October 1973, pp. 554–575.

R.C. Higgins and L.D. Schall. "Corporate Bankruptcy and Conglomerate Merger." *Journal of Finance,* March 1975, pp. 93–113.

E.H. Kim and J.J. McConnell. "Corporate Merger and the Co-Insurance of Corporate Debt." *Journal of Finance,* May 1977, pp. 349–365.

T. Langetieg. "An Application of a Three-Factor Performance Index to Measure Stockholder Gains from Merger." *Journal of Financial Economics,* December 1978, pp. 365–383.

H. Levy and M. Sarnat. "Diversification, Portfolio Analysis and the Uneasy Case for Conglomerate Merger." *Journal of Finance,* September 1973, pp. 795–802.

W.G. Lewellen. "A Pure Financial Rationale for Conglomerate Merger." *Journal of Finance,* May 1971, pp. 521–537.

G. Mandelker. "Risk and Return: The Case of Merging Firms." *Journal of Financial Economics,* December 1974, pp. 303–335.

H. Markowitz. "Portfolio Selection." *Journal of Finance,* March 1952, pp. 77–91.

———. *Portfolio Selection.* New York: Wiley, 1959.

R.W. Melicher and D.F. Rush. "Evidence on the Acquisition-Related Performance of Conglomerate Mergers." *Journal of Finance,* March 1974, pp. 141–149.

I.G. Morgan. "Stock Prices and Heteroscedasticity." *Journal of Business,* October 1976, pp. 496–508.

E.F. Renshaw. "The Theory of Financial Leverage and Conglomerate Mergers." *California Management Review,* Fall 1968, pp. 79–84.

J.H. Scott. "On the Theory of Conglomerate Mergers." *Journal of Finance,* September 1977, pp. 1235–1250.

K.V. Smith and J.C. Schreiner. "A Portfolio Analysis of Conglomerate Diversification." *Journal of Finance,* June 1969, pp. 413–427.

10 Financial Characteristics of Acquired Firms

Robert S. Harris,
John F. Stewart, and
Willard T. Carleton

The continued presence of merger activity in the United States has spawned tremendous interest in the topic. Public officials are concerned about the ultimate impacts of such combinations on the conduct and efficiency of corporate enterprise. Many private parties are excited about the possibilities of cashing in on the large premiums often offered in acquisitions.

This chapter studies the financial characteristics of acquired firms (1974–1977) to determine if (1) such characteristics differ markedly from the characteristics of nonacquired firms and (2) such characteristics might be useful in predicting which companies will be acquired.

Earlier studies similar to this research (Stevens 1973; Monroe and Simkowitz 1971) focus on the characteristics of firms acquired in the 1960s. The wave of mergers in the 1970s occurred in an inflationary and often sluggish economy—quite a different scenario from the earlier stream of mergers in the mid- and late 1960s. A major purpose of this study is to determine if previous findings hold for the mid-1970s.

The first section briefly reviews previous empirical studies and discusses methodological difficulties with these works. The second section describes an empirical technique (probit). After a discussion of sample construction in the third section, specific empirical measures of financial characteristics of companies are discussed in the fourth section. The fifth section presents empirical results, and the last section offers conclusions and suggestions for future research in this area.

Specific conclusions reached are that:

Statistical models (probit) to estimate the probability of acquisition do achieve statistical significance. These models indicate that smaller firms and firms with lower price-earnings ratios are more likely to be

We wish to thank the Federal Trade Commission and Small Business Administration (SBA) (Research Contract LO636) for their assistance in developing the data and their consent to its use here. All opinions expressed are those of the authors and do not necessarily reflect the position of the FTC and SBA. We also wish to thank Jeff Bass, Dave Guilkey, and Nick Calley for valuable assistance in the research.

223

acquired. Other factors (for example, liquidity and indebtedness) have effects that change over time.

Despite this statistical significance (99 percent level), only a very small portion of the factors contributing to acquisition is captured by the statistical models based only upon acquired-firm characteristics.

Empirical studies to predict merger targets must be careful in selecting the sample of firms to be studied. It is crucial to keep the ratio of acquired to nonacquired firms in the sample approximately equal to the ratio found in the firm population.

If one views mergers as marriages of firms, then it is crucial to look for areas of complementarity between the two firms. Such complementarity may be missed by a statistical investigation such as the present one based solely upon the characteristics of the acquired firm.

Previous Studies and Methodological Issues

Though most studies examine firms that merge (and especially measure the financial effects of merger), many of the studies focus either exclusively on acquiring firms or solely on stock market returns to owners of the participating firms.[1] Studies that explicitly try to predict the firms that will be acquired include Monroe and Simkowitz (1971) and Stevens (1973). Both of these studies used discriminant analysis to study the financial attributes of acquired firms.[2] Monroe and Simkowitz studied takeover targets for the year 1968 and concluded that acquired firms (relative to nonacquired firms) were smaller, had lower price-earnings ratios, lower dividend payout, and lower growth in equity. Unlike Monroe and Simkowitz, Stevens (1973) found that neither dividend payout nor price-earnings ratios seemed to be important variables. Stevens did, however, claim that a discriminant model based on financial characteristics of acquired firms provided useful classifications.

Specifically, studying a sample of forty acquired firms (acquired in 1966) and forty nonacquired firms (matched by size to the acquired), Stevens developed a discriminant model (table 10-1) that demonstrated 70 percent classification accuracy (acquired versus nonacquired). The same model was also able to classify with 67.5 percent accuracy on a set of acquired firms from subsequent years. The major difference between acquired and nonacquired firms was that acquired firms used significantly less debt than nonacquired firms. Some evidence of more liquidity for acquired firms was also present.

For the purpose of this study, five properties of these studies are impor-

Table 10-1
Stevens's Ratios for Forty Acquired Firms (1966) and Forty Nonacquired Firms

			Means	
Measurement	Ratio	Significant in Discriminant Model	Acquired	Nonacquired
Profitability	Earnings before interest and taxes/Sales	Yes	.0883	.104
Liquidity	Net working capital/Total assets	Yes	.4066*	.3459
Activity	Sales/Total assets	Yes	1.41	1.36
Indebtedness	Long-term liabilities/Total assets	Yes	13.77**	22.31
Dividend policy	Cash dividends/Net income	No	.37	.34
Stock value	Price/Earnings per share	No	15.0	17.5

Source: Stevens (1973).
*Difference in means significant at approximately .10 level.
**Difference in means significant at .01 level.

tant: (1) time period studied, (2) normalization of financial variables, (3) construction of sample, (4) coverage of variables, and (5) characteristics of acquiring firms.

Time Period Studied

Both Monroe and Simkowitz and Stevens study mergers in the late 1960s. Given the changes in financial climate, it is important to determine if characteristics of acquired firms change over time. We develop samples of acquired firms in two separate time periods, 1974–1975 and 1976–1977, to check for changes through time. These two time periods correspond to quite different economic climates in the United States.

Normalization of Financial Variables

As is widely accepted, financial ratios for individual firms often have little meaning in isolation. Use of time trends of such ratios and their relationships to industry averages are common methods of enhancing the explanatory power of financial ratios. In our study, financial variables are normalized by industry averages to see if this changes results obtained when such variables are not normalized.[3]

Construction of Sample

In Stevens's work, the sample used for analysis contained as many acquired firms as nonacquired firms; furthermore, acquired and nonacquired firms were matched by size. The matching by size prevents analysis of the effects of size on the likelihood of acquisition. We explicitly include size as a variable.

The ratio of acquired to nonacquired is a much more fundamental problem with matched samples if the models are to be used for predictive purposes. If a model is to be used as a successful method of predicting any event (in this study the event is a merger), it must be able to deal with the underlying population of firms that may participate in that event. After all, the ultimate test of such a model would be to make predictions based upon a sample of firms for which one does not know the ultimate outcome. Sample designs such as that employed by Stevens that use equal-sized samples of acquired and nonacquired firms when the underlying population is not in such an equal ratio may produce seriously misleading results. Given a sample of which one a priori knows that one-half will be acquired, a naive guess would classify 50 percent of the acquired correctly. Given a population in which one knew 90 percent would not be acquired, the naive classification (and one that is 90 percent accurate) is to classify all companies as not acquired. The problem, of course, is misclassifying all of the firms that were ultimately acquired. In the work presented here, data reflecting the percentage of acquired and nonacquired firms in the population are used.

Coverage of Variables

Characteristics not reflected in financial-statement representations of firms undoubtedly play very important roles in mergers. Product-market industry concentration, advertising intensity, and concentration of firm ownership all may crucially affect the likelihood of a firm's being acquired. This study restricts itself to financial-statement variables though we hope that future research will improve upon this.

Characteristics of Acquiring Firms

As did Monroe and Simkowitz and Stevens, the present study looks at mergers using information based only on half of the participants—the acquired firms. The implied assumption is that the acquiring firms value the characteristics in a merger partner in basically the same fashion. In fact, given the diversity of acquiring firms, it is probable that important factors in merger activity may go undetected by estimating a model over all acquired firms. For example, a firm with low liquidity may acquire one with high liquidity, while a firm with high liquidity may acquire one with low liquidity; both mergers may be based on an important role of corporate liquidity. This role for liquidity, however, may not be detected by looking only at the acquired entities; instead, it may be found that acquired firms have liquidity that on average is indistinguishable from that of the non-acquired firms.

Our findings based only upon acquired-firm characteristics must be viewed in this light. Further reseach on matching between acquired and acquiring firms is needed.

Empirical Methodology

The basic empirical problem is to identify those characteristics of a firm that have a statistically significant impact on the probability that the firm will be acquired. The difficulty is that it is not possible to observe and measure the probability that a firm will be acquired. It is only possible to observe a sample of firms over a specified period of time and to identify which of those firms were acquired and which were not; thus, one must estimate a model with a binary dependent variable that can be expressed as

$$y = g(X),\qquad(10.1)$$

where y is a variable representing whether or not the event occurred ($y = 0$ if the firm was not acquired, $y = 1$ if the firm was acquired), and X is a vector of financial characteristics of the firm. A number of techniques can be used to estimate relationships of the type described in equation 10.1. These include linear probability functions, logit analysis, probit analysis, and discriminant analysis. A discussion of these techniques can be found in Johnson (1972), Kmenta (1971), Theil (1971), and Watson (1974).

While earlier studies have used discriminant analysis, we use probit for our empirical work. Probit provides a means for estimating the probability that a firm will be acquired as well as the contribution of a particular financial characteristic to that probability. Probit assumes that potential acquiring firms will judge the attractiveness of all potential acquisitions. This unobservable index of attractiveness is assumed to be the same for all potential acquiring firms and can be written

$$Y_t^* = X_t B + U_t\qquad(10.2)$$

where Y_t^* is the unobserved dependent variable describing the attractiveness of firm t as a potential acquisition,

X_t is a vector of variables describing the relevant characteristics of firm t

B is a vecor of coefficients, and

U_t is an unobserved random variable assumed to be independently distributed with mean zero and variance.

Probit estimates the coefficients (B) by maximum likelihood techniques, given the pattern of the events observed in the sample. These coefficients then can be used to estimate the probability that a particular firm (given its financial characteristics) will be acquired. Coefficients have the statistical properties of consistency and an asymptotically normal distribution. The statistical significance of the probit model can be tested by looking at the negative ratio of the log likelihood function times two. This quantity is distributed chi-squared (degrees of freedom equal to the number of parameters estimated) and is the logical equivalent of the F test in the linear regression to test the hypothesis that all estimated coefficients are equal to zero.

Sample Design

To use the probit technique described in the previous section, one must have data on the financial characteristics of a sample of firms, some of which were acquired and some of which were not. The sample used here consists of:

A sample of 61 firms acquired in 1976 and 1977,

A sample of 45 firms acquired in 1974 and 1975,

A sample of approximately 1,200 nonacquired firms.[4]

Primary data sources were (1) the COMPUSTAT Expanded Annual Industrial Tape (May 1979—Primary, Supplementary, and Tertiary Files); (2) the COMPUSTAT Expanded Annual Industrial Research File (May 1979—Primary, Supplementary, and Tertiary Files); and (3) the Federal Trade Commission's Merger Series (Overall and Large).

The COMPUSTAT Industrial Research File covers firms that have been deleted from the COMPUSTAT Industrial File since 1970. It thus provides an excellent source of data for companies no longer in existence (for example, as a result of merger or bankruptcy).

The FTC merger series covers acquired firms classified in manufacturing and mining. The FTC definition of merger requires that "the acquisition must represent the purchase of 50.1 percent or more of the stock or assets of the company acquired," and (b) "an independent company, subsidiary, or division of another company must be acquired."[5]

Acquired Firms

To be included in the study, an acquired firm satisfies these characteristics:

COMPUSTAT information exists for the acquired firm,

COMPUSTAT classifies the firm as being in a four-digit industry from 2000 to 3999 (manufacturing),

The firm is recorded as an acquired firm by the FTC during the period 1974–1977.

In a few cases, firms satisfying all of these criteria were eliminated from the sample. This typically occurred if further examination (for example, using *Moody's Industrial Manuals*) indicated that the merger was complicated by additional factors.

Nonacquired Firms

The nonacquired firms were selected from the COMPUSTAT Annual Industrial File. The only restrictions placed on the firms were that they were in manufacturing (SIC 2000–3999) and that they were not in the acquired-firm sample. Since the Annual Industrial Tape used was for May 1979, the nonacquired firms had not disappeared by merger as of that date.

Ratio of Acquired and Nonacquired in the Sample

The set of nonacquired firms is representative of those COMPUSTAT firms that did not disappear by merger (or for any other reason). As a consequence, the ratio of acquired to nonacquired in our sample is, at least roughly, in line with the ratio of acquired and nonacquired firms in the manufacturing sector. It should be realized, however, that use of COMPUSTAT data restricts the study to firms that are, on average, larger than firms in the entire universe of U.S. corporations.

Measuring Financial Characteristics of the Sample: Merger Motives

The literature on merger motives is voluminous, and it is not our purpose to enumerate and to discuss all possible incentives for merger.[6] Rather, we simply provide (table 10-2) a listing of frequently mentioned financial characteristics that might make a company a desirable merger target along with plausible empirical measures of these characteristics. Table 10-3 displays specific empirical measures used in this study. This chapter focuses on financial characteristics; thus, no attempt has been made to measure product-market characteristics such as industry concentration.

The variables in table 10-3 require some explanation. First, no diversification variables are reported. Since we use only annual data, such measures are highly unreliable and are not used in the final stages of our empirical work. Second, all variables (except for FGRTH and CTAX) are developed in two fashions: (1) based solely on individual company data (designated by having the first letter C and (2) normalized by the industry average (designated by the first letter N). For example, CL1 represents the company's net working capital divided by its assets—a measure of liquidity. NL1 is CL1 divided by the industry average of this variable. COMPUSTAT four-digit industries are used in all cases.[7]

Third, the time period over which variables should be measured presents difficulties. The probit model as described previously is basically a cross-sectional model. Firms with given characteristics at a point in time are either acquired or not acquired over some specified time period. In practice it is not possible to determine how far ahead of the actual acquisition data the information appeared that ultimately resulted in that firm's acquisition. In this study, two-year time periods are used for measurement. Specifically, using the variables in table 10-2, the characteristics of the sixty-one firms acquired in 1976 and 1977 are measured by averaging 1974 and 1975 data for those companies. The characteristics of firms acquired in 1974-1975 are measured by using averages for the years 1972-1973. The interpretation of this convention is as follows: At the end of 1975, two years of data are used to measure the financial characteristics of two sets of firms (acquired in 1976 or 1977, or nonacquired); these characteristics are then used in an attempt to see which of the firms will be acquired in the subsequent two years. A similar interpretation holds for the 1974-1975 sample of mergers.

Table 10–2
Merger Motives, Variables, and Hypotheses

Motives	Variables	Hypotheses
Finance		
Economies in obtaining funds		
Financial leverage	Long-term debt/Total assets, Total debt/Total assets, Interest coverage ratio.	Acquired firms use less financial leverage than nonacquired firms.
Corporate liquidity	Net working capital/Total assets, Cash and market securities/ Total assets.	Acquired firms are more liquid than nonacquired firms.
Internal versus external financing	Funds from operation/Capital expenditures, Dividend-payout ratio.	Acquired firms have different amounts of internal financing than nonacquired firms.
Tax Savings	Tax-loss carry-forward.	Acquired firms have different tax-loss carry-forward positions than nonacquired firms.
Profitability	Return on assets, Return on equity.	Acquired firms differ from nonacquired firms in terms of profitability.
Diversification	Variability of returns to stockholders, Variability of corporate returns (for example, cash flow or profits), Covariability of returns to stockholders to a stock market index, Covariability of corporate returns with aggregate-profit index.	It is often claimed that firms diversify via merger. Such arguments call upon the correlation of returns between the acquiring and original firm. Since such measures are not possible with the current research design, accompanying variables are offered as rough measures of risk.
Earnings-per-share manipulation	Price per share/Earnings per share.	Acquired firms have lower price-earnings ratios than nonacquired firms. However, low price-earnings ratios allow the creation of growth in earnings per share for the acquiring entity.
Miscellaneous		
Managerial	Growth in sales (firm).	Firms under managerial control may use mergers as a way to further growth goals.
Assorted motives	Size.	Acquired firms are smaller than nonacquired.
Valuation	Book value per share/Market value per share.	Acquired firms have different book-to-market ratios than do nonacquired firms.

Table 10–3
Variable Definitions

Variable	Definition
Liquidity	
L1	Net working capital ÷ Assets
L2	Cash and equivalent ÷ Assets
Indebtedness	
ID1	Long-term debt ÷ Assets
ID2	Total liabilities ÷ Assets
ID3	Interest coverage
Profitability	
P1	Operating income after depreciation ÷ Assets (preinterest, pretax)
P2	Operating income after depreciation ÷ Sales
P3	Return on equity
Activity	
A1	Sales ÷ Assets
Internal versus external financing	
IE1	Profits after tax + Depreciation + Capital expenditures
IE2	(Profits after tax + Depreciation + Deferred taxes) ÷ Capital expenditures
Dividend policy	
D1	Dividends share ÷ Earnings per share
Price-earnings ratio	
PE1[a]	Market value ÷ Total earnings
Size	
Log Assets	Firm size
Valuation	
B1	Book value per share ÷ Market value per share
Additional variables (firm level)	
FGRTH	Average annual growth rate in sales for a firm
CTAX	Tax-loss Carry-forward ÷ Total assets

Note: First letter C denotes a variable calculated solely on individual company data. First letter N denotes a variable normalized by the industry average: for example, NL1 = CL1 ÷ L1, where L1 is the industry average for L1.

[a]All negative PEs or PEs in excess of 100 have been eliminated by deleting the company from the sample.

This use of time periods is still subject to a number of difficulties (for example, definition of fiscal year). Experimentation with five-year averages of data produced the same sort of results reported here.

Table 10-4
Probit Analysis for Firms Acquired and Nonacquired, 1976–1977

Constant	CL1	NID2	CD1	CA1	CPE1[a]	CP2	Log Assets	CP1	Likelihood Ratio x(−2)
− .543	− .101	− .424*	− .484	− .108	− .061*	.151			26.36*
(−1.23)	(− .22)	(−1.85)	(−1.64)	(− .99)	(−3.19)	(.128)			
.160	− .612	− .348	.236	− .154	− .059*	.335	− .139*		35.09*
(.318)	(−1.22)	(−1.55)	(.27)	(−1.35)	(−3.054)	(.283)	(−2.89)		
− .637	− .140	− .464*	.446		− .059			− .188	25.22*
(−1.63)	(− .30)	(−2.04)	(−1.60)		(−3.11)			(− .24)	
− .026	− .624	.412*	.238		− .056*		− .127*	− .189	32.80*
(− .06)	(−1.25)	(1.85)	(− .89)		(−2.94)		(−2.70)	(− .24)	

Note: Figures in parentheses are coefficients divided by standard errors; sample includes 1,199 nonacquired and 61 acquired firms.
*Significantly different from zero at the 90 percent level.
[a]Screened to exclude negative values or extremely larger values brought about by abnormally low earnings (PEs in excess of 100).

Table 10-5
Probit Analysis for Firms Acquired and Nonacquired, 1974–1975

Constant	CL1	NID2	CD1	CA1	CPE1[a]	CP2	Log Asset	CP1	Likelihood Ratio x(−2)
−2.171*	1.767*	.112	−.015	−.057	−.018*	0.867			16.04*
(−4.557)	(3.199)	(.49)	(−.096)	(−.46)	(−1.95)	(−.65)			
−1.812*	1.533*	.141	.022	−.082	−.018*	−.708	−.068		17.87*
(−3.35)	(2.66)	(.63)	(.181)	(−.64)	(−1.91)	(−.338)	(−1.35)		
−2.233*	1.808*	.102	−.017		−.018*			.83	16.31*
(−5.36)	(3.262)	(.45)	(.107)		(−1.97)			(−.893)	
−1.90	1.571*	.123	.020		−.018*	(−1.33)	−.066	−.838	18.12*
(−3.97)	(2.71)	(.55)	(.161)		(1.893)		(−1.33)	(−.913)	

Note: Figures in parentheses are coefficients divided by standard errors; sample includes 1,211 nonacquired and 45 acquired firms.

*Significantly different from zero at the 90 percent level.

[a]Screened to exclude negative values or extremely large values brought about by abnormally low earnings (PEs in excess of 100).

Empirical Results

Tables 10-4 and 10-5 report selected probit results. Numerous other specifications have been estimated, but those presented are sufficient to display the nature of the results.

The four models reported are variants of Stevens's (1973) basic model (with and without size entered as an explanatory variable). The variations include using a measure of debt use relative to the industry average (NID2) and return on assets (CP1) as a measure of profitability (models 3 and 4 only). Looking at tables 10-4 and 10-5, we see that the likelihood ratios of the probit models all have a very high degree of statistical significance. All are significant at the 95 percent level, most at the 99 percent level. In general, the models show that price-earnings ratios (CPE1) and firm size (log assets) have a strong negative effect on the probability of acquisition in both time periods (the effect of size is weaker in the 1974-1975 period). Liquidity (CL1) and indebtedness (NID2) have effects on the probability of acquisition, but these effects change between the two time periods. In the 1974-1975 period (table 10-5), higher liquidity increases the probability of acquisition; in 1976-1977, the effect is reversed and is statistically insignificant. A high use of debt relative to the industry average significantly lowers the chance of being acquired during the 1976-1977 period (table 10-4) but has a weak and statistically insignificant positive effect in the 1974-1975 period.[8] The same role for debt (that is, negative coefficient) is also found when debt is not normalized by industry average (results not reported).

The univariate results shown in table 10-6 display the differences between current findings and earlier findings by Stevens (table 10-1). Acquired firms do seem to use less debt (even when normalized NID2 is used) than nonacquired firms for both the 1976 and 1977 and 1974 and 1975 samples. The differences, however, are not nearly as dramatic as those found by Stevens for 1966 mergers. Acquired firms have significantly more liquidity (CL1) in the 1974-1975 period but not for the latter period, suggesting that the role for liquidity changes over time. Stevens's findings of higher liquidity in the 1960s do not hold for all later periods. As table 10-6 illustrates, the differences in size and price-earnings ratio between acquired and nonacquired firms are the patterns that hold for both periods in the mid-1970s.

Perhaps the best insight into the meaning and significance of the probit estimates can be obtained by calculating probabilities of acquisition based on the specific probit models. Tables 10-7 and 10-8 provide estimates of these probabilities for two probit specifications. If the probit model were a perfect representation of the world, all acquired firms would be assigned a probability of one and all nonacquired firms a probability of zero. In a sense, the probit model's usefulness can be gauged by how much better it can assign probabilities than a naive model that takes the probability of

Table 10-6
Selected Variables Means (Standard Deviation)

Measurement	Variable	1976-1977			1974-1975		
		Acquired (61 firms)	Nonacquired (1,199 firms)	Probability[a]	Acquired (45 firms)	Nonacquired (1,211 firms)	Probability[a]
Profitability	CP1	.142 (.075)	.133 (.084)		.132 (.079)	.134 (.084)	
	CP2	.097 (.052)	.091 (.058)		.089 (.064)	.094 (.059)	
Liquidity	CL1	.365 (.143)	.351 (.155)		.413 (.118)	.346 (.144)	.002
Activity	CA1	1.53 (.718)	1.56 (.635)		1.558 (.524)	1.520 (.650)	
Indebtedness	NID2	.918 (.286)	.985 (.349)	.075	.968 (.309)	.993 (.357)	
Dividend policy	CD1	.191 (2.28)	.310 (.521)	.005	.243 (.305)	.259 (.530)	
Stock value	CPE1	5.48 (3.23)	8.56 (7.53)	.001	11.42 (6.56)	14.32 (10.19)	.006
Size	Total assets	131.3	536.7	.0001	107.5	445.7	.0001
Taxes	CTAX	.0094 (.035)	.0164 (.080)	.17	.018 (.064)	.0157 (.071)	
Internal versus external	CIE1	2.25 (2.17)	2.49 (7.74)		4.50 (11.77)	2.47 (7.81)	
Growth	FGRTH	.109 (.144)	.124 (.1721)		.152 (.132)	.211 (.361)	.0093

[a]Result of t test for equality of means.

Table 10-7
Probability of Being Acquired (1976–1977), Using Probit Model

Case	Probability of Acquisition	Probability of Acquisition with Increase (Decrease) of One Standard Deviation from the Mean				
		CL1	NID2	CA1	CPE1	Assets
A firm with the characteristics of the mean acquired firm.	.06621	.05564 (.07827)	.05434 (.07999)	.05317 (.01860)	.04494 (.09454)	.04686 (.09123)
A firm with the characteristics of the mean nonacquired firm.	.03265	.02634 (.04018)	.02472 (.04258)	.02615 (.04044)	.01106 (.08104)	.01875 (.05412)

Note: Sixty-one firms were acquired out of a total sample of 1,260. Thus, the sample probability is 61/1,260 = .04841. For probit model, see second equation, table 10–4.

Table 10-8
Probability of Being Acquired (1974–1975), Using Probit Model

Case	Probability of Acquisition	Probability of Acquisition with Increase (Decrease) of One Standard Deviation from the Mean		
		CL1	CPE1	Log Assets
A firm with the characteristics of the mean acquired firm.	.0443	.06424 (.02987)	.03444 (.05663)	.03711 (.05287)
A firm with the characteristics of the mean nonacquired firm.	.02914	.04719 (.01724)	.01893 (.04357)	.02230 (.03765)

Note: Forty-five firms were acquired out of a total sample of 1,256. Thus, the sample probability is 45/1,256 = .03583. For probit model, see second equation, table 10–5.

acquisition to be the same for all firms (and equal to the percentage of firms acquired during the time period).

During the 1976–1977 period, 4.841 percent of the firms in the estimation were acquired firms.[9] Table 10–7 reports the types of probability statements that can be made about these firms using selected probit models. Using the model represented by the second equation, we see in the first column of table 10–7 that the firm with the characteristics of the mean acquired firm is assigned a 6.621 percent (.06621) probability of being acquired.[10] The mean nonacquired firm is assigned a 3.265 percent probability of acquisition. Thus, for the 1976–1977 period, the probability of acquisition is roughly twice as great for a firm with the characteristics of the mean acquired firm (low price-earnings ratio, low indebtedness, small size) as it is for a firm with the characteristics of the mean nonacquired firm. This type of increase in probability also holds (though a bit less striking) for models estimated on 1974–1975 data (table 10–8).

Effects of changes in individual characteristics on the probability of acquisition can be gauged by the numbers reported in tables 10–7 and 10–8. For example, looking at the top entries of the last column of table 10–7, a firm that is one standard deviation larger than the mean nonacquired firm (as measured by the standard deviation of the log of assets for nonacquired firms) would have a 4.686 percent (.04686) chance of being acquired. This is 1.935 percent (.01935) smaller (that is, .06621 − .04686 = .01935) than the probability for the mean nonacquired firm. A firm one standard deviation smaller than the mean nonacquired firm would have a 9.123 percent chance of being acquired—2.502 percent (.02502) larger than the probability for the mean nonacquired firm (that is, .09123 − .06621). Table 10–6 reports selected means and standard deviations of the variables in the probit models.

While providing some statistical significance, the basic thread of evidence in tables 10–4 through 10–8 is that the probit models are not capable of providing substantive discriminatory power. For example, looking at the 1976–1977 data reported in table 10–7, the probabilities of acquisition assigned to acquired firms are very low. While the reported 6.621 percent (.06621) chance of acquisition for such a nonacquired firm is greater than the naive probability of 4.841 percent (percentage of sample acquired) and is twice as great as the assigned probability for nonacquired firms (3.265 percent), it is still extremely small. The probit model predicts that, on average, one firm in fifteen (about 6.6 percent) with the characteristics of the mean acquired firm will be acquired.

Conclusions

Three major conclusions follow from the empirical work presented here:

1. In sample design, it is important to keep the ratio of acquired to nonac-

quired firms approximately equal to the ratio found in the firm population.

2. The estimated probit models are statistically significant but are not very powerful in explaining the determinants of acquisition activity.
3. A focus on characteristics of only the acquired firms may miss important phenomena that involve specific matchings of acquired and acquiring firms.

If a model is to be used as a successful method of predicting any event (in this study the event is a merger), it must be able to deal with the underlying population of firms that may participate in that event. After all, the ultimate test of such a model would be to make predictions based upon a sample of firms for which one does not know the ultimate outcome. Sample designs such as that employed by Stevens (1973) that use equal-sized samples of acquired and nonacquired firms, when the underlying population is not in such an equal ratio, may produce seriously misleading results.

The estimated probit models are statistically significant and do suggest that measurable characteristics exist that affect the probability of acquisition. Despite inclusion of numerous variables, however, the models are not powerful in increasing the ability to assign probabilities of acquisition. Additionally, coefficients on variables change from one period to the next. We have not explored in detail the predictions made by the model. Given our results, however, there does not appear to be a sound basis for out-of-sample attempts at predicting mergers based on the variables studied here.

Finally, as has been noted earlier, the research design used in generating the estimates presented in this chapter uses only acquired-firm characteristics. The results suggest that no strong generalizations can be made from these characteristics alone. Such a research design may miss important matching phenomena between acquired and acquiring firms—phenomena that are instructive in understanding merger activity. Given that markets are not perfect and that firms are not simply collections of separable and marketable factors of production, a firm is not necessarily a good merger partner for any other firm; its outstanding features may be desirable only to other particular types of firms. This suggests that further insights into merger behavior may be gleaned by studying the matching of acquired and acquiring firms.

In its most general form, a matching theory of merger behavior must explain why two specific firms pair in a merger. Empirically, the specification of this matching (which may be multidimensional) is fraught with difficulties. One approach is to look for relationships between acquired-firm characteristics and those of the acquiring firm. A shortcoming of this approach is its inability to explain why one firm (rather than many other candidate firms) disappeared through merger. An alternative empirical approach to the study of matching is a priori to classify mergers based on the characteristics of those firms doing the acquiring, thus separating firms into a three or more categories: nonacquired, acquired by acquiring-firm type A, acquired by acquiring-firm type B, and so on. While empirical research along the lines of a matching study may prove difficult, our results suggest that such research is needed to gain a better understanding of mergers.

Notes

1. For a sampling, see Ellert (1976), Halpern (1973), Haugen and Langetieg (1975), Mandelker (1974), Melicher and Rush (1973, 1974), and Weston, Smith, and Shrieves (1972).

2. Related empirical studies attempt to predict firm failure rather than merger. See, for example, Altman (1968; 1971) and Beaver (1968).

3. In his comment on Stevens's work, Monroe (1973) criticized Stevens for failure to normalize ratios by industry averages.

4. These data are part of a larger data set described in Carleton, Harris, and Stewart (1980).

5. FTC, Bureau of Economics, *Statistical Report on Mergers and Acquisitions* (Washington, D.C.: U.S. Government Printing Office, November 1976), p. 5.

6. See Scherer (1980) and Copeland and Weston (1979) for treatments of the economics (primarily industrial organization) and financial motives frequently mentioned.

7. Ratios were averaged over companies for which the relevant ratio could be formed. For example, to calculate the average sales ÷ assets, the following procedure was used: Using only companies that have both sales and assets figures for the year in question, the total sales and total assets in the industry were calculated. The ratio of these totals was the industry average for the year (for example, the average is weighted by assets for this calculation). Other calculations followed a similar procedure (for example, weighting by the denominator of the ratio).

8. The same role for debt (that is, negative coefficient) is also found using unnormalized debt ratios.

9. Data for 61 acquired firms and 1,199 nonacquired firms were used for the 1976–1977 period. $61/1,260 = .04841$.

10. All independent variables are set at the mean value of the variables for the 61 acquired firms used in the estimation.

References

Altman, E.I. *Corporate Bankruptcy in America*. Lexington, Mass.: Lexington Books, D.C. Heath and Company, 1971.

————. "Financial Ratios, Discriminant Analysis and the Prediction of Corporate Bankruptcy." *Journal of Finance,* September 1968.

Beaver, W.H. "Market Prices, Financial Ratios, and the Prediction of Failure." *Journal of Accounting Research,* Autumn 1968.

Carleton, W.T.; R.S. Harris; and J.F. Stewart. "An Empirical Study of Merger Motives." Prepared for the Federal Trade Commission and Small Business Administration under Contract LO636, 1980.

Copeland, T.E., and J.F. Weston. *Financial Theory and Corporate Policy.* Reading, Mass.: Addison-Wesley Co., 1979.

Ellert, J.C. "Mergers, Antitrust Law Enforcement and Stockholder Returns." *Journal of Finance,* May 1976.

Halpern, P.J. "Empirical Estimates of the Amount and Distribution of Gains to Companies in Mergers." *Journal of Business* 46 (October 1973).

Haugen, R., and T. Langetieg. "An Empirical Test for Synergism in Merger." *Journal of Finance,* September 1975.

Johnson, T. "Qualitative and Limited Dependent Variables in Economic Relationship." *Econometrica* 40 (May 1972).

Kmenta, J. *Elements of Econometrics.* London: Macmillan, 1971.

Mandelker, Gershon. "Risk and Return: The Case of Merging Firms." *Journal of Financial Economics,* January 1974.

Melicher, Ronald W., and D.F. Rush. "Evidence on the Acquisition-Related Performance of Conglomerate Firms." *Journal of Finance,* March 1974.

————. "The Performance of Conglomerate Firms: Recent Risk and Return Experience." *Journal of Finance,* May 1973.

Monroe, R.J. "Comment: Financial Characteristics of Merged Firms: A Multivariate Analysis." *Journal of Financial and Quantitative Analysis,* March 1973.

Monroe, R.J., and M. Simkowitz. "Investment Characteristics of Conglomerate Targets: A Discriminant Analysis." *Southern Journal of Business,* November 1971.

Scherer, F.M. *Industrial Market: Structures and Economic Performance,* 2d ed. Chicago: Rand McNally, 1980.

Stevens, Donald L. "Financial Characteristics of Merged Firms: A Multivariate Analysis." *Journal of Financial and Quantitative Analysis,* March 1973.

Theil, H. *Principles of Econometrics.* New York: John Wiley & Sons, 1971.

Watson, P.H. "Choice of Estimated Procedures for Models of Binary Choices." *Regional and Urban Economics* 4 (1974).

Weston, J.F.; K.V. Smith; and R.E. Shrieves. "Conglomerate Performance Using the Capital Asset Pricing Model." *Review of Economics and Statistics,* November 1972.

11

The Role of Employment and Capital Expenditures in the Merger and Acquisition Process

John B. Guerard, Jr.

Managers are interested in mergers and acquisitions that boost the firm's price per share of common stock. The share price will rise if the discounted future earnings of the acquired firm exceed the cost of the acquisition. Financial theorists, however, have found that mergers, as a whole, do not increase stockholder wealth;[1] but the lack of guaranteed merger profits would not be apparent to the financial manager in the current period of enormous merger activity (1967-1979).

The creation of verifiable economic profits through mergers is suggested by the management literature. Mergers create organizations that exhibit economies of scale in management. The growth in the organization fosters organizational differentiation, which increases manpower requirements. Theoretically, mergers should reduce employment because the administrative economies of scale exceed the increasing complexity of costs of large organizations.[2]

The role that changes in the number of employees and the amount of capital expenditures play in the acquisition process is examined in this study. These two variables are inputs to the production process. The growth of capital and labor is necessary for long-term firm expansion. If synergy is generated by a merger, the market value of the merged firm exceeds the sum of the market values of the unmerged firms, and the productive inputs are used more efficiently. The most efficient use of capital and labor is shown through reductions in the employment-to-sales ratio and the capital-expenditures-to-sales ratio. The increases in input productivity should benefit both the firm and the economy.

Firms, if faced with underemployment of capital and labor, operate below capacity. The labor-to-capital ratio may be too low for the most effi-

This study is taken largely from the author's dissertation, completed at the University of Texas at Austin, December 1980. I am indebted to my chairman, Ernest Walker, and committee members, Frank Bean and Charles Franckle. I am grateful to the Institute of Conservative Capitalism at the University of Texas for its financial support. I appreciate the comments of Tom Cable and Charles Clark.

243

cient production when excess capital capacity exists. This is the first hypothesis concerning mergers' increasing the employment-to-sales ratio. Firms would expand labor inputs relative to capital inputs to generate an increase in output or sales. If firms have excess capital capacity, or an adequate capital stock, then the increase in employment to expand sales increases the employment-to-sales ratio. The increase in labor drives down the marginal product of labor, which usually decreases with additional labor if the firm is operating in the area of increasing marginal and average costs. The increase in the employment-to-sales ratio suggests that the capital stock is not expanded as rapidly as employment, thus the capital-expenditures-to-sales ratio is reduced.

A second hypothesis concerning the increasing employment-to-sales ratio is that acquiring firms expect to grow more quickly than nonmerging firms and initially increase their employment and capital expenditures to generate the increase in sales and output. Both inputs are initially increased relative to sales, although the ratios should fall when the additional sales are generated. In this case of expected future growth, the capital-to-labor ratio is held constant, as are initial sales.

Purpose of This Study

The question of the relationships between mergers and employment and mergers and capital expenditures has not been examined in the financial literature. The purposes of this study are (1) to test empirically the hypothesis that employment and capital expenditures are significant variables in the acquisition process and (2) to test whether mergers and acquisitions affect the firm's capacity for utilizing the employment and capital resources acquired in the merger. Thus, both premerger managerial intentions and postmerger managerial utilization of resources are studied.

The principle hypothesis of this study is that mergers affect employment and capital expenditures. It is important to examine this hypothesis since a lessening of the acquired firm's capacities could account for the lack of expected synergy occurring in mergers. Although financial managers expect added returns, evidence does not support the likelihood of these returns. This study concentrates on mergers and acquisitions occurring during the period from 1967 to 1974.

This study differs from the existing literature on mergers and acquisitions because it examines the discriminating power of employment and capital expenditures in the merger process; these variables are examined to determine whether they aid in classifying the sample groups. The theoretical financial literature has been dominated by the belief that mergers reduce the possibility of bankruptcy, which in turn expands corporate debt capacity.

Moreover, the evidence on mergers is consistent with the additive principle of value, meaning that the value of the merged firm is expected to equal the sum of the market values of the unmerged firms. If synergy exists, however, then the value of the merged firm exceeds the sum of its unmerged individual firms.

If economies of scale exist in manpower, capital expenditures, or access to capital markets, then these economies generate operating efficiencies. The possibility of scale economies' existing in employment and capital expenditures is examined in this study.

Capital and Labor in the Merger Process

In a previous study, this author showed that a structural shift occurred in the annual merger series during the period from 1967 to 1974.[3] In this section we investigate the economic differences between the acquiring and acquired firms during this period of transition. Discriminant analysis is employed to identify the differing financial characteristics of the twenty-one acquiring and twenty-one acquired firms examined in this study. The purpose of this section is to find out if capital expenditures and employment are significant variables in the acquisition process. If the inclusion of the capital-expenditures and employment variables aids in the construction of the discriminant models, then these variables should be of interest to the financial manager in the acquisition decision.

Characteristics of the acquiring and acquired firms are examined from five years prior to the merger until the year before the merger. Classification models are constructed, using indicators of capital expenditures and the number of people employed. In addition, traditional financial-analysis variables are used to classify the firms as acquiring or acquired.

Selection of Firms and Variables

The acquired firms are selected from the research COMPUSTAT tapes. These tapes include the firms that have been removed from the industrial COMPUSTAT tapes because they have been acquired or have merged. The acquired firms in this study represent firms acquired or merged during the period from 1967 to 1974. The acquired firms tend to be small businesses with sales less than $50 million. The acquiring firms, those that actually acquired these small businesses, are firms on the industrial COMPUSTAT tapes and tend to be larger. The acquiring firms made only one acquisition during the period from 1967 to 1974. The single acquisition case is a very special case because acquiring firms usually made multiple acquisitions during this study's period. The sample is composed of twenty-one acquiring and twenty-one acquired firms. The acquiring firms are predominantly manufacturing firms as shown in table 11-1.

After defining the sample of firms to be classified as either acquiring or acquired and after selecting the firms, financial data were collected from the respective COMPUSTAT tapes. The variables selected for the analysis were chosen because of their relative importance in financial theory. The traditional financial variables used in this study are the debt-to-equity ratio, the price-earnings multiple, the asset-turnover ratio, the current ratio, and the operating return on total assets.

The debt-to-equity ratio is selected because the reduction in the variability of a firm's earnings resulting from the merger can increase its market value of debt.[4] The reduction in risk will increase the corporate debt capacity; thus, an acquiring firm might desire to acquire another firm if the acquired firm's debt-to-equity ratio is less than that of the acquiring firm. The acquisition of a firm with less debt may provide the acquiring firm with its previous debt ratio; the acquiring firm may, following merger or acquisition, issue additional debt.

Financial researchers have developed and tested the hypothesis that the acquiring firm's price-earnings multiple exceeds that of the acquired firm, in which case the acquired earnings are capitalized by investors at the acquiring firm's capitalization rate.[5] The capitalization of the acquired earnings at a higher price-earnings multiple creates an increase in the acquir-

Table 11-1
Number of Acquiring Firms in Sample Industries

Industry	Acquiring Firms
Copper ores	1
General building contractors	1
Food and kindred products	1
Dairy products	2
Bottled/canned soft drinks	1
Apparel and other finished products	1
Drugs	1
Soap and other detergents	1
Paving and roofing materials	1
Valves and pipe fittings	1
Pollution-control machinery	1
Electric and electric machinery	1
Electric transmission and distribution	1
Industrial measurement and tests instruments	1
Toys and amusement, sport goods	1
Retail stores	1
Wholesale/nondurable goods	1

ing firm's earnings per share and in the price of its common stock. The increase in earnings per share, which creates an illusion of growth, necessitates the inclusion of the price-earnings multiple as a financial variable.

The current ratio is included in this study because the liquidity constraint is likely to be a motivating force in merger activity. Smaller firms, strapped for cash and marketable assets, might be content to be acquired or merged to alleviate a liquidity problem. It is expected that the acquiring firm's current ratio usually exceeds that of the acquired firm.

The asset-turnover ratio is an activity ratio, showing the relatively efficient use of the firm's assets. The higher the ratio, the more sales the firm's assets can sustain. A firm with a relatively high asset-turnover ratio may be the object of merger talks; the high ratio can be interpreted as a sign of expert asset management. In such a case, one would expect the acquired firm's asset-turnover ratio to exceed that of the acquiring firm.

A profitability variable should be included in this study; the operating return on assets is a relevant measure. While managers probably dream of acquiring a relatively more profit-efficient firm, in the sense of dollars of profit per investment, one would expect to find that the acquiring firm tends to be more profitable.

The most important variables in this study in classifying the acquiring and acquired firms will be employment, the number of employees per sales dollar, and capital expenditures per sales dollar. The hypothesis is that the acquired firms are relatively more employment intensive and engaged in relatively greater capital expansion than the acquiring firms. Little economic theory relates the capital-to-labor ratio of the acquiring and acquired firms. No assumptions are made in this study concerning the acquiring and acquired firms' capital-to-labor ratios. Empirical evidence does not support the notion that the cost of equity is a function of firm size.[6] The capital-to-labor ratio thus should not be a function of firm size.

Empirical Results

Discriminant functions to classify firms as acquiring or as acquired are calculated. The annual models are constructed with annual balance-sheet and income-statement data using the five previously discussed variables. The annual models are calculated and used to classify firms from five years prior to the merger to the year preceding the merger. The use of annual models to classify firms in the merger activity is analogous to Altman's bankruptcy study.[7]

The discriminant function is of the following general form:

$$Z = d_1x_1 + d_2x_2 + d_3x_3 + d_4x_4 + d_5x_5 + d_6x_6 + d_7x_7,$$

where x_1 = Debt-to-equity ratio,

x_2 = *capital expenditures per sales dollar,*

x_3 = price-earnings multiple,

x_4 = number of employees per sales dollar,

x_5 = asset-turnover ratio,

x_6 = current ratio,

x_7 = operating return, which equals earnings before interest and taxes divided by total assets.

The variable means must be calculated before the discriminant functions may be found. The variable means are presented in table 11-2.

The users of discriminant analysis attempt to classify observations according to differences in the means of the samples. A glance reveals that the acquired firms' means for expenditures and employment exceed those of the acquiring firms. The acquiring firms tend to be more profitable as the merger time approaches; the acquiring firms' earnings multiples tend to rise

Table 11-2
Variable Means for Acquired and Acquiring Firms

Variable					
	Means in the Year Prior to Merger				
	1	*2*	*3*	*4*	*5*
	Acquired Firms				
x_1	1.161	.695	.791	.834	.842
x_2	.054	.048	.0415	.048	.075
x_3	13.235	20.190	12.850	23.675	15.147
x_4	.00005	.00004	.00005	.00006	.00008
x_6	1.437	1.423	1.437	1.541	1.567
x_6	2.359	2.980	3.011	3.760	2.430
x_7	.087	.148	.146	.147	.146
	Acquiring Firms				
x_1	.780	.695	.667	.723	.658
x_2	.045	.040	.038	.041	.047
x_3	17.006	17.525	18.525	15.905	17.153
x_4	.00004	.00004	.00005	.00006	.00008
x_5	1.232	1.397	1.552	1.552	1.506
x_6	2.441	2.437	2.797	2.630	2.676
x_7	.134	.156	.158	.158	.131

as the merger approaches. However, none of the means of the variables is statistically different for any of the years preceding the merger. In the year preceding the merger, the average price-earnings multiple of the acquiring firms exceeds that of the acquired firms. The acquiring firms enjoyed greater profitability. The acquired firms tend to be relatively more debt intensive. The acquired firms' debt-to-total assets ratio is unusual when compared to the debt-to-total-assets ratio of 49 percent for small firms found by Walker and Petty in their study of the differences between large and small businesses.[8] The debt policy of the acquired firms is not materially different from the debt policy of other small firms. The linear discriminant models are presented in table 11-3.

The discriminant functions can be used to classify more accurately the acquiring firms. The Wilks lambda values and the corresponding chi-square values indicate that the discriminant functions are not statistically significant. The chi-square values of the annual discriminant functions are shown in table 11-4. The discriminant function only classified 47.4 percent of the firms correctly in the year prior to the merger using the Lachenbruch method of providing a holdout sample.[9]

The purpose of this section is to examine the relative importance of capital expenditures and employment in the acquisition process. To determine the relative importance of the variables in classifying the firms as acquiring or acquired, the standardized discriminant coefficients are examined. The higher the values, the greater the importance of these coefficients. The standardized discriminant coefficients are shown in table 11-5.

The current ratio is the most important variable in the discriminant function for year -1, although capital expenditures and the operating return are also important variables. Employment is of some importance, while the asset-turnover and the debt-to-equity ratios are the least important variables.

Employment, the variable of primary concern in this study, is completely insignificant in years -2 and -5. The employment variable is not of major significance in any of the discriminant functions since it is never one of the top four variables in any function. Thus, the employment variable is of little assistance in classifying the firms. Employment is assumed to be of little interest to the financial manager in the acquisition process.

The capital-expenditures variable makes substantial contributions to the discriminant functions in years -1, -2, and -5. Because capital expenditures aid in the classification of the acquiring and acquired firms, they should be of interest to the financial manager. The current ratio dominates the capital expenditures in years -1 and -2, whereas the debt-to-equity ratio is the most important variable in the discriminant functions for years -3 and -4 and the operating return is the dominant variable in year -5.

Table 11-3
Linear Unstandardized Discriminant Functions and Classification Tables

Year before merger: 1

$$Z = 4.204 + .000x_1 - 15.488x_2 + .031x_3 - 20949.2x_4$$
$$- .814x_5 - 1.004x_6 + 3.277x_7$$

		Predicted Group			
		Acquiring		Acquired	
Actual Group	N	N	Percent	N	Percent
Acquiring	18	13	(72.2)	5	(27.8)
Acquired	18	8	(44.4)	10	(55.6)

The model correctly classified 63.9 percent of the firms.

Year before merger: 2

$$Z = 4.579 - 1.333x_1 - 7.628x_2 + .0003x_3 + .000x_4$$
$$- .814x_5 - 1.004x_6 + 3.277x_7$$

		Predicted Group			
		Acquiring		Acquired	
Actual Group	N	N	Percent	N	Percent
Acquiring	20	15	(75)	5	(25)
Acquired	20	7	(35)	13	(65)

The model correctly classified 70 percent of the firms.

Year before merger: 3

$$Z = 1.666 - 2.299x_1 - 2.883x_2 + .015x_3 + 3154.68x_4$$
$$+ .926x_5 - .431x_6 - 2.627x_7$$

		Predicted Group			
		Acquiring		Acquired	
Actual Group	N	N	Percent	N	Percent
Acquiring	20	15	(75)	5	(25)
Acquired	20	9	(45)	11	(55)

The model correctly classified 65 percent of the firms.

Table 11-3 continued

Year before merger: 4

$$Z = 1.999 - 1.241x_1 + .000x_2 - .014x_3 - 5723.46x_4$$
$$+ .741x_5 - .144x_6 - 6.484x_7$$

		Predicted Group			
		Acquiring		Acquired	
Actual Group	N	N	*Percent*	N	*Percent*
Acquiring	20	15	(75)	5	(25)
Acquired	20	8	(40)	12	(60)

The model correctly classified 67.5 percent of the firms.

Year before merger: 5

$$Z = .983 + .741x_1 + 4.883x_2 + .002x_3 + .000x_4$$
$$+ .277x_5 - .460x_6 + 6.603x_7$$

		Predicted Group			
		Acquiring		Acquired	
Actual Group	N	N	*Percent*	N	*Percent*
Acquiring	19	11	(57.9)	8	(42.1)
Acquired	19	9	(47.4)	10	(52.6)

The model correctly classified 55.3 percent of the firms.

Effects of Mergers on Capital and Labor

In this section, discriminant analysis is employed to classify the acquiring firms analyzed in the previous section and a control group of twenty-one nonmerging firms. The purpose of this section is to examine whether changes in the acquiring firm's capital expenditures and number of employees resulted from the merger or if these changes were a result of influences' also affecting firms not engaged in merger activities. We establish a control group to examine directly the effects of mergers and acquisitions on capital expenditures and employment.

Table 11-4
Discriminant Functions' Chi-Square Values and Significance

Year of Function	Chi-Square Value	Significance
-1	6.372	.383
-2	3.579	.733
-3	2.555	.923
-4	2.535	.865
-5	2.157	.905

Table 11-5
Standardized Discriminant Coefficients

	Year Prior to Merger				
Variable	1	2	3	4	5
x^1	.000	- .577	-1.155	- .865	.528
x_2	- .690	- .422	- .080	.000	.532
x_3	.635	.069	.479	.437	- .088
x_4	- .542	.000	.146	- .508	.000
x_5	- .511	-3.883	.492	.445	.190
x_6	- .790	-1.228	- .731	- .590	- .395
x_7	.679	.329	- .329	- .708	.617

Selection of the Control Group

In order to select the nonmerging firms to pair with the acquiring firms, a sample was created by matching firms that were in the same four-digit SIC codes and that employed a similar number of people.[10] Because this study is concerned with employment, the firms had to be paired on the basis of employment to account for any changes in the variable. However, since this study is utilizing the number of employees per dollar of sales, a difference may exist in the employment means of the two samples prior to the merger. The employment differences between the two samples is not statistically significant prior to the merger, as can be calculated from table 11-6. The nonmerging firms were drawn from the COMPUSTAT tapes to create a sample of firms of similar size to the acquiring firms.

Classification of the Nonmerging and Acquiring Firms

This section uses the identical variables to classify the nonmerging and acquiring firms that were used in the previous section. The use of similar

Table 11-6
Variable Means for Acquiring and Nonmerging Firms

	Year Prior to Merger				
Variable	*1*	*2*	*3*	*4*	*5*
	Acquiring Firms				
x_1	.741	.707	.716	.721	.628
x_2	.046	.041	.038	.039	.046
x_3	17.276	17.547	16.711	16.361	17.556
x_4	.00004	.00004	.00005	.00006	.00008
x_5	1.375	1.378	1.524	1.515	1.478
x_6	2.394	2.495	2.867	2.671	2.695
x_7	.154	.139	.139	.141	.131
	Nonmerging Firms				
x_1	.937	.929	.658	.706	.763
x_2	.053	.053	.053	.056	.055
x_3	18.352	18.274	15.789	29.661	14.561
x_4	.00003	.00003	.00003	.00003	.00003
x_5	1.904	1.943	1.789	1.813	1.748
x_6	3.160	2.814	2.831	2.886	2.698
x_7	.188	.191	.186	.196	.181

variables allows consistency in the examination of the merger for effects on the acquiring firm's capital expenditures and employment. The employment and capital expenditures reported for the acquiring firms represent the pooled employment and capital expenditures prior to the merger of the acquiring and acquired firms. The variables are the total number of employees and dollars of capital expenditures per sales dollar. The pooled data are necessary for comparisons of the acquiring firms prior to and after the merger. The examination of the variable means prior to the merger indicates that the acquiring firms tended to be less debt intensive and less capital-expenditures intensive, less efficient in asset turnover, less profitable on assets, and more employment intensive than the nonmerging firms. The acquiring firms grew faster than the nonmerging firms during the post-merger period, but the movements in the capital and labor ratios occurred as a result of changes in capital expenditures and employment. The examination of the evidence of the respective means does not lead to a conclusion prior to the merger as to whether nonmerging and acquiring firms behave in different manners with respect to employment and capital expenditures. The variable means for the respective samples prior to the merger are shown in table 11-6.

The nonmerging firms, relative to the acquired firms examined in the previous sections, are more profitable, more efficient in asset turnover, and have a higher return on equity. The nonmerging firms have approximately the same debt-to-equity ratio, current ratio, and price-earnings multiple. The primary discriminating variable between the nonmerging and acquired firms is the operating return on assets. The low profitability and approximately equal liquidity of the acquired firms relative to the nonmerging firms is not in accord with the Stevens study of mergers.[11]

Employment is statistically greater for the acquiring firms in year -2 ($F = 3.576$), and the current ratio is statistically greater for the nonmerging firms in the year -1 ($F = 4.118$). The variable means are not statistically different at the 10 percent level for the two samples prior to the merger.

The calculation of a linear discriminant function based on the pooled samples for the five years prior to the merger yields

$$Z = 3.950 - .368x_1 - 16.145x_2 + .008x_3 + 3351.25x_4 \\ - .706x_5 - .493x_6 - 4.000x_7$$

The discriminant function is significant at the 5 percent level since its Wilks-lambda measure of .841 corresponds to a chi-square value of 35.570. The discriminant function is quite useful in the classification of nonmerging and acquiring firms, as shown in table 11-7, although no reclassification tests are performed. The study of the diagonals of the contingency table, table 11-7, reveals that an average of 67 percent of the nonmerging and acquiring firms were correctly classified.

The discriminant function's standardized coefficients are presented in table 11-8, and the study of these coefficients indicates that the primary discriminating variables prior to the merger are the asset-turnover ratio and capital expenditures. The inclusion of the employment variables contributes relatively little to the use of discriminant functions to classify the nonmerging and acquiring firms prior to the merger.

The classification of the respective samples concentrates on the usefulness of the capital-expenditures and employment variables. We again begin our discussion of the application of the discriminant analysis by the presentation of the variable means following the merger, shown in table 11-9.

Table 11-7
Classification of Nonmerging and Acquiring Firms, Postmerger

| | | Predicted Group | | | |
| | | Nonmerging | | Acquiring | |
Actual Group	N	N	Percent	N	Percent
Nonmerging	94	55	(58.5)	39	(41.5)
Acquiring	94	23	(24.5)	71	(75.5)

Table 11-8
Standardized Discriminant Coefficients, Premerger

Variable	Coefficient
x_1	$-.271$
x_2	$-.640$
x_3	$.137$
x_4	$.218$
x_5	$-.771$
x_6	$-.537$
x_7	$-.443$

Table 11-9
Variable Means for Acquiring and Nonmerging Firms

Variable	Year after Merger			
	1	2	3	4
	Acquiring Firms			
x_1	.859	.894	1.300	1.306
x_2	.054	.058	.049	.049
x_3	14.310	15.067	10.538	11.329
x_4	.00003	.00003	.00002	.00002
x_5	1.403	1.436	1.459	1.529
x_6	2.311	2.246	2.395	2.272
x_7	.157	.155	.142	.148
	Nonmerging Firms			
x_1	1.045	.986	.947	.892
x_2	.048	.046	.049	.036
x_3	21.519	21.805	15.595	10.167
x_4	.00003	.00003	.00002	.00002
x_5	1.888	1.824	1.932	1.987
x_6	3.256	2.948	2.987	2.854
x_7	.187	.182	.174	.170

Following the merger, the acquiring firms utilize more debt, employment, and capital expenditures than the nonmerging firms. The acquiring firms have fallen, relative to the nonmerging firms, in asset turnover, current ratio, and profitability on assets. The current ratio is statistically greater for the nonmerging firms in the year of the merger. There is no statistically significant difference in the capital expenditures' means for the respective samples following the merger. Employment is statistically greater then the acquiring firms in year 2. The pooled means following the merger are shown in table 11-10.

Table 11-10
Pooled Means, Postmerger

Variable	Nonmerging	Acquiring	F
x_1	.942	1.167	.78
x_2	.049	.052	1.62
x_3	15.856	12.311	1.37
x_4	.00002	.00003	3.89*
x_5	1.908	1.475	4.34**
x_6	2.930	2.282	12.71**
x_7	.175	.148	2.01

*Significant at the 10 percent level.
**Significant at the 5 percent level.

Applying discriminant analysis to the pooled sample for the three years following the merger produces a statistically significant linear discriminant model. The linear discriminant function for the pooled postmerger period is

$$Z = 2.713 - .087x_1 - .000x_2 + .002x_3 + 26.307x_4 - .506x_5 - .985x_6 + .449x_7.$$

The classification table for the nonmerging and acquiring firms following the merger, table 11-11 is useful in correctly classifying 65.1 percent of the firms. The standardized discriminant coefficients, shown in table 11-12, reveal that the capital-expenditures variable is of no use in the discriminant function. Employment, as suggested by the F test, is relatively significant in the discriminant function. The current ratio and the asset-turnover ratio are the only variables in the discriminant function of more importance than employment.

Table 11-11
Classification of the Nonmerging and Acquiring Firms, Postmerger

Actual Group	N	Predicted Group			
		Nonmerging		Acquiring	
		N	Percent	N	Percent
Nonmerging	63	37	(58.7)	26	(41.3)
Acquiring	63	18	(28.6)	45	(71.4)

Table 11–12
Standardized Discriminant Coefficients, Postmerger

Variable	Coefficient
x_1	− .124
x_2	.000
x_3	.034
x_4	.369
x_5	− .599
x_6	− 1.050
x_7	.049

Net Effect of Mergers on Capital and Labor

The previous section showed that postmerger employment increased for the acquiring firms relative to the nonmerging firms. There was no statistically significant difference between the acquiring and nonmerging firms' capital expenditures following the merger. Mergers and acquisitions thus appeared to increase employment and not alter capital expenditures relative to firms not engaged in merger activities. In this section, a closer examination is undertaken to see if mergers and acquisitions significantly alter employment and capital expenditures when we adjust for time (before and after the merger). The sample of twenty-one acquiring and twenty-one nonmerging firms used in the previous section serves as the relevant sample for this section.

Multiple regression models are used to test whether dummy variables representing time (before and after the merger) and firm class (acquiring and nonmerging) are statistically significant determinants of employment and capital expenditures. The dummy variables are employed in models with traditional financial variables, some of which were used in the first and second sections, as the principal determinants of employment and capital expenditures.

The models hypothesized for employment and capital expenditures are quite basic. It is assumed in this section that employment is a function of firm class, time cash flow, the operating return on assets, the current ratio, the asset-turnover ratio, and capital expenditures. Because the primary hypothesis of this study is that mergers and acquisitions affect employment, the regression coefficients on the firm-class and time variables should have significant signs. Employment is expected to be a positive function of cash flow, the operating return on assets, the current ratio, and capital expenditures. Because of the statistical significance of the operating return on assets and the current ratio in the discriminant functions in the previous section, these variables are included in the regression models. The dummy variable for firm class assumes a zero for the nonmerging firms and a one for the acquiring firms. The negative coefficient on the firm-class variable would indicate that employment falls relatively for the acquiring rather than the nonmerging firms. If the hypothesis is correct that merger and acquisitions affect employment, the time variable coefficient should be negative since the variable assumes a zero prior to the merger and a one following the merger.

The model hypothesized for capital expenditures includes firm class, time, cash flow, a cost-of-capital variable, the current ratio, and the asset-turnover ratio. The two most important variables in the discriminant model presented for capital expenditures in the previous section—the current ratio and the asset-turnover ratio—are included in the regression models. It is assumed that capital expenditures are positively related to cash flow, the previous period's cash flow, the current ratio, and the asset-turnover ratio. The cost-of-capital variable, firm class, and time should be negative determinants of the capital-expenditures variable. A negative coefficient on the firm-class variable would mean that capital expenditures have fallen for the acquiring firms relative to the nonmerging firms. The negative coefficient on the time variable would mean that this relative fall in capital expenditures by the acquiring firms has occurred following the merger.

The hypothesized relationships discussed in the preceding arguments for employment and capital expenditures were regressed five years prior to the merger and three years following the merger using the sample of twenty-one acquiring and twenty-one nonmerging firms. The complete multiple-regression results for the employment equation are presented in table 11–13.

Table 11–13
Multiple Regression Results for Employment

EMPLOYMENT$_t$ .00006 − .00002TIME + .00001FIRM

(t values)   (4.37)*   (2.74)*   (1.94)*

− .00013$_{x7_t}$ − .00000$_{x5_t}$ + .00000$_{x6_t}$ + .00002CASH FLOW$_t$

(−4.22)*   (−.37)   (.72)   (.35)

− .00014$_{x2_t}$

(−1.68)**

$R^2 = .129$, $F = 6.475$*

*Significant at the 5 percent level.
**Significant at the 10 percent level.

The study of the coefficients of the multiple regression model for employment reveals that employment is significantly reduced following the merger after adjusting for firm class and other employment determinants ($-.00002$). However, employment in the acquiring firms increased significantly relative to the nonmerging firms (.00001). Employment is not a positive function of capital expenditures ($-.00014$) and the operating return on assets ($-.00013$) as hypothesized; the asset-turnover ratio, the cash-flow variable, and the current ratio are insignificant in the employment equation. The overall regression model for employment is statistically significant. The importance of the regression results of the employment equation is that employment falls significantly following a merger but rises for the acquiring firms relative to the nonmerging firms.

The multiple regression results of the capital expenditures are presented in table 11–14. The study of the multiple regression model for capital expenditures reveals that time is not a statistically significant determinant of capital expenditures; capital expenditures do not rise significantly following the merger or acquisition ($t = .42$). However, capital expenditures decrease significantly for the acquiring firms relative to the nonmerging firms ($-.00669$). Capital expenditures are significant, positive functions of the current (.22344) and previous period's cash flow (.11658) and a significant negative function of the cost of capital ($-.01190$), the current ratio ($-.00706$), and the asset-turnover ratio ($-.00810$). The positive hypothesized relationships among capital expenditures, the current ratio, and the asset-turnover ratio are not found.

An examination of the regression coefficients indicates that some net economies of scale result from mergers and acquisitions with respect to

Table 11–14
Multiple Regression Results for Capital Expenditures

$CAPITAL\ EXPENDITURES_t = .05751 + .00155 TIME$

(t values)   (6.95)   (.42)

$-.00669 FIRM + .22344 CASH\ FLOW_t + .11658 CASH\ FLOW_{t-1}$

(-1.78)**   (3.84)*   (2.22)*

$-.01190 COST\ OF\ EQUITY_t - .00706_{x6_t} - .00810_{x5_t}$

(-1.15)   (-4.06)*   (-4.39)*

$R^2 = .333, F = 21.837*$

*Significant at the 5 percent level.
**Significant at the 10 percent level.

capital expenditures and employment; the capital-expenditures-to-sales ratio decrease for the acquiring firms relative to the nonmerging firms (the $-.00669$ coefficient on the FIRM dummy variable) exceeds the employment-to-sales relative increase for the acquiring firms (the .00001 coefficient on the FIRM dummy variable).[12] Apparently, the acquiring firms use efficiently the acquired capital and labor resources. The economies of scale exist in capital, not in labor, as hypothesized by management scholars.

If the cost of capital for the merged firm decreased, then we should expect to see an increase in capital expenditures and the capital-expenditures-to-sales ratio. A multiple regression analysis of the cost of capital is shown in table 11–15. The basic result is that, following the merger, the cost of capital falls $(-.04065)$ but rises relatively for the acquiring firms (.04937).

The net economies of scale do not appear to have reduced the firm's cost of equity, nor is there any reason to suspect the scale economies would initially affect the cost of equity. The net scale economies should produce greater cash flows and hence higher market value of the firms, holding constant the cost of equity and capital. The important consideration is that a reduction in the interest rate resulting from a merger could increase the capital-expenditures-to-sales ratio despite the existence of scale economies in capital; the cost-of-capital problem does not exist in this study.

Conclusions

The purposes of this study have been to test the hypothesis that employment and capital expenditures are significant variables in the acquisition process and to test whether capital and labor are affected by the merger. The capital-expenditures variable aids in the construction of the discriminant function to classify the acquiring and acquired firms and is of interest to the

Table 11–15
Multiple Regression Results for Cost of Capital

$$\text{Cost of Equity}_t = -.02069 - -.04065\text{TIME} + .04937\text{FIRM}$$

(t vales) $(-.63)$ $(-.20)$ $(2.49)^*$

$$+ .61757_{x7_t} - -.01433_{x6_t} + .97014\text{CASH FLOW}_t$$

   $(5.67)^*$ $(-.1.50)$ $(4.68)^*$

$R^2 = .278, F = 23.697^*$

*Significant at the 5 percent level.

acquiring firm's management. Employment is not of interest in the acquisition process.

Economies of scale exist in capital expenditures—that is, the capital-expenditures-to-sales ratio falls for the acquiring firms relative to the non-merging firms following the merger. The economies of scale in capital exceed the diseconomies of scale in labor, providing a rationale for mergers.

Notes

1. Mossin (1973) argued that the additive principle of value holds in mergers. Mandelker (1974) and Frankes, Broyles, and Hecht (1977) have produced empirical evidence supporting the lack of synergy resulting from mergers.

2. Blau and Schoenherr (1971), Blau (1974), and Galbraith (1977) have formulated organization behavioral models for economies of scale in mergers and the size of organizations.

3. Guerard (1980) showed that the annual mergers occurring from 1967 to 1974 could not be modeled in terms of annual mergers that had occurred from 1895 to 1966.

4. Galai and Masulis (1976) used the option pricing model to support the debt-expansion theory of Lewellen (1971).

5. Gort (1969) found a significant difference between the acquiring and acquired firms' price-earnings multiple but attributed the difference to three unusual observations.

6. Archer and Faerber (1966) found little correlation between the size of the firm and the reciprocal of the firm's price-earnings multiple. The assumption of no relationship between the larger (acquiring) firm and the smaller (acquired) firm's capital-to-labor ratio is based on the firm-size argument.

7. Altman (1968) classified firms as bankrupt or nonbankrupt firms using annual data for five years prior to the firm's bankruptcy.

8. Walker and Petty (1978) found that small firms (acquired firms) use more debt than larger (acquiring) firms.

9. Lachenbruch (1967) developed a method for creating holdout sample when there are few observations in each group. A discriminant function is calculated with N-1 observations, and the function is used to classify the remaining observation.

10. Firms were paired on the number of employees primarily according to the following classification scheme: 1–1,000 employees, 1,001–5,000 employees, 5,001–15,000 employees, 15,001–over employees.

11. Stevens (1973) used acquired versus nonacquired groups in classifying firms.

12. The net economies-of-scale result with regard to the regression coefficients on the firm variable is also found in analysis-of-variance employment and capital-expenditures models. In the ANOVA models, the regression coefficients on the firm variable are the same as the multiple regression coefficients when adjusting for the other covariates.

References

Altman, E. "Financial Ratios, Discriminant Analysis, and the Prediction of Corporate Bankruptcy." *Journal of Finance* 23 (September 1968): 589–609.

Archer, S., and L. Faerber. "Firm Size and the Cost of Externally Secured Equity Capital." *Journal of Finance* 21 (March 1966):69–84.

Black, F., and M. Scholes. "The Pricing of Options and Corporate Liabilities." *Journal of Political Economy* 81 (May/June 1973):637–654.

Blau, Peter M. *On the Nature of Organizations.* New York: John Wiley and Sons, 1974.

Blau, Peter M., and Richard A. Schoenherr. *The Structure of Organizations.* New York: Basic Books, 1971.

Butters, J. Keith; John Lintner; and William L. Cary. *Corporate Mergers.* Boston: Division of Research, Graduate School of Business, Harvard University, 1951.

Conn, R.; and J. Nielsen. "An Empirical Test of the Larson-Gonedes Exchange Ratio Determination Model." *Journal of Finance* 32 (June 1977):749–760.

Franks, J.; J. Broyles; and M. Hecht. "An Industry Study of Profitability of Mergers in the United Kingdom." *Journal of Finance* 32 (December 1977):1513–1523.

Galai, D., and R. Masulis. "The Option Pricing Model and the Risk Factor of Stock." *Journal of Financial Economics* 3 (January/March 1976): 53–82.

Galbraith, Jay R. *Organizational Design.* Reading, Mass.: Addison-Wesley, 1977.

Gort, M. "An Economic Disturbance Theory of Mergers." *Quarterly Journal of Economics* 83 (November 1969):724–742.

Guerard, J., Jr. "Mergers and Acquisitions: The Effects of Employment and Capital Expenditures." Ph.D. dissertation, University of Texas at Austin, December 1980.

Haley, Charles W., and Lawrence D. Schall. *The Theory of Financial Decisions,* 2d ed. New York: McGraw-Hill, 1979.

Halpern, P. "Empirical Estimates of the Amount and Distribution of Gains to Companies in Mergers." *Journal of Business* 46 (October 1973): 554–575.

Halpern, P., and T. Hogarty. "New Evidence on Mergers." *Journal of Law and Economics* 13 (April 1970):167–184.

Haugen, R., and T. Langetieg. "An Empirical Test for Synergism in Mergers." *Journal of Finance* 30 (September 1975):1003–1013.

Hogarty, T. "The Profitability of Corporate Mergers." *Journal of Business* 43 (July 1970):317–327.

Lachenbruch, P.A. "An Almost Unbiased Method of Obtaining Confidence Intervals for the Probability of Misclassification in Discriminant Analysis." *Biometrics,* December 1967, pp. 639–645.

Langetieg, T. "An Application of a Three-Factor Performance Index to Measure Stockholder Gains from Merger." *Journal of Financial Economics* 5 (December 1978):365–384.

Larson, K., and N. Gonedes. "Business Combinations: An Exchange Ratio Determination Model." *Accounting Review* 44 (October 1969): 720–728.

Levy, H., and M. Sarnat. "Diversification, Portfolio Analysis and the Uneasy Case for Conglomerate Mergers." *Journal of Finance* 25 (September 1970):795–802.

Lewellen, W.G. "A Pure Financial Rationale for the Conglomerate Merger." *Journal of Finance* 26 (May 1971):521–537.

Lewellen, W.G., and Blane Huntsman. "Management Pay and Corporate Performance." *American Economic Review* 40 (September 1970): 710–720.

Lintner, J. "Expectations, Mergers, and Equilibrium in Purely Competitive Markets." *American Economic Review* 91 (May 1971):101–112.

Mandelker, G. "Risk and Return: The Case of Merging Firms." *Journal of Financial Economics* 1 (December 1974):303–335.

Melicher, R., and D. Rush. "Evidence on the Acquisition-Related Performance of Conglomerate Firms." *Journal of Finance* 29 (March 1974): 141–149.

———. "The Performance of Conglomerate Firms: Recent Risk and Return Experience." *Journal of Finance* 28 (May 1973):381–388.

Merton, R.C. "On the Pricing of Corporate Debt." *Journal of Finance* 29 (May 1974):449–470.

Morrison, Donald F. *Multivariate Statistical Methods, 2d ed. New York: McGraw-Hill, 1976.*

Mossin, Jan. *The Theory of Financial Markets.* Englewood Cliffs, N.J.: Prentice-Hall, 1973.

Mueller, D.C. "A Theory of Conglomerate Mergers." *Quarterly Journal of Economics* 83 (November 1969):743–759.

Nelson, Ralph L. *Merger Movements in American Industry, 1895–1956.* Princeton, N.J.: Princeton University Press, 1959.

Pfeffer, J. "Merger as a Response to Organizational Interdependence." *Administrative Science Quarterly* 17 (September 1972):382–394.

Rappaport, Alfred. "Strategic Analysis for More Profitable Acquisitions." *Harvard Business Review* 79 (July/August 1979):99–100.

Scherer, F.M. *Industrial Market Structure and Economic Performance.* Chicago: Rand McNally, 1970.

Scott, J. "On the Theory of Conglomerate Mergers." *Journal of Finance* 32 (September 1977):1235–1249.

Shrieves, Ronald E., and Donald L. Stevens. "Bankruptcy Avoidance as a Motive for Merger." *Journal of Financial and Quantitative Analysis* 14 (September 1979):501–515.

Stevens, Donald L. "Financial Characteristics of Merged Firms: A Multivariate Analysis." *Journal of Financial and Quantitative Analysis* 8 (March 1973):149–158.

U.S. Federal Trade Commission Staff Report. *Annual Report of the Federal Trade Commission.* (Washington, D.C.: Bureau of Economics, August 1970; 1978).

―――. *Statistical Report on Mergers and Acquisitions.* (Washington, D.C.: Bureau of Economics, August 1974).

Walker, Ernest W., and J. William Petty, II. "Financial Differences between Large and Small Firms." *Financial Management* 7 (Winter 1978):61–68.

Weston, J.F., and S. Mansinghka. "Tests of the Efficiency Performance of Conglomerate Firms." *Journal of Finance* 26 (September 1971): 919–936.

Appendix 11A:
Division of the Firms

Acquiring	Acquired	Nonmerging
Freuhauf	Kelsey Hayes	General Motors
Phelps Dodge	Western Nuclear	Hanna Mining
Elgin National	Langley Corp.	Turner Construction
Consolidated Foods	Val D'or	Amalgamated Sugar
Borden	North American Sugar Industries	RCA
Carnation	Herff Jones	Rath Packaging
Pepsi Co., Inc.	Rheingold Corp.	Dr. Pepper Co.
Phillips Van	Botany Industries	Jantzen, Inc.
Schering-Plough	Plough, Inc.	Polaroid
Clorox Co.	Grocery Store Products Co.	Johnson Products
Johns-Mansville	Holopane	Standard Oil—California
General Tire	Byers AM	Cooper Tire & Rubber
Crane Co.	CF&I Steel	Pettibone
Wheelabrator-Frye, Inc.	A.L. Garber	Acme Electric
North American Phillips Co.	PEPI, Inc.	Ford
Gould, Inc.	Allied Control	Maytag Co.
Esterlin Corp.	Astrodata	Foxboro Co.
Tektronix, Inc.	Grass Valley	Teradyne, Inc.
AMF, Inc.	Head Ski Co.	Wurlitzer Co.
ARA Service	Geriatrics	Frank's Nursery
KDI Corp.	Industrial Electronics	MPO Video

12 Interfirm Tender Offers and the Market for Corporate Control

Michael Bradley

It is commonly believed that the interfirm cash tender offer is an attempt by the bidding firm to purchase the target shares and profit from their subsequent market appreciation. This belief is inconsistent with the available evidence. While acquiring firms earn a positive return from the tender offer, they do not realize a capital gain from the target shares that they purchase.

In the 161 successful offers in this study, bidding firms paid target stockholders an average premium of 49 percent for the shares they purchased. This premium is calculated relative to the closing price of a target share 2 months prior to the announcement of the offer. The average appreciation of the target shares through 1 month subsequent to the execution of the offer was 36 percent, relative to this same benchmark. In sum, target stockholders realized a 49 percent capital gain on the shares purchased by acquiring firms and a 36 percent capital gain on the shares they retained. Thus, bidding firms suffered a 13 percent loss on the target shares they purchased. However, these same acquiring firms realized an average 9 percent increase in the market value of their own shares as a result of the offer.[1]

The paradoxical result that acquiring firms profit from the successful completion of an interfirm tender offer, yet suffer a capital loss on the target shares that they purchase, can be reconciled by considering an alternative model of tender offers. This theory views the acquisition of the target

This chapter is based on my Ph.D. dissertation, entitled "An Analysis of Interfirm Cash Tender Offers" (University of Chicago, August 1979). I would like to thank my dissertation committee, Myron Scholes, Merton Miller, Eugene Fama, Roger Kormendi, John Gould, and Robert Hamada, for their many insightful comments and helpful suggestions. I have also benefited from the comments of the participants of the finance workshops at the University of Chicago and the University of Rochester, particularly Michael Jensen, William Meckling, and G. William Schwert. I would especially like to thank Gregg Jarrell for many hours of detailed discussion which led to original conception of final completion of this study. The financial support of the Center for Research in Government Policy and Business and the Managerial Economics Research Center, both at the University of Rochester, is gratefully acknowledged.

shares as a means of securing control of the target firm. The target shares are demanded by the bidding firm only insofar as they confer control. The (post-execution) premium paid tendering stockholders is viewed as payment for the right to control the assets of the target firm.

The model developed and tested in this chapter assumes that the tender offer is an attempt by the bidding firm to secure control of the target firm and implement an operating strategy that will increase the value of both firms. These gains are assumed to stem from a synergy created by consolidating the two firms. The increase in the equity values of the acquiring and target firms—in the wake of a successful offer—is compelling evidence for a synergy theory of tender offers. In the successful offers of this study, the equity value of the average acquiring firm increased by $7.7 million, in spite of the average offer premium of $7.7 million paid to tendering stockholders.[2] This capital gain is calculated over the period from 2 months before the offer through 2 months thereafter. The value of the outstanding shares of successful target firms increased an average of $31 million over the same period. These data indicate that consolidating the control of the two firms via an interfirm tender offer is a wealth-increasing investment for the stockholders of both firms.

The theory of tender offers that is advanced in this chapter recognizes the existence of rivalrous firms that compete for the right to control the target resources. It is assumed that the information produced as a result of an interfirm tender offer enables other firms—including the managers of the target firm—to make a value-increasing change in the operations of the target firm. In other words, it is assumed that at least a portion of the return to preparing and effecting a tender offer becomes appropriable with the formal offer announcement. Thus, the announcement of a tender offer is presumed to alert other firms to the general intent of the bidding firm and initiate a competitive (auction-type) process for the target shares.

Target stockholders are assumed to be a diffuse group of homogeneous, wealth-maximizing price takers. If follows that the target shares will flow to that firm (management team) that makes the best offer in terms of the price offered for the sought-after or controlling shares and the expected post-execution value of the target shares that are not demanded.

Viewing the tender offer in terms of the model sketched above yields several implications that are at once consistent with the available data and contrary to some popular notions concerning the nature of interfirm tender offers. The first is that successful bidding firms will be forced to pay a premium—relative to the pre-announcement as well as the post-execution market price—for the target shares that they purchase. Under the assumptions of the analysis, acquiring firms cannot consistently earn abnormal returns through the market appreciation of the target shares. The data of this study indicate that they do not; on average they suffer a 13 percent capital loss on the target shares that they purchase. This is not to say that acquiring firms will not profit from the tender offer. On the contrary, the underlying synergy is presumed to have a value-increasing effect on the shares of both firms.

A second implication of the theory advanced in this chapter is that acquiring firms cannot profit from purchasing a simple majority of the target shares and "raiding" the assets of the target firm. Such offers will be anticipated by the target shareholders and competing bidding firms. Competitive alternatives will preclude such bids from being successfully executed. The fact that the post-execution market price of the target shares is 36 percent higher than the pre-announcement level indicates that corporate "raiding" is not an important explanation for interfirm tender offers. A corporate raiding strategy would result in a post-execution fall in the market price of the target shares. The data reveal no such price decrease.

Finally, the theory of this chapter provides an explanation for the empirical fact that not all tender offers are accepted by the target stockholders. Of the 258 offers in this study, 97 were rejected by the stockholders of the target firm. According to the theory of this chapter, an unsuccessful tender offer can be explained as a rational response to the alternatives that arise in a competitive market for corporate control. Clearly, bidding firms will not make an offer if they do not expect to be successful. However, once the offer is announced and new information regarding the value of the target resources is revealed (produced), the ultimate allocation of these resources is uncertain. Competing bidding firms or the target managers themselves may be able to exploit this new information and effect the optimal (highest valued) allocation of the target resources.

Target stockholders will reject those offers that become dominated by a higher bid or a higher-valued production/investment plan proposed by the target managers. If this explanation for the occurrence of unsuccessful tender offers is correct, then on average, the value of a target share after the expiration of the offer will be greater than the rejected offer price. The data show that this is in fact the case.

In a sample of 97 unsuccessful tender offers, target stockholders realized an average capital gain of 45 percent. This average post-offer return exceeds the average premium of these rejected offers, which is 29 percent. The data support the contention that refusing a given tender offer may be a value-maximizing investment for the target stockholders—even though the rejected offer price is significantly greater than the pre-offer market price of a target share.

This finding lends support to an implication of the theory that target managers may be acting in their stockholders' interests by opposing an outstanding offer. Target managers may have information that would induce a higher bid or a higher valuation of the target resources if disclosed. Lodging a formal opposition to an outstanding offer would be an effective means of communicating this type of information.

The distinction between target managers' opposing an outstanding offer and preventing a bidding firm from even making an offer should be appreciated. While the theory admits that the former can increase the welfare of target stockholders, the theory assumes that the latter cannot. Opposing an outstanding offer is viewed as a means of communicating information to the target stockholders and other market participants. However, precluding an offer (by, for example, using the powers of the state) can only be viewed as a way of limiting the alternatives facing target stockholders. According to the theory, this cannot increase their welfare.

Target managers and the managers of bidding firms are treated equally within the context of the theory. Each management group represents an alternative allocation of the target resources. Ex ante, no one group is presumed to have a comparative advantage in utilizing these resources. The theory implies that target stockholders will tender their shares to that management group that will put the target resources to their most-productive (highest-valued) use. Thus, any restrictions on the opportunity set facing the target stockholders can only serve to decrease their welfare.

The empirical tests of the theory reflect the central role that has been ascribed to the rational (wealth-maximizing) response of the target stockholders to an interfirm tender offer. The data of this study include only those offers that were actually acted on by the target stockholders. Offers that were precluded by court action or withdrawn because of target management opposition are not included in the data. Unsuccessful offers in this sample are those that were made to and rejected by the stockholders of the target firms. Consequently, many of the celebrated conflicts for corporate control are not included in the sample. Informal overtures like the Carter bid for Marshall Field, the Anderson Clayton bid for Gerber Food, and the American Express bid for McGraw-Hill—bids that never reached the target stockholders—are not part of the data base of the study.

The remainder of the chapter is organized as follows. The theoretical model sketched above is developed more extensively in the first section. The implications of this theory and the relevant empirical tests of the data are presented in the second section. The conclusions are stated in the last section.

An Analysis of the Interfirm (Cash)-Tender Offer

The interfirm cash tender offer is a proposal made by the management of one firm to purchase a significant fraction of the outstanding common stock of another legally independent corporate entity. The offer is made by the managers of the bidding firm, on behalf of their stockholders, directly to the stockholders of the target firm.

The standard analysis of the interfirm tender offer typically involves a presumption that the bidding firm is attempting to exploit some special information pertaining to the potential value of the target firm. An analogy between this situation and that of an investor who is buying on the basis of inside information is often drawn. However, this is a false analogy and one that has led to many misconceptions concerning the nature of interfirm tender offers.

One major distinction between insider trading schemes and interfirm tender offers has been generally acknowledged in the literature. The notion that control over the target resources is a central issue in the latter (and not in the former) is reflected in the works of several authors.[3] Unlike the inside trader who takes a position in an "undervalued" security and waits for the market to learn of its true value, a successful bidding firm is expected to initiate this revaluation itself, by implementing a new, presumably higher-valued operating strategy. Thus, it is generally understood that the bidding firm must secure a controlling interest in the target firm in order to realize a positive return from the acquisition.[4]

The control-seeking motive that is typically attributed to the managers of bidding firms is based on the public nature of the tender offer and the assumed existence of an efficient capital market. Since a bidding firm is required by law to purchase the target shares via a public offer, market participants will be costlessly alerted to the intentions of the firm's managers with the announcement of the offer. Moreover, federal regulation enacted in 1968 requires that all tender offers must remain open for at least 10 trading days. Thus, it is highly likely that any inside information concerning the operations of the target that the bidding managers may have will surface during the waiting period that must elapse between the announcement and the execution of an offer. Target managers as well as target stockholders have an incentive to produce and disseminate this type of information. To the extent that this inside information becomes part of the domain of publicly available information, the price of the target shares will be bid up and a profitable insider trading scheme precluded. It is therefore deduced that the demand for the target shares by the bidding firm reflects a demand to secure control of the target resources, and not an attempt to exploit some inside information.

Although the distinction between the intentions of an inside trader and the managers of a bidding firm is widely recognized, the full implication of this insight has not been developed in the literature. The important difference between the two is not whether the buyer expects to change the production/investment strategy of the target firm. Rather, the important difference is the means by which the buyer expects to profit from the acquisition of the target shares. Presumably, the inside trader can clandestinely buy the target shares at their current market price and expect to realize a capital gain once the market learns of his special information. In other

272   Mergers and Acquisitions

words, the return to his specialized information is realized through the
market appreciation of the purchased target shares.

The conventional view of tender offers is that the returns to successful
acquiring firms are realized in this same fashion—that is, through the
market appreciation of the target shares. For example, Manne (1965) argues
that the interfirm tender offer provides an incentive for a (bidding) firm to
secure control of a (target) firm that is being managed suboptimally. He
argues that the return to the acquisition is given by the difference between
the (currently depressed) price at which the target shares could be purchased
and the market price that would prevail once control has been achieved and
the suboptimal practices eliminated.

As discussed in the previous section, the testable implications of this insider trading paradigm of tender offers are not borne out by the available
evidence. The data indicate that, contrary to what this scenario predicts,
bidding firms do not profit from the subsequent increase in the market price
of the purchased target shares.

The inability of the traditional view of tender offers to explain the positive returns realized by acquiring firms is a consequence of not abandoning
the insider trading paradigm completely. Under standard neoclassical
assumptions, the public nature of a tender offer precludes bidding firms
from being able to systematically realize a capital gain on the target shares
that they purchase. Bidding firms do not enjoy the veil of secrecy that inside
traders do. This is the fundamental implication of the model that is
presented below.

The fact that acquiring firms cannot theoretically and do not empirically profit from the appreciation of the target shares implies that control of
the target resources is a valuable asset to a successful bidding firm. Whether
this increase in value is the result of more efficient production or less competitive markets is unclear. Nevertheless, both the theoretical model
developed below and the data presented in the next section imply that the
value of an acquiring firm increases as a result of securing control of the
target resources and not due to a capital gain realized on the target shares
that they purchase.

The theoretical model of this chapter is based on the following set of
assumptions. Target stockholders are a *homogeneous* group of wealth-maximizing price takers. No one stockholder can affect the outcome of the
offer. The capital market is efficient in that security prices reflect all publicly available information. Corporate managers act so as to maximize the
market values of their firm's outstanding securities.

The tender offer process is divided into three discrete time periods: pre-
announcement, post-announcement but pre-execution, and post-execution.
Typically, offers are announced two to three weeks in advance of the date
of execution. Federal law, which was enacted in July of 1968, requires that

this interim period between announcement and execution be at least 10 trading days.[5]

Subsequent to the announcement of a tender offer all capital market agents—including the target stockholders—are assumed to form rational expectations concerning the ex post value of a target share should the offer succeed. Market participants determine an expected post-acquisition market value of a target share by deducing the value-maximizing operating strategy that the bidding managers would implement should they obtain control of the target. The strategy that maximizes the value of the bidding firm, subject to any legal or contractual constraints, implies the post-acquisition market price of the target firm's shares.

Since most tender offers involve only a fraction of the outstanding target shares,[6] the value of an announced tender offer (to the target stockholders) is given by the sum of two factors. The first, and most apparent, is the offer price times the number of target shares demanded. The second factor, which is less obvious, is the expected post-acquisition market price of a target share times the number of target shares that are not purchased.

The relevance to target stockholders of this second term, the post-execution value of the target shares that are not purchased, highlights an important difference between an interfirm tender offer and a corporate merger. A merger proposal is essentially a bid for all outstanding target shares. If the acquisition is successful, all target shares will be exchanged for either cash or shares of the acquiring firm. Once the acquisition has been effected, the target shares—claims to the net cash flows generated by the target resources—will cease to exist. Consequently, when evaluating a merger proposal, target stockholders need only concern themselves with the offer price and not the subsequent behavior of the managers of the acquiring firm. However, since most tender offers involve only a fraction of the outstanding target shares, the post-execution behavior of the acquiring managers is of utmost concern to the target stockholders.

Subsequent to the execution of most tender offers, the allocation of the target resources and hence the market value of the target shares is under the control of the managers of the acquiring firm. Of course, laws governing the fiduciary responsibilities of corporate managers and the rights of minority stockholders limit the discretion acquiring managers have in determining the post-execution value of the target shares. In addition, federal regulations require that bidding firms must fully disclose, in a prospectus accompanying the formal offer, any material changes in the operations of the target that would be made should they gain control of the firm.[7] Nonetheless, there are many ways that the acquiring managers can have a predictable impact on the post-execution market price of the target shares. The acquiring managers can increase the value of the target shares simply by

selling factors of production to the target at below-market prices or by buying products from the target at above-market prices. The value of the target
shares could be decreased (and the value of the acquiring firm increased) by
reversing the terms of these contracts. It is assumed that these post-execution contracts are correctly anticipated by all market participants prior to
the execution of the offer. It therefore follows that from the perspective of a
target stockholder the rational evaluation of an outstanding tender offer involves the amount offered by the bidding firm for the demanded shares and
the implied post-acquisition value of the remaining interest in the target. If
each target share has an equal probability of being accepted, and if all target
shares are eventually tendered, then the post-announcement but pre-
execution market price of a target share is given by

$$P_A = F \cdot T + (1 - F) \cdot P_E, \tag{12.1}$$

where P_A = the interim (post-announcement but pre-execution) market
price of a target share; T = the per share offer price; P_E = the expected
post-execution market price of a target share; F = the fraction of outstanding target shares demanded by the bidding firm.

Equation 12.1 reflects the federal requirement that oversubscribed
offers must be executed on a pro rata basis—that is, if all shares are
tendered and only a fraction are demanded by the bidding firm, then this
fraction must be purchased from each tendering stockholder, and the fraction $(1 - F)$ returned.[8]

In the absence of a more profitable alternative, target stockholders
would evaluate and respond to an outstanding bid in terms of the offer price
relative to the expected post-execution market price of a target share. Since
no one stockholder can affect the outcome of the offer, the wealth-maximizing decision rule facing each is clear. If T, the offer price, is less than the
expected post-execution market price, P_E, then wealth-maximizing target
stockholders would not tender their shares. Rather, each would hope to
realize this differential on all shares held. Obviously, if all target
stockholders were to react in this same fashion no shares would be tendered
and the offer would be certain to fail.[9] It follows that if target stockholders
are atomistic, rational wealth maximizers, a necessary condition for a successful tender offer is that the offer premium be at least as large as the expected ex-post market revaluation of the target shares. Symbolically,

$$T \geq P_E \tag{12.2}$$

is a necessary condition for a successful tender offer.

Inequality 12.2 is a necessary but not sufficient condition for a successful tender offer. Competition in the market for corporate control places

additional restrictions on the properties of a successful bid. In a world of atomistic target stockholders who trade in a frictionless capital market, the supply price of the target shares is determined by the next best allocation of the target resources. One obvious alternative to an outstanding offer is the operating strategy being pursued by the current target managers. Presumably, the pre-announcement market value of the target firm represents the minimum value of the alternative opportunity facing target stockholders.

But there is no reason to expect that the bidding firm is the only firm that could effect a value-increasing change in the operations of the target firm. The announcement of the offer is assumed to generate new information regarding the value of the target. To allow for the possibility that another management team could also increase the value of the target shares relative to their pre-announcement level, define P_E^U as the expected per share value of the target resources employed in their next best allocation relative to the outstanding bid.[10] Thus, competition for control of the target resources imposes a second necessary condition for a successful tender offer:

$$F \cdot T + (1 - F)P_E^S \geq P_E^U \geq P_0, \qquad (12.3)$$

where the left-hand side of inequality 12.3 is equation 12.2, which defines the interim price of a target share if the offer is fully subscribed;[11] P_0 is the pre-announcement market price of a target share.

The model of tender offers sketched above implies two conditions for a successful tender offer. These requirements are captured by equations 12.2 and 12.3 above and are reproduced here below:

$$T \geq P_E^S \qquad (12.2)$$

and

$$F \cdot T + (1 - F) \cdot P_E^S \geq P_E^U \geq P_0. \qquad (12.3)$$

The first condition, equation 12.2, states that the offer price, T, must be at least as large as the expected post-acquisition market price of a target share, P_E^S. Rational, atomistic target stockholders would not tender their shares for $10 if they were expected to be worth $15 subsequently. The second condition, equation 12.3, states that the per share value of the offer, in terms of the offer price and the expected post-execution price of a target share, must be greater than the share price that would obtain if the offer were rejected, P_E^U. The latter term represents the per share value of the (highest valued) alternative opportunity facing target stockholders and must necessarily be at least as large as the pre-announcement market price of a target share, P_0. This condition is implied by the rational evaluation of a given offer which is based on the alternatives available to target stockholders in a competitive market for corporate control.

The conditions for a successful tender offer—equations 12.2 and 12.3—imply that successful bidding managers will be forced to pay a premium for the target shares that they purchase. More specifically, the per share value of the offer must represent a premium relative to the pre-acquisition ($T > P_0$) as well as the post-acquisition ($T > P_E^S$) market price of a target share. This immediately implies that the gains from the acquisition will not be realized through the target shares (the insider trading paradigm) but rather will be capitalized by the market directly into the price of the shares of the acquiring firm.

Inequality 12.3 reflects an important implication of the theory regarding the so-called corporate raiding strategy of tender offers. Consider an offer where the recognized objective of the bidding firm is to secure 51 percent of the target shares for a price that is just above market, liquidate the firm, and expropriate completely the value of the remaining minority interest. Equivalently, consider an offer where the bidding firm is unable to adequately assure target stockholders that such post-acquisition wealth transfers will not take place. In terms of 12.3 this bid implies an offer price of $T = P_0 + \epsilon$ and an expected post-execution value of $P_E = 0$.

In the absence of an alternative offer, the wealth-maximizing response of each target stockholder to this bid is to tender his shares. If the offer is unsuccessful his wealth will remain the same whether he tenders his shares or not. But, if the offer is successful and he does not tender, his entire interest in the target will be worthless, since it is assumed that $P_E = 0$. On the other hand, if he tenders his shares and the offer is successful, he will receive, at a minimum, 51 percent of the pre-announcement market value of his holdings. Since the decision of any one target stockholder cannot affect the outcome of the offer, the rational response of each is to tender his shares to the bidding firm. Consequently, since target stockholders are assumed to be a homogeneous group, this optimizing behavior will insure the success of the outstanding offer even though the acquisition will decrease the wealth of the initial target stockholders.

The solution of this apparent prisoner's dilemma is a competitive market for corporate control. If the preceding offer were made, there would be an incentive for another firm or the target managers themselves to make a higher offer for the 51 percent interest. Abstracting from differential abilities in expropriating wealth and the costs of making a tender offer, competition to become the successful acquirer will bid up the price for 51 percent of the target to the market value of 100 percent of the firm's securities. According to 12.3, if F is less than one and P_E is equal to zero, then the offer price T must be sufficiently "grossed up" to compensate for the eventual wealth decrease that is expected after the execution of the offer. Algebraically, $T = P_0/F$ is the minimum per share price that a bidding firm would have to pay in order to secure control of the target. Note that this price eliminates all potential gains from the acquisition. A price less than this would permit an arbitrage profit for any competing bidder that would be willing to raise T and lower his return. Thus, competition in the market for corporate control theoretically precludes corporate raiding strategies from being positive net present value projects.

Implications and Empirical Results

The implications of the analysis of the previous section for the price behavior of the shares of firms involved in interfirm (cash) tender offers depend on the outcome of the offer under study. If the offer is successful, the security holders of both firms will experience a capital gain, reflecting the synergy resulting from combining the control function of the two firms. The gains to the target stockholders will be realized through the premium $(T - P_0)$ received for the purchased shares and through the post-execution revaluation $(P_E^S - P_0)$ realized on those target shares not purchased. While stockholders of acquiring firms are expected to realize a positive return from the acquisition as well, these gains are not expected to result from the subsequent appreciation of the target shares. In other words, the analysis predicts that T, the per share offer price, is at least as large as P_E^S, the post-execution market price of a target share.

For unsuccessful offers, the analysis price of the target shares will be greater than the value of the rejected bid. A tender offer will only be rejected if another, more profitable alternative materializes. In contrast, if the post-expiration market price of the target shares were at (or below) the pre-announcement level, then it could be reasoned that target stockholders are in general irrational in rejecting an interfirm tender offer. Relatedly, a negative post-expiration revaluation of the target shares may be interpreted as evidence that an inefficient and entrenched target management has been successful in thwarting a profitable takeover.

The Data Base and Statistics Used
in the Empirical Tests of the Study

In order to test the implications of the model, a sample of 258 cash tender offers that occurred over the period July 1962–December 1977 has been collected.[12] The empirical tests of the model involve the following statistics that have been taken from this sample.

Equity Price Index (ρ). An equity price index has been calculated for each firm in the data base.[13] Each price index is defined relative to the closing market price of the firm's common stock 41 trading days (2 calendar months) prior to the announcement of the offer. It is assumed that this lead time is sufficient to capture any "leakage" of information that might precede a forma offer. Define $r_{i,D}$ as the value of the price index of the shares of the ith firm on (event) day D. Algebraically,

$$r_{i,D} = \prod_{d=-41}^{D-1} \left(\frac{V_{i,d+1}}{V_{i,d}} \right),$$

where $V_{i,d}$ is the per share value of the equity of the ith firm on day d, adjusted for all splits and dividends over the 2-month period prior to offer announcement.

A time series of the mean value of these price indexes has been calculated for each of the relevant subsets of the data base. For example, define $\rho_{T,D}^S$ as the mean value of the price indexes of the shares of target firms (T) involved in successful tender offers (S) on day D. Algebraically,

$$\rho_{T,D}^S = \frac{1}{N} \sum_{i=1}^{N} r_{i,D},$$

where N is the number of target firms in the data base involved in successful tender offers. Note that D is defined relative to the tender offer announcement date for each of the offers in the study.

Abnormal Equity Price Index ($X\rho$). An abnormal price index has been calculated for each security in the data base. These abnormal price indexes have been developed from an excess returns file compiled by the Center for Research in Security Prices (CRSP) of the University of Chicago. A complete description of the construction of this excess returns series can be obtained directly from the center. Briefly, a daily excess return for each security listed on the NYSE and the ASE has been calculated according to the following algorithm. For each year, the listed securities are grouped into 10 equal portfolios according to a measure of their underlying risk. Each security is thus assigned to a particular control portfolio based on its estimated risk. Invoking the theory and assumptions of the Capital Asset Pricing Model, an estimate of the daily excess return to a given security is given by the difference between the realized return to the security and its companion control portfolio – each adjusted for splits and dividends.

Define $XR_{i,d}$ as the excess return (taken from the CRSP data file) to the shares of the ith firm on day d. The abnormal price index for security i on day D is given by

$$Xr_{i,D} = \prod_{d=-40}^{D} (1 + XR_{i,d}).$$

Note that this index is also defined relative to the closing market price of the security 41 trading days prior to the offer. In other words, $Xr_{i,-41}$ is defined equal to one.

The mean of these abnormal price indexes for a given subset of the data base, on a given day, is defined as $X\rho_{G,D}$, where G is the designation of the particular group of securities under study. For example, $X\rho_{B,D}^{S}$ defines the mean abnormal price index for successful (S) bidding firms (B) on day D and is given by

$$X\rho_{B,D}^{S} = \frac{1}{N} \sum_{i=1}^{N} Xr_{i,D},$$

where N is the number of successful bidding firms in the sample.

Offer Price Index per Target Share Purchased (π). A mean offer price index has been calculted for each of the relevant subsets of the offers in the data base. Define π as the mean offer price relative to the market price 41 trading days prior to the announcement of the offer. Then,

$$\pi = \frac{1}{N} \sum_{i=1}^{N} \left(\frac{T_i}{V_{i,-41}} \right),$$

where N is the number of offers in the subset under study, T_i is the offer price of the ith bid, and $V_{i,-41}$ is the market price of the shares of the ith target firm 41 trading days prior to the offer, adjusted for all stock splits and dividends over the 2-month interval preceding the offer. Thus, π^S is the mean of (one plus) the market premiums paid tendering stockholders for each target share purchased.

Offer Price Index per Target Share Outstanding ($F\pi$). An index of the offer premium per target share outstanding has been calculated for the offers in each of the relevant subsets of the data base. Defined this adjusted offer premium as $F\pi$. Then,

$$F\pi = \frac{1}{N} \sum_{i=1}^{N} \left(\frac{V_{i,-41} + F_i(T_i - V_{i,-41})}{V_{i,-41}} \right),$$

where N is the number of offers in the subset under study, $V_{i,-41}$ is as defined before, T_i is the offer price of the ith bid, and F_i is the fraction of target shares demanded in the ith offer. Note that when $F = 1$—that is, all target shares are demanded—$\pi = F\pi$.

The variable F_i, the fraction of the target shares demanded in the ith offer, was taken from the published terms of each offer. The maximum number of shares that the bidding firm would accept if all were tendered divided by the total number outstanding less those already held by the bidding firm was used as the proxy for this variable.[14] Thus, like the analysis itself, this proxy presumes an all equity target firm with no convertible bonds or warrants outstanding.[15]

Successful Offers

The statistics defined in the preceding subsection can be used to test the implications of the model for the price behavior of the shares of firms involved in successful tender offers. For purposes of this study a tender offer is considered to have been successful if at least 50 percent of the number of shares demanded was actually purchased by the bidding firm.[16]

Target Firms. The analysis of the first section predicts two movements in the price level of the target shares subsequent to the announcement of a successful tender offer. These two levels correspond to the two relevant time periods that follow the announcement of an offer. The first is the market price that would prevail during the interim period between the announcement and the execution of the offer, P_A. The second is the market price that would obtain subsequent to the execution of the offer—after control of the target resources has been transferred to the acquiring firm, P_E.

The first condition for a successful tender offer defines the first of these two levels. Define P_A^S as the post-announcement but pre-execution market price of a target share involved in a successful tender offer. Thus, P_A^S is the price that would prevail after market participants became aware that the outstanding offer would succeed but before it was actually executed:

$$P_A^S = F \cdot T + (1 - F)P_E^S \geq P_E^U \geq P_0, \tag{12.4}$$

where the subscript A refers to the interim time period between the an-

nouncement and execution of the offer and the superscript S designates that
the offer will be successfully executed.[17]

The second price movement of the target shares that is predicted by the
model occurs after the offer has been executed. Since an offer price higher
than the post-execution market price is a necessary condition for a successful tender offer, and the interim price is a weighted average of the two (see,
for example, 12.4), the analysis implies that the post-execution market
price, P_E^S, will be less than the interim price P_A^S. This predicted price drop
reflects the elimination of the offer premium $(T - P_E^S)$ that accompanies
the completion of a successful tender offer.[18]

The predicted time series of the market price of the shares of a successfully acquired target firm is illustrated in figure 12–1. This pattern of prices
reflects all of the implications of the model. A successful tender offer will
necessarily involve a positive market premium for the purchased target
shares $(T \geq P_0)$ In order to induce target stockholders to tender their
shares, this offer price must be at least as large as the post-execution market
price $(T \geq P_E^S)$. The post-execution market price is predicted to be higher
than the pre-announcement level due to a higher valued allocation of the
target resources $(P_E^S \geq P_0)$. Since the post-announcement price is weighted
average of the offer price, T, and the post-execution price P_E^S, the model
predicts that this interim price will be less than the former and greater than
the latter $(T \geq P_E^S \geq P_E^S)$. Finally, the predicted post-execution revaluation
of the target shares $(P_E^S - P_0 \geq 0)$ implies an observable minimum of a
given offer—and hence a minimum value for the post-announcement
market price of a target share. From the earlier analysis, if $P_E^S \geq P_0$, and
$P_A^S = (1 - F) \cdot P_E^S + F \cdot T$ (see equation 12.4), then it follows that $P_A^S \geq$
$P_0 + F \cdot (T - P_0)$. Intuitively, if corporate raiding $(P_E^S < P_0)$ is precluded,
then the minimum per share value of a tender offer is the pre-announcement
level P_0, plus the value of the offer premium per target share outstanding,
$F \cdot (T - P_0)$. Thus, the model predicts that the interim price will be less than
the offer premium and greater than this minimum value, $T \geq P_A^S \geq P_0 +$
$F \cdot (T - P)$. This inequality is reflected in the predicted price pattern that is
presented in figure 12–1.

The data in figure 12–2 plot the time series of $\rho_{T,D}^S$, the mean price
index for the 161 successfully acquired target firms in the sample, over the
period 40 trading days prior to the offer announcement through 40 days
thereafter. The offer price index per target share purchased, π, and the
offer price index per target share outstanding, $F\pi$, are also given in the
figure.

In order to test the implications of the analysis, let ρ_5^S be the empirical
proxy for ρ_A^S, the post-announcement but pre-execution mean price level of
the shares in the sample. This proxy presumes that the full implications of
an offer are incorporated into the price of the target shares within 5 trading
days of its announcement. Let ρ_{40}^S represent the proxy for ρ_E^S, the mean

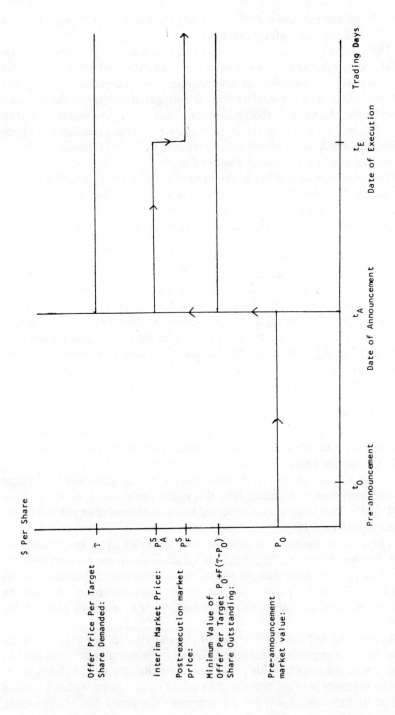

Figure 12-1. Predicted Time Series of the Price of the Shares of Target Firms Involved in Successful Tender Offers

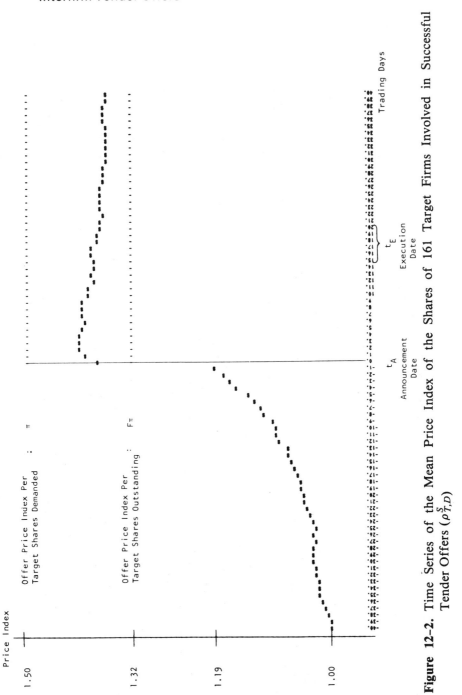

Figure 12-2. Time Series of the Mean Price Index of the Shares of 161 Target Firms Involved in Successful Tender Offers ($\rho_{T,D}^S$)

post-execution price level of the target shares. All offers in this study were either executed or withdrawn within 40 trading days of the announcement date.[19]

The data in figure 12-2 support the major implications of the analysis. Acquiring firms pay a substantial market premium for the target share that they purchase. In this sample, the mean offer premium is 49 percent ($\pi = 1.49$) with a cross-sectional standard deviation of $\sigma_x = 4$ percent.[20] The data also show that while the post-execution market price of a target share is significantly higher than its pre-announcement level ($\rho_{40}^S = 1.36$, $\sigma_x = .03$), this revaluation is significantly less than the premium paid target stockholders ($\pi - \rho_{40}^S = 1.49 - 1.36 = .13$, $\sigma_x = .03$). In this sample acquiring firms did not profit from the purchase and subsequent appreciation in the target shares; they suffered an average capital loss of 13 percent on each target share that they bought.

The data also indicate that, consistent with the implications of the model, the interim price is less than the offer price per share purchased ($\rho_A^S < \pi$) and greater than the post-execution market price ($\rho_A^S > \rho_E^S$) as well as the predicted minimum value of the offer ($\rho_A^S > F\pi$).[21] The behavior of market participants, as manifested in the market price of the target shares, is consistent with that predicted by the analysis.

Finally, it should be noted that these data are inconsistent with the corporate raiding strategy of tender offers. Recall that this argument implies that target stockholders will suffer a capital loss on the target shares that are not purchased by the acquiring firm. In terms of the model, the post-execution price, P_E^S, will be less than the pre-announcement price P_0. This implies that the price index, ρ_T^S, will fall precipitously subsequent to the execution of the offers. The data in figure 12-2 reveal no such price drop. In fact, target stockholders realized a significant 36 percent capital gain on the shares not purchased in the offer.[22] Thus, it does not appear that corporate raiding is a valid interpretation of the interfirm tender offer.

In sum the data appear consistent with the implications of the model. Compare figure 12-1 and figure 12-2. In evaluating an outstanding offer, target stockholders respond rationally to the fraction of target shares demanded, the per share offer price, and the post-execution market price of a target share. These are the parameters of the market pricing equation of the model—equation 12.4. As a more direct test of the relevance of the model developed in the first section, the market pricing equation was fitted directly to the data using multiple regression techniques. The following regression model was fitted to the 161 successful target observations in the data base: $\rho_A^S = \beta_0 + \beta_1(F\pi) + \beta_2[(1 - F)\rho_E^S]$. The predictions of the model are that $\beta_0 = 0$, $\beta_1 = \beta_2 = 1$.

The results of this analysis are given in table 12-1. Note that the model accounts for 88 percent of the cross-sectional variation in post-announce-

Table 12-1
Analysis of the Market Pricing Equation $\rho_A^S = \beta_0 + \beta_1(F\pi) + \beta_2[(1 - F)\rho_E^S]$

Independent Variable	$\hat{\beta}$	$\sigma(\hat{\beta})$
β_0	.0276	.0149
β_1	.9471	.0290
β_2	.7960	.0587

Note: $R^2 = .8750$; $N = 161$.

ment market price of the target shares. Moreover, the estimates of both β_0 and β_1 are within two standard deviations of their predicted values. However, although highly significant, the estimate of β_2 is significantly less than its predicted value of 1.

Successful Acquiring Firms. The theory of this chapter predicts that the market price of the shares of acquiring firms will increase, reflecting the synergy from gaining control of the target resources. To test this implication a time-series of the abnormal price index $X\rho_{B,D}^S$ was calculated for the shares of the 88 successful acquiring firms in this study.[23] This series is plotted in figure 12-3.

The data in figure 12-3 are consistent with the implications of the model. On average, acquiring stockholders realize an excess capital gain of 4 percent ($X\rho_{B,5}^S = 1.04$, $\sigma_X = .01$) within 5 trading days of the offer. This excess capital gain reaches 5 percent ($X\rho_{B,40}^S = 1.05$, $\sigma_X = .02$) within 40 days of the offer.[24] Note that this increase in equity value obtains in spite of the significant premium paid to tendering stockholders. In this sample, 88 acquiring firms paid target stockholders a 48 percent premium relative to the pre-announcement price ($\pi = 1.48$, $\sigma_X = .03$) and a 9 percent premium relative to the post-execution price ($\pi - \rho_{T,E}^S = 1.48 - 1.39 = .09$, $\sigma_X = .02$) for the target shares they purchased.

Taken together the data of figures 12-2 and 12-3 present a clear picture of interfirm tender offers. The stockholders of both firms realize a significant capital gain as a result of the combination. More revealingly, the gains of the acquiring firm do not obtain through the target shares per se, as the insider trading paradigm would predict. Rather, these gains are realized through the appreciation of the shares of the acquiring firm itself. This finding is consistent with a synergy interpretation of tender offers. The fact that the acquisition of the target shares is—on paper—a financial loss yet— on net—a positive value investment implies that the value of the target shares stems not from their proportional claims to the net cash flows of the target firm but rather from the control of the target resources that they confer.

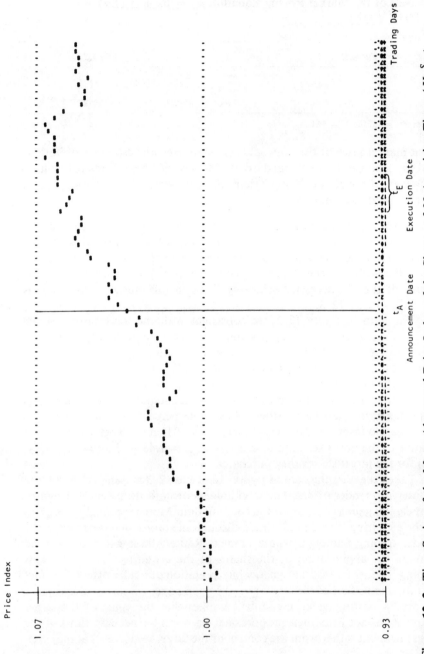

Figure 12-3. Time Series of the Mean Abnormal Price Index of the Shares of 88 Acquiring Firms ($X\rho_{B,D}^{S}$)

The synergistic gains to these corporate combinations are significant. The interfirm tender offer appears to be an important mechanism for channeling corporate resources to a higher-valued (more productive) use. These results (conclusions) are invariant to the particular time frame chosen within the 16-year period 1962 through 1977.

These findings demonstrate significant synergistic gains to interfirm tender offers. However, they provide no information as to the social welfare effects of the revealed synergy. These combinations may have either welfare-reducing or welfare-increasing consequences. Creating market power or integrating for the purpose of practicing price discrimination would reduce social welfare. Exploiting scale economies or implementing a cost-reducing operating strategy would increase social welfare.[25]

Unsuccessful Offers

Target Firms. Under the assumptions of the model, rational wealth-maximizing target stockholders will reject a tender offer only if another higher-valued alternative is available. Similarly, if target managers consistently act in their stockholders' interests they will only oppose non-value-maximizing tender offers.

The market pricing equation that was developed in the first section and tested in the last subsection reflects the rational evaluation of an outstanding tender offer. The increase in the value of a target share resulting from a given offer was shown to be a weighted average of the premium offered for the sought-after shares, π, and the post-execution revaluation of the remaining target shares, ρ_E^S. The appropriate weights for this estimate are the fraction of the outstanding target shares demanded by the bidding firm.

Define $\rho_{T,E}^U$ as the mean post-expiration price index of the target shares involved in unsuccessful tender offers. Let this variable represent the mean return to a target share assuming that the offer is rejected and the next-best alternative accepted. Note that this alternative may involve accepting another tender offer, a merger proposal, or a revised operating strategy that is proposed by the current target managers.

Using this notation and that developed earlier, the model predicts that for unsuccessful tender offers the post-expiration market price of a target share will exceed the per share value of the rejected offer. Symbolically,

$$\rho_E^U > (1 - F)\rho_E^S + F\pi. \qquad (12.5)$$

Inequality 12.5 states that an offer will be rationally rejected if the per share value of the offer is less than the market price implied by the next best allocation of the target resources—relative to the outstanding bid.[26]

In order to test the implications of this chapter for the returns to the shares of unsuccessful target firms, the sample of unsuccessful offers has been divided into two mutually exclusive groups. One group consists of those offers in which all outstanding target shares were demanded by the bidding firm, that is, $F = 1$. The second group consists of the remaining – necessarily fractional—offers; that is, $F < 1$.

An examination of inequality 12.5 reveals why this dichotomy is useful. If $F = 1$, the unobservable variable ρ_E^S, which is the post-execution price index that would have obtained had the offer been accepted, disappears from the equation. If all target shares are purchased by the acquiring firm, their subsequent value is of no consequence to tendering stockholders.[26] Only the offer premium is relevant. Thus, for unsuccessful tender offers, where $F = 1$, the prediction is that the post-expiration index of the target shares, ρ_E^U, exceeds the rejected offer premium, π.

The time series of the mean price index of the target shares involved in 33 unsuccessful tender offers where $F = 1$ is presented in figure 12–4. The offer price index, π, is also shown in the figure.

The data show that ρ_{40}^U, an estimate of the post-execution price level of a target share, is 67 percent above the pre-announcement level ($\rho_{40}^U - 1 = .67$, $\sigma_X = .07$). Moreover, this increase in the value of the target shares is greater than the rejected offer premium ($\rho_{40}^U - \pi = 1.67 - 1.52 = .15$, $\sigma_X = .04$). The data are consistent with the theory of this chapter. A tender offer will be rejected only if a higher-valued alternative materializes. The fact that the post-execution price index is significantly greater than the rejected offer price is consistent with this prediction.

As developed above, the evaluation of an unsuccessful, fractional tender offer ($F < 1$) requires the knowledge of the post-execution market price of a target share that would have obtained had the offer been successful. If the market's expectation of this price level is on average positive—a supposition supported by the empirical analysis of successful offers—then a testable hypothesis can be formulated. Under the assumption that the bidding firm would not have dissipated the value of the target shares had it secured control of the firm, the prediction is that the post-announcement price of the target shares will be greater than the minimum value of the outstanding offer per target share outstanding ($\rho_5^U > F\pi$).

Figure 12–5 presents the time series of $\rho_{T,D}^U$, the price index of the 64 firms in the data base that were the targets of unsuccessful, fractional tender offers. The minimum value of the rejected offers, per target share outstanding ($F\pi$), is also plotted.

The data show that the target stockholders of these firms realized a significant capital gain in the wake of an unsuccessful tender offer ($\rho_5^U = 1.36$, $\sigma_X = .04$). Moreover, this mean price index is significantly greater

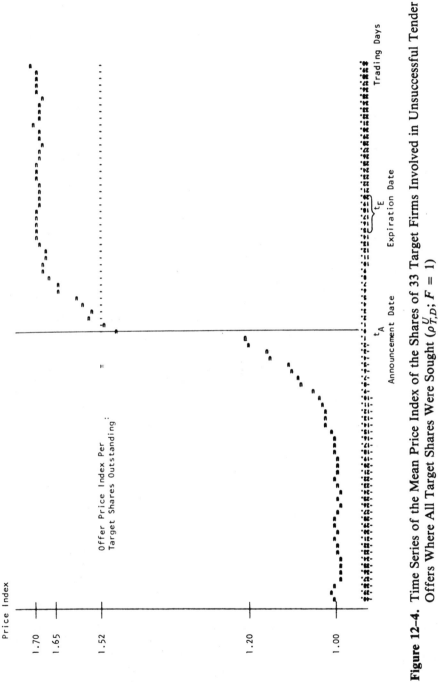

Figure 12-4. Time Series of the Mean Price Index of the Shares of 33 Target Firms Involved in Unsuccessful Tender Offers Where All Target Shares Were Sought ($\rho^U_{T,D}$; $F = 1$)

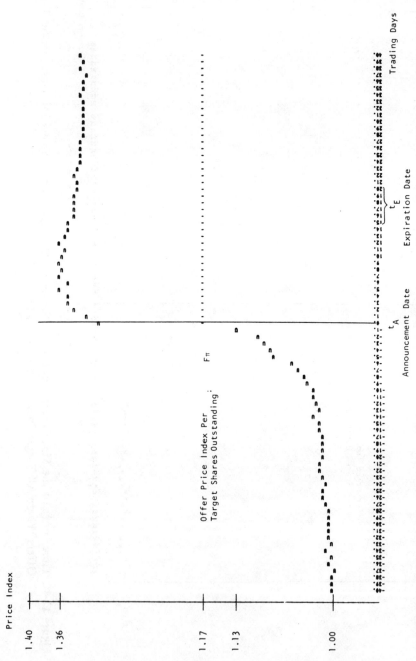

Figure 12–5. Time Series of the Mean Price Index of the Shares of 64 Target Firms Involved in Unsuccessful Tender Offers Where Less than All Target Shares Were Sought ($\rho_{T,D}^{U}; F < 1$)

than the minimum value of the rejected offer $(\rho_S^U - F\pi = 1.36 - 1.17 = .19, \sigma_X = .02)$.

The data of figures 12–4 and 12–5 support the implications of the theory concerning the returns to the shares of firms that are the targets of unsuccessful tender offers. Target stockholders display no degree of irrationality in rejecting these offers—even though π, the offer price index per target share demanded, is significantly greater than zero.

Unsuccessful Bidding Firms. The results of the analysis of unsuccessful bidding firms are reported in figure 12–6. The time series of the mean abnormal price index $X\rho_{B,D}^U$ is plotted in the figure.[28] The value of this statistic on the fortieth day after the offer is 4 percent below its pre-announcement level $(X\rho_{40}^U = .96 - 1.0 = -.04, \sigma_t = .02)$. Thus, when general market activity is netted out, an unsuccessful tender offer has a negative impact on the value of the bidding firm.

The negative return realized by unsuccessful bidding firms may be explained by examining the major costs incurred by these firms. Obviously, there are the out-of-pocket costs such as legal fees, filing fees, and advertising expenditures. A less obvious cost is the payment to investment banks for making available the substantial amount of cash that would be required if the offer had succeeded. The average offer in this sample represents a potential cash liability of almost $90 million. In addition to these out-of-pocket costs there may be other "indirect" costs of an unsuccessful bid. Suppose at some time prior to the offer the market had expected that the bidding firm would be in a position to make a profitable acquisition sometime in the future.[29] Under these conditions an unsuccessful offer might cause a revaluation in the market's assessment of the costs of an acquisition and, therefore, the (market) value of the acquiring firm.

For whatever reason, the data of the study indicate that while target firms experience a significant capital gain irrespective of the outcome of the tender offer, bidding firms profit only if the bid is successfully executed.

A Competitive Market for Corporate Control

The price behavior of the target shares (figures 12–2, 12–4, and 12–5) shows that the tender-offer process generates a significant amount of new information concerning the value of the target resources. While one can never assign causality (Did the tender offer cause the production of new information or did the discovery of new information precipitate the tender offer?), the dramatic "jump" in the price of the target shares around the announcement date indicates that it is the formal offer that initiates this production process. In many cases this information is sufficient to induce other firms to

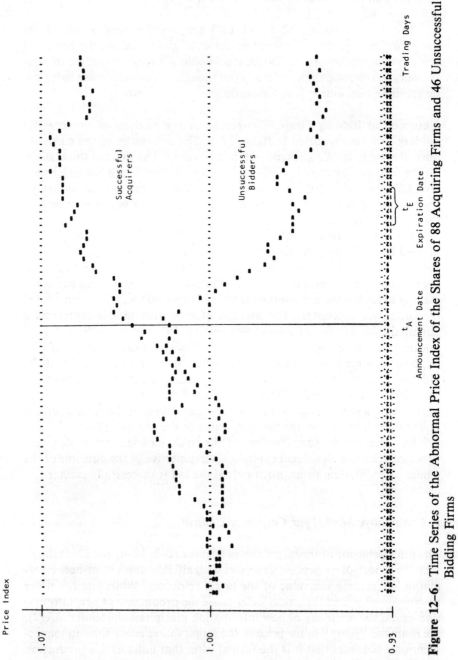

Figure 12–6. Time Series of the Abnormal Price Index of the Shares of 88 Acquiring Firms and 46 Unsuccessful Bidding Firms

enter the competition for the control of the target firm. Of the 97 unsuccessful offers that are reflected in the data of figure 12-4 and 12-5, 56 were followed by a successful tender offer or a successful merger proposal within 2 months of the initial offer; 23 of these successful offers were made by the initial bidding firm and 33 were made by other firms.[30]

The empirical evidence also indicates that the target managers themselves can implement a higher-valued operating strategy as a result of the information produced during the tender offer process. The price indexes for the shares of the 41 firms in the sample that were the target of a single unsuccessful tender offer have been computed. Thus, this sample consists of those cases where the target stockholders rejected an outside bid in favor of retaining their current managers. The mean excess capital gain to these shares through 80 trading days after the offer is 22 percent ($X\rho_{80}^{S} - 1 = .22, \sigma_t = .05$).

The ability of the target managers to capitalize on the opportunity facing the initial bidding firm may account for the fact that many tender offers are opposed by the target managers. At least for the cases in this study, one cannot reject the notion that the opposition by the target managers was in the target stockholders' interests. More generally, these findings support the assumption of a competitive market for corporate control in which the current target managers represent an important alternative to any takeover attempt.

The existence of a competitive market for corporate control (via interfirm tender offers) is also reflected in the price behavior of the shares of the bidding firms. The mean abnormal price index to the shares of all 134 bidding firms in the data base (which includes 88 successful and 46 unsuccessful bidding firms) 80 days after the offer is insignificantly different than the pre-announcement level ($X\rho_{80} - 1 = .02, \sigma_t = .02$. Thus, on average, *bidding* firms realize no abnormal returns from the tender-offer process, which is consistent with the notion of a competitive market for the right to control the target resources.[31]

Conclusions

The results of this study show that the successful completion of an interfirm cash tender offer is a value-increasing investment for both the target and acquiring firms. Target stockholders gain through the premium they receive for the shares purchased by the acquiring firm and through the capital appreciation (relative to pre-announcement market price) of the target shares they retain. This revaluation of the target shares presumably arises from a revised operating strategy that is implemented by the acquiring firm subsequent to securing control of the firm. The data also show that the stockholders of acquiring firms realize a capital gain as a result of the acquisition of the target shares. However, these gains are not realized through the market appreciation in the purchased target shares. While the post-execution market price of a target share is significantly higher than its pre-announcement level, the post-execution price is significantly less than the per share price paid by the acquiring firm. Taken together, these findings are consistent with the synergy interpretation of interfirm tender offers.

Under the assumptions of the model developed in the first section, acquiring firms cannot systematically profit from the market appreciation of the purchased target shares. This conclusion follows from the inherent public nature of the tender offer and a rational response to the bid by the target stockholders and competing management groups. Atomistic target stockholders, who individually cannot affect the outcome of an outstanding offer, will never tender their shares at an offer price that is less than the price which is expected to prevail subsequent to the acquisition. Rational target stockholders will not systematically underestimate the value of their holdings. Moreover, competing management groups, including the target managers themselves, are expected to counter any offer that does not reflect the optimal allocation of target resources. Competition for control of the target resources requires a successful bid to exceed the value of the next-best alternative. Any surplus of this value resulting from the combination will naturally accrue to the factors that give rise to the underlying corporate synergy. That is, the gain to the acquisition will be incorporated into the price of the shares of the acquiring firm directly, since these securities represent the claims to the specialized resource (of the acquiring firm) that precipitated the profitable investment opportunity. It is in this sense that the gains from the acquisition are not realized through the appreciation in the target shares, but rather through an increase in the market price of the shares of the acquiring firm itself.

The rational response to an interfirm tender offer is also reflected in the returns to the shares of firms that are the targets of unsuccessful offers. The post-expiration market price of these target shares is significantly greater than the cash offered by the bidding firm per target share outstanding. Thus, the data are consistent with an important implication of the analysis: target stockholders will reject those offers that become dominated by a more profitable investment alternative.

Notes

1. These post-execution revaluations are consistent with those reported in Dodd and Ruback (1977). These authors document an increase

in the value of target firms and a nonnegative return to successful acquiring firms.

2. This offer premium is calculated relative to the post-execution market price of a target share—40 days after the offer. Relative to the pre-announcement price—40 days before the offer—tendering stockholders received an average premium of $25 million per offer. The capital gain to the acquiring firm's shares includes an average $1.2 million increase in the market value of target shares held prior to the offer.

3. See Manne (1965), Smiley (1976), and Dodd and Ruback (1977).

4. The fact that many tender offers require that a minimum number of shares must be tendered before the terms of the offer will be honored is consistent with this control-seeking motive of the bidding managers. The target shares represent a profitable investment only if the acquiring firm can subsequently control the allocation of the underlying target resources.

5. The Williams Amendment of July 1968 to the Securities Exchange Act of 1934 brought the *cash* tender offer within the purview of the SEC. Prior to that time, only exchange offers—where the consideration is securities of the acquiring firm as opposed to cash—were governed by federal regulations. Ostensibly, the purpose of the Williams Amendment was to require bidding firms to give target stockholders sufficient time and information to make an intelligent decision as to whether or not they should tender their shares. For example, the amendment provides that the purchase of more than 5 percent of a firm's common stock must be made via a public tender offer and that the offer must be announced at least 10 trading days prior to the execution date. These public announcements must disclose the purchaser's identity, the source and amount of the funds to be used for the purchase, the purpose for which the purchase is being made, the number of shares the purchaser owns, and the details of any arrangements that the purchases has made with others regarding the purchase of the sought-after shares. In addition, target stockholders have the right to reclaim their already tendered shares should a higher-valued offer materialize within 30 days of a successful offer. Moreover, if a bidding firm elects to increase the offer price relative to an initial bid, all target stockholders, even those who have already tendered their shares, must be paid the higher price. For a more extensive discussion of the intent and extent of this piece of legislation, see Brown (1971). For an analysis of the effects of the Williams Act and the numerous state takeover statutes that have been enacted subsequently, see Jarrell and Bradley (1980).

6. It is insightful to note that in the overwhelming number of cases, successful bidding firms refuse to buy any shares that are tendered in excess of those initially sought. Also, revisions in the terms of an initial offer almost exclusively involve an increase in the demand price for the same number of target shares. These observations are consistent with the exis-

tence of a certain number of target shares that are required in order to effect a profitable tender offer. They also imply that the bidding firm does not expect a positive return through the appreciation in the target shares. If this were the case, the acquiring firm would be expected to buy all target shares tendered at the stated offer price.

7. See n.5 above.

8. To illustrate, if 51 percent of the target firm is sought—and all target stockholders tender their shares—then the acquiring firm must accept 51 percent of the holdings of each target stockholder. This implies that it is not possible for bidding managers to bribe a majority of target stockholders (via an inflated offer premium) into selling them control of the firm and, consequently, the ability to expropriate the wealth of the other (minority) target stockholders. Under existing federal regulations, all (tendering) stockholders must receive the same percentage compensation. Thus, *all* target stockholders would be left with a minority position in the target firm if a less than 100 percent tender offer were executed.

9. This criterion has been recognized by Grossman and Hart (1978) in a slightly different context. The authors use the argument to explain why closed-end mutual funds could trade at a discount from their net asset value. They argue that an offer to open up the fund by buying a 51 percent interest would never succeed at an offer price of T $< P_E =$ the per share net asset value, even if T $> P_0 =$ the current market price. The authors refer to this situation as a free-rider problem. To see their point, consider a tender offer to open up the fund, which represents an offer of T $= P_0 + \epsilon$ per share for 51 percent of the fund. Note that $0.51 \cdot N_0 \cdot (P_E - T) > 0$ represents the expected gain to the bidder from opening up the fund. However, in the wake of such an offer each stockholder would want the other investors to tender their shares so that the offer would be successful and he could earn the full capital gain of $(P_E - P_0)$ on each share held. But since all stockholders would have this incentive none would tender his shares and such an offer would necessarily be unsuccessful. The model developed herein avoids this paradoxical result since it is assumed that the acquisition yields an interactive (synergistic) gain that can be shared by the stockholders of both firms.

10. The next best alternative that is implied by P_E^U might be another tender offer, a merger proposal, a joint venture, or a new production/investment strategy proposed by the current target managers.

11. Equivalently, the left-hand side of 12.3 defines the per share value of a to-be-executed offer. Note the superscript S in this expression indicates the expected post-*execution* market price of a target share.

12. The data concerning these 258 observations have been compiled from several sources. Many of the offers occurring prior to 1969 are cited in the Austin-Fishman (1970) data base. Tender offers which have occurred

subsequent to 1974 are listed in the weekly publication *Securities and Exchange Commission News Digest* (1974-77). The remaining observations were obtained from announcements appearing in the *Wall Street Journal* (1956-77). All announcements have been verified by cross-referencing these sources with citations appearing in the *Wall Street Journal Index* (1956-77). The number of outstanding common shares of the target firms was obtained from the *Standard and Poor's Corporation Security Owners Stock Guide* (1956-77). The number of shares secured in each offer was ascertained from the Securities and Exchange Commission Official Summary (1968-77) and from articles appearing in the *Wall Street Journal* (1956-77) and from articles appearing in the *Wall Street Journal* (1956-77).

13. The return and price data used in the empirical analysis of this chapter were taken from the data files compiled by the Center for Research in Security Prices (CRSP) of the University of Chicago.

14. In the sample of 161 successful tender offers, the average acquiring firm held 5 percent of the target shares prior to the offer announcement.

15. Theoretically one would want to account for the probability that these securities would be converted into common stock and tendered to the bidding firm. To the extent that this is a common phenomenon, the denominator of F is understated. However, the numerator of F ignores the fact that many tender offer include bids for these convertible securities. This omission tends to reduce the systematic bias resulting from an underestimate of the number of target "shares" outstanding.

16. Often fewer shares are tendered than are demanded by the bidding firm. Many times acquiring firms are willing to accept those tendered rather than accept none at all. However, in this sample, the issue is not very important. The average ratio of shares purchased to shares demanded for these 161 offers is .96 with a standard deviation of .02. It should be noted that the assumption of homogeneous target stockholders is not reflected in the observed data. The homogeneity assumption of the model implies that either all target shares will be tendered or none at all. Empirically, this is not the case. Heterogeneous capital gains tax rates and/or heterogeneous expectations of the future value of the target shares would explain the absence of a unanimous response to a given tender offer.

17. Note that if P_A^S were not equal to the value given by equation 12.4, target stockholders would not be indifferent between tendering their shares and selling them in the open market—a condition required of an equilibrium market price while a successful offer is outstanding.

18. It should be noted that this systematic price decrease does not imply an arbitrage opportunity involving a post-announcement short sale of the target shares. Since all investors are assumed to know F, T, and P_E^S, the lender in a short sale would demand compensation of $F \cdot (T - P_E^S)$ per share if the shares are not returned before the execution date. A direct anal-

ogy exists in the case of short sales of securities where a dividend has been declared but not distributed. The borrower must compensate the lender for any dividend or interest which is paid while the short position is open. Thus, investors cannot profit from the fact that the post-execution market price of a target share is less than the interim price that prevails while a successful offer is outstanding.

19. As indicated by the designation of t_E along the "day" axis in the figure, the average tender offer in this sample was executed within 3 or 4 weeks (15–30 trading days) after the date of announcement.

20. Cross-sectional standard deviation are reported as σ_X, whereas standard errors calculated from time-series data are designated σ_t.

21. The empirical results for the subset of successful target shares are as follows:

$$\pi - \rho_E = 1.49 - 1.36 = .13, \sigma_X = .03,$$

$$\pi - \rho_A = 1.49 - 1.40 = .09, \sigma_X = .03,$$

$$\rho_A - \rho_E = 1.40 - 1.36 = .04, \sigma_X = .015,$$

$$\rho_A - F_\pi = 1.40 - 1.32 = .08, \sigma_X = .01,$$

22. As a more rigorous test of the raiding hypothesis, the mean abnormal price index $X\rho_{T,80}^S$ was calculated for the shares of the 98 target firms that remained listed on the NYSE or ASE for at least 80 days after the offer. This statistic is 1.20 with a standard deviation of .04.

23. The disparity between the number of acquiring firms and the number of target firms is due to lack of data for some of the former. Many bidding firms are foreign concerns or privately held firms and consequently are not included in the CRSP data base.

24. The average daily excess return (taken directly from the CRSP data file) to this portfolio was .0018 over the period $t = -15$ through $t = +15$. The standard deviation of this 21-day mean return has been estimated to be $\sigma = .0005$ based on the excess returns series preceding the offer announcement ($t = -40$ through $t = -16$). Thus, the average daily excess return is positive and significant.

Note that removing an inefficient management group is another example of a welfare-increasing change in the operations of the target firm. However, the preceding analysis implies that the returns from effecting this value-increasing change in the target must be realized through internal transfer schemes and not through the appreciation of the target shares.

25. Per the analysis of the first section, inequality 12.5 is a sufficient but not a necessary condition for an unsuccessful tender offer. An offer would fail even if it were the optimal allocation of the target resources if the offer price, T, were less than the expected post-execution market price, ρ_E^S. However, if as assumed, these prices are under control of the acquiring managers, no offer would ever be made where the offer price were less than

the anticipated post-execution market price. Therefore, in light of this consideration, inequality 12.5 is both a necessary and sufficient condition for an unsuccessful tender offer.

27. Provided of course that $\pi > \rho_E^S$.

28. This statistic for the sample of successful acquirers is plotted in the figure as well. The results for successful bidding firms are plotted as an S and those for unsuccessful bidding firms as a U in the figure.

29. Consider the case where the market value of a firm increases as a result of the creation of an internal acquisitions group.

30. It is perhaps insightful to note that in this study target stockholders realized a greater capital gain when their shares were purchased by a (second) competing bidder rather than the initial bidding firm. The mean excess price index 5 days after the offer is 1.33 for the shares of the 127 target firms that were acquired by the initial bidding firm ($X_5^S = 1.33$, $\sigma_t = .03$). For the target firms that rejected the offer of the initial bidder in favor of a competing bid (made by another firm) this statistic is 1.61 ($X_5^S = 1.61$, $\sigma_t = .09$).

31. Note that the bidding firms in this study represent a biased sample in that they are all firms that made an actual offer. Firms that incurred the costs of formulating an offer but for some reason elected not to pursue the bid are obviously not a part of the data base. This omission biases the total return to all bidding firms upwards—which could account for the positive, albeit insignificant, 2 percent return reported above. However, these data are only relevant to the extent that the sample of the study accurately reflects the true population of tender offers. Since all offers in the data base involve either NYSE or ASE common stocks, some important biases are obvious.

References

Austin, D., and Fishman, J. 1970. *Corporations in Conflict: The Tender Offer.* Ann Arbor, Mich.: Masterco Press.

Brown, M. 1971. "The Scope of the Williams Act and its 1970 Amendment." *Business Lawyer* (July):1637–1648.

Dodd, P.R., and Ruback, R. 1977. "Tender Offers and Stockholders Returns: An Empirical Analysis." *Journal of Financial Economics* 5, no. 3:351–374.

Grossman, S., and Hart, O. 1978. "Take-over Bids and the Theory of the Corporation." Working Paper, Philadelphia, University of Pennsylvania, Department of Economics.

Jarrell, G.A., and Bradley, M. 1980. "The Economic Effects of Federal and State Regulations of Cash Tender Offers." *Journal of Law and Economics* (October):371–408.

Manne, H.G. 1965. "Mergers and the Market for Corporate Control." *Journal of Political Economy* 73 (April):110–120.

Securities and Exchange Commission. 1978–1977. *Securities and Exchange Commission Official Summary.* Washington, D.C.

———. 1974–1977. *Securities and Exchange Commission News Digest.* Washington, D.C.

Smiley, R. 1976. "Tender Offers, Transaction Cost and the Theory of the Firm." *Review of Economics and Statistics* 58, no. 1. (February): 22–32.

Standard and Poor's Corporation Security Owners Stock Guide, 1956–1977. New York: Standard & Poor's.

Wall Street Journal Index. 1956–1977. Princeton, N.J.: Dow Jones Books.

Comment:
Mergers and the
Securities Industry

Jeffrey M. Schaefer

The experience of the securities industry is relevant to any discussion of mergers and acquisitions for two very different reasons. The first of these is that the so-called M&A (mergers and acquisitions) advisory fees paid by corporations have been an important source of countercyclical revenues for investment-banking firms through a very turbulent decade. The second reason is that the securities industry itself has experienced a wave of mergers during the 1970s. I focus mainly on this second topic—mergers within the securities industry—but I first comment briefly on the rise of the M&A business in the securities industry.

Usually, in a merger transaction, both the acquiring and target corporations are represented by an investment-banking firm. In major transactions, a single advisory fee can amount to millions of dollars. The M&A business has gained in complexity as companies have become more adept at fending off unfriendly takeovers and seeking higher bidders. While the most publicized mergers of the late 1960s involved acquiring companies enjoying high price-earnings multiples, the most recent emphasis has been on cash takeovers of companies having low price-earnings multiples. In effect, the M&A business adjusted itself to the bleaker equity markets of the 1970s.

The large premiums over market value paid in tenders have frequently been cited as evidence of undervaluation of common stocks. I do not discuss that here, other than to note that inflation has created uncertainty as to the quality—and, indeed, the credibility—of reported earnings per share. Acquiring companies have felt that it is cheaper to buy all of a target's outstanding stock than to buy all of its assets. Under such circumstances, the M&A business has flourished. The M&A business, however lucrative, is the domain, though, of just a handful of firms. The whole industry, in contrast, felt the effects of inflation-blighted equity markets during the 1970s.

Turning now to the securities industry itself, we find that it has experienced convulsive changes. If some downtown Rip Van Winkle were to wake up today and read a tombstone ad, he would be pretty surprised. Individual names of firms might still be present, yet their new arrangement is absolutely staggering. The three greatest factors behind these mergers are (1) the back-office legacy of the 1960s market; (2) relatively low profits, particularly when considered in terms of volatility and risk; and (3) Mayday (unfixing of commissions on May 1, 1975). Of the three, the unfixing of commissions certainly has received the most attention.

Before I discuss mergers in the securities industry, several key distinguishing industry features should be noted. The first is a matter of scale—even Merrill Lynch, the goliath of Wall Street, is medium sized by commercial-banking standards. Its $12 billion in assets place it roughly on a par with the Bank of New York, which is not considered to be an especially large bank. Comparisons with the leading companies in the *Fortune* 500 are even more dramatic. Related to smallness of scale is closeness of ownership. While more than a dozen firms are now publicly owned, few U.S. industries have ownership and management so closely intertwined. This close tie between ownership and management has strong implications for merger policy.

Another salient characteristic of the securities industry is the simple level of organizational form and control procedures found in many firms. While producer-managers are becoming a thing of the past, the chief executives of many major firms consider themselves first and foremost to be deal doers. Firms have tended to regard their operation as an indivisable whole. Prior to Mayday, unquestionably, many activities were subsidized by the institutional brokerage business. This has changed, but traces of the pre-Mayday outlook linger.

Commissions were unfixed in 1975 amid dire predictions by some observers that economies of scale in the business would lead to predatory competition and a contraction in the number of firms. A major contraction of the industry has occurred but without strong evidence of scale economies. Many mergers, no doubt, have been entered into in the hope of realizing scale economies that have since proved elusive. Studies by both the SEC and the Securities Industry Association have shown firm size to be unrelated to firm profitability. However, a major increase in volume or, more importantly, regulatory measures such as the removal of off-board trading restrictions may alter the securities business by introducing scale economies where none now exist.

An important difficulty in the past with mergers involves the need to mesh two back-office systems. A joke emerged after several mergers that one part of a combined entity will buy the shares while the other part will sell the same shares. More than any other firm in the securities industry, Shearson Loeb Rhoades is a product of mergers, and much of Shearson's success is thought to derive from its practice of integrating acquired branches a few at a time rather than en masse.

The securities industry's major resources are capital and people. The capital factor is self-evident, and mergers are a means of bolstering a firm's capital position to survive in a business increasingly oriented toward principal rather than agency transactions. When one firm acquires another, though, it is really trying to acquire people. Successful retail salesmen tend to take their accounts with them wherever they go, and post-Mayday discounting in institutional brokerage has placed a new premium on retail accounts. For those firms still active in institutional brokerage and money management, acquisition of a research house—many of which have been up for grabs since Mayday—has been an attractive alternative to building up an in-house research capacity from scratch. A research department, clearly, is little more than the people who staff it.

Another motive for acquiring a firm can be a desire to gain access to that firm's investment-banking clients. Here again, however, the real aim is to acquire that firm's personnel and financing expertise. The dominant importance of manpower and the eagerness with which recruiters descend upon the personnel of firms entering into mergers point to one of the most sensitive problems in the whole area—namely, retention of key personnel.

A notable recent development on Wall Street is a blurring of the distinction between brokerage and investment banking. Firms having strong distribution—be it retail or institutional—have used that base to gain a position in the origination of securities. Some firms that are strong in distribution have developed an investment-banking capacity in-house, while others have sought to merge their brokerage network with an originating firm. Nor is the brokerage/investment-banking frontier the only one being eroded. Firms are entering mortgage banking, real estate, insurance brokerage, and money-market-fund management as well, to name but a few. Mergers offer clear advantages for firms pursuing this kind of diversification strategy.

Diversification as a means of reducing risk is another incentive behind mergers. The securities industry's earliest diversification moves actually increased risk since these moves took firms away from the brokerage and into the dealer business. The risks in the latter business are considerably greater. A strong correlation has also existed between the different product lines securities firms offer. A weak secondary-bond market has usually meant a tapering off of underwritings, for example, and margin lending activity closely follows exchange volume.

Risk reduction for the securities industry has been made possible by improvement in hedging strategies and by moves into fields far from the world of interest rates. Neither strategy necessarily involves mergers of the kind we are discussing.

Two other circumstances conducive to mergers in the securities industry should be mentioned. The first involves the close ownership of many firms. In some cases, the desire of a major principal to withdraw his capital can create a situation in which the firm must either raise new capital very quickly, scale down its activities, or seek a merger partner. In many cases, merger has been the alternative selected.

Another factor behind mergers—far less important now than it was five or ten years ago—involves the dire straits in which the industry found itself after the 1960s boom. It was not uncommon then for a solvent firm to assume the liabilities of a failing firm in the hope of salvaging its more desirable assets. Merrill Lynch's acquisition of Goodbody & Co., involving a $30 million NYSE indemnification, was the most publicized of these shotgun combinations.

The securities industry is characterized by high leverage, both financial and operating, that gives its earnings great volatility. In recent years, it has experienced revolutionary changes on both the regulatory and technological fronts. In no sense, either, is the pace of change abating. This is the backdrop against which this feverish merger activity has taken place. Depending on the markets we have, more mergers may or may not be in the offing. It is hard to conclude that mergers' contributions to the twin goals of lowering risk and realizing economies of scale have been achieved as yet. The jury is still out on any such assumptions and will likely remain so for some time.

Panel Discussion

Louis Perlmutter

I want to comment about three specific changes that have taken place in the merger business in the last five years. First is the rise to respectability of the tender offer—cash offered directly to shareholders. Second is the rise in the number of foreign firms making acquisitions in the U.S. market. Third is the process by which companies are being valued as compared to the process during the last major merger wave of the late 1960s. This involves the whole concept of the creation of value in the marketplace and how companies perceive the ways of accomplishing their objectives in this area.

Let met start with the first, which I think is the most fundamental, change—the rise in respectability of the tender offer. Prior to 1973 or 1974, a tender offer direct to shareholders was a rather rare thing and not done by the most respectable corporations. In 1974–1975, the bear market and inflation led to very low stock prices, with companies selling far below their commercial value in the marketplace. Corporate managers charged with the responsibility of insuring growth decided that the name of their game really was not wooing people who did not want to sell to them; instead, the name of their game was to insure growth. They decided—with the help of their advisers, lawyers, and bankers—that they would go directly to shareholders. These managers were able to offer substantial premiums because of the very low stock prices. Eventually, such companies—for example, Mobile, Exxon, American Express, International Nickel—proceeded to make unilateral tender offers, thereby legitimizing this approach as a tool to accomplish corporate growth. They have been assisted by banking firms, many of which, prior to this period, took a rather hands-off and negative attitude toward participating in this sort of practice.

As a result, a cadre of lawyers and bankers now exists who spend their time planning, negotiating, defending, and litigating in the tender-offer area. A rash of legislation has occurred throughout the country as a reaction to unfriendly tender offers. Thirty-seven states now have so-called takeover statutes. As a result of this, there is some confusion as to the relationship between the Williams Act (the Federal Securities Law) and some of the state statutes. Some of the state statutes have been held unconstitutional. The SEC takes the position that the states have a legitimate role in regulating this type of activity so long as their actions are complementary to

Note: This panel discussion has been condensed by the editors.

the federal Williams Act. This evolving area will continue to be modified in the future—perhaps by legislation, perhaps by court decisions.

The second area is the dramatic rise of foreign acquisitions in the United States. In 1977, for example, there was a total of $3.2 billion in foreign acquisitions in the United States; that was a record. In 1978 the figure jumped to $6.2 billion, far surpassing the previous record. In 1979, 234 foreign acquisitions took place in the United States. This was roughly 34 percent more than the 1976 total. There is no reason to believe that this trend will not continue. The same pressures that have existed over the past several years continue to exist, though there may be ebbs and flows depending upon political, economic, currency, and other transitory pressures. Basically, the trend will continue in all areas of U.S. business, including some regulated industries such as the banking industry. We will continue to see foreign banks coming into the United States until either the process is stopped politically or the market becomes saturated.

The third area is the concept of valuation. In the last boom in the merger business, the 1960s, the game really was a game, and conglomerates led the way with creation of pieces of paper that were designed to increase the reported earnings per share on a quarter-by-quarter basis.

Corporate mergers today, I think, have a different goal, and their advisors have a different view. Firms are willing to buy companies at prices above book value, offering substantial premiums above existing stock market prices. More important considerations now are the business fit—how the acquisition fits into the long-range strategic plan of the company and where the company wants to be five years or ten years out. As a result, acquiring firms are willing to incur initial earnings dilution. At some point there is a presumed cross-over point, and there will be a contribution to earnings, either because of the company's inherent growth or because of what the combined companies can do together. There is also a concept by managers of going into a business and creating strings of earnings; even though there is some initial earnings dilution, they think the quality of earnings is higher, with the result that stockholders possibly will become richer through shares receiving a higher price-earnings ratio. I think that this concept is reflected in some of the statistics on the premiums being paid for mergers and acquisitions in the past couple of years. I do not think we would have seen these kinds of premiums, nor would they have been acceptable, in the period of the late 1960s.

Where is all this activity going? Basically, as long as there is inflation, there will be merger activity. Beyond that, most large corporations are facing a set of factors that creates more difficulties for them than they had faced in the pase—namely, shrinking markets, difficult foreign competition, currency fluctuation, lack of productivity gains—all the things that we have read about and that have been much publicized. The result is that the firms are undertaking a strategic review, business by business, to decide how to redeploy their resources. I think that many divestitures and a lot of reorganization will take place. We have seen some of that kind of activity recently, with Seagrams's divestiture of some of its properties (with the subsequent enhancement of its share price in the marketplace). These same pressures force the medium-sized and smaller companies to seek a safe haven. Thus, I think these kinds of activities are going to continue at the same rate as in the past, especially if we continue to see the entry of foreign purchasers into the U.S. market.

John A. Bulkley

My firm is Moseley, Hallgarten, Estabrook, and Weeden. We are approximately a $100 million company and are only in the securities business. I thought that, as a contrast to all of the macro looks at mergers, I would give you a worm's-eye review of the process, as somebody who has merged his company almost every eighteen months over the last ten years.

The history of all this activity began when I and two partners came out of the leveraged buy-out and mergers and acquisitions game of the 1960s and looked around Wall Street in the summer of 1970 to buy a brokerage firm. We found Estabrook, raised $2 or 3 million of private money, and bought Estabrook in August of 1970. At the time of the purchase, we were running at an annual rate of about $4 million in revenues and $6 million in costs, and, needless to say, we were being closely watched by the regulators in the stock exchanges. We were able to turn the company around and make a little money in 1971 and 1972. Then, the brokerage business really took a dive in the spring of 1973. We thought that merging with a firm called Moseley was a good idea. Moseley, as did Estabrook, had historic roots in Boston; it was also predominantly a retail brokerage firm, and from the point of view of business planning and strategy, the merger looked like a good fit.

We merged with Moseley in late spring of 1973 and started making some money; we more or less broke even by December. Then in the spring of 1974, the brokerage business again dropped off very dramatically. We found a firm called Hallgarten. Hallgarten was a local, old firm that had been in the Wall Street area since before World War I. Hallgarten had the characteristics that are relevant to mergers and acquisitions, and it was a very mature firm. (One can think of companies as somewhat like countries or people—that is, they have life-cycles. When they are young or adolescent, they have youthful entrepreneurial vigor; they reach a prime when they are adults; and then they reach an old age.) Hallgarten, as an old firm, had also gone through stages we found interesting. For example, it had gone from a strong entrepreneurial leader into a democratic structure and then into anarchy. In 1974, it was in anarchy, really going nowhere but down; but it did have capital, which was important. We merged with Hallgarten, and by that time we were up to $7 million in capital. This was early 1974, we started making money soon after, and we have had only three loss months since then.

After that we tried to get into the corporate-finance business. It seemed best to merge into the business rather than to try to start a fresh operation. We looked around for firms that did underwriting and came out of the 1960s with a lot of underwriting and underwriting background. We tried to do a merger with New York Securities. Unfortunately, however, New York Securities was being sued by many firms because it had lost one of its better clients, Equity Funding. About $500 million in litigation was hanging over the company. We hired a very good firm that specialized in bankruptcy law, and they helped us structure a deal in which we basically hired people. The name of the game is not to be a successor to a legally entangled business; rather, we acquired the human capital of New York Securities in 1975.

In 1977, we looked at C.B. Richard Ellis, which was a small New York trading firm. It was a fairly youthful, vigorous firm, making a lot of money, and having an office in Switzerland and a nice risk-arbitrage operation. Its problem was in capital resources. In the tradition of Wall Street, it was a family-owned firm. Although many family-owned firms had made provisions for what happens when the life cycle takes its inevitable course, C.B. Richard Ellis had not. A member of the Richard family had died, and with estate taxes to pay and the whole capital structure confused, the firm felt vulnerable and was open to a discussion of merger.

We then merged with C.B. Richard Ellis, combining its Swiss operation with what we got from Hallgarten. This gave us, at that time, three branches in Europe. By 1979, we were up to about $20 million in capital. The next merger that appeared on the threshold, in mid-1979, was the Weeden Company, which has been historically a very strong bond firm and a very good trading firm. It has employed a lot of prestigous people— William Simon, for example, who spent part of his career there as a trader. It has been a little unfortunate in recent years, however. It had launched into a program of upstairs trading and trying to get a third market developed. It turned out that Weeden had been advocating a destruction of the New York Stock Exchange's commission price umbrella, which would prove to be the destruction of its own firm. The firm, as an off-board trading firm, only existed because of the price umbrella of the New York Stock Exchange. That umbrella collapsed in 1975, partly as a result of Weeden's third-market efforts.

There was some good and bad years in the bond industry as well. By the time I got to Weeden in the summer of 1979, it had made one or two aborted attempts to merge. The Weeden brother in charge of the firm was in the process of telling the various Wall Street publications in our industry that a merger was not on the horizon and that he and his brothers would buckle down and pull the firm together and make it work. (An important part of any study of mergers and acquisitions is to separate what you read in the press from what is really going on.) His business objective was to hold the remaining human resources together. He did not really want to talk merger because he was in a public posture of not merging. Nevertheless, I thought it was a good idea for him to get to know us. We fit very well, in part because Weeden had an important asset—namely, a $30 million tax loss—that it had managed to create in the last couple of years of its life.

In any event, we did have a lot of other true business purposes, which included going public (Weeden already was a public firm), and we finally arranged a merger that was virtually identical with the other transactions we had done. We changed our name, which is why we now have four names, and we restructured our board and basically did a book-value merger. So, by 1979, we were a $30 million public company, and we had a $30 million tax loss carried forward.

At the time of the merger, Weeden had reduced personnel to about 100 people from well over 1,000 a few years earlier. The two remaining activities were municipal-bond activities and an upstairs trading activity. We have now restructured the upstairs-trading activity so that it works in accordance with the various rules of the New York Stock Exchange and other exchanges; in other words, orders have to touch base on these floors before they get done upstairs. In the municipal-bond area we tried to keep, and have succeeded in keeping, the basic Weeden market position intact.

The learning period in the bond business gave us an opportunity to have our first three-month loss in five years and the first down year in five years. That was the fiscal year ending in the spring of 1980. The fiscal year ending in 1981 will provide our shareholders with the assurance that we did in fact learn something in the bond business during the prior year.

What I get from our story is that mergers and acquisitions can be studied in their quantitative, academic sense perhaps, but that they are very much people things. In an industry like ours, where the industry is consolidating and firms are going out of business, I think the difference between a C.B. Richard Ellis that goes out of business and an Estabrook-Moseley combination that goes forward is in large part due to the people who work there. Firms need leadership and an ability to restructure, to consolidate, to give up some activities, which can be painful. It is often easier for a management just to give up, and merger is a way of giving up.

Certainly, as a man who is involved in mergers, I believe that those mergers are to a great extent an expression of top management's energy level, ego, and desire to build a pyramid. Some years ago, when I was looking for a job as a corporate planner, someone told me that the most important part of one's own corporate strategy was working for the right person and having a direct relationship with that person, which perhaps is another way of saying the same thing—that the person who does it has to want to do it. That is our macro story and our micro story.

Harold M. Wit

I think that the present trend in mergers and acquisitions will continue and probably will accelerate. Some of my reasons may be wrong, and certainly some are incomplete, but they are important. I think that if inflation continues, if stock prices remain below replacement costs, if easy credit is available, if the tax laws do not change, and if corporate actors continue to think the way they do, the current trend will continue and accelerate. I state some of the overall reasons or conditions that permit this; but these conditions are different in the present era than they were, say, twenty or thirty years ago.

I think one new condition is that we are in an age of middlemen who need something to do. We have a lot of people who are trained in acquisitions expertise—lawyers, brokers, investment bankers, printers, proxy solicitors, arbitrageurs, government regulators, professors, and academics—and business schools now teach the subject. There is a tremendous vested interest in the merger process now going forward, and the energy and the aggressiveness of these middlemen will help, I think, to continue this trend. If you have salespeople selling something, they are going to sell a lot of that product as long as they can make money doing it. (This is not meant to put anybody down, since I'm one of those middlemen too.) If, for example, you look around the audience of a conference on acquisitions and mergers, you will find that it is full of middlemen, or people who want to be middlemen. Where are the principals? It was very rare twenty years ago to have a conference made up of people of this sort.

I think regulators have contributed to the growth of the middlemen process. I do not think there is any collusion, but there is certainly a symbiotic relationship. For example, the law firm of XYZ a number of years ago was, in a sense, just a small provincial town; now it is an enormous city. Firms put this law firm on retainer to advise them on how to use the law to do mergers effectively and for advice on how to avoid being taken over themselves. It is a symbiotic industry.

Another factor is our age of easily available credit. The United States is in the business of manufacturing money, and there is plenty around and plenty available (though the price may seem high).

Then there is the love of action. This is an age in which people like action, and the merger and acquisition activity is an area in which plenty of action occurs. I have seen managements corrupted, in a sense, because once they get into this activity they find it interesting and exciting; it has high energy and helps them forget their real troubles.

The tax laws also abet this activity. Interest can be deducted as a cost item. Companies under the tax laws are permitted to keep much more money than they need for their ongoing activities, despite what the tax codes say about accumulated earnings and profits. That excess cash burns holds in pockets and is used partly for those activities.

The advent of the computer as a management tool gives people (in my way of thinking) the delusion that they can control and understand disparate businesses. This ties in with the new types of people who are running things. We have people who are trained to think in abstractions. We have plenty of people who are trained to think in terms of numbers and computers as valid control devices. We have lawyers and accountants who are used to thinking also in terms of abstractions and playing with pieces in an abstract way. By contrast, we traditionally had in the United States the Henry Ford types, the people who were considered result oriented, who were interested in products, who were interested in touching and feeling what they were doing.

I think large companies now are run by people who have an entirely different orientation than Henry Ford. This leads to the ability to deal with these abstract problems. It was very difficult for me. I worked on one merger years ago for months and months—fifteen or sixteen hours a day. The result of the merger was that someone went to the office of the Secretary of the State of Delaware and put a piece of paper across one of those iron gates—and that was the "conclusion" of the merger. I just could not take that anymore. I never saw a factory; I never saw anything physical or tangible. I just saw a lot of papers going back and forth.

In the mergers and acquisitions process, somebody wants to acquire another entity. It is somewhat like growing crops. You have to have something there for them to acquire. The United States has been a great place for growing new businesses. I would guess that many more businesses have been created in the United States since World War II than even existed before. Thus, in effect, you have the planting and the harvesting. If all of those businesses had not been created, there would not be anything to acquire. This certainly has been a factor in the acquisitions of brokerage businesses, for example.

Further, the antitrust laws have been a factor. The antitrust laws discourage horizontal and vertical mergers. As a result, we have a lot more conglomerate activity. The old idea was to control markets and prices; the new idea is growth for growth's sake. The antitrust laws clearly have played a role here.

Then, as Mr. Perlmutter mentioned in the first section, the international aspects are important, and the United States has become a haven for foreigners. We have a huge marketplace in the United States, a place that interests people in Europe with large amounts of capital who look for expansion and safety.

Our particular firm has taken advantage of these trends in two ways. We help arrange mergers, and we have also done quite well in the risk-arbitrage game. One particular merger in which we were involved can illustrate a number of my points. It was a small deal, involving $14 or $15 million. The middlemen did very well. Perhaps $700,000 or $800,000 in fees were paid out to various wise men like myself and to printers and accountants. It was just a marvelous thing for us. This deal also presented some new and unique legal and regulatory problems. One man owned about a third of each company, and the amusing thing to me was that this particular man, who is an old friend of mine, was one of those people who are extraordinarily fair—the sort of man who sees both sides and who wants to stay out of trouble. Because of the regulatory structure, because of the fact that we have so many keepers of the public morality who want to institutionalize various means of fairness, it was necessary to bring in about ten people to "advise" him what he had to do to be fair. Thus, this deal had the amusing aspect that all sorts of people who had absolutely no interest whatsoever, except collecting their fees and protecting the so-called public, were telling this very fair man what he had to do to be fair.

So, merger and acquisition activity is a wonderful field, not only for sociologists but also for humorists and for social critics. I think it will continue, and we will get not only more money but also more amusement, more regulations, and thicker prospectuses and the cutting down of our national forests in order to meet the paper requirements for this work.

Part IV
Strategic Planning
and Mergers

13 Diversification and Mergers in a Strategic Long-Range-Planning Framework

Kwang S. Chung and
J. Fred Weston

This analysis of diversification and mergers in the framework of the strategic long-range planning processes of firms seeks to provide perspective on a number of issues. Initially, it might be argued that taking the viewpoint of the planning activities of firms is simply to analyze the motives for mergers. This argument would then continue that motives are irrelevant—only the effects of diversification and mergers matter.

Certainly any fruitful study of mergers must be related to testable propositions on their effects. But in the merger area a wide variety of models and tests have been employed. Model development is influenced by initial assumptions. Also, the results of tests are influenced by the choice of variables, how they are measured, and how they are combined in the econometric relationships studied. These selections and interpretations are influenced by the conceptions of the underlying processes involved. For example, one of the approaches to mergers is the managerialism school, which is based on a theory of motivation (Mueller 1969; 1977). It holds that managers control corporations and that they seek mergers for growth's sake because the size, levels of sales, or total assets determine managerial compensation. Such a theory leads to particular empirical tests. Thus, alternative assumptions of managerial motivations may lead to different models or theories and different tests. The purpose of the present approach, therefore, is to provide a basis for evaluating alternative theories of mergers, their tests, and predictions from both social and enterprise perspectives.

The Managerial Capability Perspective

The literature on long-range strategic planning in purposive organizations has exploded in recent years. (See references on long-range and strategic planning at the end of the chapter.) The summary we present is not intended to be a full treatment of the subject. Rather, it represents our interpretation as oriented to the issues raised by diversifiction through mergers.

315

The literature views long-range planning and strategic planning as essentially synonymous (Steiner 1979). The emphasis of strategic planning is on areas related to the firm's environments and constituencies, not just operating decisions (Summer 1980). In our view. the modern literature on long-range planning indicates that long-range strategic planning involves at least the following elements:

Environmental reassessment;

A consideration of capabilities, missions, and environmental interaction from the standpoint of the firm and its divisions;

An emphasis on process rather than particular goals or objectives;

An emphasis on iteration and on an iterative feedback process as a methodology for dealing with ill-structured problems;

A recognition of the need for coordination and consistency in the resulting long-range-planning processes with respect to individual divisions, product-market activities, and optimization from the standpoint of the firms as a whole;

A recognition of needs to relate effectively to the firm's changing environment and constituencies;

Integration of the planning process into a reward and penalty or incentive system, taking a long-range time perspective.

Earlier, the emphasis of long-range strategic planning was on doing something about the so-called gap. When it is necessary to take action to close a prospective gap between the firm's objectives and its potential based on its present capabilities, some difficult choices must be made. For example, shall the firm attempt to change its environment or capabilities? What will be the costs of such changes? What are the risks and unknowns? What are the rewards if successful? What arc the penalties of failure? Because the stakes are large, the iterative process is employed. A tentative decision is made. The process is repeated, perhaps from a different management function orientation and at some point, the total-enterprise point of view is brought to bear on the problem. At some point, decisions are made and must involve entrepreneurial judgments.

Alternatively, the emphasis may be on broader orientations to the effective alignment of the firm with its environments and constituencies. Different approaches may be emphasized. One approach seeks to choose products related to the needs or missions of the customer that will provide large markets. A second approach focuses on technological bottlenecks or barriers, the solution of which may create new markets. A third strategy chooses to be at the frontiers of technological capabilities on the theory that some attractive product fallout will result from such competence. A fourth approach emphasizes economic criteria including attractive growth prospects and appropriate stability.

Other things being equal, a preferred strategy is to move into a diversification program from the base of some existing capabilities or organizational strengths. Guidance may be obtained by answers to the following questions: Is there strength in the general management functions? Can the company provide staff expertise in a wide range of areas? Does the firm's financial planning and control effectiveness have a broad carry-over? Are there specific capabilities such as research, marketing, and manufacturing that the firm is seeking to spread over a wider arena?

The firm should be clear on both its strengths and its limitations. To remedy weaknesses, the firm should clearly define the specific new capabilities it is seeking to obtain. If the firm does not possess a sufficient breadth of capability to use as a basis for moving into other areas, an alternative strategy may be employed. This would be to establish a beachhead of capabilities in one or more selected areas. The firm is then in a position to develop concentrically from each of these nuclei.

To understand the potential carry-over in mergers that may be termed even pure conglomerate mergers, one needs to recognize that the nature of firms and the boundaries of industries have become much more dynamic and flexible in recent years. The emphasis of traditional economic theory, as reflected in the Census Bureau's Standard Industrial Classification is on industry boundary delineation that is mainly product or process oriented. However, organization theory and the behavior of individual firms reflect an emphasis increasingly on missions and capabilities.

In a world of continuous change, managements must relate to *mission,* defined in terms of customer needs, wants, or problems to be solved. In addition to missions, another important dimension of the concept of industries is a range of capabilites. This includes technologies, embracing all processes from basic research, product design and development, and applications engineering through interrelated manufacturing methods and obtaining feedback from consumers.[1] The capabilities concept encompasses important management technologies including planning, information sciences, computerization of information flows, formal decision models, problem-solving methodologies, and behavioral sciences. Thus managerial capabilities include competence in the general management functions of planning, organizing, directing, and controlling, as well as in the specific management functions of research, production, personnel, marketing, and finance. In addition, they include a range of technological capabilities. Another important dimension is coordinating and achieving an effective organization system or entity.

The development of such a range of capabilities requires substantial investments in the training and experience of people. It includes investments in holding organizations together during periods of depressed sales. Market demand-and-supply forces place a high value on executive talent and staff expertise. Their importance in the competitive performance of firms leads to new forms of fixed investment in managerial organizations. The effective utilization of augmented fixed factors leads to firms of larger size and increased diversification. (Fixed factors are investments in plant and equipment or costs of specialist executives.)

The theory of the firm set forth by Coase (1937) predicts these developments. In explaining the role of firms in relation to markets, Coase identified two functions as determinants of the scope and size of firms. One was the relative efficiency of effecting transactions within the firm compared to transactions conducted in the external marketplace. The other was the effectiveness with which the elements of the firm were coordinated or managed. Coase described possible developments that would affect the size of firms compared to the relative scope of market transactions. Coase's model predicts that the broadening of capabilities encompassed by a firm and developments in managerial technology will result in both an increase in the absolute size of business firms and in the degree of their diversification with respect to capabilities, missions, and markets.

Potential competition has thus been enlarged. Industry boundaries defined by products become less meaningful than industries defined by the ability to perform the critical functions for meeting the customer's needs or missions. The ease of entry is increased because the critical factor for success in changing environments may be a range of technologies, experience developed in international markets, or even more general organizational-performance capabilities.

These various approaches are likely to be oriented to business goals and objectives. General goals may be formulated with respect to size, growth, stability, flexibility, and technological breadth. Size objectives are established in order to use effectively the fixed factors the firm owns or buys. Size objectives have also been expressed in terms of critical mass. Critical mass refers to the size a firm must achieve in order to attain cost levels that will enable the firm to operate profitably at market prices.

Growth objectives may be expressed in terms of sales, total assets, earnings per share, or the market price of the firm's stock. These are related to two valuation objectives. One is to attain a favorable price-earnings multiple for the firm's shares. A second is to increase the ratio of the market value of a firm's common stock to its book value.

Two major forms of instability can be distinguished. The first is exemplified by the defense market, which is subject to large, erratic fluctuations in its total size and abrupt shifts in individual programs. Another form of instability is the cyclical instability that characterizes producers of both industrial and consumer durable goods.

The goal of flexibility refers to the firm's ability to operate in a wide variety of product markets. Such flexibility may require a breadth of research, manufacturing, or marketing capabilities. Of increased interest in recent years is technological breadth. With the increased pace of technological change in the U.S. economy, a firm may consider it important to possess capabilities in the rapidly advancing technologies.

Goals may be stated in general or specific terms, but both are subject to quantification. For example, growth objectives may be expressed in some relationship to the growth of the economy or the firm's industry. Specific objectives may be expressed in terms of percentage of sales in specified types of markets. The quantification of goals facilitates comparisons of goals with forecasts of the prospects for the firm. If it is necessary for the firm to alter its product-market mix or range of capabilities to reduce or close the planning gap, a diversification strategy may be formulated.

Efforts to achieve the multiple goals suggest a broader range of variables in the decision processes of the firm. Decisions involve trade-offs and judgments of the nature of the future environments, the policies of other firms with respect to the dimensions described, and new missions, technologies, and capabilities. In short, to the requirements of operating efficiency and optimal output adjustments has been added the increased importance of the planning processes.

A number of misconceptions are held with respect to the significance of planning in the firm. The misconceptions range between two extremes. One view holds that we have always planned, that planning is nothing new, since the practice antedates biblical times. This view misses the real significance of modern planning, however. Certainly business firms have been planning for decades, with accounting and financial budgeting activities representing one kind of planning. But the important developments that set the new managerial technology of planning apart from its predecessor activities are (1) coordinating research, sales, production, marketing, facilities, personnel, and financial plans, making them consistent with one another, and resolving them into comprehensive planning for the enterprise as a whole; (2) a feedback system; and (3) integration with a reward and penalty (incentive) system. Some U.S. firms developed and practiced such integrated and coordinated planning by the 1920s, but the broad extension of the practice did not occur until after World War II, with substantial gaps still persisting in the understanding and implementation of effective planning among a large number of firms.

The other erroneous view about business planning holds that the heavy investments of capital by large corporations have led them to devise methods for controlling demand and that planning has replaced the market mechanism. Such a view has led one author to sweeping generalizations, unsupported by systematic evidence, such as the following: "It is a feature of all planning that, unlike the market, it incorporates within itself no mechanism by which demand is accommodated to supply and the reverse (Galbraith 1967, p. 35).

This represents a basic misconception. Those with experience with purposive organization planning processes recognize that the development of integrated planning is an effort to adapt more responsively to increasingly dynamic environments. Planning and management controls do not remove the uncertainty of market influences; they rather seek to help the firm adjust more sensitively to change—to new threats and opportunities.

Diversification Planning, Mergers, and the Carry-Over of Managerial Capabilities

From an economic standpoint, does any justification exist for these long-range-planning efforts of firms to achieve the regeneration of their organization systems? Particularly, does any justification exist for the use of mergers to seek continuity of firms? We shall not deal with horizontal and vertical expansion by merger activity for practical and theoretical reasons. The practical reasons are that, with the 1950 amendments to Section 7 of the Clayton Act, the ability of government authorities to block horizontal and vertical mergers has become so absolute that mergers are predominantly conglomerate. From a theoretical standpoint, the issues with respect to efficiency and market-position effects of the horizontal and vertical mergers have been well identified. We therefore focus on conglomerate mergers.

Data compiled on conglomerate mergers by the Federal Trade Commission divide them into three groups: (1) product extension, (2) market extension, and (3) others that might be called pure conglomerate mergers. Product-extension and market-extension mergers usually provide opportunities for the carry-over of specific management capabilities such as research, applications engineering, production, marketing, and so on. Pure conglomerate mergers, then, would involve, at least initially, the potential carry-over only of the general management functions of planning, organizing, directing, controlling, and so on. While finance is a specific management function, its role in the generic functions of planning and control and the broad generality of its applications suggest its treatment as a general management function as well.

One social justification for the continuity of firms whose performance is falling short of their competitors is reducing the expected present value of the costs of bankruptcy. Whether bankruptcy is due to, for example, financial causes, operating or managerial weakness, or inappropriate balance with the environment, one of the potential areas of loss is in organization learning. The dichotomy between generic and specific managerial functions can be regrouped. One form of organization learning is firm-specific managerial (and other employee) experience (Z_F), which could be described as team effects. A second form of organization learning is industry-specific managerial experience (Z_I), which refers to the development of capabilities in specific management functions related to the characteristics of production and marketing in particular industries. A third type of organization learning might be termed raw managerial experience (Z_G), which would refer to the capabilities developed in the general management-function areas as well as in financial planning and control.

In the case of pure conglomerate mergers, it may be presumed that there will be very little carry-over of either firm-specific or industry-specific managerial experience. The carry-over would have to be in the areas of the generic management functions of planning and control, research, and coordination, as well as in financial planning and control. The initial carry-over is raw managerial experience or capabilities in the more generic management functions. The motivation on the part of the diversifying or acquiring firm is an expectation that it has or will have excess capacity of general managerial capabilities in relation to its existing product-market activities. Furthermore, there is an expectation that in the processes of interacting on the generic management activities, particularly overall planning and control and financial planning and control, the diversifying firm will develop industry-specific managerial experience and firm-specific organization capital over time.

However, even this formulation is somewhat restrictive. It applies to companies such as ITT in which it is usually recognized that a high level of capability had been achieved in financial planning and control systems. But other types of carry-overs were also involved. For example, for Litton Industries the original conception was to apply advanced technologies from its defense business to industries for which such applications appeared to have a sound economic and business basis as well as to bring to organization interactions a systems approach to management (again developed out of the prior experience of the top managers of Litton). A high percentage of conglomerates came out of the defense industry, not only with organizational capital of the kinds just described and an objective to avoid the destruction of such organization capital, but also with a need for additional critical managerial capabilities to be successful in the nondefense sector of the economy. Particularly critical for the defense firms was the establishment of a capability for performing industrial marketing. This suggests that where the desired capability requires an organizational-learning and -development process that involves time and uncertainties, merger enables the firm to obtain such critical capabilities at their expected values and to avoid the risks of extreme and uncertain outcomes.

Another capability that defense firms had was the ability to manage change. The ability to manage change as such represented an important contribution to a wide range of nondefense industries that had not developed this kind of organization knowledge. Again, even though there appeared to be no relationships between the merging firms, there was a complementarity when firms are viewed as capabilities in the framework of an organization.

To summarize this discussion, let us have a production function (for output Q) defined over four factor inputs—the firm-specific learning (Z_F), the industry-specific learning (Z_I), the generic managerial capabilities (Z_G), and the capital investment (I); $Q = F(Z_F, Z_I, Z_G, I)$. The first input, Z_F, can only be supplied either by a long-term-learning effort or by acquiring existing firms. Z_I can be carried over in the market-extension mergers and potentially in product-extension mergers as well, and Z_G will be carried over even in pure conglomerate mergers. When a firm has excess capacity in Z_I (or Z_G) and another firm (in a different industry) experiences shortages in Z_I (or Z_G), the former could acquire the latter, thereby realizing more balanced factor proportions between Z_F, Z_I, and Z_G in the combined form.

The foregoing analysis of the potentials for the carry-over of some management capabilities (Z_G and/or Z_I) yields some predictions for the characteristics of acquiring and acquired firms. A relatively wide range of firms might have the potentials for carry-over of high skills in general management functions, advanced technological and managerial skills, the ability to manage change, and so on. Within a broad class of such firms, however, the ones for which diversification, both internally and externally, might yield the greatest increases in value would have the following characteristics: Acquiring firms would be operating in industries or lines of business in which demand growth and profit potentials were relatively unfavorable as compared with the economy as a whole so that they have excess Z_G or Z_I that can be utilized by diversification. These acquiring firms would have demonstrated capabilities for managing assets efficiently so that, for some periods prior to their mergers, they would show favorable market-return differentials relative to their industries.

The predictions for acquired firms would be that they belonged to industries with high demand growth and had not been performing as well as their competitors, presumably for shortages or imbalances among the factor inputs. Their growth and profitability would be below their industry averages. They become attractive merger targets because their demands for managerial inputs are greater as the potential for growth and profitability of their industries are greater than for the economy as a whole. Since acquired firms have not been performing up to their potentials, we would expect to obseve smaller abnormal market returns relative to their industry averages in their prior history.

A Pure Financial-Synergy Perspective on Conglomerate Mergers

In addition to motives for carrying over organization capital of the Z_G or Z_I type, potentials for financial synergies may also be present in conglomerate mergers.

We therefore consider next some purely financial interactions between acquiring and acquired firms. For the moment we abstract from the carry-over of managerial organization capital. The nature of the argument can be clarified with the use of figure 13–1. We assume that the marginal-efficiency-of-investment (MEI) function is unchanged upon merging because we abstract from any form of managerial carry-over. We focus on the possibility of lowering the cost-of-capital function.

The cost-of-capital function may be lowered for a number of reasons. If the cash-flow streams of the two companies are not perfectly correlated, bankruptcy probabilities may be lowered, and this may decrease the expected present value of bankruptcy costs. Considerable disagreement exists

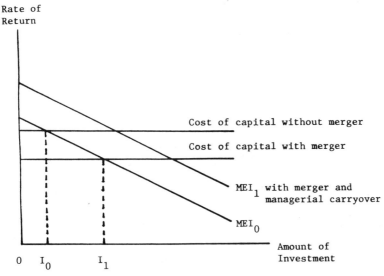

Figure 13–1. Interaction of Investment Performance and Cost-of-Capital Influences

in the literature as to whether bankruptcy costs are large or small. Previous studies on the measurement of bankruptcy costs have produced estimates of relatively low bankruptcy costs (Warner 1977). However, indirect costs including the possible loss of organizational capital were not measured, so the issue remains in doubt.

This debt coinsurance effect benefits debtholders at the expense of shareholders (Higgins and Schall 1975). However, this effect can be offset by increasing leverage after the merger, and the result will be increased tax savings on interest payments (Galai and Masulis 1976). The increase in debt capacity (defined as the maximum amount of debt that can be raised at any given interest rate) due to merger has been explicitly analyzed and shown by Stapleton (1980) in the context of the option-pricing theory. Note that the increase in debt capacity does not require the existence of bankruptcy costs.

Another effect stems from the characteristics of acquiring firms. Acquiring firms are efficient organizations in industries with growth rates less (or no greater) than the average for the economy. Hence, they may be expected to have internal cash flows in excess of current investment opportunities. Internal funds do not involve flotation costs and may have differential tax advantages over external funds. Thus, the acquiring firms may supply lower-cost internal funds to the merged firm. Again, the finance literature is in dispute on the issues involved here. To the extent that internal funds do have lower costs, this would reduce the cost of capital for the merged firm.

One might object to this rationale because the firm could simply invest the funds in new issues of the acquired firm instead of acquiring the firm. However, the acquired firm will not demand more external funds at its own cost of capital since its MEI_0 is already equalized to its cost of capital at I_0 in figure 13-1. To make the acquired firm invest I_1 using the internal funds of the acquiring firm, there would have to be a complex contract to determine the division of the extra net earnings between the two firms. Merger—that is, the outright purchase of the investment opportunity—rather than the contract may be a simpler solution since a contract may involve greater costs due to negotiating, policing, and enforcing. Merger in this case may be called financial vertical integration. Further, investment in other firms' equity securities results in extra tax liability (on some portion of dividends received).

Another dimension, emphasized by Levy and Sarnat (1970), is economies of scale in flotation and transactions costs that may be realized in conglomerate firms. Arguments may be raised with regard to the potential magnitude of these financial factors. Furthermore, questions could be raised as to why joint activities might not be taken by unmerged firms to achieve the same economies of scale in flotation and transaction costs. However, the heterogeneity of firms and the costs of contracting would seem to make such activities prohibitive, since we rarely observe them in the real world.

Thus, the pure financial factors are subject to dispute in some of their dimensions. We formulate the financial considerations as a hypothesis. A concomitant hypothesis is that these benefits are greater if the acquired firm's costs of capital are greater due to higher bankruptcy probabilities, small internal funds, or smaller firm size. The hypotheses with respect to the acquiring firm are just the opposite. The subsequent empirical tests will, therefore, have double value. First, they relate to issues with regard to the potential private and social benefits of mergers. Second, they may throw additional light on areas of dispute in finance theory.

In the analysis of the carry-over of generic management capabilities, the merger was related to the shifting of the MEI functions. Predictions of the characteristics of acquiring and acquired firms were related to industry demand growth and operating profitability. Financial synergy would operate through the cost-of-capital functions. However, the predictions for industry demand growth and profitability in the financial-synergy case are the same as in the managerial carry-over case. This is because high demand growth will tend to shift out the MEI curve, and a given reduction in the cost of capital will result in a greater increase in the net present value of an investment project.

Our hypotheses suggest that the cost of capital for acquiring firms would be equal to or lower than their industry averages, and for acquired firms it would be higher than their industry averages. Thus both total-return variance and systematic-risk measures for acquiring firms would be equal to or smaller than their industry averages and greater than their industry averages for acquired firms. These patterns would create financial-merger opportunities with the greatest potential net benefits.

Also, our pure financial-synergy model predicts that the financial-leverage ratio will be higher for the acquiring firms and lower for the acquired firms. Again, this would be consistent with lower risk and, therefore, a lower cost of capital for acquiring firms and conversely for acquired firms. The predictions on the characteristics of acquiring and acquired firms compared to their industries are summarized in table 13-1.

These particular characteristics can be specified for both acquiring and acquired firms apart from purely financial aspects. Acquiring firms have a relatively high quality of managerial capabilities and performance with some excess capacity in managerial capabilities. The industries of acquiring firms have relatively unfavorable prospects as compared with the economy as a whole. In contrast, the acquired firms have managements who have been unable to perform up to their potential, but they are in product-market areas of industries whose demand growth and profitability opportunities are above the average for the economy as a whole. Thus, their relatively

Table 13–1
Merging-Firm Characteristics

Characteristic	Acquired Firm (T)	Acquiring Firm (B)
Industry demand growth (g)	$g^{I(T)} > g^E$	$g^{I(B)} \leq g^E$
Operating profit (π)	$\pi^{I(T)} > \pi^E$	$\pi^{I(B)} \leq g^E$
	$\pi^T < \pi^{I(T)}$	$\pi^B \geq g^{I(B)}$
Risk measures:		
Beta (β)	$\beta^T > \beta^{I(T)}$	$\beta^B \leq \beta^{I(B)}$
Return variance (σ^2)	$\sigma^T > \sigma^{I(T)}$	$\sigma^B \leq \sigma^{I(B)}$
Cost of capital (R)	$R^T > R^{I(T)}$	$R^B \leq R^{I(B)}$
Premerger abnormal market return (e)	$e^T \leq e^{I(T)}$	$e^B \geq e^{I(B)}$
	$0 \leq e^{I(T)}$	$0 \geq e^{I(B)}$

Note: Superscripts E, $I(T)$, and $I(B)$ denote all industries, the acquired firm's industry, and the acquiring firm's industry respectively.

poor performance causes the acquired firms to have higher risk because of the thinness of their profitability margins and vulnerability to competitive pressures. Hence, the acquired firms have greater risk and a higher cost of capital.

The industry and firm characterizations of both the managerial and financial aspects of our model are exactly the same. Still, we should be able to distinguish the two approaches by ascertaining their relative relevance for different types of mergers. The results of a previous study are introduced later for this purpose.

Evidence from Previous Studies

Our model provides a framework for viewing previous empirical studies in relation to a more explicit theory or model to be tested.

Price-Earnings and Leverage Ratios

The price-earnings ratio will be low when a firm has a high business or operating leverage risk, a high financial risk as measured by a high debt-equity ratio, or low growth prospects. Hence if a firm's price-earnings ratio is low while its debt-equity is also low, it must be an indication that the firm has high business risk or has low growth prospects. Previous studies have found that the acquired firms employ significantly less financial leverage than acquiring firms (for example, Melicher and Rush 1974). In a study of pure conglomerate mergers covering the period 1954–1969, Conn (1973) found that the price-earnings ratio of acquired firms averaged about 13 as compared with 17 of the acquiring, the difference being statistically significant. Since the hypothesis states that the acquired firms operate in industries with expected growth rates not less than an average industry, the characterization of these firms as being risky is consistent with the evidence.

Postmerger Financial Leverage

Shrieves and Pashley (1980) provide the results of an elaborate test of the increased-leverage theory. After controlling for firm size and industry effects, they found that mergers resulted in significant increases in financial leverage. (They were also able to reject the latent-debt-capacity hypothesis as opposed to the increased debt-capacity hypothesis.) Weston and Mansinghka (1971), Melicher and Rush (1974), and Stevens (1973) find that conglomerate mergers yielded significant postmerger increases in debt-to-equity ratios. Similarly, Markham (1973, pp. 88–89) reports that the interest payment of the acquired firm (or the new division) increased after the merger, which also implies an increase in leverage. Kim and McConnell (1977) provide further evidence on increased leverage. Finally, conglomerate firms are characterized by a significantly higher degree of financial leverage compared to all other manufacturing firms (Chung 1980a)

The systematic increase in leverage following conglomerate mergers is consistent with reduced expected values of bankruptcy costs. It is also consistent with the (Higgins and Scall 1975; Galai and Masulis 1976) proposition that risk is lowered for bondholders and then is moved toward its previous level for bondholders by increased leverage. The leverage increases that take place should also yield increased tax savings.

Postmerger Capital Expenditures

Since mergers occur to internalize the investment opportunities, we should expect new capital expenditures (modernizing or scale increasing) to be increased in the acquired firms's business. In a survey study of large conglomerate firms, Markham (1973, pp. 88–89) found that the new capital outlays for the acquired companies' operations in the three-year period following acquisitions averaged 220 percent of premerger outlays for the same time span. He further reports that the managerial function of capital-expenditure planning was in most cases relocated to the corporate headquarters after acquisitions (p. 74).

Merger Gains

Some comments on the results in Nielsen and Melicher (1973) are offered as their explanations in the literature have been inadequate. One main finding was that the gains to the acquired firm (T) were greater the smaller the cash flow rate of firm T and the larger that of the acquiring firm (B). In other words, the percentage change in the acquiring firm's cash-flow rate (that is, the cash-flow-to-total-assets ratio) due to the merger was negatively correlated to the premium paid to the acquired firm. The purpose of including this variable in their discriminant-analysis model was to test the proposition that "additional gains may accrue in the form of lower borrowing costs and/ or higher corporate debt limits if a reduction in lender risk can be achieved" (p. 141) from a higher postmerger cash-flow rate.

Nielsen and Melicher interpret their results as being inconsistent with the lender-risk-reduction arguments because, contrary to their expectation, the premium (that is, the merger gain) was greater when the postmerger cash-flow rate was decreased. This erroneus interpretation simply reflects the lack of a theory to evaluate the data. A decrease in the cash-flow rate from the standpoint of firm B means an increase in the rate from the standpoint of firm T. The relevant comparison should be between the lender risk for the combined firm and that for firm T rather than for firm B, because T is the firm that needed investment funds and the merger occurred to make investments in T's business. Since their result shows that the merger gain is greater when B's cash-flow rate is greater relative to T's, this implies, when viewed from our theory, that capture of investment opportunities is easier with greater cash flow due either to the lower cost of capital for internal funds or the lowering of lender risk to T or both.

Another ad hoc interpretation of the result has appeared in the literature. Mueller (1977, p. 329) argues that this result is consistent with his managerial-motive thesis since the more cash firm B has, the larger the premium it pays to firm T's shareholders. Why is the relative premium higher for a relatively lower cash-flow rate of T? The invalidity of Mueller's contention can be seen more clearly by examining the results carefully. The premerger cash-flow rate of firm B becomes insignificant in a multiple-discriminant equation when the ratio of the combined firm's cash-flow rate to B's premerger cash-flow rate is included in the equation. Thus. what is important in creating merger benefits is the low cash flow of T and the high cash flow of B before the merger, implying redeployment of capital from B to the more favorable investment opportunities in the industry of T.

Some further empirical findings are available. Conn (1976a), for example, found that the premerger profitability change for the acquired firms was unfavorable as compared with their industries. Also, he found that the change in profitability of acquired firms' industries following merger was better than for all manufacturing (1976b).

While the evidence is mixed on beta levels, for some sample groups the average beta of acquired firms was higher than the average beta of acquiring firms. This was true for nonconglomerate acquirers as well.

Further Empirical Evidence on the Hypothesis

Acquired Firms and Their Industries

The most important aspect of the hypothesis is that the acquired firms are relatively risky but operate in industries with investment opportunities. [A more detailed discussion of the technical points of this section can be found in Chung (1980b).] Two related testable propositions have therefore been formulated. First, during some premerger period, the industry of the acquired firm will outperform the market to the extent that its demand growth and investment opportunities have not been perfectly anticipated. Second, the premerger capital-market performance of the acquired firm will be below the average for the other industry members. Therefore, our primary objectives here are to test whether the acquired firms' industries performed better than the market during some period prior to the merger event, and whether the acquired firms performed worse than their respective industries. The performance of the acquired firms relative to the market is not critical to our hypothesis.

The strategy of the test is to calculate the residuals for the firm and its industry from the market model estimated with data preceding the test period. In usual notation, the model is expressed as

$$r_{jt}^i = \alpha_j^i + \beta_j^i r_{Mt} + \epsilon_{jt}^i \qquad i = T, I,$$

where the superscripts T, I denote the acquired (target) firm and its industry, respectively, and $j = 1, \ldots n$ denotes the mergers. The industry-return index (r_{jt}^I) is constructed as an equally weighted average of returns for all firms [except the merging firms and firms delisted from the New York Stock Exchange earlier than $t = 13$ (see below)] within the same three-digit SIC industry as the acquired firm's. The market index (r_{Mt}) used is also the equally weighted one available from the CRSP tapes of the University of Chicago.

The market model is estimated for the sixty-month period -84 to -25 with the calendar month of the merger event designated as month 0

($t = 0$). The merger-event month in this study is neither the merger-completion nor the formal merger-proposal-announcement month. Rather, it is defined as the month in which the information on a possible merger of the acquired firm first became publicly available. For example, even if an acquired firm subsequently merged with a firm other than the initial pursuer, the date on which it became publicly known that the would-be acquirer sought the acquired firm is defined as the event date. An average of 5.4 months passed between the merger event and completion dates for the sample.

The final sample consists of 83 acquired firms that are involved in mergers classified as "other" in the FTC large merger series for the period 1948–1977 and whose data are available from the CRSP monthly returns file. The construction of industry indexes was possible for 62 firms (out of the initial sample of 102 New York Stock Exchange–listed acquired firms) due to the requirement of 5 firms or more per industry.

With the estimated parameters $\hat{\alpha}_j$ and $\hat{\beta}_j$, the residual or abnormal return for any month $t\epsilon(-24,K_j)$, where K_j is the completion month of jth merger, is obtained as

$$e^i_{jt} = r^i_{jt} - \hat{\alpha}^i_j - \hat{\beta}^i_j r_{Mt} \qquad i = T,I.$$

To test the differential performance between an acquired firm and its industry, for example, we calculate the cumulative paired differences $C^{TI}_j \equiv \Sigma_t(e^T_{jt} - e^I_{jt})$ over some periods contained in the interval -24 to K_j. The average of this standardized paired differences over the n sample mergers,

$$\bar{S} \equiv n^{-1} \sum_{j=1}^{n} \frac{CR^{TI}_j}{SD(CR^{TI}_j)},$$

is approximately normally distributed with $E(\bar{S}) = 0$ and $\mathrm{var}(\bar{S}) = n^{-1}$. Hence, the appropriate test statistic is $\sqrt{n}\bar{S}$. Similar statistics can be constructed for $CR^i_j \equiv \Sigma_t e^i_{jt}$ ($i = T,I$) for different periods. The results are shown in table 13–2. Also, in figure 13–2 the behavior of the cumulative average residuals is graphed for the acquired firms and their industries.

Acquired Firms. For the two years prior to the merger events, the acquired firms appear to have performed slightly worse than normal, but the abnormal returns are not significantly different from zero.

Acquired Firms' Industries. The industry average abnormal return is significantly greater than zero for the periods -12 to -4 and -3 to K_j.

Table 13-2
Relative Market Performance of Acquired Firms and Their Industries in Purely Conglomerate Mergers, Model Estimation Period: −84 to −25

Time Period Relative to Merger-Information Month 0	Acquired Firms (N = 83)		Industries (N = 62)		Paired differences (N = 50)	
	Cumulative Excess Return (Percentage)	Test Statistics	Cumulative Excess Return (Percentage)	Test Statistics	Cumulative Excess Return (Percentage)	Test Statistics
−24 to −13	−2.14	−0.65	0.18	0.07	−0.77	−0.52
−12 to −4	−2.85	−0.51	1.01	1.69*	−4.03	−1.08
−24 to −4	−4.99	−0.79	1.19	0.95	−4.80	−1.05
−3	2.35	2.24**	−0.21	−0.71	2.94	2.07**
−2	1.08	2.50**	0.04	0.57	1.37	2.37**
−1	1.31	1.81*	0.58	1.88*	1.19	1.74*
0	18.44	25.24***	−0.00	0.53	19.89	20.17***
−3 to −1	4.74	3.76***	0.41	1.01	5.51	3.52***
−3 to completion	33.05	14.85***	1.84	1.76*	35.79	12.74***
1 to completion	10.11	5.15***	1.60	1.25	10.60	4.44***
12 months following completion	—	—	−1.02	−1.24	—	—

Note: 1, 2, and 3 asterisks denote the statistical significance at the 10 percent, 5 percent, and 1 percent level, respectively.

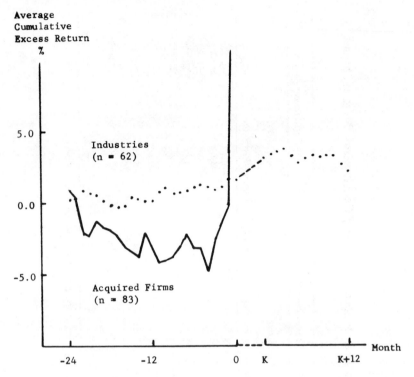

Figure 13-2. Cumulative Excess Returns of the Acquired Firms and Their
Industries in Purely Conglomerate Mergers (K = Completion
Month)

This implies that during the premerger period the industries of the acquired
firms have been characterized by favorable demand growth expectations
and greater investment opportunities than previously recognized —that is,
new information on the prospects of the industries developed in the economy. Following the merger completion, these industry returns are not significantly different than normal.

Paired Differences. As is predictable from the results for the firms and the
industries, the premerger underperformance of the acquired firms compared to the other members of their industries is noticeable although not
statistically significant.

Acquiring Firms and Their Industries

It has been hypothesized that the acquiring firms are at least as efficient as
average members of their industries and, more important, that their indus-

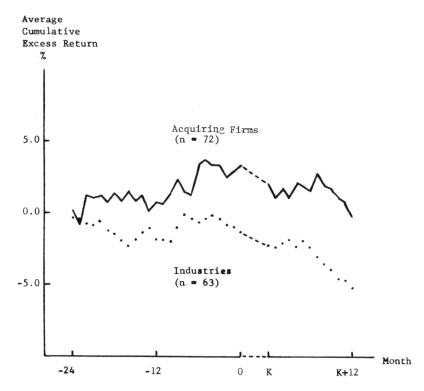

Figure 13-3. Cumulative Excess Returns of the Acquiring Firms and Their Industries in Purely Conglomerate Mergers (K = Completion Month)

tries are mature with no better demand or profitability prospects than an average industry in the economy. Following the same procedures as before, the implications of these hypotheses have been tested. The results are presented in table 13-3 and graphed in figure 13-3.

Acquiring firms. Prior to the merger event, abnormal returns of the seventy-two acquiring firms are positive and almost significant. Following the merger-information month, the residuals tend to be negative but are short of statistical significance. As discussed later, these postevent negative abnormal returns closely conform to those of their industries.

Acquiring firms' industries. For the period -23 to -4, the abnormal returns are close to zero. (However, when this period is divided into two subperiods, the residuals for -12 to -4 are almost significantly positive.) Starting in three months prior to the merger-event date, these industries show negative residuals that are significant for the period $K_j + 1$ to $K_j + 12$. According to these results, the postevent negative residuals for the acquiring

Table 13–3
Relative Market Performance of Acquiring Firms and Their Industries in Purely Conglomerate Mergers, Model Estimation Period: –84 to –25

Time Period Relative to Merger-Information Month 0	Acquiring Firms (N = 72)		Industries (N = 63)		Paired differences (N = 47)	
	Cumulative Excess Return (Percentage)	Test Statistics	Cumulative Excess Return (Percentage)	Test Statistics	Cumulative Excess Return (Percentage)	Test Statistics
–24 to –13	0.05	–0.24	–1.09	–0.91	1.81	0.61
–12 to –4	3.47	1.46	0.90	1.64	1.32	1.20
–24 to –4	3.52	0.70	–0.19	0.35	3.13	0.79
–3	–0.13	–0.23	–0.03	0.11	–1.22	–1.40
–2	–0.73	–0.56	–0.61	–0.86	1.17	1.29
–1	0.43	0.74	–0.16	–0.71	0.68	0.48
0	0.31	–0.22	–0.37	–0.83	0.67	0.00
–3 to –1	–0.43	–0.01	–0.80	–0.77	0.62	0.24
–3 to completion	–1.30	–0.42	–2.00	–1.33	0.37	0.08
1 to completion	–1.33	–0.73	–0.92	–0.96	–1.02	–0.34
12 months following completion	–2.88	–0.80	–2.95	–2.09**	1.04	0.44

Note: Two asterisks denote the statistical significance at the 5 percent level (two-tailed tests).

firms found in the preceding section and by some previous studies (for example, Malatesta 1979) are seen to be due to the performance of their industries rather than other reasons advanced by some authors.

Paired Differences. In the premerger period, the acquiring firms performed better (without statistical significance) than their industry members. Following the merger event, little difference exists between the market performances of the acquiring firms and their industries.

Comparison of Industry Performance

To allow the close examination of the qualitative differences in the market-return performances of the merging firms' industries, the cumulative residuals of the two industry residuals of the two industry groups are contrasted in figure 13-4. Up to month -4, there is no clear divergence in the behavior of residuals for the two groups except for the slightly larger residual for the acquired firms' industries accumulated in some earlier months. However, starting in month -3, the behavior of the residuals is markedly different for the two groups of industries. The cumulative residuals for the industries of the acquired firms start to increase in month -3, whereas those for the acquiring-industry group start to decrease. This divergence is statistically significant for some subperiods within -3 to $K_j +12$ (not tabulated).

The conclusion we can draw from these results is that the acquiring firms could not avail themselves of the investment opportunities in the industries in which they operate. The acquiring firms existing in mature industries choose growing industries in their pursuit of value maximization through capture of investment opportunities. If an acquired firm had been, before merger, as capable of internalizing the opportunities as other members of its industry, its merger would not achieve gains. In our hypothesis, because the firm could not adequately share in the industry demand growth, the merger can be beneficial to the firm as observed here. Thus the empirical evidence is consistent with the logic of our theory and its predictions of the characteristics of the acquired and acquiring firms and their respective industries.

Some Possible Objections and Alternative Theories

General Financial Synergy

The objection may be raised that the pure financial theory is so general that it becomes a tautology. It would imply that whenever two firms have return streams not highly correlated or differential costs of capital due to the dif-

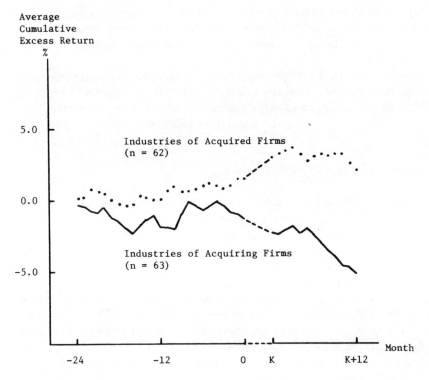

Figure 13–4. Cumulative Excess Returns of Industries of the Acquiring
and Acquired Firms in Purely Conglomerate Mergers
(K = Completion Month)

ferential availability of internal funds that a potential for a merger exists.
Individual mergers that take place may simply reflect differential costs of
capital. On average, however, pure financial synergistic conglomerate
mergers are most likely to take place where the potential benefits from the
merger are greatest so that the benefits exceed the costs of merger and
merged operations. Our model specifies the conditions under which the
potential benefits from the merger are greatest—acquired firms with industry growth rates that are higher than the economy and costs of capital that
are higher than those of other firms in their respective industries. Therefore,
statistically we should be able to discriminate between general financial-
synergy theories and our more specific delineation of it.

Related to this is that multiple bidders are likely for a given company
that will ultimately be acquired. We would predict competition in the
market for acquisitions. This is supported by other studies as well (Mandelker 1974). However, the successful bidder is more likely to be one whose
merger with the acquired firm results in the largest value creation among the

possible mergers involving the acquired firm. This implies predictable characteristics of acquiring firms as well.

Inept-Management Theory

Another possible challenge to our model is the argument that it simply formulates and is no different from the inept-management theory. It is true that our model postulates that the managements of acquired firms are not performing up to their potentials and therefore are inept in some sense. In this respect there must be some overlap between the inept-management theory and our model. However, the overlap is partial and incomplete. The differences are important for the alternative predictions and theoretical implications.

The inept-management theory has no implications for the characteristics of acquiring firms that would result in the largest benefits from a pure conglomerate merger. The inept-management theory does not make predictions with respect to the acquiring firms' industry sales and profitability potentials in relation to the economy as a whole. The inept-management theory does predict that the managers of the acquired firm will be replaced after the merger. Empirical evidence suggests, however, that this is not the case. Markham (1973, pp. 85–96) finds from his survey of thirty large acquisitions that in only 16 percent of the acquisitions two or more members of top management were replaced and that in 60 percent of the cases all top managers were retained. Similarly, based on a study of twenty-eight conglomerates, Lynch (1971) concludes that they tried to acquire companies with capable management (at least in some of the three categories of organizational learning we discussed earlier) that can be retained.

Further, a theoretical inconsistency in the inept-management theory should be noted. This theory has to admit that, at least for the acquired firms, agency costs are so large as to make their owners unable to replace the managements and thus make it necessary to invoke mergers for the purpose of replacing the inept managements. At the same time, the advocates of this theory deny the managerialism theory that requires substantial agency costs and the inability of owners to discipline management. Thus, the inept-management merger theory is internally inconsistent as a theory and cannot be a general explanation of merger activity.

Contracting

A third challenge to our model is posed by the argument that we must demonstrate why contracting could not accomplish equally well what the pure conglomerate mergers are supposed to be achieving. A number of formulations of the contracting argument may be made. One version asks, why doesn't the acquiring firm simply sell some managerial time to the firm that is not performing up to its potential? The main answer is that the acquiring firm can achieve higher net-present-value increases by improving the organizationwide planning and control process and financial characteristics of the combined firm than it could achieve by selling only managerial time. For example, the control requisite for changing the managerial- and financial-planning processes in the underperforming firm may be lacking if some managerial time were simply sold. In other words, the advice and help proffered the underperforming firm might not be implemented without bringing in new controlling management groups.

Direct Sale of Managerial Services

Another argument is that individual managers could sell their services to the underperforming companies. This was in fact done to some extent. The number of managers moving from Litton to other companies was so large that the term *LIDOS* was coined to refer to Litton Industries dropouts. Usually these managers became the chief or high-level executive officers and added other managerial resources to the firm. In terms of transferring the capabilities in the generic managerial function areas, this represents working on the expected marginal efficiency of investment curve. Two points can be made. One is that the movement of individual managers is a demonstration of our proposition that the carry-over of generic management capabilities was possible and could have a major impact on a firm whose management was not performing to its potential.

The second point is that our model predicts that both activities are plausible but that merger would take place rather than movement of individual managers when one or more of the following influences was important. If a critical mass of managerial talent or control were required for the underperforming firms, a merger rather than a movement of individual managers would take place. In addition, if the characteristics of the acquired and acquiring firms provided potentials for financial synergy, the greatest value would result from merger rather than the movement of individual managers.

A Macroeconometric Test of the Model

In order to provide an overall perspective on the theory expounded here, we introduce the results of a macroeconometric test conducted by Chung (1980b). The model was designed to explain the fluctuations in merger activity as measured by the annual numbers of mergers in the FTC's large merger series[2] and was derived from the following theoretical considerations. The profitability of mergers, which determines the rate of merger activity, will be dependent on the variables affecting the investment opportunities in the industries (of the acquired firms) and the costs of capital of individual firms.

First, investment opportunities are determined by the growth rates of industries and the real rates of interest. When the growth of a particular industry is high, the short-run fixity of some factors of production (like Z_F in our model) is likely to cause the product price as well as the output to rise. If a merger occurs to eliminate the possible constraint on generic managerial input (Z_G) or to lower costs of capital, thereby making greater investment and output feasible, the benefit will therefore be greater when the industry demand growth is faster. Thus the strength of investment opportunities from the returns side is determined by the expected growth of industries. Since the growth rate of the economy will be larger when a number of industries are expected to grow faster, the real GNP growth rate (g) is included in the econometric model.

From the point of view of firms, investment opportunities are determined relative to the cost of capital. A higher long-term cost of capital should mean fewer investment opportunities and hence the number of conglomerate mergers will be smaller. A difficulty with this variable is that it should be a real expected long-term rate of interest, which is difficult to estimate. To avoid the noise that might be introduced by using an unreliable estimate, the realized real rate of return on high-grade corporate bonds (r) as calculated by Ibbotson and Sinquefield (1979) was used. Alternatively, Tobin's q (the ratio of market value to current replacement value of a firm's nonfinancial assets) that has been used in previous studies as an important determinant of aggregate investment can substitute for these two variables—the growth rate of GNP and the real interest rate.

Second, firms are subject to different costs of capital due to differences in business risk and the availability of internal funds. The risk premium may be reduced by reducing bankruptcy risk. It is hypothesized that when the risk premium on low-grade corporate securities is higher, the absolute reduction in the risk premium through conglomerate merger is greater. The risk premium (PREM) is measured by the ratio of the returns on BAA and AAA corporate bonds.[3]

The characteristics of the acquired firm also suggest another financial variable, a measure of monetary stringency, to be included in the testing equation. To the extent that the riskiness of these firms is related to their lower profitability and lower cash-flow rate, the need for external financing is greater for them than others. When the availability of funds is tight in the financial markets, it is plausible that their cost-of-capital functions would rise differentially due to higher risk premiums that would be charged by

Table 13-4
Regression of the Numbers of Large Conglomerate Mergers, 1957–1977

Dependent Variable	Constant	PREM	SPD_{-1}	g	r	q	R^2	DW	F Test
Pure conglomerate mergers	-37.28	15.77 (6.39)	6.13 (6.79)	2.73 (6.28)	-0.43 (-4.78)		0.85	1.37	22.97
	-62.41	12.22 (2.96)	3.48 (3.01)			17.78 (3.04)	0.57	1.05	7.56
Product-extension mergers	-2.42	5.24 (1.04)	9.47 (5.15)	3.82 (4.32)	-0.46 (-2.51)		0.80	1.94	16.50
	-41.03	0.05 (0.01)	5.35 (2.93)			23.52 (2.54)	0.66	1.93	10.99
Product-extension and market-exten-	9.56	0.02 (0.04)	9.60 (4.80)	3.21 (3.34)	-0.50 (-2.48)		0.81	1.80	16.49
sion mergers	-26.96	-3.06 (-0.47)	6.39 (3.52)			22.43 (2.44)	0.72	1.40	14.32

Source: Chung (1980b).
Note: All explanatory variables are three-year sums of the current and two lagged values. The *t*-values are in parentheses.

investors, underwriters, and lending organizations. Merging with firms with larger internal cash flows and greater accessibility to the capital and money markets (or smaller costs) may be particularly attractive in periods of tight money. A measure of the tightness of external-fund availability is the spread between short- and long-term interest rates. This variable (SPD) is measured as one plus the (short-term) yield on four- to six-month prime commercial paper divided by one plus the AAA bond yield.

The results of the econometric tests using the four variables (or three when Tobin's q is used) are partly reproduced in table 13-4 and show that all variables are highly significant when the dependent variable is the number of pure conglomerate mergers. When the product-extension mergers are used as the dependent variable, an important change in the results takes place. The coefficient of the risk-premium variable becomes insignificant, while those for all other variables remain significant. For example, in one estimation, the t-value for this variable drops from 6.4 in the pure conglomerate case to only 1 in the product-extension case. When the market-extension mergers are added to the product-extension mergers, the t-value drops further and becomes practically zero and in some cases even negative.

These results strongly suggest that financial synergy in the sense of reducing the risk premium on securities is far more important for pure conglomerate than for other (conglomerate) mergers. The statistically significant coefficient for the monetary-stringency or capital-market-condition variable confirms the cross-sectional evidence of Nielsen and Melicher and attests to the importance of internal funds in determining the rates of all types of conglomerate-merger activity. Since both the carry-over of managerial resources and the pure financial rationale predict increases in merger activity in times of greater investment opportunities, it is difficult with this aggregate level of data to measure the role of managerial carry-over in explaining fluctuations in merger activity. However, the strong influence of financial synergy can be inferred from the changed results for the different groupings of mergers.

Conclusions

Markham (1973, pp. 15–16) has stated that merger activity is an alternative form of investment but that it is not necessarily a substitute for investment. This subtle but insightful statement should hopefully be more meaningful to all of us by now. This chapter has laid the conditions for determining when a merger rather than de novo entry will be observed.

We have formulated our model employing both managerial and financial carry-over or synergy. It is a priori plausible that all types of conglomerate mergers will involve both aspects. However, our objective will ultimately be to be able to predict which aspect is more important for different types of mergers.

We have already referred to some evidence that indicates that one particular aspect of financial synergy is more important for pure conglomerate mergers but less for other types of mergers. We plan to explore these relationships further by investigating additional cross-sectional merger samples. Our theory predicts that financial economies will be the major stimulus to pure conglomerate mergers and that managerial carry-over is more important for other types of conglomerate mergers.

Notes

1. Changing product requirements and changing product-market opportunities require new technologies and new combinations of technologies. To illustrate, the aircraft industry moved through stages in which the critical competence shifted from structures, to engine and other propulsion methods, to guidance, and finally to the interaction of structures, propulsion, and guidance as reflected in the concept of aerospace systems. Similarly, in office equipment, products have moved from manual operation to electromechanical, to electric, to electronic, and to the interactions of specialized units in systems. Electronics technology has moved from electron tube to semiconductors to integrated circuitry, involving a fusion with chemistry and metallurgy.

In the consumer nondurable-goods industries, product changes have characteristically been labeled product differentiation, with the unfavorable connotation that fundamental characteristics of products have not altered. Yet even in these industries, changes in consumer income patterns and tastes have created needs and opportunities for basic changes. For example, the need to understand the nature of the impact of foods on people has increased the requirements for competence in the chemical and biological sciences in food industries.

2. Since the series is affected by inflation, some adjustment was made on the numbers of mergers. See Chung (1980b) for details.

3. This variable is defined as $(1 + r_1)/(1 + r_2) - 1$, where r_1 and r_2 are the yields on BAA and AAA bonds. The variable SPD, discussed in the next paragraph, is similarly defined.

References

Diversification and Planning

Ackoff, Russell L. *A Concept of Corporate Planning*. New York: Wiley-Interscience, 1970.

Andrews, Kenneth R. *The Concept of Corporate Strategy*. Homewood, Ill.: Dow Jones-Irwin, 1971.

Ansoff, I. İgor. *Corporate Strategy*. New York: McGraw-Hill, 1965.

Biggadike, E. Ralph. *Corporate Diversification: Entry, Strategy, and Performance*. Cambridge, Mass.: Harvard University Press, 1976.

Bursk, Edward C., and D.H. Fenn. *Planning the Future Strategy of Your Business*. Cambridge, Mass.: Harvard University Press, 1965.

Caves, Richard E.; Michael E. Porter; A. Michael Spence; and John T. Scott. *Competition in the Open Economy*. Cambridge, Mass.: Harvard University Press, 1980.

Caves, Richard E., and Thomas A. Pugel. *Intraindustry Differences in Conduct and Performance: Viable Strategies in U.S. Manufacturing Industries*. New York: New York University Monograph Series in Finance and Economics, 1980.

Chandler, A.D. *Strategy and Structure: Chapters in the History of the American Industrial Enterprise*. Cambridge, Mass.: MIT Press, 1962.

Coase, Ronald H., "The Nature of the Firm," *Economica* 4 (November 1937):386–405.

Cohn, Theodore, and Roy A. Lindberg. *Survival and Growth: Management Strategies for the Small Firm*. New York: AMACOM, 1974.

Drucker, Peter F. *Management: Tasks, Responsibilities, Practices*. New York: Harper & Row, 1974.

Galbraith, John K. *The New Industrial State*. Boston: Houghton Mifflin, 1967.

Hussey, David. *Corporate Planning: Theory and Practice*. New York: Pergamon, 1974.

Laxer, Robert I., and Walter S. Wikstrom. *Appraising Managerial Performance: Current Practices and Future Directions*. New York: Conference Board, 1977.

Leontiades, Milton. *Strategies for Diversification and Change*. Boston: Little, Brown and Company, 1980.

Lorange, Peter, and Richard F. Vancil. *Strategic Planning Systems*. Englewood Cliffs, N.J.: Prentice-Hall, 1977.

Lynch, Harry H. *Financial Performance of Conglomerates*. Cambridge, Mass.: Harvard University, Graduate School of Business, 1971.

O'Connor, Rochelle. *Planning under Uncertainty: Multiple Scenarios and Contingency Planning*. New York: Conference Board, 1978.

Pfeffer, Jeffry, and Gerald Salancik. *The External Control of Organizations*. New York: Harper & Row, 1978.

Quinn, James Brian. *Strategic Change: Logical Incrementalism*. Homewood, Ill.: Dow Jones-Irwin, 1980.

Rumelt, R.P. *Strategy, Structure, and Economic Performance*. Cambridge, Mass.: Harvard University Press, Division of Research, Graduate School of Business Administration, 1974.

Steiner, George A. *Top Management Planning.* New York: Doubleday, Doran & Co., 1941.

———. *Strategic Factors in Business Success.* New York: Financial Executives Research Foundation, 1969.

———. *Strategic Planning: What Every Manager Must Know.* New York: Free Press, 1979.

Summer, Charles E. *Strategic Behavior in Business and Government.* Boston: Little, Brown and Company, 1980.

Weston, J. Fred. *The Scope and Methodology of Finance.* Englewood Cliffs, N.J.: Prentice-Hall, 1966.

Woodward, Joan. *Industrial Organization.* Fair Lawn, N.J.: Oxford University Press, 1965.

Merger Theory and Mergers

Alchian, A.A., and Demsetz, H. "Production, Information Costs, and Economic Organization." *American Economic Review* 62 (December 1972):777–795.

Auerbach, A. "Wealth Maximization and the Cost of Capital." *Quarterly Journal of Economics* 93 (August 1979):433–446.

Beckenstein, A.R. "Merger Activity and Merger Theories: An Empirical Investigation." *Antitrust Bulletin* 24 (Spring 1979):105–128.

Becker, G. *Human Capital.* New York: National Bureau of Economic Research, 1964.

Boyle, S.E. "Pre-Merger Growth and Profit Characteristics of Large Conglomerate Mergers in the United States: 1948–1968." *St. John's Law Review Special Edition* 44 (Spring 1970):152–170.

Brozen, Y. "A Comment on Weston's Industrial Concentration, Mergers and Growth." Manuscript, March 1980.

Chung, K.S. "Tests of Synergies from Diversification." Working paper, GSM-UCLA, August 1980a.

———. "A Financial Synergy Theory of Conglomerate Mergers." Working paper, GSM-UCLA, October 1980b.

Conn, R.L. "Performance of Conglomerate Firms: Comment." *Journal of Finance* 28 (June 1973):754–758.

———. "The Failing Firm/Industry Doctrines in Conglomerate Mergers." *Journal of Industrial Economics* 24 (March 1976a):181–187.

———. "Acquired Firm Performance after Conglomerate Merger." *Southern Economic Journal* 43 (October 1976b):1170–1173.

Copeland, T.E., and Weston, J.F. *Financial Theory and Corporate Policy.* Reading, Mass.: Addison-Wesley, 1979.

Dodd, P. and Ruback, R. "Tender Offers and Stockholder Returns." *Journal of Financial Economics* 5 (1977):351–373.

Evans, M.K. *Macroeconomic Activity: Theory, Forecasting, and Control.* New York: Harper & Row, 1969.

Federal Trade Commission. *Statistical Report on Mergers and Acquisitions.* Washington, D.C.: U.S. Government Printing Office, November 1978.

Feldstein, M., and Green, J. "Why Do Companies Pay Dividends?" Working Paper no. 413, National Bureau of Economic Research, December 1979.

Fisher, L. "Determinants of Risk Premiums on Corporate Bonds." *Journal of Political Economy* 67 (June 1959):217–237.

Fuchs, V.R. "Integration, Concentration, and Profits in Manufacturing Industries." *Quarterly Journal of Economics* 75 (May 1961):278–291.

Galai, D., and Masulis, R.W. "The Option Pricing Model and the Risk Factor of Stock." *Journal of Financial Economics* 3 (January/March 1976):53–81.

Gordon, R.J. *Macroeconomics.* Boston: Little, Brown and Company, 1978.

Hall, M., and Weiss, L. "Firm Size and Profitability." *Review of Economics and Statistics* 49 (August 1967):319–331.

Halpern, P.J. "Empirical Estimates of the Amount and Distribution of Gains to Companies in Mergers." *Journal of Business* 46 (October 1973):554–575.

Higgins, R.C., and Schall, L.D. "Corporate Bankruptcy and Conglomerate Merger." *Journal of Finance* 30 (March 1975):93–113.

Ibbotson, R.G., and Sinquefield, R.A. *Stocks, Bonds, Bills, and Inflation: Historical Returns (1926–1978).* Charlottesville, Va.: Financial Analysis Research Foundation, 1979.

Jensen, M.C., and Meckling, W.H. "Theory of the Firm: Managerial Behavior, Agency Costs and Ownership Structure." *Journal of Financial Economics* 3 (October 1976):305–360.

Kim, E.H., and McConnell, J.J. "Corporate Mergers and the Coinsurance of Corporate Debt." *Journal of Finance* 32 (May 1977):349–365.

Kraus, A., and Litzenberger, R.H. "A State-Preference Model of Optimal Financial Leverage." *Journal of Finance* 27 (September 1972):911–922.

Langetieg, T.C. "An Application of a Three-Factor Performance Index to Measure Stockholder Gains from Merger." *Journal of Financial Economics* 6 (December 1978):365–383.

Levy, H., and Sarnat, M. "Diversification, Portfolio Analysis and the Uneasy Case for Conglomerate Mergers." *Journal of Finance* 25 (September 1970):795–807.

Linter, J. "Expectations, Mergers and Equilibrium in Purely Competitive Securities Markets." *American Economic Review, Proceedings* 61 (May 1971):101–111.

Lynch, H.H. *Financial Performance of Conglomerates.* Boston: Harvard University, Graduate School of Business Administration, 1971.

Malatesta, P.H. "Corporate Mergers." Working paper, University of Rochester, December 1979.

Mandelker, G. "Risk and Return: The Case of Merging Firms." *Journal of Financial Economics* 1 (December 1974):303-335.

Manne, H.G. "Mergers and the Market for Corporate Control." *Journal of Political Economy* 73 (April 1965):110-120.

Markham, J.W. *Conglomerate Enterprises and Public Policy.* Boston: Harvard University, Graduate School of Business Administration, 1973.

Mead, W.J. "Instantaneous Merger Profit as a Conglomerate Merger Motive." *Western Economic Journal* 7 (December 1969):295-306.

Melicher, R.W., and Rush, D.F. "Evidence on the Acquisition-Related Performance of Conglomerate Firms." *Journal of Finance* 29 (March 1974):141-149.

Meyer, J.R., and Kuh, E. *The Investment Decision: An Empirical Study.* Cambridge, Mass.: Harvard University Press, 1957.

Miller, M.H., and Modigliani, F. "Dividend Policy, Growth, and the Valuation of Shares." *Journal of Business* 34 (October 1961):411-433.

Miller, M.H., and Scholes, M.S. "Dividends and Taxes." *Journal of Financial Economics* 6 (December 1978):333-364.

Milne, F. "Choice over Asset Economies: Default Risk and Corporate Leverage." *Journal of Financial Economics* 2 (June 1975):165-185.

Mueller, D.C. "A Theory of Conglomerate Mergers." *Quarterly Journal of Economics* 83 (1969):643-659.

————. "The Effects of Conglomerate Mergers." *Journal of Banking and Finance* 1 (1977):315-347.

Nielsen, J.F., and Melicher, R.W. "A Financial Analysis of Acquisition and Merger Premiums." *Journal of Financial and Quantitative Analysis* 8 (March 1973):139-162.

Penrose, E. *The Theory of the Growth of the Firm.* Oxford: Basil Blackwell, 1959.

Prescott, E.C., and Visscher, M. "Organization Capital." *Journal of Political Economy* 88 (June 1980):446-461.

Roll, R. "A Reply to Mayers and Rice (1979)." *Journal of Financial Economics* 7 (December 1979):391-400.

Rosen, S. "Learning by Experience as Joint Production." *Quarterly Journal of Economics* 86 (August 1972):366-382.

Rubin, P. "The Expansion of Firms." *Journal of Political Economy* 81 (July/August 1973):936-949.

Scherer, F.M. *Industrial Market Structure and Economic Performance,* 2d ed. Chicago: Rand McNally, 1980.

Shrieves, R.E., and Pashley, M.M. "A Test of Financial Economics through Increased Leverage Merger Theories." Working paper, University of Tennessee, August 1980.

Smith, V.L. "Default Risk, Scale, and the Homemade Leverage Theorem." *American Economic Review* 62 (March 1972):66–76.

Stapleton, R.C. "Mergers, Debt Capacity and the Valuation of Corporate Loans." Working paper, Manchester Business School, October 1980.

Stevens, D.L. "Financial Characteristics of Merged Firms: A Multivariate Analysis." *Journal of Financial and Quantitative Analysis* 8 (March 1973):149–165.

Stiglitz, J.E. "A Re-Examination of the Modigliani-Miller Theorem." *American Economic Review* 59 (December 1969):784–793.

————. "On the Irrelevance of Corporate Financial Policy." *American Economic Review* 64 (December 1974):851–866.

Warner, J. "Bankruptcy Costs: Some Evidence." *Journal of Finance* 32 (May 1977):337–347.

Weston, J.F. "The Nature and Significance of Conglomerate Firms." *St. John's Law Review Special Edition* 44 (Spring 1970):66–80.

————. "Industrial Concentration, Mergers, and Growth." Mimeo. 1980.

Weston, J.F., and Mansinghka, S.K. "Tests of the Efficiency Performance of Conglomerate Firms." *Journal of Finance* 26 (September 1971): 919–936.

Yawitz, J.B.; Marshall, W.J.; and Greenberg, E. "Negatively Correlated Income as an Incentive for Conglomerate Merger." Working paper no. 33, Center for the Study of American Business, Washington University, St. Louis, July 1978.

14

Implementation of the Mergers and Acquisitions Program at United Technologies Corporation

Richard B. Curtiss

This chapter begins with an overview of the business-development function at United Technologies Corporation (UTC). The business-development department has responsibility for the corporation's merger and acquisition programs, joint venture programs, and the handling of divestitures for UTC. The divestiture activity is becoming a more important factor of the department's total activities. In my opinion, UTC's track record in mergers and acquisitions exemplifies a classic case of how a large, successful organization can diversify itself and become a major multinational corporation.

The Program

The diversification program was initiated during the 1972 period when our chairman, Harry J. Gray, and the company's board of directors developed a strategy to diversify the corporation in order to reduce its dependency on aerospace activities, which at that time accounted for between 75 to 80 percent of the annual revenues. Aerospace profitability was good, and the board of directors felt that excess cash was being generated that could be used successfully to diversify the corporation.

The program was obviously implemented on an established set of parameters that were well conceived. Mr. Gray indicated four major areas into which he wanted to consider diversifying: (1) the energy industry, (2) the transportation industry, (3) the electronics industry, and (4) the telecommunications industry. All of UTC's acquisitions could be categorized into one of these four areas. (A recent article in *Fortune* on Mr. Gray suggested that the current emphasis of the corporation's diversification program would be to identify appropriate acquisition opportunities in the energy and telecommunications fields.) Obviously, as one would expect, a number of candidates could be reviewed in any one of these four industries. Therefore, it became very critical that the corporation identify certain criteria that it would use as guidelines for its acquisition program. Some of the more

349

important characteristics established at that time included, first that the corporation was going to try to emphasize its effort in identifying companies that had a high technology content. Second, UTC was going to be looking primarily for companies that could be categorized as market leaders in their industries, such as Otis Elevator Company and Carrier Corporation. Third, UTC was primarily interested in trying to identify those companies that had a strong management capability; if a company is a market leader, it is likely to have strong management. The corporation was only going to identify and try to review companies that were considered leading basic industrial corporations.

As we all know, a diversification program can be implemented in many different ways. We at UTC have a strong preference to expand our business activities through friendly transactions. The Essex, AMBAC, and Mostek transactions represent friendly approaches in diversifying the corporation. However, at other times, UTC has had to be a little more aggressive in its approach to mergers and acquisitions and has made unfriendly tender offers. Obviously we felt that being more aggressive in going after companies such as Carrier and Otis was warranted because of the unique characteristics of these fine entities. Also, as we have been expanding the corporation overseas, it becomes very important for our board of directors and senior management to realize that in many instances joint ventures and minority equity participations are going to be the ways by which UTC can proceed. Many governments overseas have strong biases in assuring that foreign entities such as UTC have local partners in order to gain access to their markets. Local partners will also help governments maintain some national control over emerging technologies that could accelerate economic growth.

I should also mention that UTC has an active program in trying to identify appropriate divestiture candidates. In many instances, large corporations such as UTC have small entities within the overall corporation that no longer fit the established growth objectives of the company. Hence, our board of directors and senior management prudently try to divest these activities and utilize the proceeds to grow more important strategic business units within the total portfolio of our activities.

Program Operation

I now identify and summarize how the business-development function operates within the UTC environment. My department reports directly to the chief financial officer of the corporation, Stillman B. Brown, and as one would expect, we have almost daily interaction with the senior management of the corporation. We maintain a very small staff in order to maintain close scrutiny over potential problems that could arise with disclosure requirements. I use the analogy in trying to get this point across by saying that, inevitably, as chapter 7 indicated, there are problems with stock price increases before official announcements are made. We take pride at UTC in trying to minimize beforehand the likelihood of any problems. Over the years, UTC has maintained close working relations with a number of leading financial intermediaries that have been very helpful to us in trying to expand the corporation's total capabilities both in the United States and abroad.

Some earlier chapters emphasized the importance of coordination in the merger and acquisition field. This is very important at UTC and is another area in which we emphasize tight control in all of the various functions. There are many reasons for this—one being the number of people we call in to help us in formalizing the presentation for our board to review. Many different disciplines, both internal and external, complement the skills of our staff in assuring that our board of directors and senior management have the best information possible to make prudent decisions regarding mergers and acquisitions. For example, at UTC, we have available senior corporate executives, the controller, the treasurer, the legal department, operating-unit staffs, and other UTC staffs. External help includes public accountants, intermediaries, marketing consultants, and investment bankers. Apparently, most of UTC's efforts in mergers and acquisitions are following what other professionals in this field would like to see in the corporate environment. It works very effectively. We have various models, and strategic planning plays a very important function in making sure that the acquisition proposals identified would be prudent directions for the corporation to pursue.

Program Results

I now turn to the specific results of the UTC merger and acquisition program since it was implemented in 1972. Since then we have consummated approximately nine acquisitions (see table 14–1). In the 1972 period, specific corporate objectives were established. Mr. Gray indicated that he would like to reduce the company's dependency on the aerospace activities; this has been accomplished. Second, he wanted to make sure that UTC's high technical base was expanded; thus, most of the acquisitions consummated represent technical leaders in their fields. Third, he wanted to make sure that the financial strength of the corporation was maintained while the acquired companies enhanced the growth performance of UTC. At that time, a sales-goal objective of $10 billion by 1982 was established; our sales in 1980 reached $12.3 billion. As indicated before, nine acquisitions have

Table 14-1
Past Activities

Acquisitions	Divestitures	Interests
Aismalibar	Allied Bronze	Babcock-Wilcox
AMBAC	TCI	ESB
Carrier	TMX	Signal
Dynell		Unitrode
Essex		
Homogenious Metals		
Maisa		
Mostek		
Otis		

been consummated during this time period, and many of the names of those companies acquired will be familiar to readers—Essex, Otis Elevator, Carrier Air Conditioning, AMBAC, Mostek.

Divestitures are becoming an increasingly important activity at UTC. The first company on the list, Allied Bronze, was sold during 1980. TCI was sold in 1976, and TMX was liquidated in 1980. The Dempster Dumpster activities of Carrier Corporation were divested late in December 1980. Again I think it indicates an awareness by our senior management of the funds that could be freed up by making prudent divestitures and then by using those funds to grow other strategic business units possessing better growth opportunities.

In the last column of table 14-1 are listed various organizations in which we have indicated an interest in the past. Babcock and Wilcox did not become part of UTC. At the time we lost this entity to J. Ray McDermott, we were somewhat chagrined. However, Mr. Gray has subsequently reported to our shareholders at an annual meeting that he would rather be lucky than smart. We made a concerted effort to acquire ESB, a leading battery manufacturer. However, competition from INCO suggested that our bid was not as acceptable as INCO's, and as a prudent investor, our management felt that it would not be mutually beneficial to consider a higher bid. The same can be said about Signal Companies but from the perspective of the Signal shareholder. UTC had reached an agreement to acquire the Signal Companies in 1973. Shortly before the formal closing was to occur, there was a large oil discovery in some of the oil fields in which Signal participated. Upon uncovering these additional resources, Signal felt a higher valuation was justified. UTC did not agree.

UTC Acquisitions

I now provide a little more detail on some of the major acquisitions UTC has consummated. Otis Elevator Company, for example, represented the first unfriendly tender offer the corporation made. At the time of the UTC tender offer, Otis' annual sales were approximately $1.2 billion, the construction industry was depressed, and many followers of UTC did not understand why it was interested in going after a company like Otis at that time. Our analysis suggested that Otis was a unique situation. As one would expect, the stock market was discounting the worst in the construction industry, and the Otis common stock was selling below its theoretical book value. More important, as one continued to analyze Otis, it became clear that the majority of the profits generated by this fine organization was the result of its service contracts. It is important to keep that in mind because we feel that Otis will continue to have a good cash flow and therefore will help UTC capitalize on its overall growth potential. Strong cash flow was an important consideration because Pratt & Whitney was engaged in some intense competition in certain engine markets during the same time period.

In addition to the cash flow and the financial considerations of Otis, Otis also had been in existence for over 100 years. Management appeared to be very competent, and the company conducted operations in more than 120 countries throughout the world. Since one of UTC's stated acquisition criteria was to expand the corporation beyond U.S. boundaries, a company such as Otis helped establish UTC as a true multinational.

Carrier was acquired during 1979. Again our analysis indicated that it represented a major U.S. company serving attractive markets. It possessed established technical capabilities and an in-place management team, and it afforded good growth potential.

Mostek Corporation is the last major acquisition we have made. It, like Carrier, was acquired in 1979. My department spent about a year and a half prior to August 1979 attempting to find ways to expand UTC's capabilities in the semiconductor industry. The semiconductor industry was attractive since the trends in electronics suggested that, if UTC was going to become an established factor in the electronics markets, it had to have a strong capability in semiconductor technology. As fate would have it, just as we were focusing on Mostek, GK Technologies announced that it was going to sell its shares of Mostek to Gould. The immediate reaction from Mostek, when informed about the GK Technologies announcement, was negative. UTC was cast in the role of a white knight, and quite frankly, it was a good experience for Mr. Gray and UTC to be the preferred candidate. We felt that, in order to bring Mostek into a large corporate environment, we had to use a unique approach in trying to motivate these entrepreneurial individuals. What we did first was to establish a unique management-incentive program based on Mostek's future performance. In addition, Mostek needed additional capital investments in order to continue its rapid growth. Part of UTC's agreement with Mostek stipulated that UTC would make $200 million available to Mostek to finance future growth and capital-equipment requirements. Furthermore, Mostek was a very important acquisition for UTC in developing a strong cornerstone for further expansion into the electronics field. UTC's new electronics group, which was formed last year, has an annual sales volume of about \$2.5 to \$3 billion. UTC hopes to be a major competitive factor in electronics in the years to come.

Divestitures

As I indicated before, as cash becomes a scarcer commodity, a prudent divestiture program can help raise additional capital to assist in financing the growth potential of more dynamic parts of UTC. This raises another interesting point—that is, at certain times within a large corporation, certain small business units exist that do not fit the overall growth objectives of the company. Some of these business units represent very good growth opportunities, but as they grow, it will be very important for them to become larger in size to maintain their competitive status. Management is therefore confronted with a business decision of whether to sell some of these rapidly growing units to raise capital or to invest to enhance the entities' competitive position—a difficult decision. UTC is currently making a concerted effort to identify certain business activities that no longer meet the total corporate growth objectives.

Foreign Activities

Our foreign-expansion activities in the nonaerospace industries are relatively new but successful. A few small joint ventures have been consummated primarily for our electronics operations, and we continue to monitor many activities both in Europe and Far Eastern markets that might represent good complementary acquisitions for some of the business units.

Conclusions

Let us finally look at the scoreboard. We have completed five major acquisitions since UTC's program was initiated by Mr. Gray in 1972, and I think it is fair to say that the diversification program has been successful. We have reduced our aerospace dependency from around 75 to 80 percent of revenues to the range of 20 to 25 percent. UTC's aerospace operations have achieved good growth during the same period. The overall technical capabilities of UTC have also been enhanced, particularly through the acquisitions of AMBAC and Mostek. Sales and profit growth objectives have been achieved. Our financial condition remains healthy, and the company continues to have the financial wherewithal to maintain a very competitive posture.

I hope these remarks on UTC's acquisition program have given a better perspective on why we feel mergers and acquisitions have played an important role in the company's diversification program.

List of Conference
Participants
and Contributors

Edward I. Altman, New York University
Ernest Bloch, New York University
Michael Bradley, University of Rochester
Ivan E. Brick, Rutgers University
John A. Bulkley, Moseley, Hallgarten, Estabrook, & Weeden, Inc.
Willard T. Carleton, University of North Carolina
Kwang S. Chung, University of California, Los Angeles
W. Scott Cooper, Securities and Exchange Commission
Richard B. Curtiss, United Technologies Corporation
Kenneth M. Davidson, Federal Trade Commission
Eleanor M. Fox, New York University
John B. Guerard, Jr., University of Virginia
Lawrence J. Haber, Rutgers University
Robert S. Harris, University of North Carolina
John J. Huber, Securities and Exchange Commission
Michael Keenan, New York University
Robert Lessin, Morgan Stanley & Co.
Martin Lipton, Wachtell, Lipton, Rosen and Katz
Michael E. Moses, New York University
Dennis C. Mueller, University of Maryland
Louis Perlmutter, Lazard Freres & Co.
Joshua Ronen, New York University
Jeffrey M. Schaefer, Securities Industry Association
George H. Sorter, New York University
Richard C. Stapleton, University of Manchester
John F. Stewart, University of North Carolina
M. Jane Barr Sweeney, Vanderbilt University
Benjamin M. Vandegrift, Securities and Exchange Commission
Daniel Weaver, Rutgers University
J. Fred Weston, University of California, Los Angeles
Lawrence J. White, New York University
Harold M. Wit, Allen & Co.

About the Editors

Michael Keenan is associate professor of finance at the Graduate School of Business Administration, New York University. He received the B.S. at Case Western Reserve University in Cleveland and the Ph.D. at Carnegie Mellon University in Pittsburgh. After teaching for three years at the University of California, Berkeley, he joined the faculty at NYU, where his primary teaching areas have been corporation finance and investments. Professor Keenan's current research interests include mergers and acquisitions analysis, the economic structure of the securities industry, and the growth of the service-sector economy.

Lawrence J. White is professor of economics at the Graduate School of Business Administration, New York University. He received the B.A. from Harvard University (1964), the M.Sc. from the London School of Economics (1965), and the Ph.D. from Harvard University (1969). His major fields of research include industrial organization, regulation, and antitrust policy. He is the author of *The Automobile Industry Since 1945; Industrial Concentration and Economic Power in Pakistan; Reforming Regulation: Processes and Problems;* and articles in leading economics journals, including *American Economic Review, Quarterly Journal of Economics,* and *Bell Journal of Economics.* He is the coeditor of an earlier conference volume published by Lexington Books entitled *Deregulation of the Banking and Securities Industries.*